Adam Zamoyski is a freelance historian and author of over a dozen books on figures and subjects taken from European history, including two *Sunday Times* bestsellers. He lives in London and Poland, and is married to the painter Emma Sergeant.

From the reviews of *Poland: A History*:

'An excellent book'   *Financial Times*

'For the past 25 years, thanks to the efforts of Adam Zamoyski, we have been better informed about the history and character of Poland than about any other East European country . . . Zamoyski's new perspective on an old culture and its modern political liberty is . . . presented with a new, confident sense of freedom'   *The Times*

'Shrewd . . . an excellent section on the country and its politics since '89'   *Independent on Sunday*

T0381956

By the same author

Chopin: A Biography

The Battle for the Marchlands

Paderewski

The Polish Way

The Last King of Poland

*The Forgotten Few: The Polish Air Force
in the Second World War*

*Holy Madness: Romantics, Patriots and Revolutionaries,
1776–1871*

1812: Napoleon's Fatal March on Moscow

Rites of Peace: The Fall of Napoleon and the Congress of Vienna

Warsaw 1920: Lenin's Failed Conquest of Europe

Chopin: Prince of the Romantics

*Phantom Terror: The Threat of Revolution
and the Repression of Liberty 1789–1848*

POLAND

A HISTORY

ADAM ZAMOYSKI

WILLIAM
COLLINS

William Collins
An imprint of HarperCollins*Publishers*
1 London Bridge Street
London SE1 9GF
WilliamCollinsBooks.com

HarperCollins*Publishers*
Macken House, 39/40 Mayor Street Upper
Dublin1, D01 C9W8, Ireland

This William Collins paperback edition published 2015

First published by William Collins in 2009

14

Copyright © Adam Zamoyski 2009

The Polish Way published by John Murray in 1987

Adam Zamoyski asserts the moral right to be identified as the author of this work

A catalogue record for this book is available from the British Library

ISBN 978-0-00-755621-2

All rights reserved. No part of this publication may be reproduced, stored in a
retrieval system, or transmitted, in any form or by any means, electronic, mechanical,
photocopying, recording or otherwise, without the prior permission of the publishers.

This book is sold subject to the condition that it shall not, by way of trade or otherwise,
be lent, re-sold, hired out or otherwise circulated without the publisher's prior consent
in any form of binding or cover other than that in which it is published and without a
similar condition including this condition being imposed on the subsequent purchaser.

Typeset in Minion by Palimpsest Book Production Ltd, Falkirk, Stirlingshire
Printed and bound in the UK using 100% renewable electricity at CPI Group (UK) Ltd

Without limiting the author's and publisher's exclusive rights, any
unauthorised use of this publication to train generative artificial intelligence
(AI) technologies is expressly prohibited. HarperCollins also exercise their
rights under Article 4(3) of the Digital Single Market Directive 2019/790 and
expressly reserve this publication from the text and data mining exception.

This book is produced from independently certified FSC™ paper
to ensure responsible forest management.

For more information visit: www.harpercollins.co.uk/green

CONTENTS

LIST OF ILLUSTRATIONS

The bronze doors of Gniezno Cathedral, made by local craftsmen in the 1170s, depicting the life of St Wojciech (Adalbertus).

The Benedictine Monastery at Tyniec on the Vistula. (*Światosław Lenartowicz*)

Sword made for Bolesław of Mazovia in the early thirteenth century, which became the coronation sword of the kings of Poland after 1320.

The Battle of Legnica (1241), in which the Tatar army routed the forces of Henryk Probus of Silesia. Panel from a triptych by the Master of Wielowieś (c.1430). (*Teresa Żółtowska*)

The Church of St Catherine in Kraków, one of many built by King Kazimierz the Great (1333–70). (*Edmund Kupiecki*)

The Old Synagogue in the Kazimierz district of Kraków, built in the reign of Kazimierz the Great.

The stronghold of the Teutonic Knights at Marienburg (Malbork). (*Wojciech Karliński*)

Presumed portrait of Władysław Jagiełło, depicted as one of the Three Kings on the altar of Our Lady of Sorrows in Kraków Cathedral (c.1480).

King Kazimierz IV. Detail from his sarcophagus by Veit Stoss in Kraków Cathedral (1492).

Memorial to Philippo Buonaccorsi (Callimachus) by Veit Stoss in the Dominican Church in Kraków (1496).

Mikołaj Kopernik (Copernicus).

King Zygmunt Augustus. Contemporary portrait from the workshop of Lucas Cranach the Younger.

Barbara Radziwiłł. Contemporary portrait from the workshop of Lucas Cranach the Younger.

Brussels tapestry with the arms of Poland and Lithuania, commissioned by King Zygmunt Augustus in the 1550s.

Renaissance courtyard of the Royal Castle on Wawel Hill in Kraków, begun in 1507 by Francesco Fiorentino and completed in the 1530s by Bartolomeo Berecci. (*Edmund Kupiecki*)

Grain store in the Polish mannerist style at Kazimierz Dolny on the Vistula, dating from 1591. (*Wojciech Karliński*)

King Zygmunt III. Contemporary portrait by an unknown artist.

Władysław IV taking the surrender of the Muscovite army outside Smolensk in September 1633.

The Lubomirski stronghold of Wiśnicz, built by Matteo Trapola between 1615 and 1621. (*Światosław Lenartowicz*)

Łukasz Opaliński, Grand Marshal of the Crown, by an unknown artist.

The body armour of a soldier of the winged cavalry, the *husaria*, with the cross and a medallion with the Virgin on the breast.

A provincial sejmik taking place in a church. Pen-and-ink drawing by Jean Pierre Norblin de la Gourdaine.

Wooden Church of St Joseph, Baborów (c.1700), a typical baroque village church.

King Stanisław Augustus, by Marcello Bacciarelli.

View of Warsaw, by Bernardo Bellotto (1772). (*Archiwum Zamku Krolewskiego*)

General Wincenty Krasiński.

List of Illustrations

MAPS

TABLES

NOTE ON POLISH PRONUNCIATION

Polish words may look complicated, but pronunciation is at least consistent. All vowels are simple and of even length, as in Italian, and their sound is best rendered by the English words 'sum' (*a*), 'ten' (*e*), 'ease' (*i*), 'lot' (*o*), 'book' (*u*), 'sit' (*y*).

Most of the consonants behave in the same way as in English, except for *c*, which is pronounced 'ts'; *j*, which is soft, as in 'yes'; and *w*, which is equivalent to English *v*. As in German, some consonants are softened when they fall at the end of a word, and *b*, *d*, *g*, *w*, *z* become *p*, *t*, *k*, *f*, *s*, respectively.

There are also a number of accented letters and combinations peculiar to Polish, of which the following is a rough list:

ó = *u*, hence *Kraków* is pronounced 'krakooff'.
ą = nasal *a*, hence *sąd* is pronounced 'sont'.
ę = nasal *e*, hence *Łęczyca* is pronounced 'wenchytsa'.
ć = *ch* as in 'cheese'.
cz = *ch* as in 'catch'.
ch = guttural *h* as in 'loch'.
ł = English *w*, hence *Bolesław* becomes 'Boleswaf, *Łódz* 'Wootj'.
ń = soft *n* as in Spanish '*mañana*'.
rz = French *j* as in '*je*'.

ś = *sh* as in 'sheer'.

sz = *sh* as in 'bush'.

ż = as *rz* (Z is the accented capital).

ź = A similar sound, but sharper as in French '*gigot*'.

The stress in Polish is consistent, and always falls on the penultimate syllable.

PREFACE

The idea that a historian should radically alter his view of the past over the space of a couple of decades is, on the face of it, preposterous. But when I reread my history of Poland, *The Polish Way*, first published in 1987, which I meant to revise and update for a new edition, I became convinced of the contrary. History did not, as some have argued, come to an end in the intervening two decades, but they have completely changed the perspective.

When I sat down to write that book, few people in western Europe, let alone further afield, had any idea of where Poland lay, and fewer still had any sense of its having a past worth dwelling on. Given that history is made up of an intricate interaction of land, people and culture, Poland presented unique problems. How was the historian to approach a country whose territory had expanded and contracted, shifted and vanished so dramatically, which currently existed as an almost random compromise resulting from the Second World War, and which lay within the imperial frontiers of another power? How was he to treat a people which, from ethnic, cultural and religious diversity had been purged by genocide and ethnic cleansing into a homogeneous society? How to represent a culture which had been largely obliterated, whose remains survived only underground or in exile?

Matters were made no easier by the fact that the entire geo-political space in which Poland existed was also in an unnatural state of suspension, with Germany divided, Russia a bureaucratic totalitarian monstrosity, and the areas inhabited by the Lithuanians, Belorussians and Ukrainians a kind of limbo.

Although the election of a Pole, Karol Wojtyła, to the Holy See as Pope John Paul II, the dramatic rise of Solidarność and a number of books and articles published in the West, along with increased travel, had recently brought Poland into the consciousness of greater numbers of people, it was not until the collapse of the Soviet project in 1989 that the situation began to alter significantly. It was only then that Poland and the other countries of the region came back to life as political entities. And that fundamentally altered the way in which they are perceived.

The concurrent process of globalisation and the huge shifts in economic and military power taking place around the world have also made it easier for the historian to represent a foreign country to his readers. The fact that what were then viewed as 'developing countries' (with all the condescension that term implied) are now emerging as the major players of the future has radically altered attitudes in the hitherto dominant nations of the West. Put simply, the historian has less to explain and fewer prejudices to break down. But the real significance of the events of 1989 only began to make itself felt later.

When I was writing my book, Europe was divided by the Iron Curtain. Crossing it was an awesome and bizarre experi-ence for anyone brought up in the West – the coils of barbed wire, the watchtowers, the machine guns aimed at the traveller and the ubiquitous guards with their Alsatian dogs were richly redolent of Nazi concentration camp and Soviet gulag. Not surprisingly, since this absurd barrier was one of the last surviving vestiges of a long historical process that had reached its apogee in the twin abominations of Soviet communism and German fascism.

Only two hundred years before, the whole area between the Rhine and the Dnieper had been inhabited by a variety of peoples with wildly differing cultural, religious and political affiliations, organised into an equally variegated miscellany of empires, commonwealths, kingdoms, duchies, principalities, republics, bishoprics, city states, baronies and lesser sovereignties. In a process that began with the eighteenth-century partitions of Poland, these polities had been subjugated and then reorganised into a small number of highly competitive states and the peoples inhabiting them into largely fictitious nations which saw their survival in Darwinian terms. This initiated a struggle that culminated in the two world wars and the Cold War.

If the Iron Curtain disfigured Europe physically, the process which had led up to it had distorted history even more fundamentally. No history more so than that of Poland, which was the first and greatest casualty of the process. Two years after Russia, Prussia and Austria had divided the country up among themselves, on 26 January 1797 they signed a convention containing a secret article which stressed the absolute 'necessity of abolishing everything which might recall the existence of a Polish kingdom in face of the performed annihilation of this political body'. In this spirit, the Prussians melted down the Polish crown jewels, the Austrians turned royal palaces into barracks, and the Russians grabbed everything they could lay their hands on and shipped it out, particularly documents. All three rewrote history to give the impression that Poland had never been a fully sovereign state, only a backwater which needed civilising.

Throughout the nineteenth century the Poles who struggled to reverse this process and recover their independence were generally viewed in the West as troublemakers impeding the orderly march of progress. In the twentieth century, by contrast, when they once again fell victim, to the Soviet Union, they came to be seen as reactionary and backward because of their resilience to supposedly progressive doctrines such as communism.

Looking back on the way history was written in the twentieth century, particularly in its middle decades, one cannot avoid being struck by how deeply politicised it was. Not only did nationalism or dominant state orthodoxy select and distort facts; various interpretations of Marxist theory reinvented them to suit visions of the future.

Not surprisingly, considering the country's position at the geographical and ideological interface of such disputes, Poland's past received the full treatment. And given that it was a battle-ground for political and nationalist passions of great intensity, it was impossible, even for supposedly uncommitted historians in faraway universities, to write about it entirely dispassionately. That did not change until the disintegration of the Soviet experiment robbed the most vociferous combatants of their arguments.

What was not immediately apparent even at that point was that the disintegration of the Soviet Union held a deeper significance: it marked the end of the era of state-based Darwinism that had begun with the rise of Prussia in the early eighteenth century (arguably even earlier). This model had been discredited by the Great War and was abandoned by most of Europe after 1945, as one country after another divested itself of its national pretensions and imperial attributes to pool its sovereignty in the interests of a united Europe. But the Soviet Union remained wedded to the old mindset of paranoid nationalist/ideological struggle for dominance. Its implosion released the nations of East Central Europe from this, and although large sections of society within those nations, particularly in the Balkans, are still affected by it (for understandable historical reasons), most of the inhabitants of the area have been able to, or even been obliged to, take an entirely fresh view of the past.

This mirrors an analogous process that has been taking place in Western societies. While most young Britons would probably still enjoy watching a 1940s war film glorifying British pluck and derring-do, the overwhelming majority might as well, for all their empathy, be watching an Arthurian romance or a piece of science fiction, and the concept of laying down their lives for their country is largely alien to them. The same is even more true of the French and Germans, while to young Italians the very myths of the *Risorgimento*, the founding faith of their country, now appear laughable. The majority of the population of the European Union now thinks in terms of societies rather than nations.

Histories written a few decades ago now appear strangely obsessed with political achievements, dominions established, battles won – in essence, with national success. They can seem embarrassingly patronising on the subject of all those who did not win out according to the rules of the day. Those rules have changed, and this is particularly welcome to the historian of Poland.

In the early modern period, the Poles failed spectacularly to build an efficient centralised state structure and they paid the price, being swallowed up by their more successful neighbours. The history of Poland has therefore, up until now, been written as that of a failed state. Like some distorting lens or filter, that failure coloured and deformed the historian's view of the whole of Polish history.

He is now no longer, as he was only a couple of decades ago, writing the history of an enslaved and to all intents and purposes non-existent country. There is a great difference between writing up a bankrupt business and writing up one that has been through hard times and turned the corner. He is no longer writing the history of a state that failed, but of a society that created a social and political civilisation of its own, one which was occluded by the success of a rival model (now utterly discredited) but whose ideals are close to those the world values today.

All this convinced me that I could not just brush up and update *The Polish Way*. But since I still stand by that book, as far as it goes, and indeed its basic structure, I did not see any point in beginning a new history of Poland from scratch, and used that earlier book as the basis for this one. At the same time, I have so thoroughly reworked the text, removed so much of the old and added so much that is new, that I had no qualms about submitting it under a new title.

Some readers may be surprised to find no references to sources in the text. This is an essay rather than a textbook. It is based on well-known and undisputed facts, and is not in any sense meant to break new ground. I therefore saw no reason to clutter the text with numbers, which many readers find off-putting.

I owe a debt to Miłosz Zieliński, who helped me research the recent past, and to Jakub Borawski, who helped me place it in perspective. I should like to thank my editors Richard Johnson, who gave me invaluable support when I began to entertain doubts about the venture, Arabella Pike, who took the project over with enthusiasm, and Robert Lacey, whose editorial skills are nonpareil. I must also thank Shervie Price for reading the text and making useful suggestions, and my wife Emma for her sensible comments and her love.

Adam Zamoyski
London, 2009

ONE

People, Land and Crown

In the Middle Ages, when people favoured simple explanations, Polish folklore had it that the German nation had been deposited on this earth through the rectum of Pontius Pilate. Sadly, the Polish nation boasts no such convenient and satisfying founding myth, and its origins were something of a mystery even to its neighbours.

While most of Europe evolved from the Dark Ages in mutual interaction, with Celtic monks from Ireland carrying the religion of Rome to Germany, and Vikings from Scandinavia linking England and France with Sicily and the Arab world or sailing down the rivers of Russia to Kiev and Constantinople, the area that is now Poland existed in a vacuum.

Along with eastern Germany, Bohemia and Slovakia, it had been settled by a number of Slav peoples. Roman merchants who had come from the south in the first century in search of amber, the 'gold of the north', had recorded that they were unwarlike and agricultural, living in a state of 'rural democracy'. The most numerous of these peoples even took their name from their trade, being known as 'the people of the fields', *Polanie* in their language. There is some evidence that in the sixth century the area was overrun or partially settled by Sarmatians, a warrior people from the Black Sea Steppe, who may have provided a

1

new ruling class, or perhaps only a military caste for the Polanie.

Be that as it may, the Polanie were cushioned from the outside world by other Slav peoples. To the north, the Pomeranians (*Pomorzanie*, or people of the seaboard) and others were linked by Viking trade with much of Europe and the Arab world. To the south, the *Vislanie* of the upper Vistula were alternately attacked and evangelised by Christian Moravians. To the west, the Lusatians and the Slenzania of Silesia warred and traded with the Germans and Saxons. Sheltered by this buffer zone, the Polanie remained undisturbed throughout the eighth and ninth centuries.

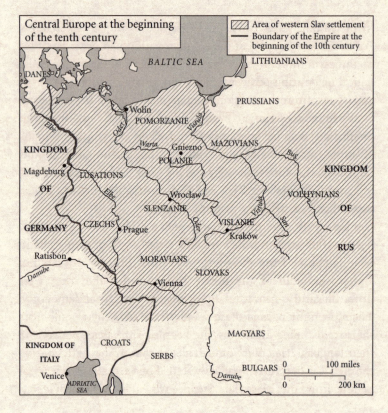

The Polanie shared a common language with the other western Slavs which differed slightly from that spoken by the Bohemians or Czechs to the south-west and that of the eastern Slavs of Rus. They also shared a common religion based on much the same pantheon as other Indo-European cults, worshipped through objects in nature – trees, rivers, stones – in which they were held to dwell, and less so in the shape of idols, or in circles and temples. As practised by the Polanie, this religion was neither organised nor hierarchical, and was not a politically unifying force. What set the Polanie apart from their sister peoples were their rulers, the Piast dynasty established in Gniezno at some time during the ninth century.

Throughout the second half of the ninth century and the beginning of the tenth, these princes gradually extended their sway over neighbouring peoples. Most of these were under some kind of pressure from the outside world, which made it easier for the Piast princes to assume control, and by the middle of the tenth century they reigned over a considerable area. This dominion was described in the first written source of any worth, by Ibrahim Ibn Yaqub, a Jewish traveller from Spain, who noted that the ruler, Prince Mieszko, had imposed a relatively sophisticated fiscal system, and exercised control through a network of castles and a standing army of 3,000 horsemen.

It was these troops and castles that Otto I, King of the Germans, encountered in the year 955. Otto had won a series of victories over his eastern neighbours and fortified his boundaries with a string of bastion-provinces known as marches. He then crossed the Elbe. As he advanced eastward, routing small bands of Slav warriors on the way, he eventually came up against something resembling an army and a system of defences. For the Polanie, the period of isolation had come to an end, and Prince Mieszko could no longer ignore the outside world.

He could even less afford to do so after 962, when Otto was crowned Roman Emperor by the Pope. This was a largely symbolic act, but one charged with significance, and Mieszko, who was aware of the political and cultural benefits Christianity had brought his Czech neighbours of Bohemia, appreciated this. Only by adopting Christianity himself would he be able to avoid war with the Emperor, and at the same time provide himself with a useful political instrument. In 965 he sought the approval of Otto and married the Bohemian Princess Dobrava. The following year, 966, Mieszko and his court were baptised. The Duchy of Polonia became part of Christendom.

Mieszko nevertheless continued to pursue his own aims, even where they conflicted with those of the Empire. One of these was to gain control of as much of the Baltic coast as possible. He invaded Pomerania, but this led to confrontation with the Margrave of the German northern march, who was attempting to conquer the area for the Empire. Mieszko defeated him at Cedynia in 972 and reached the mouth of the Oder in 976. The Margrave called on his new master Otto II for assistance, and the latter mounted an expedition against the Poles. Mieszko defeated him too in 979, and became master of the whole of Pomerania. He continued to advance along the coast until he joined up with the Danes, who had been extending their dominion eastward. He ensured good relations with his new neighbours by giving his daughter Świętosława in marriage to King Eric of Sweden and Denmark (after Eric's death, she would marry Swein Forkbeard, King of Denmark, and bear him a son, Canute, who visited Poland in 1014 to collect a force of three hundred horsemen who would help him reconquer England).

The first ruler of Christian Poland was a remarkable man. Consistently successful in war, Mieszko did not neglect diplomacy, involving powers as distant as the Moorish Caliphate of Cordoba

4

in Spain in his schemes. His last enterprise was to invade and absorb the lands of the Slenzanie. There in 992 he drew up a document, *Dagome Iudex*, laying down the boundaries of his realm, which he dedicated to St Peter and placed under the protection of the Pope.

The Pope was to prove immensely useful to Mieszko's son and successor, Bolesław the Brave, who carried on his work with flair. In 996 a monk called Adalbertus (originally Vojteh, a Bohemian prince) appeared at Bolesław's court. As he had been sent by Pope Sylvester I on a mission to evangelise the Prussians, a non-Slavic people inhabiting the Baltic seaboard to the east of the mouth of the Vistula, Bolesław received him with due honours before sending him on his way. The Prussians made short work of putting the missionary to death. On hearing the news, Bolesław sent to Prussia and bought the remains of the monk for, allegedly, their weight in gold. He then laid them to rest in the cathedral at Gniezno.

When Pope Sylvester heard of this, in 999, he canonised Adalbertus. He also took the momentous step of elevating Gniezno to the level of an archbishopric, and creating new bishoprics at Wrocław, Kołobrzeg and Kraków. This effectively created a Polish province of the Church, independent of its original tutelary German diocese of Magdeburg. It also strengthened the Polish state, as ecclesiastical networks were prime instruments of communication and control. In Poland, the first parishes were established beside castles which were centres of royal administration, a connection between religious and temporal power which is enshrined in the etymology of the Polish word for 'church' – *kościół*, which derives from the Latin *castellum*.

The new Emperor Otto III had been a friend of Adalbertus, as well as of Pope Sylvester, and in the year 1000 he came on a pilgrimage to the saint's shrine at Gniezno. His visit is described by the chronicler Gallus, who wrote:

Bolesław received him with such honour and magnificence as befitted a King, a Roman Emperor and a distinguished guest. For the arrival of the Emperor he prepared a wonderful sight; he placed many companies of knights of every sort, and then his dignitaries, in ranks, every different company set apart by the colours of its clothes. And this was no cheap spangle or any old stuff, but the most costly things that can be found anywhere on earth. For in Bolesław's day every knight and every lady of the court wore not linen or woollen cloth, but coats of costly weave, while furs, even if they were very expensive and quite new, were not worn at his court unless lined with fine stuff and trimmed with gold tassels. For gold in his time was as common as silver is now, silver was as cheap as straw. Seeing his glory, his power and his riches, the Roman Emperor cried out in admiration: 'By the crown of my Empire! What I see far exceeds what I have heard!' And taking counsel with his magnates, he added, before all those present: 'It is not fit that such a man should be titled a prince or count, as though he were just a great lord, but he should be elevated with all pomp to a throne and crowned with a crown.' Taking the Imperial diadem from his own brow, he placed it on the head of Bolesław as a sign of union and friendship, and for an ensign of state he gave him a nail from the Holy Cross and the lance of Saint Maurice, in return for which Bolesław gave him the arm of Saint Adalbertus. And they felt such love on that day that the Emperor named him brother and associate in the Empire, and called him the friend and ally of the Roman nation . . .

Otto had come not only to pray at the tomb of his saintly friend. He needed to assess Poland's strength and establish its status within the Holy Roman Empire. He was impressed by what he saw, and decided the country must be treated not as a tributary duchy, but as an independent kingdom, alongside Germany and Italy.

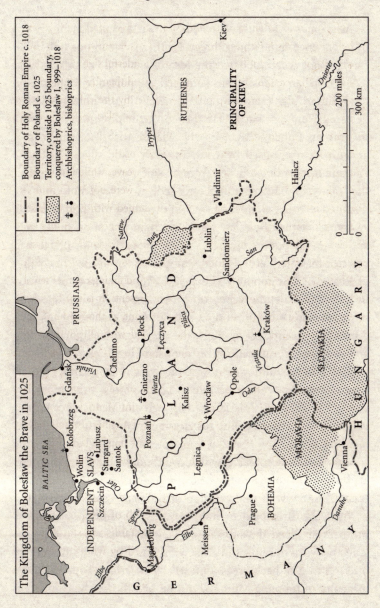

The Kingdom of Bolesław the Brave in 1025

BALTIC SEA

Boundary of Holy Roman Empire c. 1018
Boundary of Poland c. 1025
Territory, outside 1025 boundary, conquered by Bolesław I, 999–1018
Archbishoprics, bishoprics

PRUSSIANS

INDEPENDENT
SLAVS

Wolin
Kolobrzeg
Szczecin
Lubusz
Stargard
Santok
Gdańsk
Chelmno
Plock
Poznań
Gniezno
Leczyca
Kalisz
Wrocław
Opole
Legnica
Meissen
Magdeburg
Prague
Kraków
Sandomierz
Lublin
Vladimir
Halicz
Kiev
Vienna

POLAND

MORAVIA
SLOVAKIA
BOHEMIA
GERMANY
HUNGARY

RUTHENES

PRINCIPALITY
OF KIEV

Elbe
Spree
Elbe
Oder
Warta
Vistula
Vistula
Pilica
Oder
Danube
Narew
Bug
San
Prypet
Dniester

0   200 miles
0   300 km

7

As soon as Otto was succeeded by the less exalted Henry II this independence came under threat. Neither German nor Bohemian *raison d'état* accommodated the idea of a strong Polish state, and a new German offensive was launched, supported by Bohemia on the southern flank, and some pagan Slavs in the north. Bolesław defeated Henry in battle. He then brought diplomatic pressure to bear on Bohemia by a timely alliance with the Hungarians, and on Henry himself by arranging a dynastic alliance with the Palatine of Lorraine. Pressed from all sides, Henry was obliged, at the Treaty of Bautzen (1018), to cede to Poland not only the disputed territory along the Elbe, but the whole of Moravia as well.

Like his father, Bolesław was not a man to rest on his laurels, and when an opportunity for action arose, he took it. He had married his daughter to Prince Svatopolk, ruler of the Principality of Rus. When Svatopolk was ousted by rebellion from his capital in Kiev, Bolesław intervened on his son-in-law's behalf. He took the opportunity of annexing a slice of land separating his own dominions from those of Kiev, the area between the rivers Bug and San, which rounded off his own state in the east.

The Polish realm was now large by any standards, and its sovereign status seemed beyond doubt. To stress this, in the last year of his life, 1025, Bolesław had himself crowned King of Poland in Gniezno Cathedral. But his death revealed that the empire-building policies of Mieszko and Bolesław had outstripped the means of the nascent state, which could not digest their conquests at this rate. At the same time, strong regionalist tendencies made themselves felt with the accession of Bolesław's son Mieszko II.

While he attempted to hold together his dominions, jealous brothers obtained the support of Kiev by promising to cede the lands between the Bug and San rivers, and that of the Empire by offering to give back areas annexed by Bolesław. They had little difficulty in toppling Mieszko, and he had to flee the country in

1031. The unfortunate man was then set upon by some Bohemian knights who, according to the Polish chronicler, 'used leather thongs to crush his genitalia in such a way that he would never sire again'. Although he managed to return and regain his throne, Mieszko died in 1034, leaving the country divided.

His son, Kazimierz I, was hardly more successful, and he too had to flee when civil war broke out. Duke Bretislav of Bohemia took advantage of this to invade. He seized Gniezno, whence he removed not only the attributes of the Polish crown, but also the body of St Adalbertus (Wojciech in Polish), which put in jeopardy the very survival of Poland as an independent unit.

At a moment when boundaries were theoretical, cultural distinctions imperceptible and concepts of nationhood in their infancy, the first Czech chronicler, Cosmas of Prague, and his Polish contemporary the monk Gallus, both saw the other nation as the worst enemy of his own.

This raises the question of what we mean by terms such as 'Poland' at this point in history, let alone by 'Poles', 'Germans' and 'Czechs'. Frontiers, such as they were, were fluid, changing each time one ruler or another asserted his rights by force. Ethnic distinctions did not impose any deeper loyalty, and Germans fought amongst themselves more often than they fought Slavs, while the Slavs were constantly at war with each other. Nor were they well defined. When the Germans occupied the lands up to the Oder, they absorbed so much Slav blood that the population of what would become Brandenburg, the cradle of German racial myths, was heavily mixed. When the area later known as Mecklenburg became part of the German world, the Slav ruling classes became the German aristocracy. On the other hand, the rulers of Poland repeatedly intermarried with Germans.

The underlying conflict that ranged the Poles against Bohemia and the Empire was over the question of Poland's position in the

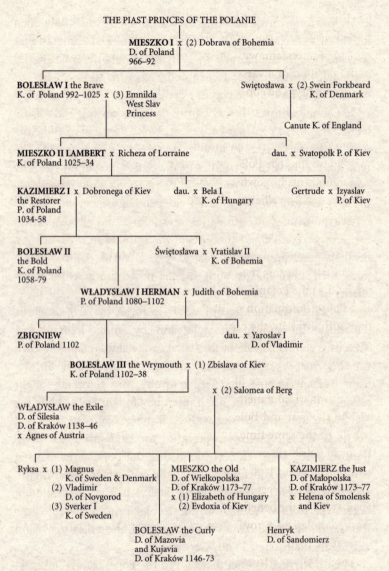

Poland – A History

THE PIAST PRINCES OF THE POLANIE

MIESZKO I x (2) Dobrava of Bohemia
D. of Poland
966–92

BOLESŁAW I the Brave
K. of Poland 992–1025 x (3) Emnilda
West Slav
Princess

Świętosława x (2) Swein Forkbeard
K. of Denmark

Canute K. of England

MIESZKO II LAMBERT x Richeza of Lorraine
K. of Poland 1025–34

dau. x Svatopolk P. of Kiev

KAZIMIERZ I x Dobronega of Kiev
the Restorer
P. of Poland
1034-58

dau. x Bela I
K. of Hungary

Gertrude x Izyaslav
P. of Kiev

BOLESŁAW II
the Bold
K. of Poland
1058-79

Świętosława x Vratislav II
K. of Bohemia

WŁADYSŁAW I HERMAN x Judith of Bohemia
P. of Poland 1080–1102

ZBIGNIEW
P. of Poland 1102

dau. x Yaroslav I
D. of Vladimir

BOLESŁAW III the Wrymouth x (1) Zbislava of Kiev
K. of Poland 1102–38

x (2) Salomea of Berg

WŁADYSŁAW the Exile
D. of Silesia
D. of Kraków 1138–46
x Agnes of Austria

Ryksa x (1) Magnus
K. of Sweden & Denmark
(2) Vladimir
D. of Novgorod
(3) Sverker I
K. of Sweden

MIESZKO the Old
D. of Wielkopolska
D. of Kraków 1173–77
x (1) Elizabeth of Hungary
(2) Evdoxia of Kiev

KAZIMIERZ the Just
D. of Małopolska
D. of Kraków 1173–77
x Helena of Smolensk
and Kiev

BOLESŁAW the Curly
D. of Mazovia
and Kujavia
D. of Kraków 1146-73

Henryk
D. of Sandomierz

Fig. 1 The early Piast Kings. (Only the more important members of the dynasty are shown.
Dates given are those of reigns. The family tree continues on pages 24–5.)

10

Christian world. For a century and a half after Otto III had sanctioned Bolesław the Brave's royal ambitions, Poland's status remained uncertain, with the Empire repeatedly trying to place it in the position of a vassal state, and Poland struggling to preserve its sovereignty. The ebb and flow of this struggle is reflected in the way Polish monarchs are variously referred to as *dux*, *princeps* or *rex* in contemporary Western sources. In spite of its own internal dissensions and wars, the Empire was the theoretical arbiter on such questions. The Polish monarch could strengthen his position by building up his own power, by seeking the support of other countries and by alliance with the Pope against the Emperor. The problems involved are clearly illustrated by the hundred years after the death of Kazimierz I in 1058.

After regaining his throne in 1039, Kazimierz had made Kraków his capital. Gniezno, the centre of Wielkopolska (Greater Poland), the land of the Polanie, needed a strong boundary along the Oder and Polish domination of Pomerania in the north and Silesia in the south. Kraków, the capital of Małopolska (Lesser Poland), was likely to be more affected by what happened in Kiev than what was going on in Pomerania. Both Kazimierz, who was married to the sister of the Prince of Kiev, and his son Bolesław II, the Bold, who also married a member of that royal house, had turned their eyes to the east and Bolesław occupied Kiev twice on his uncle's behalf. At the same time, Hungary was emerging as an important factor in Polish affairs. It was an obvious ally against both Bohemia and the Empire. It was also an element in a great web of papal diplomacy aimed against the Empire, stretching from Poland to Spain. One of the benefits of joining this alliance was that the Pope granted Bolesław a royal crown, with which the latter crowned himself in 1076.

The fiery king's friendship with the Papacy came to grief only three years after this event. Less than a century after his namesake had made such mileage out of a saint, Bolesław lost his throne over one. A number of magnates, including Stanisław, Bishop of Kraków, had started to plot against him. When Bolesław uncovered the conspiracy he reacted with violence, putting to death several of the conspirators, including the Bishop. This aroused widespread indignation, and the unfortunate King was obliged to abandon his throne to his brother Władysław Herman. The killing of the Bishop (who would be canonised in 1258) undermined the prestige of the Polish dynasty, and in 1085 the Emperor Henry IV allowed the Duke of Bohemia to crown himself King of Bohemia and Poland. Although this was a purely symbolic act, it was an affront to Władysław.

At home, Władysław was unable to curb the rising power of local lords, who stipulated that Poland should be divided between his two sons at his death. But when this came, in 1102, the younger son, Bolesław the Wrymouth, drove his brother out of the country. As his name suggests, he was an ugly man, but he was extremely capable, and quickly earned the respect of his subjects, in spite of his determination to rule with a strong arm. He was aided in this by his military prowess. In 1109 he won a victory over the Emperor and the Duke of Bohemia at the Battle of Psie Pole near Wrocław, forcing them to renounce their claims to Polish territory. He also invaded Pomerania, where a gradual German incursion had over the years weakened Polish influence. He recaptured the area up to and well beyond the Oder, as far as the island of Rügen.

The last years of his reign brought defeat during expeditions in support of his Hungarian allies, provoking renewed Bohemian invasions. A group of nobles took advantage of the situation, forcing Bolesław to make a political testament which carved Poland up into duchies. Each of his five sons was to rule over one of these. Pomerania, whose dukes were closely related to but not of the main Piast line, was given equal status. The eldest son, Władysław, was

The Division of Poland, 1138

0   200 miles
0   300 km

‧‧— Boundary of the state under
   Bolesław the Wrymouth, 1138
— — Provincial boundary
- - - Boundary of Province of
   Sandomierz, 1146
✝ ✝ Archbishoprics, bishoprics

SWEDEN

BALTIC SEA

DENMARK

Rügen

Lübeck

Wolin

Szczecin

MARCH OF
BRANDENBURG

Brenna

Magdeburg

MARCH OF
MEISSEN

KINGDOM OF BOHEMIA

Prague

Kołobrzeg

POMERANIA

Gdańsk

PRUSSIANS

CURONIANS

LITHUANIANS

LATVIANS

LETTS

Riga

Lubusz

Chelmno

Gniezno Włocławek MAZOVIA

Poznań

WIELKOPOLSKA

Konin

Kalisz

Legnica

Wrocław

SILESIA

Opole

Płock

Lublin Vladimir

SANDOMIERZ

MAŁOPOLSKA

Kraków Sandomierz

Cieszyn

MORAVIA

Halicz

KINGDOM OF
HUNGARY

Vienna

13

to reign in the small but theoretically paramount duchy of Kraków as well as his own and exert suzerainty over the others. Thus when Bolesław the Wrymouth died in 1138, the country embarked on a political experiment designed to compromise between regionalist tendencies and an underlying sense of kinship and political unity.

Ironically, considering the frequent interruptions in the succession and the consequent fragmentation of the realm, this sense of unity was based primarily on the Piast dynasty. They had established over eighty castle-towns by the end of the eleventh century and endowed market towns with royal charters granting rights and protection. They encouraged the replacement of barter with their own coinage, and provided the security necessary for the development of international trade routes through the country. Cities such as Kraków, which became the capital in 1040, Sandomierz, Kalisz, Wrocław, Poznań and Płock flourished.

Another unifying element was the Church, which was instrumental in the spread of new technologies and of the Romanesque style in architecture. It was also central to the spread of culture and education, providing as it did technical expertise, administration and schooling for would-be priests and young noblemen. The arrival of the Benedictines, whose monastery at Tyniec on the Vistula dates from the second half of the eleventh century, and later of the Premonstratentian and Cistercian orders, added impetus to this process. Most of the cathedrals had schools attached to them, and through the institution of the Church it was possible for Polish students to travel to other counties in search of learning. A local Latin *chanson de geste* made its appearance, and between 1112 and 1116 the first Polish chronicle was written in Kraków by Gallus, probably a Benedictine monk from Provence.

A distinction must be drawn between the great impact of the

Church's educational and even political activities, and the considerably lesser one it produced at the strictly religious level. Pagan cults survived the official conversion of the country in 966, and the next two centuries witnessed several major revivals, during which churches were burnt and priests put to death. The pagan survivals were particularly strong in areas such as Pomerania, which maintained a measure of autonomy in the face of pressure to submit to either Polish or Imperial overlordship.

The Church could do little about this in the face of a general lack of zeal, which is well illustrated by the Polish response to Rome's summons to the Crusades. Apart from Prince Henryk of Sandomierz, few heeded it. Duke Leszek the White explained in a long letter to the Pope that neither he nor any self-respecting Polish knight could be induced to go to the Holy Land, where, they had been informed, there was no wine, mead, or even beer to be had. There were other reasons for staying at home, since there were troublesome pagans on Poland's own frontiers in the shape of the Prussians and Lithuanians. But little was being done to convert them, and this lack of zeal was characteristic. A major motive propelling European knights across the seas to fight crusades in Palestine and the Baltic (and settlers to follow them) was the population explosion of the Middle Ages which produced overcrowding in some areas. The far from populous Poland felt no such need for expansion, and her rulers welcomed the immigration of Jews, Bohemians and Germans who provided useful services.

The realm continued to fragment after the death of Bolesław the Wrymouth in 1138 had transformed it into five duchies. The eldest of his sons, Władysław, made an attempt at reuniting it from his position as ruler of Kraków, but he came up against the resistance not only of his brothers but of most of the local lords as well. Over the next hundred years successive dukes reigning in Kraków proved less and less able to enact the formal suzerainty which went with the position, and eventually abandoned the attempt altogether. The various branches of the royal family established local dynasties, in some cases subdividing the original five duchies of Wielkopolska, Mazovia-Kujavia, Małopolska, Sandomierz and Silesia into smaller units in order to accommodate their offspring.

There was more to such fragmentation than sibling rivalry. Regional lords and the larger towns yearned for autonomy, and the trend towards devolution went hand in hand with a demand for wider power-sharing. Władysław of Wielkopolska, also known as Spindleshanks on account of his bony legs, made a valiant attempt to reassert his authority as Duke of Kraków, but powerful barons forced him to grant them substantial prerogatives by the Privilege of Cienia in 1228, thirteen years after a similar document, the Magna Carta, had been extorted from a king of England.

There was nevertheless a marked difference between the barons of England and the magnates of Poland. The power of an English or French lord at this time was held from the crown and fitted into a system of vassalage. This feudal system was never adopted in Poland, except with respect to some nobles who had migrated from western Europe. This set Polish society apart from the rest of the Continent in fundamental ways.

The highest estate were the gentry, the *szlachta*, who inherited both status and land. They were obliged to perform military service for the king and to submit to his tribunals, but they were the independent magistrates over their own lands. They upheld the customary laws of the country, the *Ius Polonicum*, based entirely on precedent, and resisted attempts at the imposition of foreign legal practices by the crown. Beneath the szlachta were a number of estates, including the *włodyki*, who were knights without noble status, and the *panosze*, who formed a kind of yeoman class. The peasants were mostly free and able to rise to a higher status. While the land they tilled belonged to the sovereign, they enjoyed defined rights. A small number were enserfed, but these gained greater personal freedom during the first half of the thirteenth century, and were not generally tied to the land as in western Europe. The adoption of the three-field system at the beginning of the thirteenth century and the agrarian boom it brought about differentiated between those who had land and those who did not. Those who did grew richer, those who did not were revealed to have nothing to offer except their labour. Thus while they gained greater personal freedom and legal protection, the poorer peasants were caught up in the mesh of economic bondage.

The cities were, literally, a law unto themselves. Most of them had been either founded by or endowed with special charters which gave them a measure of autonomy. As they grew, they attracted foreigners – Germans, Italians, Walloons, Flemings and Jews – whose presence served to increase this independence. The Germans imported with them the *Ius Teutonicum*, which was first adopted for Silesian towns in 1211, and subsequently, in the modified form of 'Magdeburg Law', for others all over Poland. These laws, which regulated criminal and civic offences and all trade practices, meant that the area within a city's walls was both administratively and legislatively in another country from that lying without. The city-dwellers evolved as a separate class having nothing in common with the others. The same was true of the growing Jewish community, which was granted a royal charter by Bolesław the Pious in 1264, the Statute of Kalisz. This recognised all Jews as *servi camerae* (servants of the treasury) and afforded them royal protection. It was the first of a number of such privileges which were to turn them into a nation within a nation.

Since there was no framework of vassalage there were no natural channels for the exercise of central authority. Royal control therefore depended not on a local vassal as elsewhere in Europe, but on a functionary appointed by the king. He was known by his function, and his title of Castellan (*Kasztelan*) derived from the royal castle from which he exercised judicial, administrative and military authority on the king's behalf. There were over a hundred of these castellans administering the Polish lands by 1250, but their importance waned along with central authority when the country was divided. In terms of power, they began to be superseded by the ministers of the individual dukes, the Palatines (*Wojewoda*).

This divergence from European norms is significant. Unlike Bohemia, which had faced similar challenges and choices, Poland had not been fully absorbed into the framework of European states. One consequence of this was that it remained more backward. But it maintained a greater degree of independence. And while it was divided into duchies it remained more uniform and cohesive as a society than many others, because it was not subjected to the mixed overlordships that placed large tracts of geographical France under the sovereignty of the king of England, areas of Germany under that of the French dynasty, or Italy at the mercy of a succession of Norman, French and German warlords. It was probably this that ensured the survival of Poland as a political unit.

TWO

Between East and West

In 1241 the horde of the legendary Genghis Khan, now commanded by his grandson Batu, broke over eastern Europe in a great wave. It overran and put to fire and sword the principalities of southern Russia and then divided into two. The larger force swept into Hungary, the other ravaged Poland. The knighthood of Małopolska gathered to face it at Chmielnik, but were swamped and massacred. The Duke of Kraków, Bolesław the Chaste, fled south to Moravia.

The Tatars sacked Kraków, then rode on westwards into Silesia. Here Duke Henryk the Pious had massed all his own forces, as well as those of Wielkopolska, a contingent of foreign knights, and even the miners from his goldmines of Złotoryja. On 8 April 1241 he led them out of the city of Legnica to face the oncoming Tatars. His forces were defeated and Duke Henryk himself was hacked to pieces.

Happily for western Europe, the Tatars veered south to rejoin their brothers in Hungary and there news reached them of the death of their Khan Ugedey. They abandoned their westward advance and rode back whence they had come. Although they never again attempted a conquest of Europe, they would keep the whole of Russia under their yoke for the next three centuries and

19

continued to harass Poland. In 1259 they sacked Lublin, Sandomierz, Bytom and Kraków. They returned in 1287, wreaking similar devastation. The horror of these raids was vividly captured in chronicle, legend and song, and is kept alive to this day in the hourly trumpet-call from the tower of St Mary's Church in Kraków, which breaks off in the middle to commemorate the Tatar arrow that cut short the medieval trumpeter's call. And it established the barbaric eastern infidel as a bogeyman in the Polish political mind.

The Tatar incursions showed up the vulnerability of a country divided. Although there was a community of interest, there had been no coordination of action, and regional militias were defeated one by one. Just as the Tatar threat died away, this vulnerability was beginning to be demonstrated on the other side of the country, where the other great bogeyman of modern Polish history was born, swaddled in steel marked with the black cross.

At a time when Poland had already been a Christian state for two hundred years, much of the southern and eastern Baltic coastline was still inhabited by pagans and was the scene of a fierce struggle carried on by Denmark, the Scandinavian kingdoms, Brandenburg and the Polish Dukes of Gdańsk-Pomerania and of Mazovia. Denmark, Brandenburg and other German princes vied with each other to conquer the area which would be known as Mecklenburg, with its valuable port of Liubice (Lübeck). Further east, where the Baltic coast curves northwards, the Danes and Scandinavians were making inroads into the lands of the Lithuanians, the Latvians, Lettigalians and Semigalians, and the Curonians. In between, the Poles battled against the Prussians, another Baltic people. The motives were the desire for land and trade, thinly disguised as missionary by local bishops who could not afford to have the Church excluded. This changed when St Bernard of Clairvaux started preaching the crusade all over Europe.

It was he who persuaded Pope Alexander III to use north European crusaders in northern Europe rather than the Middle East, and to issue, in 1171, a bull granting the same dispensations and indulgences to those who fought against the heathen Slavs or Prussians as to those fighting the Saracens. The advantage of a crusade was that any local duke who launched what was in effect a private war against his enemies could, by making an arrangement with his bishop, recruit foreign knights who would come and fight for him as unpaid soldiers. And the fruits of this crusade whetted the appetites of Danes, Poles and Germans alike. Although the first northern crusade was a failure, the heathen Slavs in Western Pomerania were gradually subjugated by the Germans and the Danes over the next fifty years.

Throughout the early 1200s the Dukes of Mazovia made inroads into Prussia, but this only provoked counter-raids from the Prussians. A methodical military takeover of the area was needed, and the only armies which could take up such a challenge were the military orders, the most famous of which, the Templars and Hospitallers, had proved their efficacy in Palestine. The Bishop of Riga had, in 1202, formed the Knighthood of Christ, better known as the Sword Brothers, to help him conquer and evangelise the Latvians. With the approval of Duke Konrad of Mazovia, the Bishop of Prussia followed suit by founding Christ's Knights of Dobrzyn as the regular army of the Polish 'mission' to Prussia. But this was too small to cope with the task.

A more radical solution was called for, and so, in 1226, Konrad of Mazovia took a step whose consequences for Poland and for Europe were to be incalculable. He invited the Teutonic Order of the Hospital of St Mary in Jerusalem, known as the Teutonic Knights, to establish a commandery at Chełmno and help him conquer Prussia. The Teutonic Knights, founded at Acre in Palestine on the model of the Templars, were attracted by the idea of a mission nearer home. They thought they had found one in Hungary, where they were given the task of holding the Tatars at bay, but King Andrew II of Hungary grew wary of their ambitions and shortly expelled them.

They could see the advantages of the Polish offer, but this time the Grand Master Hermann von Salza was determined to guarantee their future. He obtained documents from the Emperor Frederick II and a bull from Pope Gregory IX authorising the order to conquer Prussia and thereafter to hold it in perpetuity as a papal fief. Before he realised what he had let himself in for, Konrad of Mazovia discovered that the lease he had granted the order on the territory of Chełmno had become a freehold.

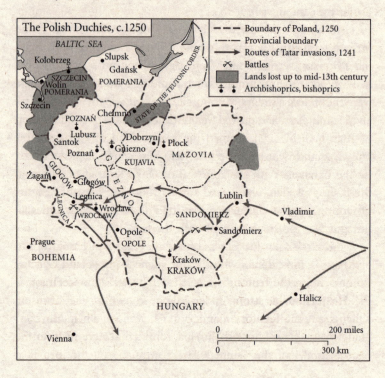

The Polish Duchies, c.1250

- - - Boundary of Poland, 1250
-·-·- Provincial boundary
→ Routes of Tatar invasions, 1241
⚔ Battles
▨ Lands lost up to mid-13th century
✝ Archbishoprics, bishoprics

Hermann von Salza, who still kept his sights on the Holy Land, originally saw the Prussian theatre of operations as a sideshow. He despatched a few knights there in 1229, and a further contingent took part in a crusade into Prussia in 1232–33, preached by the Dominicans, in which several Polish dukes, the margraves of Meissen and Brandenburg, the Duke of Austria and the King of Bohemia took part, along with hundreds of German knights. The order's involvement grew when, in 1237, it took over the Sword Brothers. And it was encouraged to take a greater interest in the area by successive Popes, whose wish to see the conversion of the pagan Balts was complemented by a desire to bring as much of northern Russia as possible into the fold of the Roman Church.

This placed the order in a position to organise annual forays (*reysas*) against the pagans for kings, princes and knights who wished to acquit themselves of the duty to bear arms for Christ. These *reysas* were like safaris for the visiting grandees, who not only fulfilled their crusading vows but enjoyed a good campaign. They also took away a favourable impression of the order, which they subsequently expressed by giving it grants of land in their own countries and by supporting it diplomatically. At the same time, the increase in crusading activity in the region created tensions and problems of its own, as it was now drawing in not only Denmark, Sweden, Norway and the Polish duchies, but also the emerging state of Lithuania and the Russian principalities of Novgorod and Muscovy.

By 1283 most of Prussia had been conquered. Although it was settled by a considerable number of landless Polish and German knights, it was the Teutonic Order that ruled the province. It established a formidable stronghold at Marienburg, a number of castles throughout the territory and a port at Elbing (Elbląg) to carry trade from the province. It proved an efficient administrator, as monastic discipline precluded venality and its structure provided

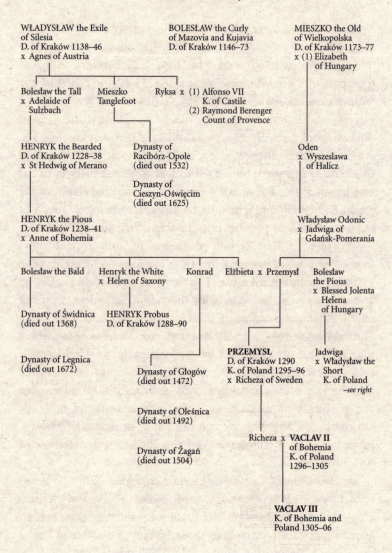

Fig. 2 The division and reunification of Poland under the later Piasts

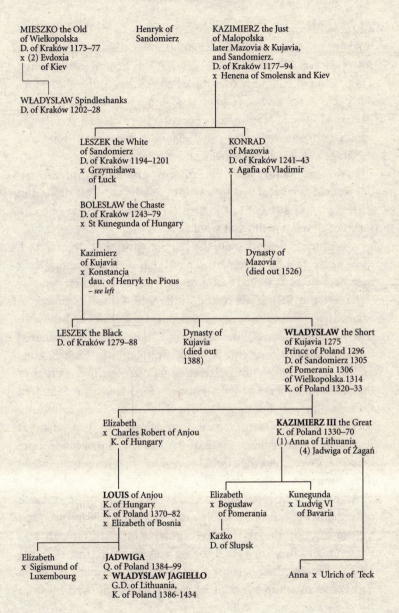

MIESZKO the Old
of Wielkopolska
D. of Kraków 1173–77
x (2) Evdoxia
      of Kiev

Henryk of
Sandomierz

KAZIMIERZ the Just
of Małopolska
later Mazovia & Kujavia,
and Sandomierz.
D. of Kraków 1177–94
x Henena of Smolensk and Kiev

WŁADYSŁAW Spindleshanks
D. of Kraków 1202–28

LESZEK the White
of Sandomierz
D. of Kraków 1194–1201
x Grzymisława
   of Łuck

KONRAD
of Mazovia
D. of Kraków 1241–43
x Agafia of Vladimir

BOLESŁAW the Chaste
D. of Kraków 1243–79
x St Kunegunda of Hungary

Kazimierz
of Kujavia
x Konstancja
   dau. of Henryk the Pious
   – *see left*

Dynasty of
Mazovia
(died out 1526)

LESZEK the Black
D. of Kraków 1279–88

Dynasty of
Kujavia
(died out
1388)

WŁADYSŁAW the Short
of Kujavia 1275
Prince of Poland 1296
D. of Sandomierz 1305
of Pomerania 1306
of Wielkopolska 1314
K. of Poland 1320–33

Elizabeth
x Charles Robert of Anjou
   K. of Hungary

KAZIMIERZ III the Great
K. of Poland 1330–70
(1) Anna of Lithuania
     (4) Jadwiga of Żagań

LOUIS of Anjou
K. of Hungary
K. of Poland 1370–82
x Elizabeth of Bosnia

Elizabeth
x Bogusław
   of Pomerania

Kaźko
D. of Słupsk

Kunegunda
x Ludvig VI
   of Bavaria

Elizabeth
x Sigismund of
   Luxembourg

JADWIGA
Q. of Poland 1384–99
x WŁADYSŁAW JAGIEŁŁO
   G.D. of Lithuania,
   K. of Poland 1386-1434

Anna x Ulrich of Teck

a degree of continuity which dynastic states (with their disputed successions, minorities and likelihood of feckless or incompetent rulers) lacked. The knights' rule was relatively benign to begin with. They favoured voluntary over forced conversion of the autochtonous population, and were pragmatic enough to use local pagans to fight alongside them when necessary. But repeated revolts and apostasies made them take a more jaundiced view with time, and the autochtones were gradually all but exterminated.

In the space of fifty years, the Prussian nuisance on the Mazovian border had been replaced by a well-ordered state. This did not in itself represent a threat to the Polish duchies. But it was one of a series of developments that would.

A century earlier, in 1150, the last Slav prince of Brenna died, to be succeeded by a German. The March of Brandenburg, as it then became, encroached eastwards, driving a wedge between Slav states on the Baltic, where the outflanked Prince Bogusław of Szczecin was forced to accept German overlordship, and those to the south, like the small principality of Lubusz, which was annexed to Brandenburg outright. In 1266 Brandenburg took Santok, and in 1271 Gdańsk, thus extending its own territory to that of the Teutonic Order. The Poles retook both Gdańsk and Santok in the following year, but they would never push the German advance back to the river Oder. From the stronghold they had set up at Berlin on the river Spree in 1231, the margraves of Brandenburg looked eastward, and they would seize every opportunity to extend their dominion in that direction.

At the same time, settlers from all over Germany came in search of land and opportunity, usually well received by Polish rulers, and by the end of the thirteenth century not only Silesian and Pomeranian cities such as Wrocław and Szczecin, but even the capital, Kraków, had become predominantly German. In Silesia and Pomerania, the influx of landless knights and farmers from

Germany also made itself felt in rural areas, radically affecting the will as well as the ability of local Piast rulers to stand by a disunited Poland. Like so many small shopkeepers, these minor rulers had to pay tribute to whoever was strong enough to impose protection. One by one the princes of Pomerania, outflanked by German states and undermined by the German ascendancy in their cities, particularly Hanseatic centres such as Szczecin and Stargard, had to accept the German Emperor instead of the Duke of Kraków as their overlord. This process weakened the greater Polish duchies as well, as a result of which even their independence came under threat. In 1300 King Vaclav II of Bohemia was able to invade Wielkopolska, and with the blessing of the Emperor have himself crowned King of Poland.

If the experience of the Tatar invasions had provided a powerful argument in favour of reuniting the Polish duchies into a single kingdom, this was given added weight by increasing resentment of the encroaching Germans and foreigners in general. After Bohemia's capture of Kraków with the connivance of some of the townspeople in 1311, the Polish troops which retook it the following year rounded up all the citizens and beheaded those who could not pronounce the Polish tongue-twisters they were made to repeat.

It was also supported by the Church. Until now, this had not played a political role, merely an administrative one. Under the early Piast kings, the bishops had been little more than func-tionaries with no power-base of their own. The devolution of the country into separate duchies changed this, as the individual dukes needed the support of their local bishops. These were quick to perceive that if the Polish duchies were absorbed into Bohemia or Germany, the Polish Church would lose its autonomous status, and they took steps to counter the creeping Germanisation. At the Synod of Łęczyca in 1285 the Polish bishops adopted a resolution that only Poles could be appointed as teachers in church schools.

After the canonisation of Stanisław, the Bishop of Kraków put to death by Bolesław II and recognised as patron of Poland in 1253, the monk Wincenty of Kielce wrote a life of the saint in which the alleged miraculous growing together of his quartered body is described as prophetic of the way in which the divided Poland would become one again. Similarly patriotic sentiments can be detected in the chronicle of another Bishop of Kraków, Wincenty Kadłubek, written in the first years of the thirteenth century, and in the more reliable *Kronika Wielkopolska*, written by a churchman in Poznań in the 1280s.

The message was taken up by some of the dukes, who decided to abandon the hereditary principle and to elect from their number an overlord who would rule effectively in Kraków. Henryk Probus of Silesia was the first to be chosen in this way, and on his death in 1290 the Kraków throne was given to Przemysł II of Gniezno, who was actually crowned King of Poland in 1295, but was assassinated two years later by agents of Brandenburg. He was succeeded in 1296 by a prince of the Mazovian line, Władysław the Short, who was to become one of the most remarkable of Polish kings.

The Bohemian invasion of 1300 forced Władysław to flee the country for a time, and he went to Rome in search of allies. As his sobriquet suggests, he was a small man, but he knew what he wanted and how to get it, laying his plans with skill. The Papacy was locked in one of its perennial conflicts with the Empire, and therefore looked kindly on the anti-Imperial Polish prince. Władysław sought the support of Charles Robert of Anjou, the erstwhile King of Naples and Sicily who had just succeeded to the Hungarian throne. With the Pope's support he sealed an alliance by marrying his daughter to the Angevin. Having also secured the cooperation of the princes of Halicz and Vladimir he set off to reconquer his realm from the Czechs.

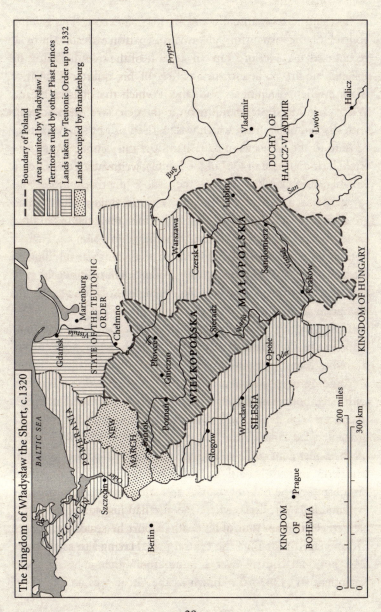

The Kingdom of Władysław the Short, c.1320

Boundary of Poland
Area reunited by Władysław I
Territories ruled by other Piast princes
Lands taken by Teutonic Order up to 1332
Lands occupied by Brandenburg

BALTIC SEA

Gdańsk

Marienburg

STATE OF THE TEUTONIC ORDER

Chełmno

Prypet

Vladimir

DUCHY OF HALICZ-VLADIMIR

Lwów

Halicz

Bug

San

Lublin

Warszawa

Sandomierz

Czersk

Wisła

MAŁOPOLSKA

Kraków

Sieradz

Warta

WIELKOPOLSKA

Płowce

Gniezno

Poznań

NEW MARCH

POMERANIA

Santok

Noteć

Odra

Głogów

Wrocław

Opole

Oder

SILESIA

Szczecin

SZCZECIN

Berlin

KINGDOM OF BOHEMIA

Prague

KINGDOM OF HUNGARY

0   200 miles
0   300 km

29

In 1306 he took Kraków and in 1314 Gniezno, thus gaining control of the two principal provinces, while a third, Mazovia, recognised his overlordship. In 1320 he was crowned King of Poland, the first to be crowned at Kraków. By making an alliance with Sweden, Denmark and the Pomeranian principalities, Władysław forced Brandenburg on to the defensive while he dealt with the Teutonic Order, which was in a difficult position. The fall of Acre to the Saracens in 1291 had deprived it of its headquarters. The indictment in 1307 of the Templars, on whom the Teutonic Knights were closely modelled, their subsequent dissolution and savage persecution, were a chilling warning to any order which grew too powerful. Władysław lost little time in taking the Teutonic Order to a Papal court not only on charges of invasion and rapine, but on more fundamental questions of whether it was fulfilling its mission. The Papal judgement went against the order, but the very fact that the Knights had been cornered brought about a subtle change in their attitude.

Their headquarters, located in Venice after the fall of Acre so as to be ready for future crusades in the Holy Land, was quickly moved to Marienburg in Prussia in 1309. Prussia now became not a crusading outpost, but a state, and it would settle its disputes with neighbours not through Papal courts but on the battlefield. In concert with its ally John of Luxembourg, King of Bohemia, the order invaded Poland. The Silesian Duke Bolko of Świdnica held off the Bohemians while Władysław marched against the order and defeated it in a costly battle at Płowce in 1331. Too weak to pursue his advantage, he did not manage to reassert a Polish ascendancy in Pomerania or Silesia, where the German hegemony persisted. Nevertheless, by the time of his death in 1333, Władysław the Short had managed to reunite the central provinces and to establish at least nominal control over a number of other areas. His son Kazimierz III (1333–70), known as the Great, was able to carry through this process and to place the sovereignty of Poland beyond question.

In this he was assisted by an unusually favourable conjunction of circumstances. As a minor ice-age reduced yields and ruined harvests throughout much of Europe, Poland basked in a more than usually warm and temperate spell, which produced not only bumper crops but also conditions in which Mediterranean fruit could be grown and wine produced. While the Hundred Years' War devastated the richest lands in western Europe and wrought financial havoc as far afield as Italy, Poland was spared lengthy conflicts. Finally, as the entire Continent was engulfed by the plague of 1348, the Black Death, most of Poland remained unaffected. The populations of England and France, of Italy and Scandinavia, of Hungary, Switzerland, Germany and Spain were more than halved. Poland's grew, partly as a consequence of conditions elsewhere. The depredations of the plague were accompanied by widespread famine, which provoked an exodus from towns, and refugees roamed Europe in search of food and a safe haven. In addition, the need for a scapegoat had provoked the greatest wave of anti-Jewish atrocities in medieval history, and terrified survivors also fled, mainly eastwards. All were welcomed in Poland, which insisted only on a period of quarantine.

Kazimierz was a fitting ruler for these halcyon days. Physically handsome, with a broad forehead and a remarkable head of hair, he was a regal figure, combining courage and determination with the tastes of a voluptuary. He launched a building programme which, along with the cathedrals of Kraków and Gniezno and churches all over the country, gave rise to sixty-five new fortified towns, the fortification of twenty-seven existing ones, and fifty-three new castles. He also rerouted the Vistula at Kraków, and constructed a canal linking the salt-mines of Wieliczka with the capital. In 1347 he codified the entire corpus of existing laws in two books: one, the Statute of Piotrków, for Wielkopolska; one, the Statute of Wiślica, for Małopolska. He reformed the fiscal system, created a central chancellery, and regulated the monetary situation with the introduction in 1388 of new coinage. In the towns, he established guilds and extended Magdeburg Law. He granted a separate law to the Armenians living in Polish cities and gave the Jews their own fiscal, legal, and even political institutions.

These measures laid the foundations of a new boom. Polish cities gained considerable numbers of merchants and skilled artisans, while the influx of Jews provided them with banking and other facilities. This stimulated industry. Newly-discovered deposits of iron, lead, copper, silver, zinc, sulphur and rock salt were exploited and mining techniques improved. The traditional exports of grain, cattle, hides, lumber and other forest produce were supplemented by manufactured goods such as finished cloth, which was carried as far west as Switzerland.

Contact with the outside world was increasing, largely thanks to the Church, whose activity, both missionary and educational, brought foreign clerics to Poland and sent Polish ones abroad, some, like the friar Benedictus Polonus, as far as the capital of the Mongol Khan Guyuk in 1245, but most to study, particularly at the universities of Bologna and Paris. King Kazimierz exerted a personal influence on the development of learning and culture, and laid the foundations of the flowering of the next century by establishing, in 1364, a university at Kraków. Coming just after the foundation of the Charles University of Prague and before those of Vienna and Heidelberg, this was the second such academy in central Europe. Unlike most English, French and German universities, which evolved from religious institutions, it was based on the Italian models of Padua and Bologna, which were secular establishments.

While he lavished care on domestic projects and encouraged

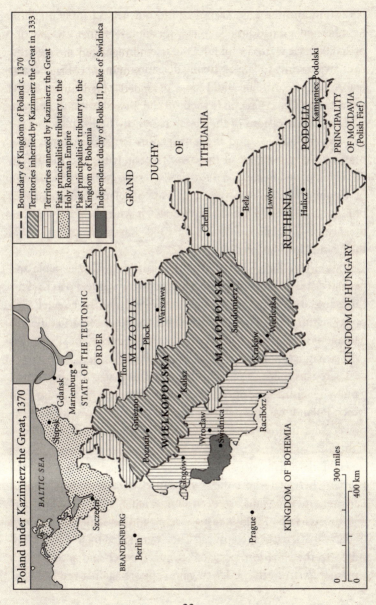

Poland under Kazimierz the Great, 1370

Legend:
- Boundary of Kingdom of Poland c. 1370
- Territories inherited by Kazimierz the Great in 1333
- Territories annexed by Kazimierz the Great
- Piast principalities tributary to the Holy Roman Empire
- Piast principalities tributary to the Kingdom of Bohemia
- Independent duchy of Bolko II, Duke of Świdnica

BALTIC SEA

BRANDENBURG
Berlin

Szczecin
Słupsk
Gdańsk
Marienburg

STATE OF THE TEUTONIC ORDER

GRAND DUCHY OF LITHUANIA

Głogów
Wrocław
Świdnica
Racibórz

Poznań
Gniezno
Kalisz

WIELKOPOLSKA

Toruń
Płock

MAZOVIA

Warszawa

Sandomierz
Kraków
Wieliczka

MAŁOPOLSKA

Chełm
Bełz
Lwów
Halicz

RUTHENIA

Kamienec Podolski

PODOLA

PRINCIPALITY OF MOLDAVIA (Polish Fief)

KINGDOM OF HUNGARY

Prague

KINGDOM OF BOHEMIA

0   300 miles
0   400 km

33

education and the arts, Kazimierz did not neglect foreign affairs: he inherited a kingdom of 106,000 square kilometres, and left one of 260,000. He warred with John of Luxembourg, King of Bohemia, over rival claims to Silesia, finally defeating him in 1345, one year before the unfortunate blind king lost his ostrich feathers to the Prince of Wales at Crécy. He then turned his attention to the east.

The Tatar invasions of the previous century had annihilated the Principality of Kiev, and the smaller Russian principalities were only allowed to survive at the cost of yearly tribute to the Tatars, who had settled in southern Russia. Two such principalities, those of Halicz and Vladimir, were adjacent to Poland's south-eastern border. Both were dynastically connected with Poland, and after the princes of Halicz died out, in 1340, Kazimierz incorporated their lands into his own dominion.

This elongation of Poland to the south-east was inevitable and permanent. The move of the Polish capital from Gniezno to Kraków three hundred years before was now beginning to affect Polish policy significantly. The king viewed his dominions from a different vantage point, and the most pervasive influence at court was that of the magnates of Małopolska, the 'Kraków Lords'.

There was more at stake in this eastern theatre than territorial gain. The disintegration of Kiev had left a power vacuum into which Poland was inevitably drawn, all the more so since another power was taking more than a passing interest in the area – Lithuania.

The Lithuanians were a Baltic people like the Prussians and the Latvians, between whom they were settled. Long after their kindred Latvians and Prussians had been subjugated by the Sword Brothers and the Teutonic Knights respectively, the Lithuanians continued to defy all attempts at conquest. They were ruled by a dynasty well suited to the situation, prepared to make peace and accept token Christianity from the order to gain support against the Russians of Novgorod, and from Novgorod to defeat the order. Their conduct of policy was so wily and volatile that none of their neighbours could ever rest easy. After the débâcle of Kiev, the Lithuanians annexed vast tracts of masterless land. In 1362 their ruler Grand Duke Algirdas defeated the Tatars at the Battle of the Blue Waters, and in the following year he occupied Kiev itself.

In less than a hundred years the Lithuanian state had quadrupled in size, but while this made it more formidable to its enemies, it endeared it to none and enmeshed it in problems which, for once, were too great for its rulers. They could not hope to administer the huge area populated with Christian Slavs by whose multitude they were to be eventually swamped. Their seizure of these lands had brought them into conflict with the Tatars on one front, while the Teutonic Knights were straining all their resources to crush them on the other. The Russian principalities were hostile, while the Poles, who now shared a long frontier with Lithuania, were growing tired of sporadic border raids. Lithuania needed an ally. The problem of which to choose was the most pressing issue facing Grand Duke Iogaila when he came to the Lithuanian throne in 1377. And that same year had placed Poland in a dilemma, for different reasons.

Kazimierz the Great had died in 1370. Although married four times, he had no heir, and left the throne to his nephew, Louis of Anjou, King of Hungary. King Louis attended his uncle's funeral and then went back to Hungary, leaving his mother, the late king's sister, to rule in his name. She could not rule without the support of the more powerful nobles of Małopolska, the 'Kraków Lords'. They exploited this opportunity to assume a greater share not only in the running of the country, but in the definition of its very status.

A new concept of the Polish state had been evolving from the beginning of the fourteenth century whose gist was that sovereignty

The Combined Kingdom of Poland and Lithuania in 1466

```
0                    300 miles
0            400 km
```

SWEDEN

DENMARK

BALTIC SEA

Riga

NOVGOROD

PSKOV

TVER

Moscow

MUSCOVY

Vitebsk

Gdańsk

Königsberg

Wilno

Smolensk

RIAZAN

Marienburg

Toruń

Poznań

Warszawa

KINGDOM

GRAND DUCHY

OF

LITHUANIA

Wrocław

OF

KINGDOM
OF
BOHEMIA

Kraków

Lwów

Kiev

GOLDEN HORDE

POLAND

KINGDOM OF
HUNGARY

PRINCIPALITY

OF

MOLDAVIA

*WILD
PLAINS*

KHANATE

OF THE

CRIMEA

*Azov
Sea*

TRANSYLVANIA

Kilia

VALLACHIA

BLACK SEA

- - - Boundary of the Kingdom of Poland
and her vassal states c. 1466
▥ Duchy of Słupsk
▨ State of Teutonic Order
▦ Piast duchies of Silesia
⣿ Lands nominally belonging to Lithuania

should be vested not in the person of the monarch, but in a specific
geographical area, the *Corona Regni Poloniae*, an expression meant
to embrace all the Polish lands, even those which had fallen under
foreign domination. In 1374 the Polish nobles wrested from King
Louis the Statute of Košice, which stressed the indivisibility of
this patrimony, and stipulated that no part of it was his to give
away. They were looking to a future which remained uncertain,
since Louis, too, had no male heir.

He did, however, have two daughters. He had married the elder, Maria, to Sigismund of Luxembourg, and intended him to take the Polish throne. The younger, Hedwig, was betrothed to Wilhelm of Habsburg, who was to have Hungary. But when Louis died in 1382, the Kraków Lords refused to bow to these wishes and made their own plans.

They rejected the already married Maria and brought her ten-year-old sister Hedwig, Jadwiga in Polish, to Kraków, where in 1384 she was crowned emphatically king (*rex*). The chronicler Długosz noted: 'The Polish lords and prelates were so taken with her, so greatly and sincerely loved her that, almost forgetting their masculine dignity, they did not feel any shame or degradation in being the subjects of such a gracious and virtuous lady.' In fact, they saw her principally as an instrument, and they disregarded her feelings entirely. When young Wilhelm of Habsburg turned up to claim his betrothed, she was locked in the castle on Wawel hill. After fruitless efforts to see her he left, and she was prepared by the Polish lords for the bed of another: they had found a husband for her in Iogaila, Grand Duke of Lithuania.

The idea of a union between Poland and Lithuania had germinated simultaneously in both countries. On 14 August 1385 a basic agreement was signed at Krewo. This was followed by more specific pledges at Wołkowysk in January 1386, and at Lublin a few weeks later. On 12 February, Jagiełło, as his name had crystallised in Polish, entered Kraków, and three days later he was baptised as Władysław. On 18 February he married Jadwiga, and on 4 March was crowned King of Poland.

THREE

The Jagiellon Experience

Queen Jadwiga died young, having borne her husband no heir. Yet the fruits of her marriage to Władysław Jagiełło were prodigious. In the first instance, it sounded the knell for the Teutonic Order: with the conversion of Lithuania the need for crusading vanished, and with it the whole *raison d'être* of the Knights in Prussia. The union of two enemies whom the order had often played off against each other in the past only compounded this.

The order responded by trying to undo it. Władysław Jagiełło unwittingly helped when he installed his fiercely ambitious and unaccountable cousin Vytautas (Witold) as regent in Lithuania. Vytautas championed pagan separatist opposition to the union with Poland, at the same time accepting baptism and the alliance of the order. But while the order continued to intrigue with Vytautas and negotiate with Władysław, it could not hope to avoid confrontation with the Polish–Lithuanian alliance indefinitely. When this came in the war of 1409–10, it resulted in the devastating defeat of the Order on the battlefield of Grunwald (Tannenberg) by a combined force under the command of Władysław and Vytautas.

The battle was one of the longest and bloodiest of the Middle Ages. The Grand Master Ulrich von Jungingen and all the order's officers but one lay dead on the field, and the whole of Prussia was there for the taking. Much to the exasperation of the Polish commanders, Władysław reined in the pursuit and in the treaty signed later he demanded only a thin strip of land to be ceded to Lithuania, and nothing for Poland, while taking a vast cash indemnity from the order for himself. A decade later the knights made war again, were again defeated, and again got away with insignificant losses. In 1454 a revolt against the order by local knights and cities, aided by Poland, initiated a war which dragged on for thirteen years. The knights were defeated, and were once again spared, by the Treaty of Toruń in 1466. Poland took the coastline around Gdańsk and Elbing, the province of Warmia (Ermland), and even the stronghold of Marienburg, but did not suppress the order, which moved its capital to Königsberg and retained the rest of its dominions as a vassal of the king of Poland. Such forbearance might seem surprising, particularly as the Teutonic Knights were ruthless in war, raping and murdering, and even burning churches. There were, however, factors involved in the relations between Poland and the order that touched on a religious debate of European proportions.

The Teutonic Order had representatives and friends at every court, and was a master of propaganda. Its first line of attack had been that the betrothal of Jadwiga to Wilhelm of Habsburg had been consummated and that her marriage to Władysław Jagiełło was therefore bigamous. It also argued, with some justification, that the alleged conversion of Lithuania was a sham, and that Catholic Polish knights had been the minority at Grunwald in an army made of Lithuanian pagans, Christians of the Eastern rite, and even Muslims (the Tatars who had settled in Lithuania some time before). The order suggested that Władysław Jagiełło's army was hardly more Christian than Saladin's.

The Teutonic Knights had a point, and that point assumed importance in the context of a minor reformation which was sweeping Europe, a nationalist, anti-clerical, anti-Imperial movement whose greatest exponent was the Bohemian Jan Hus. The Hussite movement was itself connected with John Wycliffe's Lollards in England, and both causes enjoyed considerable sympathy in Poland.

Matters came to a head at the Council of Constance, convoked in 1415 to combat the Hussite heresy. The Teutonic Order saw in this a perfect forum at which to discredit Poland and reconfirm the validity of its own crusading mission, judging that if this were endorsed by Christian Europe, it would have placed itself beyond the reach of Polish attempts to destroy it.

The Polish delegation to the Council of Constance, led by Paweł Włodkowic (Paulus Vladimiri) of Kraków University, included a number of Lithuanians and schismatics, which caused uproar and favoured the order's case. Włodkowic ran rings around its representatives and managed to discredit it. But there was no clear-cut victory. The Teutonic Knights enjoyed wide diplomatic support, including that of the Empire, which had political objections to the Polish–Lithuanian union.

The arrangement itself was under frequent review. In 1413, after Grunwald, a new treaty of union was signed at Horodło. This attempted to bind the two states together more firmly, and was epitomised by the Polish szlachta adopting the Lithuanians as brothers in chivalry, bestowing on them their own coats of arms. In 1430, Vytautas' successor as Grand Duke of Lithuania, Svidrigaila, undid all this by allying himself with the Teutonic Order and adopting an anti-Polish policy. Ten years later, the union was formally dissolved, but this made little difference, since the ruler of Lithuania was the son of the King of Poland, whom he succeeded in 1446, reuniting the two states under one crown.

The unstable nature of the union was largely the result of incompatibility. Poland was a nationally based Christian state with

The Jagiellon Experience

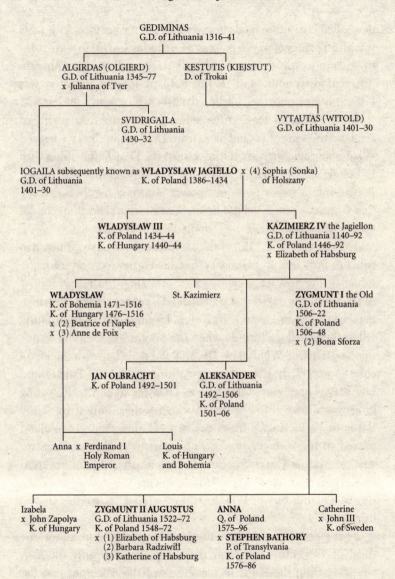

Fig. 3 The Jagiellon dynasty of Poland-Lithuania

developed institutions and strong constitutional instincts. Lithuania was an amalgam of pagan Balts and Orthodox Christian Slavs ruled by an autocratic dynasty. The two states pulled each other in different directions, and in the field of foreign policy it was Lithuania, or rather the Jagiellon dynasty, which pulled the hardest.

It is no coincidence that the oldest extant letter from a king of England to a king of Poland dates from 1415, when Henry V begged Władysław Jagiełło to assist him against the French: the union with Lithuania and the victory over the Teutonic Order had turned Poland into a major European power. And it is hardly surprising that with such power behind them, the ambitious Jagiellons should have taken advantage of the opportunities on offer.

The extinction in 1437 of the Luxembourg dynasty, which had ruled in Bohemia and Hungary, heralded a new contest for hegemony in the area between two new arrivals – the Habsburgs of Austria and the Jagiellons of Poland-Lithuania. Hungary, which had been ruled successively by Anjou, Luxembourg and Habsburg, fell to the Jagiellons in 1440 when the Magyars offered the throne to the stripling Władysław III of Poland, Władysław Jagiełło's eldest son. Władysław did not rule long as King of Poland and Hungary. Three years after he was crowned at Buda, the young king was drawn into the anti-Turkish league, and slain at the Battle of Varna on the Black Sea in 1444. The throne of Poland passed to his younger brother, Kazimierz IV. That of Hungary went to Mattias Corvinius, but after his death in 1490 it reverted to Kazimierz's eldest son, Władysław. This Władysław was king not of Poland, but of Bohemia, the Czech Diet having elected him in 1471.

By the end of the century the Jagiellons ruled over about one third of the entire European mainland. Their gigantic domain stretched from the Baltic to the shores of the Black Sea and the Adriatic. In the next generation they would lose all the thrones outside Poland to the Habsburgs, and Poland would find itself none the richer for the experience of having been at the heart of a great empire.

Yet, as the szlachta were quick to appreciate, there were advantages in having wayward and often absentee kings. It permitted them to assume a greater share in the running of the country, and the crown's frequent demands for funds and armies supplied them with the levers for extorting the concessions which shaped the emerging forms of parliamentary government.

The principle of government by consensus was already enshrined in practice under the early Piast kings. By the beginning of the thirteenth century this practice was established firmly enough to survive in the governance of the various provinces when the Kingdom was divided. Provinces such as Wielkopolska and Mazovia would hold an assembly called *sejm*, at which the entire szlachta of the district could join in discussion and vote.

The consent of the sejm of every province was crucial to the process of reunification of the Polish lands, and by the time this was achieved the sejms had become part of the machinery of government. Władysław the Short convoked them four times during his reign (1320–33), and his successor Kazimierz the Great (1330–70) almost as often, acknowledging them as the basis of his right to govern.

The heirless death of Kazimierz and the ensuing regency of Elizabeth furnished the opportunity for one group of szlachta to steal a march on their fellows. These were the dignitaries of the realm, the castellans who had been the mainstay of royal authority in the regions, and the palatines, who had grown into virtual governors of their provinces – the provinces themselves came to be known as 'palatinates' as a result. Representing as they did the forces of regional autonomy, the palatines were poor instruments of royal control, and Władysław the Short when reuniting the country had been obliged to bring in a new tier of royal administration, the *starosta*, a kind of royal sheriff, who henceforth represented the king in his area. The palatines assumed a political rather than a purely administrative role, and, in alliance with the bishops, formed a new oligarchy. Over the years, a number of them had assumed the function of royal council, and in the critical moments following the death of Kazimierz the Great they took the fate of Poland into their own hands, deciding on Jadwiga rather than Maria and choosing her a husband in Władysław Jagiełło. And they made it clear that it was they who would select his successor. His failure to produce an heir with Jadwiga strengthened their hand.

All the palatines and castellans were allowed a seat in the Grand Council (*consilium maius*), but policy-making was jealously guarded by those palatines and bishops who sat in the Privy Council (*consilium secretum*). A typical figure is Zbigniew Oleśnicki, Bishop of Kraków, secretary to Władysław Jagiełło, regent during the minority of Władysław III and mentor of his successor Kazimierz IV. Educated, tough, absolutist in his convictions, a cardinal who was a born statesman, guided by a vision which combined his own advancement with that of Poland and the Church, he had no room in his scheme of things for a vociferous sejm.

The szlachta were not fond of him or the oligarchy he stood for, and made it clear to Władysław Jagiełło that he needed their support as well as that of the magnates in order to secure the succession of his son. This enabled them to extort a number of privileges and rights during the 1420s, the most important of which, granted at Jedlnia in 1430 and confirmed at Kraków three years later, was the edict *Neminem captivabimus nisi iure victum*. An equivalent to the later English *Habeas corpus* act, it meant that nobody could be held or imprisoned without trial. This placed the szlachta beyond the reach of intimidation by the magnates and officers of the crown. Once it had become clear that the crown's prerogatives were being ceded, the magnates and the szlachta leapfrogged each other to claim them. This race had the twofold effect of accelerating the development of the parliamentary system, and of defining the two groups which were eventually to crystallise into the upper and lower chambers.

Hemmed in by the magnates, Kazimierz IV sought the support of the szlachta, which was eager to give it, at a price. The price was the Privilege of Nieszawa, granted in 1454, which stipulated that the king could only raise troops and taxes with the approval of the district assemblies, the sejmiks (lesser sejms) of the eighteen palatinates of Poland. This enshrined the principle of no taxation without representation for the ordinary szlachta, who all had a vote at these assemblies, but it also made the sejms of Wielkopolska and Małopolska more directly answerable to their electorate. In 1468, these decided to meet together, at Piotrków, and henceforth constituted the national Sejm, bringing together dignitaries of the kingdom, and the representatives of all the provinces and the major towns (Lithuania was still ruled autocratically by the grand duke, and Mazovia, ruled by a vassal Piast, kept its own separate sejm for another century). The next step came in 1493, when the national assembly divided into two chambers: the Senate, consisting of eighty-one bishops, palatines and castellans, and the Sejm proper, which consisted of fifty-four deputies of the szlachta and the largest cities.

The death of Kazimierz IV in the previous year afforded the new parliament an opportunity to flex its muscles and demonstrate that the existence of a natural heir to the throne did not infringe its right to choose who would rule over them. For two weeks the Sejm discussed the merits of a number of candidates, including the king's sons and a Piast prince from the Mazovian line, and finally chose Kazimierz's son, Jan Olbracht.

From now on not even the only son of the deceased king would sit on the Polish throne before being vetted by the Sejm. After the death of Jan Olbracht in 1501 his brother Aleksander was elected, and forced to sign over yet more royal power before he could take his throne. Four years later, in 1505, the Sejm sitting at Radom passed the act *Nihil novi*, which removed the king's right to legislate without the approval of the two chambers.

The constitutional developments of the fifteenth century are mirrored in the legal system. The regional castellans' courts had declined steadily in influence. Their jurisdiction was encroached upon by the starostas' courts, which dealt with the affairs of the szlachta and their tenantry, elective courts, whose judges were appointed by the regional sejmiks, and, most of all, by the ecclesiastical courts. The latter, which originally governed those living on Church-owned lands, gradually extended their competence to cover all cases involving a cleric or Church property, as well as those with a religious dimension (marriages, divorces, sacrilege, etc.). The division of the country allowed the ecclesiastical courts to encroach on other areas, by providing what was in effect an independent legal system embracing the whole country, which proved convenient in cases where the litigants were residents of different provinces. They complemented the rising power of the Church hierarchy, and directly challenged the influence of the central legal system. This was reinforced through the new county courts (*sąd ziemski*), whose judges were appointed by the crown, and which had permanent executive officers. The crown also re-established its jurisdiction, through the Supreme Crown Court, over the gravest criminal and civil offences, and retained the role of supreme court of appeal. But these functions would ultimately be taken over by the Sejm.

Jagiellon rule had provided greenhouse conditions for the growth of parliamentary institutions. At the death of Kazimierz the Great in 1370, Poland had been in advance of most European countries in this respect, but only 150 years later it had surpassed even England. The power of the crown was so hamstrung by a series of checks and balances that it could never be used arbitrarily. The Sejm had taken over all legislative functions. The degree of representation, with some 7 per cent of the population having a vote, would not be bettered until the British Reform Act of 1832. Yet the basis of Polish democracy was flawed at the outset, as the running had been made exclusively by the noble estate, the szlachta, and this was as restricted in its interests as it was varied in its make-up.

One cannot substitute the terms 'nobility' or 'gentry' for szlachta because it had little in common with those classes in other European countries either in origin, composition or outlook. Its origins remain obscure. Polish coats of arms are utterly unlike those of other European nobles, and lend weight to the theory that the szlachta was of Sarmatian origin. They were also held in common by groups of families, which suggests clan-based origins. The attitude of the szlachta begs analogies with the Rajputs of India or the Samurai of Japan. Like both of these, and unlike any other gentry in Europe, the szlachta was not limited by nor did it depend for its status on either wealth, or land, or royal writ. It was defined by its function, that of a warrior caste, and characterised by mutual solidarity and contempt for others.

'The Polish gentry,' writes the contemporary historian Długosz, 'are eager for glory, keen on the spoils of war, contemptuous of danger and death, inconstant in their promises, hard on their subjects and people of the lower orders, careless in speech, used to living beyond their means, faithful to their monarch, devoted to farming and cattle-breeding, courteous to foreigners and guests, lavish in hospitality, in which they exceed other nations.' But the outlook of the szlachta was changing, largely under the influence of economic factors.

The Vistula and its tributaries provided a natural conduit for all Poland's overseas trade, effortlessly concentrating the country's agricultural produce at the port of Gdańsk. This was also the point of entry for imports, of herrings from Scandinavia, salt from western France, and cloth from Holland, Flanders and England. The Teutonic Order had used its position straddling the lower Vistula to promote its own exports at the expense of Polish trade and to impose heavy duties on inbound goods. Its defeat and removal from the area in 1466 altered the situation radically. Trade with England through Gdańsk quadrupled, and by the end of the century the number of ships calling there had risen to eight hundred a year, most of them bound for Bruges.

Increased demand for grain as populations grew in western Europe raised prices, while the rapid expansion of seaborne trade pushed up those of timber and other forest produce by some 4,000 per cent. Polish landowners responded by intensifying production. Meadows were drained, scrub woods cut back, and acreages under cultivation increased, but while there was no lack of land available, there was a shortage of people to work it.

Most szlachta estates were worked by peasant tenants who paid part of their rent in labour. The size of their holdings and the rent varied enormously around the country, but as a general illustration one can take an example from 1400: the annual rent for a unit of seventeen hectares (forty-two acres) was fifteen *grosze* (the price of a pig or a calf) and a few bushels of grain, plus twelve days' work a year by the tenant in the landlord's fields – using his own implements and horses, usually at the busiest times.

The dramatic fall in the value of the coinage in the early 1400s halved the real value of money-rent received from tenants, while the productivity of a day's work did not fluctuate. And money was useless to the landlord in view of the shortage of casual labour in the countryside, exacerbated by the drift of the poorest peasants to the towns. It therefore made sense for the landlords to trans-

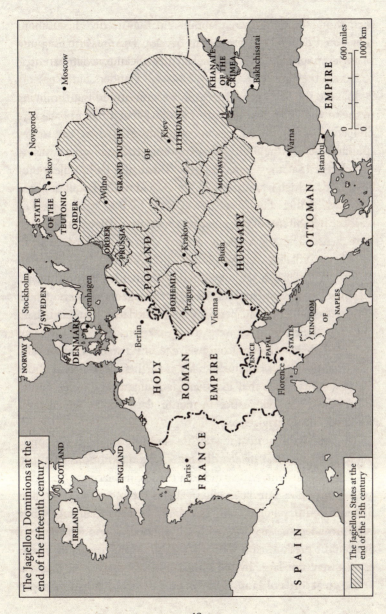

The Jagiellon Dominions at the end of the fifteenth century

form money-rent into purely labour-rent: they needed cheap labour they could depend on in order to develop what was turning into a cash-crop agricultural economy, and they used their political muscle to ensure they got it.

In 1496 the Sejm passed measures preventing peasants moving to the towns. Tenants who wished to move to a different area were obliged to put their tenancies in order, pay off all dues, and to sow the land before they left. The economic effort involved was so prohibitive that they were in effect tied to the land, unless they absconded, which was not easy in the case of whole families. Those who owned their land were not affected by this legislation. Nor were the inhabitants of free villages, sometimes referred to as 'Dutch settlements'. These had arisen in areas where a landlord, eager to found new villages on unexploited land, enticed peasants (often of foreign origin) to settle by offering them advantageous terms, set down in special charters. There were tenants rich enough to employ casual labour to perform the labour-rent on their behalf, but even their resources were strained when, in 1520, the Sejm increased the labour-rent from twelve to fifty-two days per annum. The legal position of the peasants was further weakened at about the same time, when they lost their right of appeal to other courts and could only seek justice in manorial courts, in which their landlords sat as magistrates.

The ease with which the szlachta could promote its economic interests by political means did not encourage notions of thrift, risk and investment, and spawned a rustic complacency that set it aside from other European elites. This is the more unexpected as fifteenth-century Poland was essentially an urban culture. While land provided the majority with a livelihood, it was not the only or even the predominant source of wealth for the magnates, whose estates were not large by the standards of the barons of England or the great lords of France. So far, only the Church had managed to build up extensive *latifundia* through the monastic orders and the dioceses, which made prelates such as the Bishops of Kraków the richest men in the land.

The magnates only started accumulating property on a large scale at the beginning of the fifteenth century. Jan of Tarnów (1367–1432), Palatine of Kraków, built up an estate of one town, twenty villages and one castle. His son, Jan Amor Tarnowski, Castellan of Kraków, increased this to two towns and fifty-five villages – more than doubling it in the space of fifty years. Jan of Oleśnica, father of Cardinal Zbigniew Oleśnicki, only had one village in 1400, yet by 1450 his other son owned fifty-nine, along with a town and a castle.

Taken alone, the revenues from such estates were not great enough to support rampant ambition. The magnates were obliged to supplement them by lucrative or influential public office, and by various business ventures, such as mining, in which fortunes could be made with a little influence at court and some capital. It was necessary first to obtain a concession from the crown, which owned all underground deposits. Personal capital or that of specially set up joint-stock companies was then used to employ engineers and build machines to work the mines, which were among the deepest in Europe. These were ambitious operations, but the rewards were abundant – salt, sulphur, tin, lead, zinc, and even gold. It was only by being on the spot that noblemen could make fortunes, and the great families of the fifteenth century based themselves in or near the cities. In this, as in other things, they were more akin to the civic magnates of Italy than to the regional nobility of France or England.

The cities were not large. Only Gdańsk, with 30,000 inhabitants, could rival those of western or southern Europe. Kraków had a paltry 15,000; Lwów, Toruń and Elbląg 8,000; and Poznań and Lublin only some 6,000. What they lacked in numbers they made up in diversity. Kraków was a Babel in which German predominated in the streets over other languages, while patrician circles rang with Polish, Italian and Latin.

One consequence of the Jagiellon forays into Hungary and southern Europe was that for the best part of the century their dominions bordered the Republic of Venice, opening up new vistas for Polish society at a decisive juncture in its relationship to the rest of Europe.

The previous century had radically altered the balance between Poland and the more developed countries of Europe. As a consequence of the Black Death, the population of the Continent fell by some twenty million during the fourteenth century, and it took the whole of the fifteenth to make up this loss. Poland's population did not drop significantly during the fourteenth, and rose sharply during the fifteenth. The gap also narrowed in economic terms, and Poland was attracting people as well as capital from other parts of Europe.

This process was mapped out in cultural terms. In the north, Flemish architects originally brought in by the Teutonic Order and the Hanse left their mark in the churches, town halls and city walls of Gdańsk and other cities. In Poznań, Warsaw and Kalisz, the Flemish style was mitigated by local variants – themselves marked by Franconian and Burgundian examples of an earlier age. In Kraków the most remarkable cross-breeding took place, dominated at first by a strong Bohemian influence which was superseded by that of German artists, most notably by one of the greatest sculptors of the Middle Ages, the German Veit Stoss, who settled in Kraków in 1477.

Polish thought and literature remained encased in the limits of medieval parochialism, their primary expression being religious verse. The only notable prose to be written at the time were the annals of Jan Długosz, a church canon and tutor to the royal family, begun in 1455. Długosz was a creature of the Middle Ages.

As he painstakingly wrote his last *Annales* in the 1470s, he took every opportunity to carp at what he saw as the newfangled ideas and practices invading the venerable cloisters of medieval Kraków. His successor as tutor to the royal family could not have presented a greater contrast, or better summed up the transformation taking place in Poland. He was Filippo Buonaccorsi, a native of San Gimignano in Tuscany obliged to flee after incurring the Pope's displeasure, was a leading humanist and, from 1472, a professor at the University of Kraków.

Although it had been founded by the Piast Kazimierz the Great and lavishly endowed by the Angevin Queen Jadwiga, it had come to be known as the Jagiellon University. It was under this dynasty that it received funds necessary for expansion and the patronage of kings who recognised its uses. Foreigners from as far afield as England and Spain came to study or teach in its halls, while native graduates went abroad to widen their learning, one of them, Maciej Kolbe of Świebodzin, becoming rector of the Paris Sorbonne in 1480. During the reign of Kazimierz IV (1446–92) some 15,000 students passed through the university, including the major dignitaries, prelates and even soldiers of the time.

The Church, and particularly its prelates, also encouraged the dissemination of the new ideas emanating from Italy. Piotr Bniński, Bishop of Kujavia, devoted his own fortune and that of his diocese to patronage of the arts, paying more attention to arranging symposia by humanist poets than to the spiritual duties of his position. Grzegorz of Sanok, Archbishop of Lwów, who had studied in Germany and Italy, established at his residence of Dunajów near Lwów a small court modelled on that of Urbino, nurtured by a stream of visitors from Italy. It was there Buonaccorsi first came when he had to flee his native country.

Buonaccorsi later moved to the royal court in Kraków and wrote, among other things, a set of counsels for the king, like some Polish Machiavelli. His writings, which he published under the pen name of Callimachus, his position at the Jagiellon University, and his part in founding, along with the German poet Conrad Celtis, a sort of Polish writers' workshop, the *Sodalitas Litterarum Vistulana*, made him a key figure of the Polish Renaissance.

The Italian connection grew stronger as Poles travelled to study or to visit cities such as Padua, Bologna, Florence, Mantua and Urbino. Italians came to Poland, bringing with them amenities and refinements, ranging from painting to postal services. The impact was omnipresent and lasting, nowhere more so than on the language. The first treatise on Polish orthography appeared in 1440, and the Bible was first translated in 1455, for Jagiełło's last wife, Sophia. In their search for words or expressions to describe hitherto unknown objects or sentiments, the Poles more often than not borrowed from Italian, particularly in areas such as food, clothing, furnishing and behaviour, as well as in the expression of thought. These words rapidly passed from speech into writing, and from writing into print.

The year 1469 saw the first commercial use of Gutenberg's invention of moveable type, in Venice. The idea was taken up throughout Europe with breathtaking speed: printing presses began operating in Naples, Florence and Paris in 1471; in Spain, the Netherlands and Kraków in 1473; in Wrocław, where the first book in Polish was printed in 1475; and in London in 1476.

By the end of the fifteenth century Poland had become an integral part of late-medieval civilisation. Lithuania, on the other hand, was largely left out of the picture, contributing nothing and gaining little from its association with Christian Europe. Lithuania proper was inhabited by no more than half a million people still pagan in spirit, while the vast expanses it had taken over to the south and east were thinly populated with some two million Slavs who practised Christianity in its eastern rite. At the moment of Władysław Jagiełło's conversion, this vast dominion boasted five stone castles, at Vilnius (Wilno), Kaunas (Kowno) and Trakai (Troki) in Lithuania; and at Kamieniec and Łuck in what had been Kievan lands. Leaving aside the more fertile south, the land produced little wealth and most of the population subsisted from scratching the topsoil with wooden implements, living in dugouts or timbered cabins.

In 1387 Władysław Jagiełło granted the Lithuanian nobles the first element of personal freedom, the right to hold property. In 1434 he extended the act *Neminem captivabimus* to the Grand Duchy, but it was some time before the principle was translated into practice. While Poland achieved power-sharing and representation, Lithuania continued to be ruled autocratically. While Jan Ostroróg, Palatine of Poznań, Master of the Jagiellon University and Bachelor of those of Bologna and Erfurt, applied himself in 1467 to writing a treatise on the Polish system of government and a programme for social reform, the average Lithuanian nobleman hardly knew what such words meant.

The only link between the two societies was the Jagiellon dynasty itself, and it was its interests that prevailed. Władysław Jagiełło's loyalties, to Lithuania and to Poland, were largely subjected to his own dynastic vision. His son Władysław III, killed at the Battle of Varna in 1444 in his twentieth year, never had the opportunity to show his mettle as a ruler. Władysław's younger brother Kazimierz IV reigned for forty-six years and established himself as a power to be reckoned with – he was, significantly, the only Pole ever to wear the English Garter. His wife Elizabeth of Habsburg bore him seven daughters, who make him the ancestor of every monarch reigning in Europe today, and six sons: one saint, one cardinal, and four kings. Kazimierz was succeeded in Poland by Jan Olbracht, a young prince with a passion for reading who drank, danced and loved hard, dressed like a peacock and worshipped pleasure. His brother Aleksander was a much-loved lightweight who died in 1506 having done little to be remembered or cursed for.

While the Jagiellons acquired a high degree of culture, they did not develop the political maturity demanded by their new role. Throughout this formative century, when the magnates and the szlachta were erecting the structure of their democracy, the Jagiellon kings failed to define the prerogatives of the crown, wasting their resources on foreign adventures instead.

Kazimierz IV's dynastically-minded foreign policy enmeshed Poland in a number of pointless and damaging conflicts. Turkey and Poland shared a common interest, and in 1439 an embassy from Murad II came to Kraków to negotiate an alliance against the Habsburgs of Austria, who had taken over Hungary. This failed to materialise, since Władysław III took Hungary himself and proceeded to make war on Turkey over Moldavia, a war which cost him his life at the Battle of Varna. Eighty years later, in 1526, Louis Jagiellon, also King of Hungary, was to lose his life in the same way. He was trampled to death in a muddy stream at the Battle of Mohacs, fighting against Suleiman the Magnificent over a Hungary which passed to Ferdinand of Habsburg after the battle.

The feud with Muscovy was equally pointless. After the Tatar invasions, the Lithuanian dukes had occupied the remains of Kievan Rus. The remaining Russian principalities were too weak to think of anything but survival, but with time Muscovy began to nurture ambitions. After the fall of Constantinople in 1453 the princes of Muscovy, who were linked by marriage to the Byzantine Emperors, declared their city to be Constantinople's successor, the 'Third Rome', protector of the Eastern Catholic Faith, and spiritual mother of all the Russias – most of which were under Lithuanian dominion. In the fifteenth century, Poland and Lithuania could afford to ignore such posturing. Apart from their own strength, they could count on the Tatar Golden Horde to keep Muscovy in check. In the latter part of the century, however, the Golden Horde went into decline, and its stranglehold over Muscovy was broken.

The Jagiellons' rivalry with the Habsburgs over Hungary and Bohemia also proved counter-productive, provoking a rapprochement between the Habsburgs and Muscovy, forcing Poland to sign her first treaty with France, in 1500. An English alliance was also considered, but in 1502 the Sejm rejected this on the grounds that England 'is in a state of continual revolution'. Henry VII and Henry VIII would repeatedly angle for an Anglo-Polish alliance against Turkey but nothing would come of this, as by then Poland needed the support of Turkey, with which she eventually signed an Eternal Peace in 1533.

Whatever international advantages they may have forfeited, the last two Jagiellon kings did give their subjects and their country something of inestimable value. Zygmunt I (known as 'the Old'), the youngest son of Kazimierz IV, succeeded in 1506 and died in 1548. His son Zygmunt II Augustus became Grand Duke of Lithuania in 1522 and King of Poland after his father's death. Their combined reign from 1506 to 1572 displayed a certain continuity, even if their persons did not. The strong Solomon-like father was strikingly different from his glamorous, refined son who stands out, along with Francis I and Charles V, to whom he was often compared, as the epitome of the Renaissance monarch. But they both encouraged every form of creative activity and helped to institutionalise a spiritual and intellectual freedom which endured. Above all, they ensured that the murderous Reformation and Counter-Reformation never grew into anything more dangerous in Poland than an unruly debate.

FOUR

Religion and Politics

The Jagiellon realm was theoretically a Roman Catholic kingdom like every other in Christendom, yet the majority of its population was not Catholic. Large numbers of Christian Slavs living within its borders practised the Orthodox rite, acknowledging the Patriarch of Constantinople rather than the Pope. Another group of Christians who paid no heed to Rome were the communities of Armenians living in the major cities of south-eastern Poland.

A significant proportion of the population was not Christian at all. The Jewish community multiplied each time there was an anti-Semitic witch-hunt in other countries, and its numbers soared in the decades after the expulsions from Spain in 1492 and Portugal in 1496. If visiting foreign prelates were shocked to see synagogues in every Polish township, they were hardly less so to see mosques standing on what was supposed to be Christian soil. These belonged to the descendants of Tatars who had settled in Lithuania in the fifteenth century and become loyal subjects of their adopted country. Many of them had been admitted to the ranks of the szlachta but clung to the Islamic faith. By the mid-sixteenth century there were nearly a hundred mosques in the Wilno, Troki and Łuck areas.

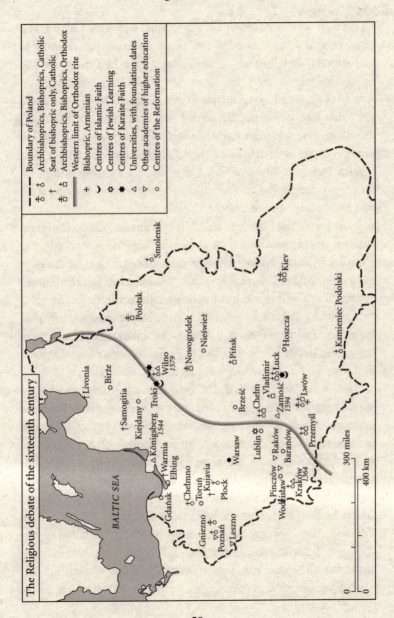

The Religious debate of the sixteenth century

Boundary of Poland
Archbishoprics, Bishoprics, Catholic
Seat of bishopric only, Catholic
Archbishoprics, Bishoprics, Orthodox
Western limit of Orthodox rite
Bishopric, Armenian
Centres of Islamic Faith
Centres of Jewish Learning
Centres of Karaite Faith
Universities, with foundation dates
Other academies of higher education
Centres of the Reformation

BALTIC SEA

Smolensk
Polotsk
Nowogródek
Nieśwież
Kiev
Pinsk
Birże
Livonia
Samogitia
Kiejdany
Königsberg 1544
Troki
Wilno 1579
Warmia
Elbing
Chełmno
Toruń
Kujavia
Płock
Gdańsk
Gniezno
Poznań
Leszno
Warsaw
Lublin
Raków
Baranów
Pińczów
Wodzisław
Kraków 1364
Brześć
Chełm
Vladimir
Zamość 1594
Łuck
Hoszcza
Lwów
Przemyśl
Kamieniec Podolski

300 miles
400 km

One of the conditions of the union between Poland and Lithuania in 1385 had been the conversion of that country to Christianity. But, formal gestures apart, little had been done to bring this about, and 150 years later, Grand Duke Zygmunt Augustus recorded that 'Outside Wilno . . . the unenlightened and uncivilised people generally accord that worship which is God's due, to groves, oak-trees, streams, even serpents, both privately and publicly making sacrifices to these.' A hundred years after that, Bishop Melchior Gedroyc noted that he could hardly find in his diocese of Samogitia 'a single person who knows how to say a prayer or make the sign of the Cross'.

That the Polish hierarchy had failed to impose religious observance on the population is not altogether surprising. According to a special arrangement, its bishops were appointed not by the Pope but by the King of Poland, who submitted his candidates for Rome's approval. When this was not forthcoming it was ignored. In 1530, for instance, Pope Clement VII violently objected to the anti-Habsburg and pro-Turkish policy of the Primate Archbishop Jan Łaski, and insisted King Zygmunt dismiss him on pain of excommunication. But no action was taken.

The King was guided by political considerations when appointing bishops and this led him to choose either powerful magnates whose support he needed, or, more often, trusted men of his own. These were drawn from his court, which was imbued with a humanistic and empirical spirit. A high proportion of his secretaries was of plebeian stock, and Zygmunt felt no compunction in ennobling those, like his banker Jan Boner, whom he favoured. This favour transcended creed as well as class. The Jew Abraham Ezofowicz, whom Zygmunt elevated to the rank of Treasurer of Lithuania, did convert to Christianity, albeit the Orthodox rite, before being ennobled, but his brother Michał remained a practising Jew when he was elevated to the szlachta in 1525 – a case without parallel anywhere in Christian Europe.

Most of the bishops were at home in this milieu. The Polish clergy were no more debauched than those of other countries at this time, and possibly less so – the last quarter of the fifteenth century saw the foundation of no fewer than eighteen new fundamentalist and strict Franciscan monasteries in the provinces of Mazovia and Małopolska alone. What did set them apart was an unusual element of realism in the face of other religions and of candour with respect to corruption. Bishop Krzycki, for instance, left a poem concerning the gossip that surrounded a fellow bishop caught in the act of lowering a girl from his bedroom window in a net. 'I fail to see what shocks everyone so,' the poet-bishop wrote, 'for no one can deny that the Gospels themselves teach us to use the Net of the Fisherman.' Krzycki wrote much erotic verse before he became bishop, and this did not affect his career any more than it did that of another, who ended up as Prince-Bishop of Warmia.

Jan Dantyszek was a good example of what the times could offer a clever man. A plebeian by birth, he entered the king's service, becoming a secretary and later a diplomatic envoy. After a life which took him around Europe and brought him into contact with Francis I of France, Henry VIII of England, assorted popes, Ferdinand Cortes, Martin Luther, with whom he formed a friendship, the Emperor Charles V, who tried to keep him in his service, and Copernicus, who became a close friend and protégé, Dantyszek settled down to his episcopal duties with a degree of worldly wisdom.

The conversion of Poland by Mieszko I had been primarily an act of political wisdom which had brought him status and security within the Christian world. The usefulness of the Christian Church had subsequently revealed itself more than once, helping to reunite the country in the thirteenth century, and to outmanoeuvre the Teutonic Order in the fourteenth. But this had been accompanied by an unwelcome extension of its influence and wealth. And the Church's foreign connections no less than its persecution of movements such as the Hussite heresy made the szlachta uneasy.

An institution which raked in bequests, exacted tithes, and contributed nothing in taxes to the state was bound to be unpopular. By the sixteenth century, the Church owned just over 10 per cent of all arable land in Wielkopolska, 15.5 per cent in Małopolska, and 25 in Mazovia. The share owned by the crown in the same provinces was 9, 7.5 and just under 5 per cent respectively. The Church wielded political power through its bishops who sat in the Senate and through its tribunals, which exercised jurisdiction over those living on its lands, and kept attempting to exercise it on wider areas. This power was also potentially at the disposal of Rome, a state often allied with Poland's enemies. The Church was therefore a focus for a number of the szlachta's phobias. The following is a typical complaint, uttered by a deputy during a Sejm debate of the 1550s.

> The gentlemen of the clergy summon us, citing their titles and invoking some foreign, Romish law, contrary to the laws and freedoms of our Realm, attempting to extend their jurisdiction and that of their master, the Roman Pope, which jurisdiction we, not finding it in our statutes, neither can nor will bear; for we know no other jurisdiction than the supremacy of his majesty the King our master.

The tone and the sentiments expressed are characteristic of a 'national Catholicism' which was the spiritual heir of Hussitism. Many of the Bohemian followers of Hus had taken refuge in Poland, and their ideas were well known to writers such as Biernat of Lublin

(1465–1529), who denounced the discrepancies between the Scriptures and the practices of the Church.

In view of all this, it is not surprising that when Martin Luther nailed his famous declaration of war on the Papacy to the church door in Wittenberg in 1517, setting off a chain reaction which was to shake the whole Christian world, he produced little more than a tremor in Poland. His teachings rapidly penetrated northern and western areas, enthusiastically received by the preponderantly German population of the towns, but elsewhere they met with little response.

Calvinism was another matter. Enhanced by its more sympathetic Francophone associations, it rapidly gained ground all over the country. The democratic spirit of Calvinism which placed the lay elder on a par with the minister could hardly fail to appeal to the instincts of the szlachta, while the absence of pomp and ceremony from its rites made it a pleasingly cheap religion to support.

By the 1550s a dominant proportion of the deputies to the Sejm were Protestants. But their number is not representative of the population as a whole, since the most ardently Catholic palatinates often returned Protestant deputies. By 1572 the Senate provided a similar picture. Of the 'front-bench' seats, thirty-six were held by Protestants, twenty-five by Catholics and eight by Orthodox, which again meant only that many magnates had converted to Calvinism. It was they who provided the conditions for its growth in Poland. The Oleśnicki family founded a Calvinist academy in their town of Pińczów, which became the foremost centre of Calvinist teaching and publishing in that part of Europe, referred to by the faithful as 'the Athens of the North'. Similar centres were established on a smaller scale by the Leszczyński family at Leszno, and the Radziwiłł at Nieśwież, Birże and Kiejdany.

Although they gained an ascendancy, the Calvinists never managed to control the Protestant movement in Poland. The northern cities stood by Luther; Anabaptists seeking refuge from persecution in Germany appeared in various areas of the country in the 1530s; and in 1551 Dutch Mennonites set up a colony on the lower Vistula.

The Protestant sect which produced Poland's most significant contribution to Christian philosophy was the Arians. Expelled from Bohemia in 1548, they settled in Poland, where they were known as 'Czech Brethren' and later Arians, since two of their fundamental beliefs – the human nature of Christ and the rejection of the Trinity – were first voiced by Arius at the Council of Nicea in AD 235. They also came to be known variously as Anti-Trinitarians, Polish Brethren and Socinians.

Theirs was a rationalist and fundamentalist response to the teachings of Christ, whom they held to be a divinely inspired man. They were pacifists, opposed to the tenure of civic or military office, to serfdom, to the possession of wealth, and to the use of money, believing as they did in the common ownership of all material goods.

They gained many converts – up to about 40,000 adherents practising in some two hundred temples scattered throughout the country. Their spiritual centre was Raków, where they established an academy, visited by students from all over Europe. It was here that the Raków Catechism was published, the work of Fausto Sozzini (Socinius), a nobleman from Siena who sought refuge in Poland and became one of the leading lights of the movement. The two most prominent Polish Arians were Marcin Czechowicz and Szymon Budny, the second of whom made a fine translation of the Bible into Polish and was also responsible for a rapprochement with the Jews, which produced some curious results.

The Jewish community had also been affected by the spirit of the times. The expulsions from the Iberian peninsula had brought many distinguished Spanish scholars to Poland, and in 1567 a

Talmudic academy was founded at Lublin, with the eminent Solomon Luria as rector, which enriched the religious debate. The Jews were by no means united, as there were considerable colonies of Karaites in eastern Poland who accepted only the Bible and rejected the Talmud.

The Arians made many converts from the ranks of Talmudic Jews, while a number of Arians and Calvinists converted to Judaism. It was one of these converts, 'Joseph ben Mardoch' Malinowski, who played the most incongruous part in this religious interaction. It was he who put the finishing touches to the Hebrew original of *The Fortress of the Faith*, a Karaite catechism by Isaac ben Abraham of Troki, which was subsequently published in a number of countries, and was later rediscovered by Voltaire, who believed it to be the greatest demolition of the divinity of Christ ever written.

In other countries the established Church reacted with violence to the slightest departure from dogma, let alone to apostasy. The reaction of the Polish hierarchy was pragmatic, often cynical, sometimes vehement, but never hysterical. Bishop Drohojowski of Kujavia, a region profoundly affected on account of its many German-dominated towns, went out of his way to meet prominent Lutherans and sanctioned their takeover of the Church of St John in Gdańsk since most of the parishioners had gone over to the heresy. Elsewhere in his diocese he allowed the sharing of parish churches by Catholics and Lutherans.

A considerable proportion of the clergy were genuinely interested in the reform of the Church. The Christians of the Orthodox rite had always enjoyed three of the demands of the Protestant movement: the marriage of priests, the use of the vernacular in the liturgy, and communion in both kinds. The Protestant demands were therefore less shocking and novel in Poland than in other Catholic countries. It was not uncommon for Catholic priests to emulate their colleagues of the Orthodox rite by having common-law wives, and these were keen to regularise their position and legalise their broods. Stanisław Orzechowski (1513–66) married while Canon of Przemyśl, and defended his action in a long debate with his bishop and with Rome, published in pamphlet form.

Apart from the practical demands concerning marriage and the vernacular, Luther's revolt aroused strong feelings among the clergy against the medieval practices of the Church. Marcin Krowicki (1501–73) left the priesthood and published his *Defence of True Learning*, a fiercely anti-clerical work in which the Papacy is referred to as the whore of Babylon. Bishop Uchański, on the other hand, did not forsake a career which was eventually to make him Primate of Poland, but nevertheless wrote vituperative diatribes against the practices of the Church. In 1555 he declared himself in favour of the marriage of priests, communion under both kinds and the use of the vernacular. He also mooted the idea of a joint synod of all confessions in Poland, to bring about reconciliation on common ground. When the King promoted him to the bishopric of Kujavia the Pope refused to ratify the appointment, but neither the King nor the Polish hierarchy took any notice.

King Zygmunt the Old (1506–48) felt that the religious debate was none of his business. He came under considerable pressure from Rome and from those of his own bishops who were in favour of stamping out the heresy. He was even reproached by Henry VIII of England for not taking a more energetic line against the Protestants. Whenever this pressure became overwhelming, he would take some action to satisfy the zealots, but his edicts were invalid without the approval of the Sejm. His attitude is summed up in the words of his successor, who shared it fully. 'Permit me to rule over the goats as well as the sheep,' he told one Papal envoy who was demanding arrests and executions.

In many countries the Reformation had social and political overtones. In Poland it was above all a constitutional issue. As the Papal

Nuncio's secretary noted after witnessing the debates of a Mazovian sejmik, the assembly seemed staunchly Catholic when the discussion turned on the faith, the sacraments and the sacred rites, but when the talk was of the privileges of the clergy, a number of 'Protestant' voices could be heard, and when it came to the subject of the Church's immunity from taxation, the entire assembly appeared to have become fanatically Calvinist. In 1554, Bishop Czarnkowski of Poznań sentenced three burghers to death by fire for heresy, but they were rescued by a posse of mostly Catholic szlachta. The same bishop later sentenced a cobbler to the same fate, and this time over a hundred armed szlachta of all denominations, led by the foremost magnates, laid siege to the episcopal palace and freed the condemned man. On one or two occasions, the ecclesiastical courts managed to execute the sentence before anyone could take preventive action. In 1556 Dorota Łazewska, accused of stealing a host from a church and selling it to some Jews for alleged occult rites, was burnt at the stake in Sochaczew. The execution caused uproar, and this came in time to save the lives of the three Jews who were to be burnt on the next day. They too were saved by the intervention of Catholic as well as Protestant szlachta. As Jan Tarnowski pointed out, 'It is not a question of religion, it is a question of liberty.'

All were agreed that there could be no liberty while a body independent of the parliamentary system was able to judge people, and the ecclesiastical tribunals' jurisdiction was duly annulled by act of the Sejm in 1562. Two years later, when a young Arian, Erazm Otwinowski, snatched the monstrance from the prelate during a religious procession in Lublin, threw it on the ground and stamped on the Blessed Sacrament, shouting obscenities, he was brought before the Sejm tribunal. This body, made up of Catholics and Calvinists, heard the case and agreed broadly with the defence, ably conducted by the poet Mikołaj Rej, who argued that if God was offended, God would punish, and as for Otwinowski, he should be ordered to pay the priest 'a shilling, so he can buy himself a new glass and a handful of flour' with which to repair the monstrance and bake a new host.

At a time when torture and death awaited anyone caught reading the wrong book in most European countries, such dispassionate adherence to the notion of the primacy of individual rights over all other considerations was extraordinary. But neither the Catholic nor the Protestant leaders were happy with this state of affairs. There was a general desire to reach consensus and to decide on a state religion. At the Sejm of 1555 a majority of deputies demanded the establishment of a Church of Poland with rites in the vernacular, the right of priests to marry and communion under both kinds, to be administered by a Polish Synod independently of Rome. The prospect of a break with Rome loomed, but the King of Poland was no Henry VIII.

Zygmunt Augustus, the only son of Zygmunt the Old, was a melancholy figure. Painstakingly educated – some say debauched – by his mother Bona Sforza, he was dubbed 'Augustus' by her and brought up to rule accordingly. She was a forbidding creature. The first cousin of Francis I and a close relative of Charles V, she had been brought up at the court of her father the Duke of Milan, which had an evil reputation for intrigue and poison. In an unprecedented move, she arranged for Zygmunt to be elected and crowned heir to the throne during his father's lifetime. But she did not contribute to his happiness, and he did not live up to her ambitions.

In 1543 he married Elizabeth of Habsburg, daughter of the Emperor Ferdinand I, who died only two years later, allegedly poisoned by Queen Bona. He then fell in love and eloped with Barbara Radziwiłł, the sister of a Lithuanian magnate. Only four years after this marriage, which was opposed by virtually everyone in Poland for a variety of reasons, Barbara Radziwiłł died, and again the Queen Mother was suspected of using her Milanese skills. After considering at length the possibility of marrying Mary Tudor, in 1553 Zygmunt married his first wife's sister, Katherine of Habsburg, widow of the Duke of Mantua. It was a disastrous marriage. The epileptic Queen physically repelled him and, unlike the others, she did not die – perhaps because Queen Bona, feeling more unpopular than ever, had loaded herself up with gold and jewels and fled to Bari in Italy where, appropriately enough, she was herself eventually poisoned.

Since neither of his first two wives had borne him any children, the fact that Zygmunt Augustus refused to touch his third was a matter of some concern to his subjects. The extinction of a dynasty is always cause for alarm, and in this instance the alarm was all the greater as the Jagiellons were still the only real link between Poland and Lithuania. The Sejm begged the King to attend to his wife, repulsive or not, and the Primate actually went down on his knees in the chamber to beseech him either to possess her or to cast her off, breaking with Rome if need be.

The King's behaviour at this point was critical to both the religious and the political future of Poland, yet he remained un-decided. His attitude to the Reformation was ambivalent. He never showed much sympathy for the Protestant movement, but took a great interest in it, avidly reading all the dissenting tracts and trea-tises and accepting the dedication of works by Luther and Calvin. In 1550 he issued an anti-Protestant decree in the hope of winning support from the bishops for his marriage to Barbara Radziwiłł, but this remained a dead letter. A few years later he rebuked the Papal Nuncio for urging a firmer line towards the Protestants, and in effect forced him to leave Poland. When asked by his subjects which way they should lean in the religious debate, he replied: 'I am not the king of your consciences.'

Unlike Henry VIII of England, Zygmunt Augustus did not want a divorce. His love for Barbara Radziwiłł had been a great passion, and her death robbed him of the will to live. He continued to carry out his duties without enthusiasm, dressed in black, and showed no desire to mould the future or perpetuate the dynasty. When pressed by the Sejm of 1555, he took the characteristically non-committal and quite extraordinary step of referring the proposal for a national Church to Rome. He sent Stanisław Maciejewski to Pope Paul IV with the four demands of the Sejm. The Pope listened to them 'with great sorrow and bitterness of heart', and then rebuked Zygmunt for allowing his subjects to formulate such heretical ideas. The matter of the national Church rested there, and the reformers were, for once, unaided by provocative behaviour on the part of the Pope.

The principal weakness of the Protestant movement in Poland was its lack of unity, and the only candidate for its leadership spent most of his active life in England. Jan Łaski, nephew of the archbishop of the same name and a member of what was briefly a rich and powerful family, became a Protestant while studying abroad. He stayed in Geneva with Calvin, who praised his 'erudition, integrity and other virtues'. In Rotterdam he drew close to Erasmus, helping him out of financial difficulties by buying his library and leaving it with him for life. He was then invited to England by Thomas Cranmer and given a pension by Edward VI, who appointed him chaplain to the foreign Protestants who had taken refuge in England. Known in England as John a Lasco, he collaborated with Cranmer on the Book of Common Prayer of 1552, but with the accession of Queen Mary he was forced to leave the country.

He reached Poland in time for the first Calvinist synod in 1554, at which he urged greater unity and a closing of ranks by all dissenters against the Catholic hierarchy. But his pleas were drowned out by disputes over minor theological and administrative questions. Łaski died in 1560, and it was not until 1570 that any kind of agreement was reached, in the Consensus of Sandomierz, but this failed to produce the sort of Protestant front he had hoped for.

The Protestant movement enjoyed the patronage of the foremost magnates, but failed to gain the support of wider sections of the population. It never touched the peasants to any significant extent, never seriously affected those towns such as Przemyśl or Lwów, which had no large German population, and left much of the szlachta indifferent, particularly in poor, populous Mazovia. Even in cases where their master went over to Calvinism the peasants clung to their old faith with surly tenacity, sometimes walking miles to the nearest Catholic church.

The Reformation in Poland was not in essence a spiritual movement; it was part of a process of intellectual and political emancipation which had started long before. The szlachta, which had done everything to curtail the power of the crown, seized eagerly on the possibilities offered by it to break the power of the Church. Straightforward anticlericalism was easily confused with a desire for a return to true Christian principles, and so was another movement in Polish politics which reached a climax in the 1550s.

A purely political reformist movement had come into existence at the beginning of the century. In spirit it was very close to the Reformation, since it placed the accent not on innovation but on stricter observance of the law, on weeding out malpractice and corruption. It was known as 'the movement for the execution of the laws', or simply the 'executionist' movement. One of its first preoccupations was that the law itself should be codified and published in clear form, and as a result much groundwork was done in the first half of the century, culminating in a number of legal reforms passed in 1578 which fixed the legal system for the next two hundred years.

The executionists waged a war of attrition on the temporal position of the Church. It was they who gave the impetus to abolish the medieval anomaly of the diocesan courts in 1562. The Sejm of the following year saw another victory, when the Church, which had always enjoyed exemption from taxation, was forced to contribute financially to the defence of the state. Much of the executionists' support stemmed from the ordinary person's revulsion at having to contribute to the treasury through taxation, and they were therefore keen to see that such resources as the crown possessed were properly adminstered. This led them into direct conflict with the magnates, over the thorny subject of royal lands and *starosties*.

The crown owned estates all over the country which it did not administer itself. Some were granted to individuals for services to the crown, to favourites, and even to merchants in return for cash advances. Others were granted with the office of *starosta*. The starostas were the linchpin of local government, the king's officers in charge of law and order in a given locality. The starosties came with profitable estates which the incumbent was supposed to administer on behalf of the king, taking 20 per cent of the profit for himself as payment for the office he carried out. The rest went to the crown. All starosties and royal lands were the inalienable property of the crown, and reverted to it on the incumbent's death. In practice, things worked differently.

The office of starosta had degenerated into a sinecure, while the administration of the lands, which was not subject to any verification, afforded endless scope for venality, with the result that most of the revenue went not to the crown but into the pocket of the incumbent. The starosties were therefore highly sought-after; their holders could increase their revenue without any extra effort or outlay of funds and at the same time enjoy the prestige and power of the office. Influential families began to collect them, with the result that a magnate might hold up to half a dozen important starosties, and a number of other royal estates, and his family would be understandably loath to give them up on his death. Although the lands were supposed to revert to the crown, successive kings found it increasingly difficult not to award them to the son of the deceased incumbent without alienating the whole family. To all practical purposes, the starosties were therefore becoming hereditary in the richer families.

This enraged the szlachta, since it both bolstered the position of the magnates and diminished the crown's financial resources. Again and again the executionists clamoured for a return to due process and the repossession by the crown of multiply-held starosties. On this issue, however, the magnates in the Senate who normally supported the executionists against the Church would vote with the bishops against the executionists, and the king, who by the middle of the century relied more and more on the magnates for support, would cooperate with them. Only minimal success was achieved in 1563, when the Sejm decreed a general inspection of all accounts and inventories to catch out corrupt administrators.

The executionist movement distracted much of the zeal which might otherwise have been concentrated on religious questions. At the same time, Catholic voters elected Calvinist deputies because they were executionists, and Catholic deputies voted with the executionist Calvinists on issues such as the demand for a national Church, the abolition of ecclesiastical tribunals, and the law forcing the Church to contribute financially to defence. Even at the height of the Reformation no Pole, be he Catholic, Lutheran, Calvinist or Arian, was prepared to place religious issues before constitutional and legal ones. That is why the Reformation failed in Poland. After raging and blustering in word and print for a few decades, the

Protestant movement gradually burnt itself out, while the energies which had fuelled it were diverted to political matters.

The Catholic Church, which had dodged the heaviest blows and avoided confrontation, slowly went over to the offensive, as the Counter-Reformation gained strength. In Poland its progress was unsensational: no inquisition, no burnings at the stake, no anathemas, no forfeitures of property, no barring from office. It could hardly have been otherwise, given the spirit pervading Polish society and the stature of the leaders of the Counter-Reformation. The greatest of these, Cardinal Stanisław Hosius, was fundamentally opposed to violence and, referring to Mary Tudor, warned in 1571: 'Let Poland never become like England.'

Hosius and his principal colleague, Marcin Kromer, were unusual among sixteenth-century Catholic prelates. Both had worked in the royal chancellery for the king before they went into the Church. Hosius then went on to play an important role at the Council of Trent. Kromer was a historian, and in his writings he demonstrated the unifying role the Church had played in Polish history. He preferred to argue with heretics rather than condemn them. Hosius favoured a similar approach, but he made a greater and more categorical statement on the matter of religion – something the Calvinists were unable to do. His *Confessio* (1551), a lucid reaffirmation of Catholic dogma, was one of the most powerful arguments of the European Counter-Reformation. It was translated into several languages, and between 1559 and 1583 ran to no fewer than thirty-seven separate editions in France alone. In 1564 Hosius brought the Jesuits to Poland, to reconquer the hearts, and more specifically the minds, of the Poles, and the most outstanding of them, Piotr Skarga (1536–1612), proved a worthy partner.

Hosius and Skarga pinpointed the principal arguments for returning to the fold, letting time do the rest. And time was on the side of Rome. In 1570 Mikołaj Sierotka Radziwiłł, son of the man who had introduced Calvinism to Lithuania and been one of its greatest financial and political supports, went back to the Church of Rome. Others followed suit, for a variety of reasons. Even the mixed marriages which the hierarchy had fulminated against worked in favour of Catholicism, since women had been largely left out of the religious debate and their conditioning led them to stand by their old faith. Jan Firlej, Marshal of Poland, had become a Calvinist, but his wife, Zofia Boner, had not. She covertly brought his sons up to love the Catholic faith, and three of the four became Catholics when they grew up. After her death, Firlej married Barbara Mniszech, another fervent Catholic. Although their son was ostensibly brought up a Calvinist, the mother's influence prevailed, and he later became Primate of Poland. As Piotr Skarga foresaw, the country would be reconquered for Rome, 'not by force or with steel, but by virtuous example, teaching, discussion, gentle intercourse and persuasion'.

As Calvin grew more strident and Protestants in various European countries began to execute not only Catholics but other Protestants, the Polish prelates showed forbearance. They pointed out that Protestantism could be more repressive than Catholicism. They explained that it was not only divisive, but irresponsible, and in this they were helped by the example of the Arians.

Under the influence of Fausto Sozzini, the Arian movement displayed a tendency to splinter while attracting all manner of dissenters and schismatics migrating from other countries. But what made the Arians really unpopular with the szlachta were the starkly political implications of their faith. 'You should not eat bread made by the sweat of a subject's brow, but make your own,' they would hector. 'Nor should you live on estates which were granted to your forebears for spilling the blood of enemies. You must sell those estates and give the money to the poor.' Since the status of the szlachta was based on their readiness to bear arms, the Arians' pacifism was downright subversive. (In an attempt to square the circle, their synod of 1604 allowed them to bear arms provided they did not use them.)

With the impending extinction of the Jagiellon dynasty, Poland and Lithuania needed unity of purpose rather than dissent and refusal to take responsibility. Nevertheless, the constitutional and legal aspects of the issue were still paramount. After the death of Zygmunt Augustus the Sejm which met in 1573 under the name of the Confederation of Warsaw to shape Poland's future passed an act whose most memorable clause ran as follows:

> Whereas in our Common Wealth there is no small disagreement in the matter of the Christian faith, and in order to prevent that any harmful contention should arise from this, as we see clearly taking place in other kingdoms, we swear to each other, in our name and in that of our descendants for ever more, on our honour, our faith, our love and our consciences, that albeit we are *dissidentes in religione*, we will keep the peace between ourselves, and that we will not, for the sake of our various faith and difference of church, either shed blood or confiscate property, deny favour, imprison or banish, and that furthermore we will not aid or abet any power or office which strives to this in any way whatsoever . . .

The freedom to practise any religion without suffering discrimination or penalty was henceforth enshrined in the constitution. This law would be observed rigorously by Catholic kings and an increasingly Catholic population. Some illegal executions did take place, but they were few. When no criminal offence had been committed, even acts of extreme provocation went unpunished. In 1580 the Calvinist Marcin Kreza snatched the host from a priest, spat on it, trampled it, and then fed it to a passing mongrel, for which he was reprimanded by the king and told not to do it again.

The Calvinist writer who chronicled the course of the Counter-Reformation in Poland, listing every execution or sectarian killing of a Protestant between 1550 and 1650, came up with a total no higher than twelve. During the same period, over five hundred people were legally executed for religious reasons in England, and nearly nine hundred were burnt in the Netherlands, while hundreds more suffered confiscations and attainders. This unique absence of violence stemmed partly from the Polish attitude to religion, partly from an obsession with legality and the principle of personal liberty, and partly from the fact that throughout this period Polish society concentrated on an attempt to build utopia on earth.

FIVE

Kingdom and Commonwealth

As the heirless Zygmunt Augustus paced the galleries of the Royal Castle on Kraków's Wawel hill dressed in mourning for Barbara Radziwiłł, his subjects thought uneasily of the future. The realm of the Jagiellons was an assemblage of territories with disparate populations, differing customs and varying forms of government co-existing within one state. They were held together by no feudal bond, administration, constitution or military hegemony, but by a consensus whose only embodiment was the dynasty itself. Its possible extinction raised the question not just of who would rule the country, but whether it would even continue to exist in its current form.

The only thing which could prevent the realm from falling apart was a constitutional expression of the consensus which had created it. But who was to formulate this? Who represented the population of this mongrel conglomerate? The answer, as they were not slow to make clear, was the szlachta.

By the mid-sixteenth century the szlachta included Lithuanian nobles and Ruthene boyars, Prussian and Baltic gentry of German origin, as well as Tatars and smaller numbers of Moldavians, Armenians, Italians, Magyars and Bohemians, and was diluted by intermarriage with wealthy merchants and peasants. The szlachta made up around 7 per cent of the population. Since they extended from the top to the bottom of the economic scale, and right across the board in religion and culture, they represented a wider cross-section as well as a greater percentage of the population than any enfranchised class in any European country. To be a member of the szlachta was like being a Roman citizen. The szlachta were the nation, the *Populus Polonus*, while the rest of the people inhabiting the area were the *plebs*, who did not count politically.

While the score of patrician families and the princes of the Church attempted to establish an oligarchy, the mass of the 'noble people' fought for control of what they felt to be their common weal. It was they who pressed for the execution of the laws, for a clearly defined constitution, and for a closer relationship with the throne. They met with little support from Zygmunt the Old or Zygmunt Augustus, both of whom tended to seek support in the magnates. While the executionists struggled with increasing desperation to arrive at a definition of the powers of the Sejm and the role of the monarch and his ministers, the magnates stalled, meaning to take matters into their own hands when the time came.

A complicating factor was Lithuania, whose dynastic bond with Poland would have to be replaced with a constitutional one. In spite of being granted a senate of their own (*Rada*) at the beginning of the century, and a sejm in 1559, the szlachta of the Grand Duchy were politically immature and dominated by their magnates. One Lithuanian family, the Radziwiłł, had shot to prominence at the beginning of the century. They accumulated wealth by means of marriages with Polish heiresses, and held most of the important offices in the Grand Duchy.

In 1547, Mikołaj Radziwiłł 'the Black' (to distinguish him from his cousin and brother of Barbara, Mikołaj 'the Red') had obtained from the Habsburgs the title of Prince of the Holy Roman Empire, and as the extinction of the Jagiellons approached he dreamed of detaching the Grand Duchy from Poland and turning it into his own fief. But this was not likely to survive on its own: in 1547 the ruler of Muscovy, Ivan IV 'the Terrible', took the title of Tsar and made it clear that he meant to realise his forebears' mission of gathering all the Russias under one crown, and his methods, ranging from boiling people in oil to putting cities to the sword, amply demonstrated the firmness of his resolve. Without Polish support, Lithuania, which had already lost Smolensk to Muscovy, would sooner or later experience them too.

While the Lithuanian magnates and szlachta hesitated, the Poles forced the issue, by the administrative sleight of hand of transferring Lithuania's Ukrainian lands from the Grand Duchy and annexing them to Poland. The Senate and Sejm of Lithuania and those of Poland met at Lublin on the border between the two states, and on 1 July 1569 unanimously swore a new act of union. At the practical level, the Union of Lublin was hardly revolutionary. It stipulated that henceforth the Sejms of both countries should meet as one, at Warsaw, a small town conveniently placed for the purpose. The combined upper house would contain 149 senators and the lower 168 deputies. Poland and Lithuania would share one monarch, not, as had been the case hitherto, *de facto* (because the Jagiellon elected to the Kraków throne was already the hereditary Grand Duke of Lithuania) but *de jure*. The Grand Duchy was to keep its old laws, codified in the Statutes of Lithuania in 1529, a separate treasury, and its own army, to be commanded by a Grand Hetman and a Field-Hetman of Lithuania. The ministers of the crown (marshal, chancellor, vice chancellor, treasurer and marshal of the court) were joined by identical officers for Lithuania. The Union was a marriage of two partners, with the dominant position of Poland diplomatically effaced. It was the expression of the wishes of the szlachta, the embodiment of their vision of a republic in which every citizen held an equal stake. The combined kingdom

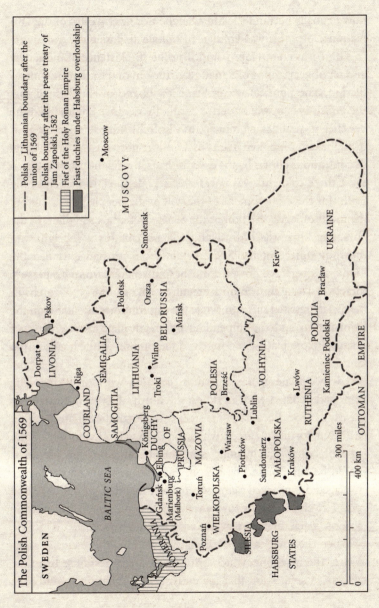

The Polish Commonwealth of 1569

Polish – Lithuanian boundary after the union of 1569

Polish boundary after the peace treaty of Jam Zapolski, 1582

Fief of the Holy Roman Empire

Piast duchies under Habsburg overlordship

SWEDEN

MUSCOVY

• Moscow

• Smolensk

• Pskov

Dorpat •

LIVONIA

• Riga

UKRAINE

• Polotsk

Orsza •

BELORUSSIA

• Mińsk

• Kiev

SEMIGALIA

COURLAND

LITHUANIA

Troki • • Wilno

PODOLIA

• Bracław

SAMOGITIA

POLESIA

Brześć

VOLHYNIA

• Lwów

Kamieniec Podolski •

BALTIC SEA

Königsberg •

DUCHY OF

Elbing •

PRUSSIA

RUTHENIA

OTTOMAN

EMPIRE

Gdańsk •

Marienburg

(Malbork)

• Toruń

MAZOVIA

• Warsaw

Lublin •

• Piotrków

Sandomierz •

MAŁOPOLSKA

• Kraków

Poznań •

WIELKOPOLSKA

SILESIA

HABSBURG

STATES

300 miles

400 km

0

0

81

now formally became 'the Most Serene Commonwealth of the Two Nations', '*Serenissima Respublica Poloniae*' to foreigners.

There was an obvious paradox in the co-existence of monarchy and republic, yet the Poles made a virtue out of the seeming contradiction. The political writer Stanisław Orzechowski claimed that the Polish system was superior to all others, since it combined the beneficent qualities of monarchy, oligarchy and democracy. That it might combine their faults as well was not considered. In spite of continuous efforts by the executionists, the relationship between these three elements was never precisely defined. In principle, the Sejm was the embodiment of the will of the people, and therefore the fount of legislative power; the Senate were the custodians of the laws; the king was both a political unit in his own right and the mouthpiece of the Sejm. While the Sejm had curtailed the monarch's personal power, it meant to invest its own in his person, thereby turning him into its executive. The would-be oligarchs in the Senate resisted this aim, while the uncertainties attendant on the Reformation and the impending interregnum made the deputies hesitate before placing too much of their power in the hands of the king.

There was never any question of doing without a king. The Sejm had debated what to do on the death of Zygmunt Augustus as early as 1558. Because of the stalling tactics of the Senate, nothing had been formally agreed when, on 7 July 1572, the last of the Jagiellons died. The burning issue thus became how his successor should be chosen, and by whom. Early suggestions on procedure envisaged an enlarged Sejm, where each member would have one vote. The eleven major towns were to be represented, but not the bishops, since they were agents of a foreign power.

When the time came, the Senate demanded the exclusive right to elect the new king, which brought an angry response from the szlachta. A suggestion that the entire political nation should have an equal vote was seized on by the bishops, who realised that an overwhelming majority were Catholic and therefore likely to support a Catholic candidate. The cry for universal suffrage was taken up by an ambitious young deputy to the Sejm, Jan Zamoyski, who captivated the szlachta with his rhetoric and became their tribune. With their support, he forced the proposal through the Convocation Sejm which met after the king's death, in 1573. From now on every single member of the szlachta, however poor, was a king-maker. More than that: each one carried a royal crown in his saddlebag, for it was stipulated that only a Polish nobleman or member of a ruling foreign dynasty could be a candidate to the throne of the Commonwealth.

The procedure for choosing the king was improvised at the first election of 1573. On the death of the sovereign, the Primate of Poland assumed the title of *interrex*, provisionally taking over the functions of the monarch, and summoned the Convocation Sejm to Warsaw. This fixed the date of the election, restated the rules, and vetted all the proposed candidates. It also set down the terms on which the king elect was to be invited to take the throne. Then came the Election Sejm, which met at Wola outside Warsaw, and to which every member of the szlachta was entitled to come. Since tens of thousands of voters might turn out, along with their servants and horses, this was often a remarkable gathering. The representatives of the various candidates set up 'hospitality tents' in which they plied the voters with food, drink and even money in the hope of gaining their vote. Rich magnates fraternised with the poorest members of the szlachta in order to gain their support for a favoured candidate.

The centre of the Election Field was taken up by a fenced rectangular enclosure. At one end of this there was a wooden shed for the clerks and senior dignitaries, including the Marshal of the Sejm, who supervised the voting and policed the whole gathering.

The electors remained outside the enclosure, on horseback and fully armed, drawn up in formation according to the palatinate in which they lived. This symbolised the *levée en masse*, the obligation to fight for the country which was the basis of all the szlachta's privileges. It says a great deal for the restraint of the proverbially quarrelsome szlachta that the occasion did not degenerate into a pitched battle. Each palatinate sent ten deputies into the enclosure, where they and the assembled senators listened to the representatives of the various candidates make an election address on behalf of their man, extolling his virtues and making glittering election pledges. The deputies would then go back to their comrades outside the enclosure and impart what they had heard. When this had been mulled over, the voting began. Every unit was given sheets of paper, each with the name of a candidate at the top, and the assembled voters signed and sealed on the sheet bearing the name of the candidate of their choice. The papers were then taken back into the enclosure, the votes counted, and the result officially proclaimed by the *interrex*. The whole procedure took four days at the first election, in 1573, which was attended by 40,000 szlachta, but subsequent elections were often less well attended and could be over in a day or two.

The king thus chosen could hardly entertain any illusions about Divine Right. To make sure that all remnants of any such idea should be banished from his mind, his prospective subjects made him swear an oath of loyalty to them and their constitution, as well as to a set of other conditions laid down in two documents: one, the *Acta Henriciana*, immutable; the other, the *Pacta Conventa*, drawn up specifically by the Convocation Sejm before every new election. In swearing to these, the king abdicated all right to a say in the election of his successor and agreed not to marry or divorce without the approval of the Sejm. He undertook not to declare war, raise an army, or levy taxes without its consent, and to govern through a council of senators chosen by it, which he had to summon at least once in every two years. If he defaulted on any of these points, his subjects were automatically released from their oath of loyalty to him – in other words, he could forfeit his throne if he did not abide by the terms of his employment.

The king was, in effect, a functionary, the chief executive of the Commonwealth. He was not by any means a mere figurehead, but his power was not arbitrary, and he was not above the law. Although he had no aura of divinity surrounding him, the king could, and many did, build up a strong position and elicit unbounded respect and devotion from his subjects. And no elected King of Poland would suffer the fate of a Charles I or Louis XVI, however bad his behaviour.

Like all others affected by the new learning of the Renaissance, the Poles had been fascinated by the rediscovery of the artistic and political culture of the Hellenic world and ancient Rome. The apparent similarities between some of their own institutions and those of the republics of antiquity tickled the national vanity. Without looking too closely at the pitfalls that led to the demise of the Roman Republic, the *Senatus Populusque Polonus* drew further on this model. The Polish political vocabulary bristled with terms such as 'liberty', 'equality', 'brotherhood', 'nation', 'citizen', 'senate', 'tribune', and 'republic'. Like the makers of the French Revolution of 1789, the Poles increasingly borrowed the style, the symbolism and the concepts of the Roman Republic.

The difference between the Poles of the sixteenth century and the French revolutionary leaders, however, was that the Polish system was based almost entirely on precedent. The notion of electing a monarch had evolved with Poland's twelfth-century subdivision into duchies, and had attended every royal accession since. At the very beginning of the fifteenth century, Paweł Włodkowic had put forward the thesis that the king was merely an administrator ruling the country on behalf of and by consent of his subjects, while his colleague Stanisław of Skarbimierz (d. 1431) had added that he had no right to infringe their rights. The thesis put forward by Buonaccorsi that the ruler should have absolute power and that nothing should stand in his way of acting for the greater good was confounded by the Polish constitutional jurists. After the death of Kazimierz IV in 1492, his sons and all subsequent kings of the house of Jagiełło were subjected to a regular election.

Nor was the idea of choosing a foreign prince new – it was based on the precedent of the Kraków Lords approving the accession of Louis of Anjou, and their subsequent choice of Jagiełło. Virtually every clause in the *Acta Henriciana* and most of those in the *Pacta Conventa* were a repetition of older privileges. This deference to precedent is reflected in the fact that there was no written constitution, merely a great body of legislation written into the statute books, swelling gradually by accretion over the centuries.

Yet if the Polish constitution evolved out of practical rather than theoretical motives, it was fashioned by a mentality which was idealistic rather than pragmatic. The parliamentary system relied to an inordinate extent on the integrity of the individual deputy and senator, and lacked procedures for ensuring correct behaviour. The Marshal of the Sejm (not to be confused with the Marshals of Poland and of Lithuania, who were the king's ministers) was elected at the beginning of each session by the deputies, and it was his duty to keep order. Since he had no authority to silence a deputy or expel him from the chamber, the orderly conduct of debates depended in large measure on his skill in easing tensions and steering attention back to the point at issue. His job was made no easier by the ambiguities inherent in the mandate given to the deputies by the sejmiks which elected them.

In principle, the deputies were the representatives not merely of the provincial sejmiks which had returned them, but of the corporate electorate of the whole Commonwealth, and they were supposed to cast their votes as such. At the same time, each deputy was given a set of written instructions before he left for Warsaw to take up his seat. These instructions varied from general guidelines to specific orders on how to vote on certain issues. The electorate's participation in government did not end with the election of a deputy, and he could ill afford to disregard the injunctions of his electors, since he had to face a debriefing in his constituency at the end of the parliamentary session. Sometimes deputies were instructed not to vote on any unforeseen issues without consulting their electors.

This practice tied the hands of the deputies and reduced the value of parliamentary debate, but an intelligent and experienced deputy could still vote according to his conscience and answer for it successfully to his electors. It was not until the beginning of the next century, when the electorate began to grow suspicious of central government, that the instructions became binding.

The Polish parliamentary system was more vulnerable than most, because of a principle whose perverted form, the *liberum veto*, was to become notorious: the principle that no legislation could be enacted without mutual consent. Some such convention originally existed in virtually every parliamentary body in Europe. It did not mean that everyone had to vote for a measure unanimously, but expressed the twin convictions that any measure not freely assented to by all lacked full authority and that no sincere dissenting opinion should be disregarded by the majority. Dissenting minorities were listened to, argued with and persuaded, and only when broad agreement had been reached (the word used was the Latin *consensus*) was a measure passed. In theory, a small minority, even a minority of one, could block legislation. In practice, minorities were ultimately ignored if they proved intractable.

Another curious feature of the constitution was the szlachta's right to confederate in an emergency such as the death of the monarch, foreign invasion, or some other extremity. They would form a confederation, elect a marshal, publish their aims and invite others to join. It was a form of plebiscite, and could take place within a Sejm where deadlock had been reached; it was the one political assembly in which, for obvious reasons, strict majority voting was observed and dissent ignored.

A fundamental weakness of the Polish parliamentary system was the under-representation of the towns, and therefore of trading interests, in the Sejm. This was not so much a flaw in the constitution as a reflection of the country's social structure. In the fifteenth century the towns, with their predominantly foreign populations enjoying a favourable administrative status, did not join in the scramble for power and thereby missed an opportunity for integrating their rights into the constitution. They had always dealt directly with the crown, which guaranteed their status, but when the crown began to abdicate its responsibilities to the Sejm, the towns were left without a champion. This was compounded by social barriers. A law passed in 1550 (mainly at the insistence of the merchants) barred members of the szlachta from indulging in trade, and soon the szlachta began to regulate admissions to its own ranks. In 1578 the Sejm passed a law taking away from the crown and arrogating to itself the exclusive right to ennoble people (except for battlefield grants of arms by the king). A law of 1497 preventing plebeians from buying noble estates closed a back door to noble status. This sort of legislation was impossible to enforce given the absence of any heraldic institution or register, but lines were being drawn. A merchant might join the szlachta by some means and thereby acquire voting rights, but when he did, he would find himself banned from practising anything except agriculture, politics and war.

A number of cities, including Kraków, Lublin, Lwów, Poznań, Wilno, Gdańsk and Toruń, were represented in the Sejm, and other towns were on occasion invited to send deputies. In theory, these had the same debating and voting rights as others, but the reality was often different. As the writer Sebastian Petrycy put it: 'Once upon a time a donkey was asked to a wedding feast; he marvelled and licked his chops at the thought of the new unfamiliar delicacies he would be tasting, but when the day came the donkey found he was only there to carry water and kindling to the kitchen.' The city deputies were usually intimidated by their noble colleagues and feared to say anything – with some reason, since it appears that in 1537 the Kraków deputies were physically assaulted. They often found it easier to stay away and put up with whatever taxes might be imposed, or employ the local palatine to look after their interests.

The peasants, who had also enjoyed a direct relationship with the crown, were similarly sidelined. As the judge of the supreme court of appeal, the king had been the final arbiter in all their disputes with landowners. In 1518 Zygmunt the Old was persuaded to give up his right of arbitration, and in 1578 the Sejm itself assumed the function. Since it represented almost exclusively landed interests, the peasants were unlikely to find justice here. It is worth nothing that the principles of Polish democracy were not exclusive to the Sejm, and every village had its elected communal council and officers. The squire's functions within this, usually as local magistrate, were not feudal or proprietary, but elective.

Not all the drawbacks of the Polish constitution were specific to it. All democracy breeds its own problems, and one of these is the impossibility of carrying on a successful foreign policy when decision-making is hamstrung by the devolution of power and the force of public opinion. The element of secrecy was impossible to sustain since all Sejm debates were open to the public and all its resolutions immediately printed. Defence suffered from the same problems. No democracy likes an army, because nobody likes paying for one. In the late sixteenth century about two-thirds of the entire revenue of most European states was spent on armament, almost 70 per cent in the case of Spain. In Poland, the figure was nearer 20 per cent. In the 1480s a 'Current Defence Force' of 2,000 was set up to parry Tatar raiding, and in 1520 the Sejm increased the numbers slightly. In 1563 a new system of 'Quarter Troops' was introduced, paid for out of a quarter of all revenues from starosties, but the number of men under arms remained tiny in relation to the vast area of the Commonwealth.

It was not just that the Poles did not like paying for the troops. The szlachta also wished to perpetuate the idea of the *levée en masse*, which would become unnecessary if there were an adequate standing army. More important than either of these considerations was the deep-rooted conviction that a standing army was sooner or later bound to be used by the crown to enforce absolutist government. This fear of authoritarian rule was responsible for all that is most striking about the political edifice of the Commonwealth.

The salient features of this edifice were the oath of loyalty made by the incoming monarch to his subjects, and the clause which stipulated that if he defaulted on his obligations his subjects were automatically released from their obligations to him. The latter was an obvious recipe for disaster. It amounted to a right to mutiny if the king overstepped his powers – a question open to highly subjective interpretation. But this right was never carried through to its logical end. Mutinies would take place in the spirit of this clause in 1606 and 1665, but neither of them led to the dethronement of the monarch. They were intended as a final rap on the royal knuckles to make the king desist from his plans.

The release clause was only the ultimate recourse in the whole scheme of checks and balances erected in order to make sure that power was never concentrated in too few hands. It also proclaimed the basis of the relationship between king and subject. Ruler and ruled were bound by a bilateral contract which placed obligations on both and had to be respected by both. This notion of a contract between the throne and the people, the cornerstone of the constitution, was almost entirely unknown in Europe at the time – only in England were the germs of such ideas in evidence.

While the Habsburgs of Austria, the Bourbons of France, the Tudors of England, and every other ruling house of Europe strove to impose centralised government, ideological unity and increasing control of the individual through a growing administration, Poland alone of all the major states took the opposite course. The Poles had made an article of faith of the principle that all government is undesirable, and strong government is strongly undesirable. This was based on the conviction that one man had no right to tell another what to do, and that the quality of life was impaired by unnecessary administrative superstructure. That such ideals should be held by people who simultaneously oppressed their own subjects, the peasants, is neither novel nor exceptional: the Greek founders of modern political thought no less than the Fathers of the American Revolution applied a similar double standard which cannot be equated with hypocrisy.

SIX

The Reign of Erasmus

In the sixteenth century the Polish Commonwealth was the largest state in Europe, extending over 990,000 square kilometres. The nature of this vast expanse varied from the undulating landscape of Wielkopolska to the flatness of Mazovia and the dense forests of Lithuania, from the Tatra mountains to the swamps of Belorussia, from the forests and lakes of Mazuria to the wild plains of Podolia rolling away into the distance, which the Poles referred to as 'Ukraina', meaning 'margin' or 'edge'.

The population was, at ten million, equal to that of Italy and the Iberian Peninsula, twice that of England, and two-thirds that of France. Only 40 per cent were Poles, and they were concentrated in about 20 per cent of the area. The mass of the population, the peasantry, was made up of three principal ethnic groups: Polish, Lithuanian and Belarusian or Ukrainian. The urban population too was far from uniform. The great trading emporium of Gdańsk, almost a city-state in itself, was preponderantly German. Nearby lay the smaller port of Elbląg, which had a large colony of English and Scots. Kraków had significant ones of Hungarians and Italians. Lwów, a city with an individual outlook, both politically and cultur-ally, and the only city apart from Rome to have three Christian archbishoprics, was made up of Poles, Germans, Italians and

Armenians. Six languages were recognised for legal purposes; Polish, Latin, Belarusian, Hebrew, German and Armenian.

Almost every town also had its Jewish community. In the north, where some towns enjoyed exemptions under medieval charters granted by the Teutonic Order, the Jews were confined to a specific quarter. In the rest of the Commonwealth they settled where they would, and there were quantities of small towns in the south and east in which they predominated. This Jewish community, which accounted for nearly 10 per cent of the entire population, led a life of its own, communicating almost exclusively in Hebrew or Yiddish, while the Karaite Jews spoke Tatar.

A charter of 1551 set up what was in effect a Jewish state within the state. Local Jewish communes (*Kahal*) sent deputies twice a year to a national assembly (*Vaad Arba Aracot*) which governed the whole community. It passed laws, assessed taxes, funded and regulated its own legal system and institutions, communicating directly with the crown, not the Sejm. The next hundred years saw a remarkable flourishing of this community, which grew confident and assertive. Jealous merchants in Lwów complained in 1630 of the Jews behaving 'like lords, driving in carriages, in coaches-and-six, surrounded by pages and grand music, consuming costly liquors in silver vessels, behaving publicly with pomp and ceremony'. They were rich merchants and bankers, small traders and inn-keepers, artisans and farmers, agents, factors and surgeons. Every village had one or two Jews, every little town had its community, with synagogue and ritual baths, and its own secluded life.

The most striking aspect of the Commonwealth, particularly in view of its size and ethnic diversity, was that it had no administrative structure to speak of. The only thing holding it together was the political nation, the szlachta, and that was as disparate as the Commonwealth itself. The wealthiest could compare with any grandees in Europe, the poorest were the menial servants of the rich. In between, they might be wealthy landowners or humble homesteaders ploughing and harvesting with their own hands, barefoot and in rags, poorer than many a peasant. Their level of education, religious affiliation and ethnic origin were just as varied.

The szlachta nevertheless developed a remarkably homogeneous culture and outlook, based on two influences which might be thought mutually exclusive. The first was the discovery of ancient Rome, and the analogies increasingly made between its institutions, customs and ideology, and those of the Commonwealth. This affected the Poles' attitude to government. It was also responsible for the abandonment of the long hair of the late medieval period and the adoption of the 'Roman' haircut, and the acceptance of Renaissance forms in architecture. At the psychological level it gave the Poles a sense of belonging to a European family, based not on the Church or the Empire, but on Roman civilisation.

The second influence was more nebulous but far more pervasive. It stemmed from the theory, elaborated by various writers at the beginning of the century, that the Polish szlachta were not of the same Slav stock as the peasantry, but descendants of the Sarmatians. This placed a neat ethnic distinction between the political nation and the rest of the population, the plebs. How far they really believed in it is not clear, but the myth was embraced by the multi-ethnic szlachta, who were far more at home with the 'noble warrior' Sarmatian myth than with the image of Christian chivalry, with all that entailed in terms of fealty and homage.

In time, the Sarmatian myth grew into an all-embracing ideology, but in the sixteenth century its influence was visible principally in manners and taste. As a result of contacts with Hungary and Ottoman Turkey various accoutrements of Persian origin were gradually incorporated into everyday use, and by the end of the century a distinctly oriental Polish costume had evolved.

The szlachta invested in things they could wear or use – clothes, jewels, arms, saddlery, horses, servants and almost anything else that could be paraded. Weapons were covered in gold, silver and precious stones. Saddles and bridles were embroidered with gold thread and sewn with sequins or semi-precious stones. It was common for a nobleman who had a number of fine horses and several caparisons to have them all harnessed and led along behind him by pages, rather than leave them at home where no one would be able to admire them. The Poles were close to their horses, which were symbols of their warrior status. They were tacked in fine harness, covered in rich cloths, adorned with plumes and even wings, and, on high days and holidays, dyed (usually cochineal, but black, mauve or green were favoured for funerals).

Another aspect of Sarmatism was the love of ceremony. Hospitality was a way of showing respect and friendship, and was rarely confined to providing adequate food and drink, although both featured in abundance. Vodka and other spirits were never served at table or in the home, where wine predominated, imported for the most part from Hungary and Moldavia, but also from France, Italy and even the Canary Islands and, in the following century, California.

The discovery of America flooded Europe with minerals and precious metals in the sixteenth century, and the eventual consequence of this was to raise prices of commodities such as food. The ever growing demand for ships had the same effect on timber, pitch and hemp. Over the course of the century, the price at which Poles sold their agricultural produce went up by over 300 per cent. The actual buying power of what the szlachta had to sell went up against staple imports such as cloth, iron, wine, pepper, rice and sugar, by just over 90 per cent between 1550 and 1600. During the same period, the quantity exported more than doubled. The result was that landed Poles became a great deal richer in terms of cash to spend than their counterparts elsewhere in Europe.

This permitted increasing numbers of Poles to travel abroad, primarily in order to study. Lutherans might send their sons to Wittenberg and Calvinists to Basel, for religious reasons, but the most popular universities were those of Italy: between 1501 and 1605 Polish students consistently made up at least a quarter of the student body at the University of Padua. As they grew richer, they began to mix tourism with study. The wealthy would come back loaded with pictures and sculpture, books and works of art, and once home, set about embellishing their own surroundings along the lines observed abroad.

In 1502 Prince Zygmunt returned from his travels, bringing with him a Florentine architect who would rebuild the Royal Castle in Renaissance style. Other Italians followed in his footsteps, lured by the opportunities as magnates and prelates vied with each other to build lavish new residences, in a style that subjected Italian Renaissance architecture to the demands of the Polish climate and the pretentions of their patrons. The same instincts that fed on Sarmatism are undoubtedly responsible for the extravagance and the fantasy displayed. But the new style also reflected an attempt to give form to some of the ideals the educated szlachta had embraced. Many of the important buildings of the period are public ones, and they embody the spirit that was responsible for constructing the Commonwealth, the Polish utopia.

Nowhere is this more in evidence than in the largest, the most monumental, and the most ambitious building project of the age – the city of Zamość. And few individuals offer as complete a picture of the contradictions of the age as does it creator, who was both a child of the Renaissance and a forerunner of a new Baroque plutocracy, a libertarian and an autocrat, one of the creators of the Commonwealth, who sowed some of the first seeds of its corruption.

Jan Zamoyski was born in 1542, the son of a Calvinist minor senator. As a young man he completed courses at the Sorbonne and at the new Collège de France, then at the University of Padua, of which he became Rector. While there, he published a treatise on Roman constitutional history and became a Catholic. He returned to Poland with a letter of recommendation from the Senate of Venice to Zygmunt Augustus, who employed him as a secretary. He made his mark during the first interregnum, became Chancellor in 1578, and Hetman in 1581. He married, among others, the daughter of Mikołaj Radziwiłł 'the Black', and later the niece of the second elected king of Poland. Whether he aspired to the crown himself is not clear, but he set a pattern of autonomy which would be followed by most magnates in the next century.

On the death of his father in 1571 Zamoyski inherited four villages and the rich Starosty of Bełz. He methodically enlarged this estate, squeezing out adjacent landowners and buying out the senior branch of his family from the seat of Zamość. By 1600 he owned 6,500 square kilometres in one block, as well as lesser estates, properties in all the major cities, and thirteen lucrative starosties.

In 1580 he began to build New Zamość. It was to be an ideal Platonic city, laid out according to symbolic axes and points of reference, dominated at one end by his own palace, and at the centre by the town hall. Other major buildings included the law courts, the Catholic collegiate church, the Franciscan church, the Armenian church, the Orthodox church, the synagogue, the university, and the arsenal. The city was underpinned by a sophisticated sewerage system and surrounded by star-shaped fortifications of the most modern type.

Zamość made economic sense. It was settled by large numbers

of Hispanic Jews, Italians, Scots, Armenians, Turks and Germans, who provided everything from medical facilities to a cannon foundry, from jewellery to printing presses. By endowing his domain with a capital city, Zamoyski turned it into a self-sufficient state, and all the profits, levies and dues which would otherwise have gone to the royal cities or the treasury went into his own pocket. The idea was widely copied. In 1594 the Żółkiewski family founded their administrative capital of Żółkiew, which by 1634 when it passed to the Sobieski was a flourishing centre with fifteen different guilds. Soon every magnate was building a private town for himself, a trend that undermined the position of the existing towns and cities.

Zamość is nevertheless unique. It is a model of Polish Renaissance-Mannerist style, but its purpose was not merely to achieve beauty. It was to combine functionalism with aesthetic perfection in order to create the ideal environment. Every element was of importance, and if there was one that overshadowed the others, it was probably the university, opened in 1594, which would, it was assumed, produce the ideal citizen.

This belief that utopia could be built was the product of more than a century of prosperity and security, of political self-confidence based on the civil liberties of the citizen, and of an impressive legacy of political and social thought which continued to develop and spread through the printed word. There may not have been very much awaiting publication when the first press was set up at Kraków in 1473, but by the early 1500s the urge to publish was evidenced by the proliferation of presses in provincial cities. While originally legislation demanded that all books be passed by the Rector of the Jagiellon University, the executionist movement won a notable victory in 1539 by obtaining a royal decree on the absolute freedom of the press.

Only a fraction of the existing literary heritage was in the vernacular, which was still orthographically inchoate and marked by regional variation. Atlases and geographical works published between 1500 and 1520, and works on the history of Poland that appeared in the following decades, helped to standardise the spelling of place-names. The publication of large numbers of books in Polish from the 1520s imposed uniformity of spelling and grammar. In 1534 Stefan Falimirz published the first Polish medical dictionary; in 1565 Stanisław Grzepski of the Jagiellon University published his technical handbook *Geometria*. The six translations of the New Testament – Königsberg (Lutheran, 1551), Lwów (Catholic, 1561), Brześć (Calvinist, 1563), Nieśwież (Arian, 1570), Kraków (Jesuit, 1593), Gdańsk (Lutheran, 1632) – constituted an exercise in Polish semantics. In 1568 the first systematic Polish grammar was compiled by Piotr Stojeński, an Arian of French origin; in 1564 Jan Mączyński issued his Polish–Latin lexicon at Königsberg; and finally, in 1594 the writer Łukasz Górnicki produced a definitive Polish orthography. Latin nevertheless continued in use, particularly in religious and political literature, both because it was a better tool for theoretical and philosophical writing, and because it was universal to Europe.

The most striking aspect of Polish thought at the time was the preoccupation with public affairs and government. The discussion on the Polish body politic was opened by Jan Ostroróg with his *Monumentum pro Reipublicae Ordinatione* (c.1460), which argued for a more just social and political system. It was taken up by Marcin Bielski (1495–1575) and Marcin Kromer (1512–89), who used books on the history of Poland to polemicise about the rights and wrongs of the system. Stanisław Orzechowski applied geometrical principles to constitutional projects. Andrzej Frycz-Modrzewski (1503–72), Zygmunt Augustus' delegate to the Council of Trent in 1545 and a close friend of the theologian Melanchthon, with whom he had studied at Wittenberg, published a treatise on the Polish legal system, and in 1554 a longer work, *De Republica Emendanda*, sketching a utopian political vision.

Most of this literature was idealistic, and, like the work of the eighteenth-century *philosophes*, predicated on the mirage of an ideal condition. It represented existing abuses and injustice as perversions of this condition, rather than as inherent in human affairs.

The next generation of political writers applied their ideas to specific institutions. Bartłomiej Paprocki's *O Hetmanie* was an attempt to define the role and duty of the hetman; Krzysztof Warszewicki's *De Legato* did the same for those engaged in diplomacy; Jakub Górski's *Rada Pańska*, Jan Zamoyski's *De Senatu Romano* and Wawrzyniec Goślicki's *De Optimo Senatore* all lectured on the conduct of affairs of state. Although they were more practical than their forerunners they still clung to the belief that good government depended on good people rather than on strong institutions. As Zamoyski said in the speech inaugurating the university he had founded: 'Republics will always be as good as the upbringing of their young men.'

By the end of the fifteenth century over 80 per cent of the 6,000 parishes in Wielkopolska and Małopolska had schools. The resultant upsurge in literacy was no doubt responsible for a literary flowering which took place at the same time. The first Polish lyric poet, Klemens Janicki (1516–43), was born a peasant but entered the priesthood and studied at the universities of Bologna and Padua, where he was crowned poet laureate by Cardinal Bembo. More typical was Mikołaj Rej of Nagłowice (1505–69), a country gentleman who wrote in robust Polish on religious, political and social issues. He was one of half a dozen notable poets, but they were all overshadowed by one figure who dominated the second half of the century.

Jan Kochanowski (1530–84) studied at Kraków, Königsberg and

Padua, and then spent some years at court while considering a career in the Church. He was prolific and imaginative, and his use of Polish, a language he did more than any other to enrich, was masterful and refined. While he is best known for his lyrical verse and court poems, his rendering of the psalms of David, and above all the threnody he composed on the death of his three-year-old daughter, Kochanowski did not avoid the political subjects popular with other writers. He too was preoccupied with the good of the Commonwealth. This comes out strongly in his only attempt at drama. Although there was dramatic entertainment at court from the 1520s and a number of troupes active around the country (and, from 1610, a playhouse in Gdańsk in which English actors performed Shakespeare), it was not a favoured medium. Kochanowski's short play *The Dismissal of the Greek Envoys* is the only exception. The characters in the play are not really people, but in effect the voices of collective interests, and the play is not about their feelings, but about the fate of Troy. This curious use of dramatis personae to represent the collective foreshadows nineteenth- and twentieth-century Polish drama, the mainstream of which is neither lyrical nor psychological, but ethical and political.

The state of mind defined in the words of these writers is a curious mixture of ideological bombast, emotional sincerity and healthy cynicism. The three co-exist with the two most pervasive themes. One is the almost obsessive feeling of responsibility for and compulsion to participate in the organic life of the Commonwealth at every level. The other is the quest for Arcadia. If political writing rested on the myth of an 'ideal condition' which had been perverted and must be restored, the literary imagination translated this into a quest for the state of innocence as epitomised by country life. This gave rise to a long tradition of *Sielanki*, a word the poet Szymon Szymonowicz (1558–1629) coined to express bucolic idylls. The *sielanka* theme haunted Polish thought and literature, sometimes assuming the aspect of a cult. Inspired by the quest for a lost innocence, which implied a rejection of corruption, it could take many forms. In the minds of the nineteenth-century Romantics, for instance, it would become confused with the quest for the lost motherland, and imply a rejection of political reality. More often, it took the form of intellectual withdrawal from the world, which at its worst exalted intellectual escapism and made the spirit of enquiry suspect.

There is a strong, if indefinable, connection between these states of mind and Poland's place in European culture. By the middle of the sixteenth century, the Poles were as widely travelled as the citizens of any nation. Polish and foreign painters, sculptors and musicians likened Polish cities and palaces to those of Europe. Kochanowski knew Ronsard, Stanisław Reszka and others were friends of Tasso, and a considerable number of Poles were closely associated with Erasmus of Rotterdam. Leonard Coxe, who taught at Cambridge and the Sorbonne before becoming professor at the Jagiellon University, remarked in a letter to an English friend that the Poles walked, talked, ate and slept Erasmus, beginning with the King, who wrote to him in a familiar style usually reserved for sovereign princes.

The literature of other countries was avidly read in Poland, and while Polish poetry may not have been read widely in other countries, the political and religious works penetrated far and wide. Modrzewski's *De Republica Emendanda* was available in Latin, French, Italian, Spanish and Russian. Goślicki's *De Optimo Senatore* was published in Venice, Basel and London. Kromer's *Confessio* ran into several dozen editions of the original Latin text in various countries, and was translated into Polish, Czech, German, Dutch, French and English. Technical works such as Grzepski's *Geometria* became part of the European scientific toolkit, as did those of Mikołaj Kopernik (Copernicus).

Born at Toruń in 1473, the son of a merchant, Kopernik enrolled at the Jagiellon University in 1491 to study astronomy, and later joined the priesthood, which enabled him to pursue studies at the universities of Bologna, Ferrara and Padua. After returning home, he became administrator of the bishopric of Warmia, but also worked as a lawyer, doctor, architect and even soldier, commanding a fortress in the last clash with the Teutonic Order in 1520. In 1543, the year of his death, he published *De Revolutionibus Orbium Coelestium*, in which he demonstrated that the sun and not the earth was the centre of the planetary system.

Erasmus was prompted to 'congratulate the Polish nation ... which ... can now compete with the foremost and most cultivated in the world'. But this could very well serve as an epitaph, for Polish participation in the cultural life of Europe had reached a peak. A crucial element was language. For centuries the native tongue had been supplemented by Latin, which enjoyed the twin benefit of being a developed instrument of communication and an international medium without which the Poles would have been utterly isolated. As the Scots traveller Fynes Moryson noted in 1593, 'There is not a ragged boy, nor a smith that shooes your hose, but he can speake Latten readily.' During the sixteenth century the first of these benefits dwindled as Polish rapidly evolved into a lucid, harmonious language as efficient as Latin for the expression of ideas. The second benefit of Latin also began to wane, as a general drift throughout Europe towards the vernacular tended to restrict its international usefulness. From 1543 the decisions of the Sejm were published in Polish not Latin, and the same went for legal documents. As Polish became the language of state and of literature, Polish thought became increasingly inaccessible to western Europe.

In a poem he wrote to Erasmus, Bishop Krzycki assured him that the Poles were not only reading all his works, but also passing them on 'across the Don'. The Russian world, which never had Latin, was heavily dependent on Poland for access to classical and contemporary European literature. It was from Kochanowski's translations of Tasso, for example, that the first Russian ones were made. The Commonwealth was also the printing house of eastern Europe. The first book, a Bible, to be printed in Belarusian was published in Wilno in 1517. More surprisingly, the first printed work in Romanian was published in Kraków, from which also came quantities of books in Hungarian. By the end of the century the printers of Wilno, Kraków and Lublin were making small fortunes from supplying eastern European markets. The Polish presses also printed the Hebrew religious texts used throughout the European Diaspora.

The Polish szlachta continued to learn Latin, but German, which had been a crucial link with the outside world until the end of the Middle Ages, gradually dwindled. Partly as a result of the Reformation, Germany's importance as a source of culture declined for Poland. France and Spain were in the grip of the Counter-Reformation and increasingly absolutist government, which made them unattractive to the Poles. Direct links had been forged with Italy, and Poland itself had acquired most of the amenities for which it had in the past been dependent on others. If the fifteenth-century Pole had seen himself as living on the edge of a flat earth whose centre was somewhere far away to the west, his counterpart in the late sixteenth saw Poland not as peripheral to Europe, but as central to its own world.

The East had never had much to offer except for Tatar raids and Muscovite maraudings, but in the course of the sixteenth century a new vista came into view beyond these nuisances. Persian and Ottoman culture began to fascinate Polish society. Apart from owning Turkish artefacts, Stanisław Lubomirski, Palatine of Kraków, also kept three eminent orientalists in his permanent entourage. Tomasz Zamoyski, son of the Chancellor and Hetman, was learning four languages at the age of eight: Latin, Greek, Turkish and Polish. By the time he had completed his early studies, he was fluent in not only Turkish, but also Tatar and Arabic. The Polish Commonwealth was turning into a hybrid of East and West, increasingly exotic but also baffling to western Europeans.

SEVEN

Democracy versus Dynasty

There was nothing oriental about the man the Poles chose as their new king in 1573. Nor was he the most likely candidate for the throne of the multi-denominational Commonwealth. A few months before the Confederation of Warsaw passed its act on religious freedom, Henri de Valois, younger brother of Charles IX of France, took an enthusiastic part in the St Bartholomew's Day Massacre of Protestants.

The first election went remarkably smoothly. At the news of Zygmunt Augustus's death a Convocation Sejm gathered to thrash out the details. The candidates were Ernest of Habsburg, Henri de Valois, Ivan IV of Muscovy, and the two outsiders John III of Sweden and Stephen Bàthory of Transylvania. A key figure was the late king's sister, Anna, the last surviving member of the Jagiellon dynasty. Many took it as read that the successful candidate would marry her, thereby cementing his position on the throne and emulating the precedent set by Jagiełło himself, an assumption which Anna did much to further. Others, including the majority of the Senate, suspected her ambition and saw her as an obstacle to establishing a new dynasty. Apart from being no beauty, Anna was well over fifty years old.

This did not stand in the way of the cunning agent of Henri

de Valois, Jean de Monluc, Bishop of Valence, who laid siege to her affections on behalf of his master, assuring her that the Prince, twenty-eight years her junior, was consumed with passion for her.

Ivan IV's candidature had been suggested on the grounds that the rising power of Muscovy might best be rendered harmless in the same way as that of Lithuania had. If Poland could tame Jagiełło, then perhaps the Commonwealth could do the same with the Tsar. But Ivan the Terrible was not an alluring prospect, and even the most sanguine supporters of the idea had to admit that it was unrealistic.

Some 40,000 szlachta turned up at Warsaw to vote, accompanied by as many servants and attendants, all armed to the teeth. To the astonishment of the foreign observers present, no shot was fired or steel bloodied in spite of the contentious issues involved. Henri de Valois was elected by an overwhelming majority, and a delegation was despatched to Paris.

Henri received the news as he was laying siege to the Protestants of La Rochelle, and hurried back to Paris to meet the delegation of eleven dignitaries and 150 szlachta who arrived from Warsaw on 19 August 1573. They were not there in such force just to impress the Parisians, which they did with their exotic clothes, their jewellery and their painted horses. Henri de Valois had to be fully acquainted with the conditions of his employment and obliged to accept them before he placed a foot on Polish soil. At a ceremony in Notre Dame on 10 September attended by the entire French court, he swore to observe the *Acta Henriciana*, named after him, laying down the constitutional obligations of the monarch, and the *Pacta Conventa*, which listed his personal undertakings.

The ceremony went smoothly until he came to the article in the *Henriciana* concerning religious freedom. He tried to mumble his way through, missing out the clause in question. The Poles, who had been alert to such a contingency, drew his attention politely to the fact that he had overlooked a clause. He demurred, but the head of the Polish delegation, Hetman Jan Zborowski, stepped forward, booming: '*Si non iurabis, non regnabis!*' Henri swore. The French royal family were not going to let an oath stand in their way, and Charles IX was even prepared to listen to the so-called *Postulata Polonica*, in which the Sejm admonished him on his treatment of French Protestants.

Henri de Valois and his entourage travelled to Poland overland and arrived in the middle of an exceptionally cold winter. The tight hose and light jerkins of the Frenchmen were no match for the climate, and by the time the royal party reached Kraków they were frozen and depressed by the sight of the snowy wastes. The King and his new subjects were in many respects ill-matched. The mincing, scented young man, with his earrings and his codpieces, came as something of a shock to the robust Poles. In spite of this, and although he showed unwillingness to be bound by the *Pacta Conventa*, he was not unpopular. He was gallant towards Anna Jagiellon, though he made no move in the direction of marriage, and went out of his way to charm and captivate those he saw as the most important figures. But on 30 May 1574 Charles IX died unexpectedly, and Henri became King of France.

His intention was to keep both crowns, a course of action favoured by some magnates, who assumed that they would be free to rule in his absence, and it was agreed that he would set off for France in the autumn. But Henri made his own plans. On the night of 18 June he slipped out of Kraków and left the country.

The King's behaviour raised the delicate constitutional question of whether there was now an interregnum or not. In the autumn, letters were despatched to the newly crowned Henri III of France, one from the Polish senators and deputies, one from the Lithuanians. The Poles gave him an ultimatum – if he did not present himself in Kraków by 12 May 1575 the throne would be declared vacant. The Lithuanians merely pleaded for his return. Henri replied that he had every intention of keeping the Polish throne, and suggested sending his younger brother the Duc d'Alençon as viceroy.

The Poles would have none of it, and called a new election. The experience of the first had considerably dampened the optimism of the voters, and only some 10,000 turned out. The magnates saw an opportunity of settling the question themselves as they had always aspired to do. The Senate conducted its own election and chose the Emperor Maximilian II, but as they gathered in Warsaw Cathedral to sing the *Te Deum*, the szlachta set up howls of protest. It was then that a minor candidate at the first election, Stephen Bàthory, Duke of Transylvania, was suggested, and on 14 December 1575 he was acclaimed king. Stephen reached Kraków on 23 April of the following year, and was married to Anna Jagiellon and crowned on 1 May. He arrived in Poland without finery, accompanied only by a couple of regiments of Hungarian infantry. He dutifully bedded Anna, making it clear that he did not take the Polish throne lightly. A forthright man and an able commander, he knew how to pick men who would serve him well. He appointed a new Chancellor, Piotr Wolski, and a new Vice Chancellor, Jan Zamoyski, who was to become a close partner in all his enterprises and a mainstay of his rule.

But he was in a difficult position, as Maximilian brokered an alliance with Muscovy and succeeded in getting the city of Gdańsk to declare for him. King Stephen marched north to Gdańsk, but although he defeated the army sent out head him off, the prospect of a long siege was not alluring. Tsar Ivan had invaded from the east, and the international situation was looking ugly. The King therefore lured Gdańsk back to the fold with a number of trading concessions, and switched his attention to problems that had been brewing unchecked for decades while the Poles had been absorbed by their religious and political debates.

Dramatic shifts in power had been taking place around Poland since 1515, when King Zygmunt the Old, the Emperor Maximilian I and the Jagiellon King Władysław of Hungary and Bohemia had met at Pressburg (Brno) to discuss the future of East Central Europe. The two Jagiellons were then in possession of the areas coveted by the Habsburgs, but Władysław's son Louis had no heir, and it was in order to avoid a war that the three met. The issue was settled amicably. It was agreed that Hungary and Bohemia would pass to the Habsburgs if Louis produced no heir, in return for which the Habsburgs bound themselves to eschew their traditional policy of supporting the Teutonic Order and other enemies of Poland. But other questions were left unresolved.

The last Slav prince of Szczecin-Pomerania, Bogusław X, had no heir and wished to switch his allegiance from the Empire to the Polish crown, but the issue was not addressed, and when he died his duchy reverted to the Empire. There was a similar situation in Silesia, where the towns and much of the gentry were German, but the rural population Polish. The area was still ruled by Piast princes, some of whom, like Jan III of Opole, spoke no German. They were vassals of the Bohemian crown, worn by Władysław Jagiellon. When his son Louis was killed in 1526 at the Battle of Mohacs his crown passed to the Habsburgs, so that when Jan III died in 1532 his principality of Opole went to them. Although several of the Piast dynasties in Silesia survived to the end of the following century, the area had drifted beyond Poland's field of influence.

At about the same time, the territory of the Teutonic Order also came up for the taking. Monastic orders were seminally affected by Luther's teachings, and Grand Master Albrecht von Hohenzollern (who was King Zygmunt's nephew) and most of his knights came under Luther's spell just as Poland defeated them again, in 1520. Since neither the Vatican nor the Empire would support the apostate knights, there was nothing to prevent Zygmunt from winding up the redundant crusading state and incorporating it into his kingdom. Instead, he sanctioned its transformation into a secular duchy hereditary in the Hohenzollern family, who became vassals of the Polish crown. Cardinal Hosius called the King 'a madman who, being in a position to crush the vanquished, prefers instead to show mercy'. Even the court fool Stańczyk taunted the King on his folly, taunts which would be fully justified in time.

The Livonian knights had also gone over to Luther, and found themselves in a critical position as a result. Both Sweden and Denmark, which had long-standing interests in the area, had designs on Livonia. This was also in the sights of Muscovy, which craved a coastline on the Baltic. Faced by this concert of rival interests, the Livonian knights could see no way of guaranteeing their continued existence other than by becoming vassals of the Commonwealth, which they duly did in 1561.

This deepened a conflict between Poland and Muscovy which had begun in 1512. In that year the ruler of Muscovy, Vasily III, had made alliances with the Teutonic Order and the Empire, which enabled him to field a more modern army and contributed directly to his capture of Smolensk. Although a Polish army under Hetman Ostrogski gave his forces a drubbing at the Battle of Orsza in 1514, the threat from the east would not go away. Throughout the 1550s and 1560s Ivan the Terrible made repeated attempts to slice through Lithuania to the sea.

In 1577 Ivan invaded Livonia once more, and while Lithuanian detachments managed to contain the invasion, King Stephen decided that a conclusive war was called for. In 1579 he concentrated his forces near Wilno under Hetmans Mikołaj Mielecki of Poland and Mikołaj Radziwiłł of Lithuania, and moved on Polotsk, which he quickly captured. In the following year Stephen collected an army of 30,000 which moved out in three corps, one commanded by himself, the other two by Mikołaj Radziwiłł and Jan Zamoyski. The Poles took Vielikie Luki and in the following year, 1581, besieged Pskov, which was ably defended by the brothers Ivan and Vasily Shuisky. As winter set in, King Stephen returned to Poland, leaving Zamoyski in command outside Pskov. Meanwhile negotiations had begun through the good offices of the Jesuit Antonio Possevino, acting on instructions from Rome, and on 15 January 1582 the treaty of Jam Zapolski returned the whole of Livonia, Polotsk and other areas to Poland.

The way in which he and his trusted men carried through the Muscovite campaigns is characteristic of Stephen's reign as a whole. As he declared to the Sejm at the outset of his reign, he was '*rex non fictus necque pictus*' – a king, not a statue or a painting. He abided by the constitution, but did not hesitate to use the powers it left him. He proved something of a disappointment to the executionists, who were instrumental in his election, by failing to reinforce the role of the Sejm and rejecting their demands for reform. In 1580 he even imposed censorship on political literature, which did not endear him to the deputies, but he did manage to recover some authority and respect for the crown. His unexpected death in December 1586, after a reign of only ten years, placed this in jeopardy once more.

The Commonwealth faced its third interregnum in the space of fourteen years, which fostered a feeling of impermanence and did nothing to contribute to the orderly conduct of the next election. Although the candidates included the late king's nephew Andrew Bàthory and the new Tsar of Muscovy Fyodor, the contest was essentially between the Habsburg Archduke Maximilian and Prince Sigismund Vasa of Sweden. The Habsburg faction included all those disgruntled by the firm rule of King Stephen and was strongly supported by Rome and the money of Philip II of Spain. With the Armada about to sail against England, the Habsburgs were at the height of their aspiration to dominate Europe.

The anti-Habsburg camp lent their support to Sigismund Vasa, son of King John III of Sweden and Katherine Jagiellon, second sister of Zygmunt Augustus. The pro-Habsburg party attempted to force through their candidate, but on 19 August 1587 Sigismund Vasa was elected to rule as Zygmunt III. Three days later Maximilian invaded at the head of an army and laid siege to Kraków, but he was defeated by Hetman Zamoyski, who pursued him into Silesia and took him prisoner.

When Zygmunt arrived in Kraków to take up his throne he enjoyed the accumulated popularity of his Jagiellon forebears and sealed this by his excellent command of the Polish language. But the twenty-two-year-old King's difficult childhood had marked his character and outlook. He was born in a dungeon where his parents had been imprisoned by the then King of Sweden Eric XIV, and the only ray of light in this dismal incarceration had been brought by Polish Jesuit priests who attended to his education. As the Papal Legate Annibale di Capua noted: 'King Stephen was good to soldiers, this one will be good to priests.'

His first appointments made it clear that Catholics were more likely to get the best offices. He overruled the Sejm of 1589 when it attempted to reinforce the clauses on religious freedom of the Act of the Confederation of Warsaw. A casualty of this was Chancellor Zamoyski's project for tightening up election procedure, which included limiting the interregnum to a maximum of eight weeks, introducing voting by delegation from the sejmiks (i.e. abolishing the universal vote), and, perhaps most important of all in view of later events, the introduction of majority voting. At the King's insistence, the Primate introduced the *sine qua non* that all candidates to the throne must be Catholic, which guaranteed uproar in the Sejm and rejection of the whole package. To the King the causes of parliamentary reform and religious liberty were synonymous, and he would sabotage any project which smacked of either.

He had been elected largely for anti-Habsburg reasons, and the attempt by Maximilian to usurp his throne should have entrenched him in this position. Yet Zygmunt wasted little time in freeing the Archduke, marrying a Habsburg, and signing an 'eternal peace' with Vienna whose benefits for the Commonwealth were not apparent. His intentions were locked away behind a countenance of frigid reserve, and only began to reveal themselves with time.

Zygmunt had been reared by his religious mentors as the future leader of the Counter-Reformation in Sweden, and therefore regarded the Polish throne primarily as a means to an end. It seems he even considered the possibility of handing over Poland to the Habsburgs in return for their support in reclaiming Sweden for himself and Catholicism, a Sweden possibly enlarged by Polish possessions on the Baltic such as Livonia.

Chancellor Zamoyski uncovered evidence of the King's machinations and in 1592 led the Sejm in a formal indictment of his behaviour, which amounted to breaking the *Pacta Conventa* and the *Acta Henriciana*. Zygmunt apologised and promised to behave in the future, but his subjects remained suspicious, and he grew more secretive than ever.

That same year his father John III of Sweden died, and Zygmunt determined to take up his inheritance. The Sejm allowed him to go, on condition that he returned within a year, which he did, leaving his uncle, Charles of Södermannland, as regent. The inevitable followed: Charles ruled Sweden as his own to the growing annoyance of his nephew, who went over in 1598 to reaffirm his authority, only to be humiliated. In the following year the Swedish Riksdag deposed Zygmunt, adding the proviso that his son Władysław could succeed if he became a Lutheran.

Zygmunt started a war with Sweden which led to the loss of Livonia. The Poles regained it in 1601, but four years later Zygmunt's uncle, now Charles IX, invaded once again. The province would have fallen to Sweden had it not been for the Hetman of Lithuania Jan Karol Chodkiewicz, who took on Charles at Kircholm and worsted him. He went on to recapture the whole of Livonia, retaking Riga in 1609. The Swedish defeat was compounded by the death in 1611 of Charles IX. But he was succeeded by the under-age Gustavus Adolphus, who was to prove an immeasurably superior general, while the man appointed to rule during his minority was Axel Oxenstierna, one of the most brilliant statesmen of seventeenth-century Europe.

He would exploit Sweden's peripheral situation during the Thirty Years' War, which broke out in 1618, by joining in against the Catholic-Habsburg camp when there was something tangible to be gained, and keeping out when there was not. Although Poland had declared its neutrality in this conflict, King Zygmunt considered himself a member of the Catholic League ranged against the Protestant Union. He sent the Habsburgs a reinforcement of 10,000 cavalry, which contributed to their victory at the Battle of the White Mountain against the 'Winter King' of Bohemia. This allowed Sweden to disregard Poland's neutrality and invade not only Livonia but Pomerania as well. In 1627 Hetman Koniecpolski defeated the army of Gustavus Adolphus on land and the Polish navy defeated the Swedish fleet at sea. Peace was eventually signed at Stumsdorf in 1635, but the Vasas' claim to the Swedish throne would cause more bloodshed yet.

The Commonwealth itself had no part in these wars, and no reason for fighting them. The Sejm had lost control over the King's conduct of foreign affairs, but did retain a negative influence on its outcome, since it could refuse funds for troops. Once the King's actions had provoked foreign invasion, however, the Commonwealth had no choice but to defend itself. Thus Polish foreign policy under the three Vasa kings, Zygmunt III (1587–1632) and his sons Władysław IV (1632–48) and Jan Kazimierz (1648–68), often took the form of ambitious plans which foundered either before or shortly after being put into effect, as they enjoyed little support in the Sejm.

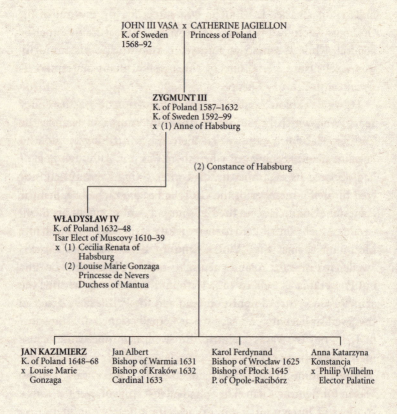

JOHN III VASA   x   CATHERINE JAGIELLON
K. of Sweden   Princess of Poland
1568–92

ZYGMUNT III
K. of Poland 1587–1632
K. of Sweden 1592–99
x (1) Anne of Habsburg

(2) Constance of Habsburg

WŁADYSŁAW IV
K. of Poland 1632–48
Tsar Elect of Muscovy 1610–39
x (1) Cecilia Renata of
        Habsburg
    (2) Louise Marie Gonzaga
        Princesse de Nevers
        Duchess of Mantua

JAN KAZIMIERZ	Jan Albert	Karol Ferdynand	Anna Katarzyna
K. of Poland 1648–68	Bishop of Warmia 1631	Bishop of Wrocław 1625	Konstancja
x Louise Marie	Bishop of Kraków 1632	Bishop of Płock 1645	x Philip Wilhelm
Gonzaga	Cardinal 1633	P. of Opole-Racibórz	Elector Palatine

Fig. 4 The Vasa Kings of Poland

Notwithstanding his apologies to the Sejm of 1592, Zygmunt continued on his own course, breaking the pledges he had made in the *Acta Henriciana* on at least three counts: contracting a marriage (twice, to a Habsburg), carrying on secret diplomatic negotiations and embarking on foreign wars, without the approval of the Sejm. In 1605 he presented the Sejm with a package of reforms that included the imposition of a permanent annual tax, the introduction of a larger standing army, the reduction of the Senate and the abolition of the lower chamber. The spokesmen of the opposition, Chancellor Zamoyski, Marek Sobieski and Field-Hetman Żółkiewski, pointed out that this was unrealistic, where-upon the King dismissed the Sejm. In the last speech he ever made, the old Chancellor told the King that he would have the absolute loyalty of his people, all the taxes he wanted and greater power if only he could bring himself to identify with the interests of his subjects and his kingdom.

The appeal went unheeded, and when the Chancellor had been laid in his grave that summer, Zygmunt called a second Sejm in the hope of having a freer hand. Another vociferous leader of the opposition, Mikołaj Zebrzydowski, Palatine of Kraków, called a rival assembly of the szlachta which threatened the King with dire consequences if he did not abide by the constitution. The Sejm sitting at Warsaw tried to hammer out a compromise, but this was scuppered by the King, who demanded the repeal of the Act of the Confederation of Warsaw which guaranteed religious freedom. More and more szlachta and some magnates such as Janusz Radziwiłł joined Zebrzydowski at Sandomierz, and with the King persisting in his demands, they voted for his dethronement in accordance with the final clause of the *Acta Henriciana*.

Their case was constitutionally watertight, but it required a man of greater intelligence than Zebrzydowski to spell it out and one of greater authority to rally opinion to it. While few people sided with the King, most were reluctant to raise arms against him. After some hesitation, the two Hetmans Chodkiewicz and Żółkiewski decided to stand by him. They assembled the royal troops and defeated, or rather dispersed, the rebellion at Guzów.

The affair had a highly detrimental effect on the political system of the Commonwealth. The szlachta had tried and failed to invoke its rights according to the constitution, which revealed how academic these rights really were. The King had been defied with armed rebellion, and as it was not ruthlessly crushed it would probably happen again. The episode highlighted a number of faults in the constitution which should have been corrected in the natural process of evolution. But the repeated interregna and rapid succession of kings had impeded the process. By the time it might have been resumed King Zygmunt was on the throne, and he had his own ideas. Opposition to these could be voiced in the Sejm, but not converted into political action. Power had been dispersed so successfully that neither the King, nor the Senate, and least of all the lower chamber of the Sejm, could act without the full support of at least one of the other two.

The King was the catalyst which made the parliamentary process function, but Zygmunt failed to understand the workings of the system, and he had fallen into the trap of thinking that the crown had no constitutional power. It did not require a Pole to see how wrong he was. As the Italian Giovanni Botero observed in 1592, 'The King has as much power as he is allowed by his own skill and intelligence.' Zygmunt possessed neither, and the result was a succession of fruitless and damaging collisions.

The source of the King's power was the right to appoint the senior officers of the Commonwealth, and the bishops, palatines and castellans who made up the Senate. His influence was based on the right to grant the lucrative and prestigious starosties. He was free to appoint whomever he wished, and was under no obligation to favour the rich or powerful. Under the last two Jagiellons most of the senior officers, senators and bishops were the King's men, many of them groomed in the royal chancellery, with the result that the crown had influence and that talent and ambition were drawn towards the royal court as an anteroom to power.

It was inevitable that elected monarchs would be driven by a sense of insecurity to seek the support of influential grandees. But while this might prove expedient in the short term, it merely compounded the King's weakness, by building up the position of the grandees, which was growing as never before.

Between 1550 and 1650 the Firlej, Tarnowski, Tenczyński and other great houses of the Jagiellon era disappeared or declined into obscurity, making way for an oligarchy which was to dominate the life of the Commonwealth over the next three centuries – families such as the Potocki, which would produce no fewer than thirty-five senators, three Hetmans and one Field-Hetman in less than two hundred years. Stanisław Lubomirski provides a good example of this new breed. He owned ninety-one villages, parts of sixteen others, and one town. He also held eighteen villages and two towns on lease from the crown, and a valuable starosty. With his two great castles of Łańcut and Wiśnicz, his Palatinate of Kraków, and his two Imperial titles, the Prince-Palatine no longer needed the King.

Any attempt by the crown to curb a magnate such as him would be sure to provoke widespread opposition, even from the poorest szlachta, who saw it as an attack on personal liberty. There was also the matter of the magnates' very real physical power. Most of them had numerous retinues, and some maintained regular regiments of foreign mercenaries as well as bodyguards of landless szlachta and a pool of supporters and clients. When a quarrel between the Koniecpolski and Wiśniowiecki families led to armed confrontation, the combined strength of the two bodies facing each other came to over 10,000 men.

The factors that contributed to the wealth of the magnates over-lapped those that furnished them with manpower. This period saw enormous fluctuations in the supply of and demand for agricultural produce. A bumper harvest in 1618 coincided with high prices on the export market, while 1619 yielded a tiny crop accompanied by low prices and a European financial crisis. Small estates benefited only marginally from a good year and suffered severely in a bad one, often going bankrupt for lack of financial reserves. Increasing numbers of minor szlachta were obliged to sell out to the local magnate, who was the only source of cash in the area. The birth rate of the minor szlachta soared in the sixteenth century owing to improved hygiene and medical care, and the resulting numerous families only compounded the slide into penury. A sort of noble *lumpenproletariat* came into being, with nothing to offer except a vote and a sword. As they could not indulge in trade, they were obliged to take service. Since there was no royal army or administration that could absorb them, they sought employment with the magnates, as agents, courtiers or soldiers. A pattern of clientage evolved, and the residences of the magnates gradually took over the functions of the royal court.

The pattern varied around the Commonwealth. In Wielkopolska a higher percentage of szlachta managed to hang on to productive estates, thereby not only maintaining their own financial independence, but also thwarting the accumulation of vast latifundia. No princely states developed there, even if the real wealth of the local magnates was on a par with that of those in Lithuania or Ukraine who owned areas the size of a small country. It was here, in the eastern reaches of the Commonwealth, that the great magnates were a law unto themselves. Their ambitions and priorities were of no interest to the rest of the country, but their ability to carry on a semi-independent policy dragged it into disastrous adventures on more than one occasion. Possibly the most spectacular of these was a private jaunt which developed into years of full-scale war with Muscovy.

Ivan the Terrible had died in 1584, leaving two sons: Fyodor, who took the throne; and Dmitry, who was exiled to Uglich, where he was murdered in 1591, probably by Boris Godunov, who became Tsar after Fyodor died, in 1598. In 1601 Muscovy was racked by severe famine, giving rise to unrest and rebellion, and dark rumours began to circulate about Boris, about his bloody deeds, and about divine retribution.

In 1603 a runaway monk by the name of Grishka Otrepiev appeared at the court of Prince Konstanty Wiśniowiecki, Palatine of Ruthenia, claiming to be Ivan's son Dmitry. He spun a yarn about his miraculous escape from Boris Godunov's cut-throats in 1591, and although this was taken with a pinch of salt, his potential usefulness was quickly perceived by Jerzy Mniszech, Palatine of Sandomierz, a man whose personal ambition was exceeded only by the fortune he had made out of salt-mines. He had married off one daughter to Wiśniowiecki, and was now seeking a match for his second, Maryna. The pseudo-Dmitry agreed to marry her in return for financial and political backing. Dmitry went to Kraków and converted to Catholicism. This earned him the support of the Jesuits, who persuaded the Papal Nuncio to introduce him to King Zygmunt. The King received him graciously, granted him a pension, and permitted him to canvass support and raise an army. The impostor then tried to persuade the Chancellor and the hetmans to back him, without success, but there was no lack of adventurers willing to follow him.

In September 1604 Dmitry set off at the head of an army of 3,000 men, paid for by Mniszech. His progress was facilitated by the chaos reigning in Muscovy. Cities surrendered to him and many boyars joined his ranks. In April 1605 Boris Godunov died suddenly in Moscow, and Dmitry entered the city without a fight. He was crowned Tsar, and Maryna Mniszech arrived to take her place at his side. In May 1606 there was a rising in Moscow, and Dmitry was killed. His Polish followers were put to the sword, his wife was locked up, and his corpse was dragged by the genitals to Lobnoie Mesto, where it was cut up, burnt, stuffed into a cannon, and shot off westwards, whence he had come.

The boyar Vasily Shuisky was elected to rule in his place, but that was not the end of the story. In July 1607 an even more disreputable impostor claiming to be the miraculously surviving Dmitry appeared on the scene (there were to be forty such pretenders between 1598 and 1613). The freed Maryna Mniszech 'recognised' him (her Jesuit confessor made them go through a second marriage ceremony just in case), and he became the rallying point for disgruntled Muscovites and Poles who had followed his namesake. They were joined by a number of Lithuanian magnates, including Samuel Tyszkiewicz and Jan Piotr Sapieha, nephew of the Chancellor of Lithuania.

So far, the war had been a private affair. In 1609, however, Tsar Vasily Shuisky made a defensive alliance with King Charles of Sweden, who proceeded to invade Livonia. The Sejm sent Chodkiewicz with an army to oust him, but would not sanction intervention in Muscovy. Ignoring it, King Zygmunt asked for and received full crusading status from Pope Paul V (anyone taking part got full remission of sins, and anyone killed went straight to Heaven), and marched out against the Muscovite schismatics at the head of his own army. He laid siege to Smolensk and soon got bogged down. The pseudo-Dmitry was besieging Moscow with an army made up of Polish adventurers, Cossacks and Russian boyars. With the intervention of Zygmunt III, most of the Poles left him in order to join their king, with the result that the impostor had to fall back to Kaluga and, in effect, drop out of a rapidly changing picture.

The bronze doors of Gniezno Cathedral, made by local craftsmen in the 1170s, depicting the life of St Wojciech (Adalbertus), including his martyrdom at the hands of the Prussians, the purchase of his body for its weight in gold by Bolesław the Brave in 998, and its entombment at Gniezno.

ABOVE: The Benedictine Monastery at Tyniec on the Vistula.

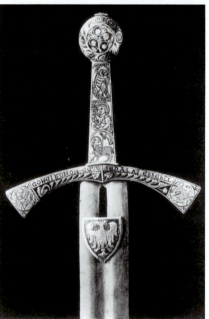

LEFT: Sword made for Bolesław of Mazovia in the early thirteenth century, which became the coronation sword of the kings of Poland after 1320.

RIGHT: The Battle of Legnica (1241), in which the Tatar army routed the forces of Henryk Probus of Silesia. Panel from a triptych by the Master of Wielowieś (c.1430). Henryk can be seen lying dead at the foot of the picture, and again at the top, being borne up to heaven by angels, along with his fallen knights.

LEFT: The Church of St Catherine in Kraków, one of many built by King Kazimierz the Great (1333–70).

BELOW: The Old Synagogue in the Kazimierz district of Kraków, built in the reign of Kazimierz the Great.

ABOVE: The stronghold of the Teutonic Knights at Marienburg (Malbork).

RIGHT: Presumed portrait of Władysław Jagiełło, depicted as one of the Three Kings on the altar of Our Lady of Sorrows in Kraków Cathedral (c.1480).

LEFT: King Kazimierz IV. Detail from his sarcophagus by Veit Stoss in Kraków Cathedral (1492).

ABOVE: Memorial to Philippo Buonaccorsi (Callimachus) by Veit Stoss in the Dominican Church in Kraków (1496).

NICOLAVS COPERNICVS

LEFT: Mikołaj Kopernik (Copernicus).

ABOVE: King Zygmunt Augustus. Contemporary portrait from the workshop of Lucas Cranach the Younger.

ABOVE: Barbara Radziwiłł. Contemporary portrait from the workshop of Lucas Cranach the Younger.

BELOW: Brussels tapestry with the arms of Poland and Lithuania, commissioned by King Zygmunt Augustus in the 1550s.

ABOVE: Renaissance courtyard of the Royal Castle on Wawel Hill in Kraków, begun in 1507 by Francesco Fiorentino and completed in the 1530s by Bartolomeo Berecci.

LEFT: Grain store in the Polish mannerist style at Kazimierz Dolny on the Vistula, dating from 1591.

Early in 1610 the Tsar's brother Dmitry Shuisky set off to relieve Smolensk. Hetman Żółkiewski made a forced march and surprised Shuisky's army at Klushino. He won a resounding victory and pursued the fleeing remnants to Moscow, where the boyars deposed their Tsar and elected in his place Władysław, the eldest son of King Zygmunt. But such a diplomatic solution did not fit in with Zygmunt III's plan of bringing the Catholic faith to Moscow on the tip of his sword. He continued to besiege Smolensk, the boyars waited for the arrival of Władysław, and the small Polish garrison in the Kremlin lived on borrowed time. Since they had not been paid for months, the soldiers offered the Muscovite crown jewels for sale, touting them round Europe by letter. As there were no takers, they divided them up amongst themselves.

On 13 June 1611 Smolensk surrendered to Zygmunt. He felt strong and refused to negotiate with the boyars, adamantly insisting that the whole of Muscovy must go over to Catholicism before he would consider allowing Władysław to become Tsar. There were several risings against the Polish garrison in Moscow, and in November 1612 the Poles capitulated and left the Kremlin

In February 1613 the boyars elected a new Tsar, Mikhail Fyodorovich Romanov, son of the Metropolitan Bishop of Rostov, an associate of the pseudo-Dmitry. As the new Tsar was crowned (with a coronet found in the baggage of a slaughtered Polish soldier), the situation remained confused. His father was a prisoner in Poland. Maryna Mniszech and her three-year-old son were entrenched in southern Russia, supported by the Don Cossacks, and in 1618 Władysław set off at the head of an army to claim his throne, having at last gained the approval of his father. He failed to take Moscow, and in 1619 a peace was signed which returned Smolensk and other areas to Poland, and permitted Władysław to style himself 'Tsar elect of Muscovy'.

The matter was not allowed to rest there. Taking advantage of the death of Zygmunt III in 1632, the Muscovites invaded and laid siege to Smolensk, but in September 1633 Władysław relieved the city and defeated them. In the following year peace was signed, and one of the principal Muscovite demands was that the document of Władysław's election by the boyars in 1610 be handed back to them. Since the document could not be found in the archives, Władysław agreed to a solemn church ceremony in Warsaw, during which he abdicated all his titles and pretensions to the Muscovite throne before a delegation of boyars.

Symbols were immensely important, and they could be very telling. As King Zygmunt III lay dying only two years previously, after the longest reign in Poland's history, he had called his son to his bedside. With the last strength of his trembling arm he placed on Władysław's brow the royal crown of Sweden. He himself lay in state wearing the crown of Muscovy. The only crown which was his to wear, the crown of Poland, had hardly figured in his scheme of things.

EIGHT

Champions of God

When the tower of Kraków's Town Hall had been rebuilt in 1556 a copy of Erasmus' New Testament was immured in the brickwork. When the same tower was repaired in 1611 the book was replaced by a Catholic New Testament, along with a picture and a relic of the first Polish Jesuit to be canonised, St Stanisław Kostka. The symbols could hardly have been more apt. One vision of life was replaced by another, the spirit of enquiry by one of piety, humanist principles by post-Tridentine conformism, and if Erasmus had been the beacon for all thinking Poles in the 1550s, the Jesuits were the mentors of their grandchildren.

Yet the Catholic Church had to tread warily as it set about the reconquest of Poland, as the battle lines criss-crossed society in the most confusing way. When Cardinal Aldobrandini, the future Pope Clement VIII, visited Wilno in 1588, he was astonished at a dinner given by a Catholic canon that the principal guest was a Calvinist, Judge Teodor Jewlaszewski of Nowogródek, whose father was the Orthodox Bishop of Pińsk, and whose son was brought up as an Arian. In such situations it was not feasible to be rigoristic. Even the bigoted Zygmunt III grudgingly had to allow his Lutheran sister Anna to install a Protestant chapel in the Royal Castle.

The most fervent Catholics tended to feel that they were, as the

125

saying went, 'born noble, not Catholic'; the political solidarity of the szlachta far outweighed religious loyalties. When the King had a Protestant book seized in 1627, there was immediate uproar. The Arian Samuel Przypkowski voiced the proto-Orwellian sentiments of the majority of the szlachta when he raged: 'The next move will be to institute torture for having thoughts . . . Our cause is bound to the cause of common freedom by a knot so tight that the one cannot be separated from the other.'

The progress of the Counter-Reformation was slow. The number of Protestant chapels dwindled by some two-thirds in the last third of the sixteenth century, and the Protestant majority in the Senate in 1569 shrank to a handful by 1600. The fact that a fervently Catholic king favoured those of this faith when making appointments was no doubt one reason. But it was not until 1658 that the Arians were banished, for having refused to bear arms at a time of national peril and allegedly siding with the enemy. In 1660 the Quakers were expelled from their colony near Gdańsk, whence they set sail for America. In 1668 the Sejm ruled that nobody could leave the Catholic Church for any other on pain of exile, and in 1673 admittance to the szlachta was barred to non-Catholics. None of these measures prevented anyone from practising the faith of his choice, and there was a twilight zone between what the Sejm decreed and what even the most zealous Catholic officer of the law was prepared to implement against a fellow citizen.

Yet the drift back to Catholicism coincided with a change of intellectual climate and a spiritual reawakening, reflected in, among other things, a spectacular resurgence of monasticism. The Dominican Order, for example, numbered no more than three hundred brothers in forty communities at its lowest point in 1579. Twenty years later there were nine hundred brothers, and by 1648 there were 110 large communities. Between 1572 and 1648 the number of monasteries in the Commonwealth rose from 220 to

565. The same period saw the foundation of new contemplative or ascetic orders such as the Benedictine nuns of Chełmno and the Barefoot Carmelites, starting a mystical tradition in Polish religious life that had seldom been in evidence before.

This was in large measure the work of the Jesuits. Their principal instruments in the battle for the soul of Poland were the colleges they established all over the Commonwealth, of which there were nearly forty by the mid-seventeenth century. They were free, they accepted Arians, Calvinists and Orthodox as readily as Catholics, and the teaching was of a high standard. The Spanish, Italian, Portuguese, English and French priests who taught in them added an element of cosmopolitanism which the poorer szlachta appreciated. In 1587, twenty-three years after the first Jesuit had set foot in Poland, the Jesuit College of Wilno had some sixty priests and novices teaching over seven hundred pupils. 'There have always been and there still are in the classes of this college very numerous sons of heretics and schismatics,' explained the Rector, Garcias Alabiano. 'Their parents send them to our schools solely to learn the Arts, and not to be taught the Catholic Faith. However, by the Grace of God, not one of them has to this day left without abjuring his parents' errors and embracing the Catholic Faith.'

Two years later the college was elevated to the status of university by King Stephen, and its influence increased accordingly. By the 1620s, with the Jagiellon University sinking into clerical sophistry and that of Zamość lapsing into provincialism, Wilno had only two rivals: the Arian academies of Raków and Leszno. Raków, founded under the spiritual aegis of Fausto Sozzini (Socinius) and the patronage of the magnate Jan Sienieński, had become the principal centre of Arian thought in the early 1600s, attracting teachers and students from all over Europe. During the next decades it gave rise to a canon of Socinian literature which was disseminated far and wide (Spinoza and Locke are among those thought to have been influenced by these writings). In 1638 two students of the academy desecrated a Catholic wayside shrine, and the ensuing scandal resulted in the closure of the academy and its press. The Brethren moved these to the estate of another Arian magnate, but they were gradually undermined by continual legal harassment from the Catholic hierarchy. The Arian college of Leszno, founded in the previous century by the Leszczyński family, was enhanced in the 1620s when the Czech philosopher Jan Amos Komensky (Commenius) joined it. His teachings were particularly influential in Holland and England, which he visited under Cromwell's Protectorate (it was during this visit that he was invited to preside over the college of Harvard in New England). Leszno was sacked during the Swedish war of 1655, just three years before the banishment of the Arians, so by the second half of the century the Jesuit University of Wilno had no serious rival.

Between their arrival in 1564 and the end of the century, no fewer than 344 books by Jesuits were published in Poland. This literature, much of it on subjects of general interest, subtly promoted their vision, political as well as spiritual. The Jesuits ranged themselves behind the crown, particularly after the accession of Zygmunt III in 1587, and displayed marked hostility towards the szlachta. This stemmed not only from the Jesuits' genuine sympathy for the peasantry, but also from the realisation that the real foe of Catholic absolutism was not so much the Arians or the Calvinists, the Jews or the Muslims, but the democratic Catholics who made up such a large proportion of the szlachta.

The constitution of the Commonwealth stood in the way of the Counter-Reformation and the szlachta were the guardians of the constitution. Little could be achieved through the power of the crown, so the Jesuits looked for other weapons. They even began to use the pulpit to incite the downtrodden to raise their heads: the spectre of a nationwide peasants' revolt in support of the King and the Church was not a pleasant prospect for the szlachta. It never came to that. The Zebrzydowski rebellion, which voiced some unequivocal intentions where the Jesuits were concerned, frightened them. As the Jesuits attracted more and more minor szlachta into their ranks, they learnt to operate more adroitly within the system, while their schools turned out thousands of young szlachta imbued with religious, social and political principles honed by them.

The magnates were a different matter. Although they had collected wealth and office with single-minded egoism, often behaving like petty tyrants, they nevertheless entertained a view of themselves as pillars of the constitution. They were fond of likening their families to the senatorial houses of ancient Rome – to the extent, in the case of the Lubomirski, of claiming descent from Drusus (the Radziwiłł, not to be outdone, published a family tree showing Hector of Troy as their ancestor). They were, in consequence, far harder for the Jesuits to snare. But even they were tamed.

A characteristic figure in this respect was Jerzy Ossoliński, born in 1595 into an old family of substance which his generation carried into the top league. After a Jesuit education, he set off on a grand tour through Holland, England, France, Italy and Austria. He distinguished himself at the siege of Moscow in 1618, and subsequently as a diplomat before embarking on a parliamentary career. In 1631 he was elected Marshal of the Sejm, an opportunity he used to put forward a project for reform of voting procedures. In 1636 he entered the Senate as Palatine of Sandomierz, two years later he was appointed Vice Chancellor, and in 1642 Chancellor of Poland. An intelligent statesman, he inspired respect for himself and the king he served by his strong yet moderate approach, but his Jesuit upbringing showed whenever there was talk of religious toleration, and he was instrumental in the closing down of the Raków Academy.

Ossoliński was a great patron, but he lacked the civic vision of his predecessors, and created little more than monuments to himself. In 1635 he built a grand residence at Ossolin, in 1643 the magnificent church of St George at Klimontów, and then a fine Palladian palace in Warsaw. It was his elder brother Krzysztof who encapsulated the spirit that guided them both in one of the greatest pieces of self-advertisement by any Polish family – the astonishing castle of Krzyżtopór. Built on a spectacular ground plan consisting of a number of courtyards of different sizes radiating from a central *cour d'honneur* superimposed on a mass of star-shaped fortifications, it looks for all the world like a beached ocean liner. The windows were ornamented with marble plaques inscribed in Latin in praise of various real and invented forebears.

Ossoliński's embassy to Rome in 1633 was an excuse to show off. He pawned and mortgaged in order to cover his servants in gold and to caparison his horses and camels in pearls for the occasion. He accepted the title of duke from the Pope, and that of prince from the Emperor in 1634, titles which only caused the bearer embarrassment at home – the cornerstone of the constitution was the absolute equality of the szlachta, and no titles were recognised (with the exception of those accorded at the Union of Lublin to Lithuanian and Ukrainian families of Jagiellon, Rurik or other dynastic descent, such as the Czartoryski, Sanguszko, Zbaraski, Zasławski and others).

Ossoliński and his peers stopped short of enforcing religious conformism. But the original text of the Act of the Confederation of Warsaw, in which the inhabitants of the Commonwealth pledged, as equals, to respect each other's religious beliefs and practices, was amended, to 'graciously permit' others to practise a different faith. The Catholic faith was, in Ossoliński's words, 'mistress in her own house', while the Protestants were no more than tolerated guests. And while there was no objection to ethnic minorities practising different rites or the Livonian szlachta remaining Protestant, Poles who were Protestants began to be viewed as eccentric, even suspicious. A psychological connection had been made between Catholicism and patriotism, a patriotism made increasingly vital by the succession of wars in the first half of the century. Since these were fought against Protestant Swedes and Orthodox Russians, Jesuit and other writers began to picture the Poles as defenders of Catholicism. When the Turks and Tatars took over as the principal enemy in the following decades, it was a short step to turn the Poles into the defenders of Christendom. A powerful myth grew up of Poland as the predestined bulwark of Christendom, the *Antemurale Christianitatis*, as Machiavelli had referred to it. 'Lord, you were once called the God of Israel,' Jakub Sobieski prayed in the 1650s. 'On bended knee we now call you the God of Poland, our motherland, the God of our armies and the Lord of our hosts.'

But while it affected this embattled sense of destiny, Polish society nevertheless remained highly cosmopolitan. Translations of French, Italian, Spanish, Turkish and Persian works were published with little delay, and plays by Shakespeare were performed in Poland as early as 1609. Zygmunt III kept an Italian *commedia dell'arte* at his court, supplemented in the 1620s by an English troupe, and during the first half of the century few courts had such good music. In 1633 Władysław IV set up a royal opera company, and Piotr Elert wrote the first Polish opera in the late 1630s.

The Jesuits themselves were responsible for much artistic patronage, including some of the best building and painting of the period. They also contributed the greatest lyric poet of the Polish Baroque, Maciej Kazimierz Sarbiewski (1595–1640). Most of his fellow poets devoted themselves to the subject of war, giving rise to a tradition of heroic and pathetic verse, a latterday *chanson de geste* inspired by the unique conditions and atmosphere in which wars against the Turks and Tatars were fought. In Ukraine or Moldavia, companies of Polish horsemen with the image of the Blessed Virgin on their breastplates and a prayer on their lips faced the Infidel in epic contest.

'Do not disturb yourself, most beloved wife, for God watches over us,' Hetman Żółkiewski wrote from his camp at Cecora in Moldavia on the night of 6 October 1620. 'And if I should perish it will be because I am old and of no further use to the Commonwealth, and the Almighty will grant that our son may take up his father's sword, temper it on the necks of pagans and, if it should come to pass as I said, avenge the blood of his father.' The next day his army was defeated and his body hacked to pieces by Turkish janissaries. His head was sent to Istanbul, where it was displayed on a pike. What sustained such attitudes was the conviction that Poland had a special part to play in God's scheme. This notion deeply marked the seventeenth-century szlachta, for warfare was their preserve.

The father of Polish military science was Hetman Jan Tarnowski, who published his *Consilium Rationis Bellicae* in 1558. He elaborated the old Hussite tactic of forming a square, a mobile fortress which could save a small army caught out in the open, and this became standard practice in all operations against Tatars and Turks. The need to move fast and to live off the land meant that Polish armies operated in divisions, while most European armies marched in a great mass until the end of the eighteenth century. Another peculiar feature was the tradition of the deep cavalry raid sweeping out ahead of the main army in a great arc behind enemy lines. The Poles were also in advance of their enemies in terms of artillery. From the Turks they had learnt much about incendiary and explosive shells, and they developed rocketry to great effect.

The core of the Commonwealth's armed forces was a small

body of infantry consisting of peasant levies, raised on and paid for by 25 per cent of revenue from the starosties and royal lands, and therefore known as 'quarter troops'. In 1579 King Stephen instituted a new system under which peasants from royal lands could volunteer to become reserve soldiers, freed from all servage and dues in return for their regular training and readiness to fight, and paid when on active service. This type of infantry, known as *Piechota Wybraniecka*, was effective on account of its regular training in peacetime and its good morale. Lightly dressed, without helmets or armour, the men were equipped with a musket, short sword and hatchet. Only one man in eight carried a pike. In the 1550s, a Polish regiment of two hundred men could deliver 150 shots in five minutes, while contemporary Spanish brigades of 10,000 men operating in the Netherlands could only deliver 750 in the same time – ten times less on a man-to-man basis. The Commonwealth also employed mercenaries – German, Scottish or French infantry drilled on standard European lines. It could also count in the hour of need on the private armies of magnates.

The infantry was outnumbered by cavalry, and, aside from a few regiments of regular dragoons, this was based on the chivalric pattern of the knight and his squires. The szlachta who fought in the front line were known as *towarzysze*, or 'companions'. Each companion would bring with him as many men as he could afford to equip, most of them poor szlachta, to make up the second and third ranks, and these were known as *pocztowi*, literally 'retainers'. Companions equipped themselves and their retainers at their own expense, but received soldier's pay when on active service.

The presence in the ranks of large numbers of volunteers, and particularly of szlachta fighting not for the cause of some king but for their own Commonwealth, gave them the same edge over their enemies as that enjoyed by the soldiers of revolutionary France in the 1790s. The gentleman-trooper carried the szlachta's democratic principles in his saddlebag and thought of his commander and the Hetman as elder brothers.

The pride and glory of the Polish cavalry, its mailed fist, was the Husaria. The companions of the front rank carried a lance of up to twenty feet in length, which outreached infantry pikes, allowing the Husaria to cut straight through a square, and a sabre or a rapier with a six-foot blade which doubled as a short lance. Each companion also carried a pair of pistols, a short carbine, a bow and arrows and a variety of other weapons. The retainers carried much the same arsenal without the lance, while the rear rank often led spare mounts into the charge.

The Husaria wore helmets, thick steel breastplates and shoulder and arm guards, or eastern scale armour. The companions also sometimes sported wooden arcs bristling with eagle feathers rising over their heads like two wings from attachments on their shoulders or the back of the saddle. Over one shoulder they wore the skin of a tiger or leopard as a cloak. These served to frighten the enemy's horses, and the wings had the added advantage of preventing Tatars eager for ransom from lassoing the Polish riders in a mêlée. But the main purpose of these accoutrements was to give an impression of splendour. The companions in the Husaria were young noblemen who liked to show off their wealth. Helmets and breastplates were chased or studded with gold and often set with semi-precious stones. Harnesses, saddles and horsecloths were embroidered and embellished with gold and gems.

For over a century, the Husaria were the lords of the battlefield. Kircholm (1605), where 4,000 Poles under Chodkiewicz accounted for 14,000 Swedes, was little more than one long cavalry manoeuvre ending in the Husaria's charge. Klushino (1610), where Żółkiewski with 6,000 Poles, of whom only two hundred were infantry, defeated 30,000 Muscovites and 5,000 German and Scottish mercenaries, was a Husaria victory, as was the Battle of Gniew (1656), in which 5,500 Polish cavalry defeated 13,000 Swedes. In many other battles, from Byczyna (1588) and Trzciana (1629) to the relief of Vienna (1683), the Husaria dealt the decisive blow.

Though hardly a maritime nation, the Poles did have a navy for a while. In 1560 Zygmunt Augustus licensed a total of thirty privateers to sail under the Polish ensign. He established a Maritime Commission and in 1569 launched a galleon and a frigate of the Polish navy. In 1620 Zygmunt III had a further twenty warships built, and in 1627 the Polish navy fought its only sea battle when it defeated the Swedish fleet off Oliwa. If the Poles did not like paying for an army, they liked digging into their pockets even less for a navy, which seemed an unnecessary luxury since cordial relations with England and Holland meant that Poland had maritime friends in the Baltic. The navy dwindled, and the only sailor of talent Poland produced, Krzysztof Arciszewski, became a Dutch admiral.

Victory was repeatedly achieved at low cost and with little apparent effort, and this had a pernicious effect. Increasingly, when money was needed for defence, voices were raised in the Sejm to the effect that 'They're scaring us with Turks and Tatars just to get money out of us,' in the belief that if any real threat materialised it could be parried easily by the noble Polish knight, armed with the superiority of his political freedom and inspired by God. There was some truth in this, but times were changing.

NINE

A Biblical Flood

'Poland is like a spectator who stands safely on the seashore, calmly looking on at the tempest raging before him,' wrote Krzysztof Opaliński, Palatine of Poznań, in 1630. With most of Central Europe caught up in the self-perpetuating butchery of the Thirty Years' War, Poland did indeed appear remarkably peaceful and stable. When Zygmunt III died in 1632, his eldest son Władysław was elected unanimously in the space of half an hour. The prestige of the Commonwealth and its king rode high, and France repeatedly urged him to take the Imperial crown after the death of the ailing Ferdinand II, offering the necessary funds and military as well as diplomatic support. When his wife died, portraits of no fewer than sixteen princesses were sent in by other courts.

The situation changed drastically when the Thirty Years' War came to an end in 1648. That same year the Commonwealth was shaken to its foundations by the explosion of formidable tensions that had been building up for over half a century in its south-eastern reaches of Ukraine. This area of formerly Kievan lands taken over by Lithuania in the thirteenth century and transferred to Poland before the Union of Lublin in 1569 had been administratively tacked on to the Kingdom of Poland without any regard for its specific nature.

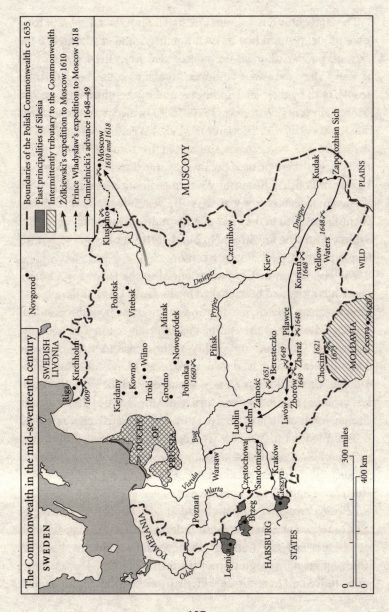

The Commonwealth in the mid-seventeenth century

Legend:
- Boundaries of the Polish Commonwealth c. 1635
- Piast principalities of Silesia
- Intermittently tributary to the Commonwealth
- Żółkiewski's expedition to Moscow 1610
- Prince Władysław's expedition to Moscow 1618
- Chmielnicki's advance 1648–49

SWEDEN

SWEDISH LIVONIA

Novgorod

Riga
Kircholm 1609

MUSCOVY

Polotsk
Vitebsk
Mińsk
Nowogródek

Moscow
1610 and 1618

Klushino 1610

Czernihów

Kiev

Kudak
Zaporozhian Sich

PLAINS

Kiejdany
Kowno
Wilno
Troki
Grodno
Połonka 1660

Pińsk

Pryper

Dnieper

Dnieper

Korsuń 1648

Yellow Waters 1648

WILD

DUCHY OF PRUSSIA

Bug

Lublin
Chełm

Zamość

Beresteczko 1651
Piławce 1648
Zbaraż 1649
Zborów 1649
Lwów

Chocim 1621 1673

MOLDAVIA

Cecora 1620

POMERANIA

Vistula

Warta

Warsaw

Poznań

Częstochowa
Sandomierz
Kraków
Cieszyn

Brzeg

Legnica

HABSBURG STATES

Oder

300 miles
400 km

The autochtonous population of Ukraine had kept a strong sense of identity and had its own nobility, some of whom, like the Ostrogski and Zasławski, were descended from the former rulers of Kiev. They were well equipped to stand at the head of their people, both by their ancient lineage and by their immense wealth. Prince Konstanty Ostrogski (1526–1608) owned a hundred towns and 1,300 villages. Prince Jarema Michał Wiśniowiecki (1612–51) owned 38,000 homesteads, inhabited by some 230,000 of his subjects. But these princes became separated from their people by the lure of Polish culture and Western civilisation. A classic pattern of alienation evolved: it was with the best intentions that Prince Zbaraski travelled in the West and spent three years studying under Galileo, returning to Ukraine to build, fortify and improve, but his people came to view him as a traitor.

The population of Ukraine belonged to the Orthodox Church, whose hierarchy had been shaken by the fall of Constantinople and the subsequent Ottoman expansion in the Balkans, and was still in a state of disarray at the end of the sixteenth century. In 1588 the Patriarch of Constantinople paid a pastoral visit to his flock in the Commonwealth and held two synods, at Wilno and Kamieniec Podolski. Chancellor Jan Zamoyski put forward the suggestion that the Patriarch settle in Kiev and turn it into the centre of the Orthodox Church. Jesuit influence thwarted this, and the Patriarch was invited by Tsar Feodor I to Moscow. There, in 1589, he created the patriarchate of all the Russias, whose purpose was to bring under its authority the whole Orthodox Church, including that part of it which lay within the Commonwealth.

Before leaving, the Patriarch had appointed Bishop Terlecki of Łuck to represent him in Poland. Terlecki started negotiations with his counterpart the Catholic Bishop of Łuck in the hope of achieving greater recognition of his own hierarchy. These negotiations moved on to embrace wider issues and aroused the interest of the Jesuits, particularly of Piotr Skarga. After consultation with Rome, agreement was reached and an Act of Union was signed in 1596 at Brześć. By this act the Commonwealth's Orthodox bishops recognised the Pope as their spiritual head in lieu of the Patriarch in Moscow, but kept their old Slavonic liturgy and rites, and the right of priests to marry.

The Jesuits congratulated themselves on having brought millions of wayward sheep into the fold, but many Orthodox priests and their flocks felt indignant at not having been consulted, and refused to adhere to the Union, with the result that there were now in effect three and not two Churches – Roman, Orthodox and Uniate, as those who had transferred to Rome were known. While the Roman and Uniate looked to the West, the Orthodox looked elsewhere. The Union had been designed to bind the Orthodox population of Ukraine to Poland. In the event, it had the effect of pushing it into the arms of Moscow. While the Uniate bishops continued in their efforts to bring the recalcitrant priests to accept the Union, the Orthodox hierarchy of Moscow was pulling them the other way.

The organisation of the Uniate Church proceeded slowly. It was not until the 1630s that metropolitan bishops were installed at Kiev and Polotsk, and by then the whole matter was coming under discussion once again. Władysław IV was keen to revise the arrangement within the framework of an entirely new formulation of religious freedoms. He wanted to replace the toleration of differing religions as enshrined in the Act of the Confederation of Warsaw (1573) by some form of ecumenical consensus on religious diversity. After much preparation, he managed to hold a congress at Toruń in 1645, in which Catholics, Lutherans and Calvinists discussed their differences. The congress was inconclusive, but, as the King himself put it, 'At least nobody insulted each other.' A similar congress between the Catholic, Orthodox and Uniate Churches was planned for 1648. Meanwhile Metropolitan Mohyla of Kiev was in the process of renegotiating the Union of Brześć with Rome. But these efforts came too late.

The drift of Ukraine's nobility towards Western culture was usually accompanied by a straightforward switch to Catholicism, which provided a bridge to that culture. In 1632 Jarema Wiśniowiecki, the last of the great Ukrainian lords to live entirely in Ukraine and to cling to its language, culture and traditions, converted to the Church of Rome. Despite the valiant efforts of Metropolitan Mohyla, who founded an academy in Kiev that same year, the Uniate Church was failing to hold people such as Wiśniowiecki, while Orthodoxy was rapidly becoming the religion of the lower orders. It was inevitable that these would eventually see in it a rallying point and a weapon.

The incorporation of the area into Poland in 1569 had been followed by an influx of landless Polish szlachta eager to carve out estates for themselves in this fertile and underpopulated land. They were closely followed by Catholic clergy and large numbers of Jews, for the most part brought in by Polish landowners to act as middlemen, agents, rent collectors and innkeepers – all of which made them odious to the locals. This was particularly true of the Cossacks, who found themselves in a position not unlike that of the American Indians in the nineteenth century – the newcomers were settling and farming land which they considered to be common, and pushing them further and further into frontier territory.

The Cossacks were not so much a people as a way of life. The very name 'Cossack' derives from a Turkish-Tatar word denoting a free soldier, and that just about defines their identity and semi-nomadic way of life. The spiritual home of the Cossacks of western Ukraine, the Zaporozhian Host, was the *Sich*, a commune ruled by elected elders on the Zaporozhe, the islands beyond the rapids of the river Dnieper. The population of the *Sich* was variable, as almost anyone could be a Cossack if he wished.

The Cossacks inhabited a frontier zone constantly open to attack from the Principality of Moldavia, whose rulers owed allegiance alternatively to Poland, Turkey and Hungary, or from the Khanate of the Crimean Tatars, with its capital at Bakhchisaray, which was separated from the Commonwealth by a broad stretch of no-man's-land known as the Wild Plains. The Tatars were nominally subjects of the Sultan. Every spring their raiding parties or *tchambouls* set off along three trails running north into Muscovy, north-west into Poland, and west into Ukraine, burning and looting as they went. They took valuables and livestock, and above all people, leaving behind only the old or infirm. They would then return to the Crimea whence the wealthy would be ransomed and the rest shipped to the slave markets of Istanbul.

Although the Tatars were a nuisance, they never represented a serious threat on their own. But they could, and sometimes did, join up with an Ottoman army marching up through Moldavia, thereby effectively outflanking any Polish defence. Ever since the 1520s, when the Turks had ousted Venice and the Knights of St John from the eastern Mediterranean and taken over much of the Balkans, Moldavia and Ukraine presented a tempting theatre for expansion. The Commonwealth was directly threatened, and responded with two moves. In 1593 a Polish expedition placed a friendly vassal on the Moldavian throne and a *pax polonica* was imposed on the area, affording some security to the south-eastern reaches of the Commonwealth.

The other measure taken in the 1590s was the transformation of the Cossack community of the Zaporozhian *Sich* into an army, defined by a 'register' listing the number and pay of serving Cossacks. But while 'His Majesty's Zaporozhian Army' wore the title with pride, it remained unaccountable, and instead of parrying Tatar raids, the Cossacks preferred to conduct their own. They would push into the Crimea or else climb into longboats, sail down the Dnieper and molest Turkish cities on the Black Sea. In 1606 they raided Kilia, Akerman and Varna. In 1608 they captured Perekop. In 1615 they sacked Trebizond and attacked Istanbul itself.

Relations between the Commonwealth and the Porte grew increasingly sour, and in 1620 Iskander Pasha invaded Moldavia. A small Polish force under Hetman Żółkiewski set off in support of the vassal prince. The Poles were defeated, Żółkiewski was killed and Field-Hetman Koniecpolski was taken prisoner. Tatar *tchambouls* swarmed into Poland as far as Lwów, in the rear of a second Polish army which had dug in at Chocim to hold off the Turks. Although the Poles managed to drive the Ottoman forces back then and on a similar occasion ten years later, the whole area remained vulnerable.

Nor had the creation of the Zaporozhian Army solved the internal problems of Ukraine. The Cossacks saw themselves as loyal subjects of the king, and they had a particular affection for Władysław IV. But they were constantly at loggerheads with local authorities, the landed szlachta and the agents of large estates who kept trying to pin non-register Cossacks down to the status of peasants. In 1630 the register was raised to 8,000, but the Poles were wary of letting the Cossacks grow too strong; relatively minor grievances were regularly translated into mutinies which were an excuse for organised banditry. In 1637, after one such mutiny, the register was reduced to 6,000. A fortress was built at Kudak on a bend in the Dnieper, from which a Polish garrison kept an eye on movements in the *Sich*.

Instead of being admitted as the third nation of the Commonwealth, Ukraine was treated, by its own elite as well as by the Poles, as a sort of colony, and the resultant sense of deprivation engendered much bitterness. It was these simmering tensions that boiled over in the late 1640s, triggering a series of events that would abort the dream of Ukrainian nationhood and break the

Commonwealth's power decisively, to the benefit of Turkey and, above all, Muscovy.

In 1640, and again in 1644, unusually large Tatar *tchambouls* ravaged Podolia and Volynia. Hetman Koniecpolski managed to defeat them, but not before they had carried off multitudes into slavery. In the winter of 1645 the Tatars sent their *tchambouls* into Muscovy in even larger numbers, and this time Field-Hetman Mikołaj Potocki was dispatched with a Polish army to help the Muscovites, the consequence of a rapprochement which had taken place between Warsaw and Moscow. This gave rise to a plan for a joint Polish–Muscovite offensive into the Crimea, which Muscovy would then incorporate into its own dominions, followed by a similar expedition into Moldavia, which would be incorporated into the Commonwealth. Two unexpected events shattered this plan. One was that Hetman Koniecpolski, now approaching his sixtieth year, absented himself to marry for the third time. His bride, Zofia Opalińska, was not only a great heiress but also a vivacious girl of sixteen. After a brief honeymoon which the Hetman described to a friend in ecstatic terms, he died of exhaustion on 10 March 1646.

The other came in May, when King Władysław unexpectedly announced that he was going to lead a crusade to recover Istanbul, an enterprise he believed would earn him lasting fame. The Sejm was in uproar, and Chancellor Ossoliński quashed the project. But Władysław had already secretly given the Cossacks money, instructing them to double the register to 12,000 and to start building longboats. The Cossacks had set to work in high spirits. Their anger was all the greater when news reached them that the Sejm had put paid to the King's plans. The agreed Crimean and Moldavian campaigns were less attractive to them than a royal licence to take to their boats and rampage around the southern shores of the Black Sea. It was at this point that one man and his personal grievances brought about an explosion. His name was Bohdan Chmielnicki.

Chmielnicki was born in 1595 into the landed szlachta, and although he was Orthodox, he had been educated by the Jesuits. He took part in the 1620 Moldavian campaign, and was taken prisoner by the Turks at the Battle of Cecora along with Koniecpolski. When they recovered their freedom, Koniecpolski obtained for him the post of Secretary to the Zaporozhian Army. Chmielnicki waged a personal vendetta with a Lithuanian neighbour who eventually killed his son. Failing to get justice from the local court, Chmielnicki went to the *Sich*, where he stirred the already indignant Cossacks into a frenzy and started negotiating with the Tatars.

The situation was not critical. The King was personally due in Ukraine, Polish forces were concentrating, and the Muscovite army had started moving south to link up with them. Hetman Potocki, however, decided that a show of strength was required, and in April 1648 he dispatched his twenty-four-year-old son Stefan with 3,500 men, half of them Cossacks, towards the *Sich*. Stefan Potocki was surrounded by the Zaporozhian Army under Chmielnicki and defeated, and his father was ambushed and taken prisoner ten days later at Korsuń. At this crucial moment, Władysław IV, the only man in a position to placate the Cossacks, died unexpectedly.

It was fortunate for the Commonwealth that both the Primate and *interrex*, Maciej Łubieński, and the Chancellor, Jerzy Ossoliński, were sagacious men. They arranged an immediate truce through Adam Kisiel, Palatine of Kiev, the only Orthodox member of the Senate, who began negotiations on a broader settlement. But hopes of an amicable resolution were dashed by Prince Wiśniowiecki, who led his own private army into the field against the Cossacks: the greatest lord of Ukraine was not interested in Ukrainian autonomy, only in putting down the rabble and restoring order. This strengthened the hand of those in the Cossack camp who wanted war rather than negotiation, and Chmielnicki bowed to the pressure.

A large Polish army had assembled, including detachments of the *levée en masse* from the threatened areas, but this fled after a short skirmish at Piławce, and the rest of the army beat a hasty retreat. News of this fanned the flames of revolt. The beleaguered garrison of Kudak capitulated and with it vanished the last vestige of Polish order in Ukraine. Large numbers of peasants joined the Cossacks, and, abetted by Chmielnicki's Tatar allies, they scoured the country, massacring nobles, priests, nuns and, in particular, Jews. The Moldavian custom of impaling alive caught on, and it was practised with relish as decades of tension erupted into mindless cruelty. Chmielnicki was no longer master of the situation, any more than Ossoliński was on the Polish side. Leading the crusade against the rabble were Prince Wiśniowiecki and Janusz Radziwiłł, Field-Hetman of Lithuania, both acting independently.

Rid of the mixed blessing of the *levée en masse*, the Polish army had dug in at Zbaraż, where it held off the combined Cossack and Tatar forces. Then came the first Polish success, at the Battle of Zborów, after which negotiations were reopened and agreement quickly reached. The three Palatinates of Kiev, Bracław and Czernyhów were to be declared Cossack territory, into which no Polish troops, Jews or Jesuits would be allowed. All dignitaries and officials in the area were to be Orthodox Ukrainian szlachta, and the register was to stand at 40,000 men.

Ossoliński and his more reasonable counterparts had managed to pour oil on the water once again, and Ukraine quietened down. It was not to last. In 1650 Chmielnicki accepted the overlordship of the Sultan, who named him vassal prince of Ukraine. Polish forces moved into Ukraine the following spring and in the three-day Battle of Beresteczko routed the Cossack army and its Tatar allies. A new peace was signed at Biała Cerkiew on 28 September

1651 annulling all previous Polish concessions, but while one Polish army set about pacifying the area, another which had gone to Moldavia to head off Chmielnicki's Turkish allies was defeated and its remnants massacred at Batoh.

Władysław IV had been succeeded by his younger brother, Jan Kazimierz, a complex character with a chequered past. He was intelligent and resourceful, but he suffered from fits of depression and listlessness. His lack of charm did not help him gain the confidence of the szlachta, while many magnates felt an intense dislike for him. They also distrusted the Queen, Louise Marie de Gonzague, Duchesse de Nevers, Princess of Mantua.

Her grandfather, a friend and collaborator of Marie de Médicis, had come to Poland with Henri de Valois, and her father, the last Gonzaga Duke of Mantua, had also spent some time in Warsaw. She was brought up at the French court. In 1645, as a result of a rapprochement between Poland and France, she married Władysław IV, and after his death, his younger brother Jan Kazimierz. He was then forty, and she thirty-eight.

She and the bevy of young French ladies she had brought with her introduced French court culture into Poland, which, Cardinal Mazarin hoped, would facilitate his plan to bring the Commonwealth within the French orbit, and if possible place a Bourbon on its throne. From the outset they aroused Polish suspicions.

One faction among the magnates, including the Radziwiłł and Lubomirski families, believed in the necessity of the removal of Jan Kazimierz, and they began to plot accordingly. In the case of the Radziwiłł, it went further: the family had thought of themselves as quasi-royal for the last century, and their dream of assuming the throne of a separate Lithuania had grown into something of an obsession with Janusz Radziwiłł. Such attitudes helped destabilise the situation.

In 1654, Bohdan Chmielnicki, who had developed dynastic

aspirations quite as extravagant as those of the Radziwiłł, negotiated the Treaty of Pereiaslav, placing himself under the protection
of Muscovy in return for military assistance against the Commonwealth. Tsar Alexey began to style himself 'Tsar of Great and Little
Russia'. There were protests from some of the Cossacks, and the
Metropolitan of Kiev announced that he for one was still a subject
of the King of Poland. Alexey invaded Lithuania, defeated Janusz
Radziwiłł and took Polotsk, Smolensk, Vitebsk and Mohilev, while
the Cossacks reached Lublin. In the following spring he took Wilno,
and titled himself 'Grand Duke of Lithuania, Belorussia and
Podolia'. Far from getting Lithuania for themselves, the Radziwiłł
were now in imminent peril of becoming Muscovite subjects, and
they reacted by appealing for help to the King of Sweden.

Charles X Gustavus had just ascended the throne. His country
was bankrupt after the Thirty Years' War, its only asset a huge and
now redundant army. In spite of the twenty years of peace with
the Commonwealth, the Swedes still dreamed of extending their
possessions on the Baltic seaboard. The discontent of many Polish
magnates, the confusion attendant on the Cossack and Muscovite
invasions, and finally the appeal from the Radziwiłł, all paved the
way for an invasion, which took place at the beginning of 1655.

The Swedes rapidly made themselves masters of Pomerania and
advanced into Wielkopolska. A Polish army barred their way, but
was made to capitulate by Krzysztof Opaliński, Palatine of Poznań,
and his colleague the Palatine of Kalisz, who officially transferred
their provinces to Swedish overlordship. The enemies of Jan
Kazimierz all over the country announced his dethronement in
favour of Charles X. With three enemy armies operating in the
country confusion reigned. Disoriented by a rumour that Jan
Kazimierz had abdicated, Hetman Stanisław Rewera Potocki
capitulated. Isolated groups of szlachta and small bodies of troops
on their way to join the army either surrendered or dispersed. Jan

Kazimierz advanced to face the enemy with a small army commanded by Stefan Czarniecki, Castellan of Kiev. In September 1655 they were defeated at Żarnowiec and fell back on Kraków. The King then took refuge in Silesia, while Czarniecki tried unsuccessfully to hold Kraków.

On 22 October Janusz Radziwiłł signed an agreement at Kiejdany detaching Lithuania from Poland and placing it under the protection of Sweden. Swedish troops appeared in every province, often accompanied by magnates or szlachta who supported Charles. Since there was little to choose between one Vasa king and another, many accepted what appeared to be a *fait accompli*.

Charles was only interested in provinces such as Pomerania and Livonia, which would give Sweden control of the Baltic, and treated the rest of Poland as occupied territory. He and his generals removed everything they could lay hands on – pictures, sculpture, furniture, entire libraries. His troops burnt down churches, having first emptied them of everything portable, and this sacrilege incensed the peasants, who were hardly concerned as to who sat on the throne. They began to massacre lone soldiers, then lone detachments. A guerrilla war developed, with bands of szlachta and peasants making life unpleasant for the Swedes.

A handful of fortresses such as Gdańsk, Lwów, Kamieniec and Zamość continued to hold out for Jan Kazimierz, while the fortified monastery of Częstochowa fought off a siege in a manner which would pass into legend. All around the country groups of szlachta only needed a signal to take up arms for the King.

The Tatars were prescient enough to see that if the Commonwealth were defeated it would only be a matter of time before Muscovy and the Cossacks would devastate the Crimea, and Mehmet Girey therefore signed an alliance with Jan Kazimierz and despatched several thousand warriors to assist the Polish army.

In January 1656, Jan Kazimierz took the offensive at the head of the army he had rallied. Although the Swedes, assisted by a large contingent of troops from Brandenburg, managed to win the three-day Battle of Warsaw in July, fortune began to turn against them. Denmark and Holland joined the Polish alliance, and in June a Dutch fleet broke the Swedish blockade and sailed in to relieve Gdańsk. The Swedes, who had already made an alliance with the Elector of Brandenburg, now enlisted the support of the prince of Transylvania and briefly managed to reoccupy Warsaw in 1657, but they and their allies were decisively beaten in the following year, when Brandenburg switched sides and joined Poland, along with the Habsburgs. In 1660 peace was signed at Oliwa on the basis of a return to the *status quo ante*.

The death of Chmielnicki in 1657 had ended the Cossack threat. He was succeeded by Jan Wyhowski, a moderate who quickly brought negotiations to a head. On 16 September 1658 the Union of Hadziacz turned the Commonwealth of Two Nations into a Commonwealth of Three Nations. Ukraine was to have its own chancellor, treasurer, marshal and hetman, chosen by the king from candidates proposed by the Cossacks. It was to have its own courts, its own mint, and its own army. Several hundred Cossacks were ennobled, and the Metropolitan of Kiev and the Orthodox bishops of Lwów, Przemyśl, Chełm, Łuck and Mścisław were to have seats in the Senate. Polish and Lithuanian troops were barred from entering the three Palatinates, in which only Orthodox Ukrainians were to hold office. Ukraine was to have two universities and a number of schools, paid for by the Commonwealth.

This project came to nothing. At the end of 1659 Wyhowski was toppled by Chmielnicki's son, who emulated his father by swearing allegiance to both the King of Poland and the Tsar of Muscovy at the same time. Muscovite forces invaded in support of the Cossacks, but both they and the Cossacks were defeated by

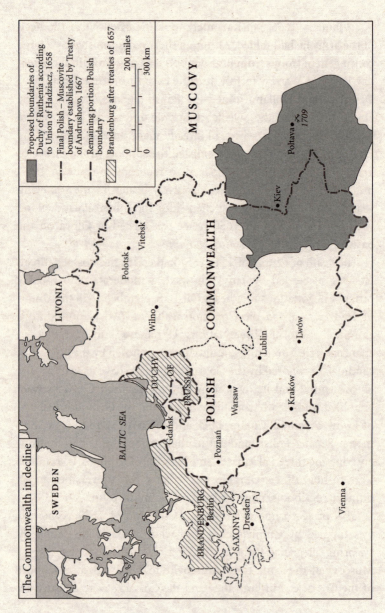

The Commonwealth in decline

Legend:
- Proposed boundaries of Duchy of Ruthenia according to Union of Hadziacz, 1658
- Final Polish – Muscovite boundary established by Treaty of Andrushovo, 1667
- Remaining portion Polish boundary
- Brandenburg after treaties of 1657

200 miles / 300 km

MUSCOVY

Poltava • 1709

Kiev •

Vitebsk •
Polotsk •

LIVONIA

Wilno •

COMMONWEALTH

Lublin •
Lwów •

DUCHY OF PRUSSIA

Kraków •

BALTIC SEA

POLISH

Warsaw •

Gdańsk •

Poznań •

SWEDEN

BRANDENBURG
Berlin •

SAXONY
Dresden •

Vienna •

Polish armies at Cudnów and Połonka in 1660. Having pacified Ukraine, Jan Kazimierz moved against Muscovy, but Poland was exhausted, and as Ottoman armies hovered in the south he made peace.

There would be no room in this for Ukrainian aspirations. Chmielnicki had been so successful in demonstrating to everyone the strategic importance of Ukraine that neither the Commonwealth nor Muscovy could countenance its existence as an autonomous province, liable at any moment to subversion by the other side. By the Treaty of Andruszowo in 1667, they divided it between themselves along the Dnieper.

TEN

Morbus Comitialis

Polish diplomatic missions were notorious throughout seventeenth-century Europe for their splendour. The ambassadors would enter the foreign capital preceded by regiments of private troops and servants decked out in lavish liveries, surrounded by attendants on prancing horses saddled and tacked with gold-embroidered velvet adorned with semi-precious stones, and followed by more detachments of often exotic household troops. When he entered Istanbul in 1622, Prince Krzysztof Zbaraski was accompanied by two regiments of Hungarian infantry and followed by page boys in Circassian dress, bodyguards in Roumelian costume, a troop of Cossacks and forty mounted musketeers.

In 1633 Rome was treated to the spectacle of Jerzy Ossoliński's embassy, consisting of some three hundred riders and ten camels decked out in feathers, gold and pearls. When Krzysztof Opaliński's cavalcade entered Paris in 1645 to collect Władysław IV's bride, Louise Marie de Gonzague, his horses were intentionally loosely shod, so that their solid gold horseshoes scattered the cobbles of the Faubourg Saint-Antoine as a gesture to the populace of the city. Both camels and gold horseshoes became *de rigueur* in subsequent embassies, and numbers went up as well. In 1676 Prince Michał Czartoryski took no fewer than 1,500 retainers on his embassy to Moscow. In the following year Jan Gniński strained the arrangements made by his Turkish hosts, one of whom quipped that he had brought too many to sign a peace, and too few to fight a war.

Both as a measure of Poland's wealth and as a symbol of its diplomatic ascendancy, these displays were highly misleading. They obscured the fact that the Commonwealth had no chancellery which could formulate a foreign policy, and gave the impression that Poland was a country of immense wealth, which was far from being the case.

While the sixteenth century saw the beginnings of capitalism take root in the West, most of Central Europe had drifted into what might best be described as industrial agriculture. Poland exported foodstuffs, cattle, wax, hemp, timber, flax, charcoal, pitch, iron and other raw materials, and only a few low-quality finished goods, such as beer, rope and cloth. It imported finished products of every description and a quantity of colonial goods. It was the sort of trading pattern that places Third World countries at the mercy of industrialised nations. The carriage of goods was predominantly in foreign hands, which meant that a large part of the profit was made outside the country. Of the ships leaving Gdańsk with Polish exports in 1585, for instance, 52 per cent were Dutch, 24 per cent Friesian, and 12 per cent English. The real marketplace for Polish grain was not Gdańsk but Amsterdam, whence it was re-exported to Spain and other countries.

While timber and other ships' stores remained in high demand, particularly from the Dutch, who had no source of their own, and the English and Spanish, who had depleted their forests, the grain trade began to decline in importance as prices of grain on western European markets fell steadily; smaller countries such as England and the Netherlands learnt to grow more intensively and to supplement their diet with rice and eventually the potato.

153

The twenty years of war in the middle of the century had a dramatic effect. Grain exports through Gdańsk in the early 1600s averaged 200,000 tonnes per annum, reaching some 250,000 tonnes in the bumper year of 1618. The figure for 1651, after three years of Cossack unrest, was only 100,000 and two years later this had fallen to 60,000, which remained the average yearly figure for the rest of the century. The import of colonial goods through Gdańsk went up by 10 per cent between 1615 and 1635, and then shot up by 50 per cent between 1635 and 1690. Only in the case of Gdańsk are such comprehensive figures available, and it is impossible to ascertain the position for other ports like Elbląg, or for overland trade with Germany and Muscovy, where the balance was more favourable. The wars also had a catastrophic effect on the export of cattle and horses reared in the south-eastern areas of the Commonwealth.

The mid-century wars were disastrous in other respects. The casualties were not in themselves remarkable, except in the south-eastern areas. The Tatars led many thousands off into slavery and Tsar Alexey deported large numbers to colonise newly conquered areas of Siberia, but the most destructive invaders were the Swedes. The wholesale razing of crops, the burning of villages and towns, and the removal of cattle brought about famine, compounded by plague. The results were devastating. Between 1600, when the population of the Commonwealth stood at over ten million, and 1650 there had been an increase of 23 per cent, but in the ten years between 1650 and 1660, it fell by at least a quarter, to below the original ten million mark. Population density in the Polish heartlands of Wielkopolska, Małopolska and Mazovia had reached 26.3 per square kilometre by 1650, but by 1660 it was down to 19.9. With war and famine destroying their villages, people wandered the countryside in search of less badly affected areas. Food production fell to disastrous levels. By 1668, when the situation had stabilised, 58 per cent of arable land on szlachta estates was lying fallow, while the figures for Church estates and royal lands were 82 and 86 per cent respectively.

The greatest casualties were the towns. At the beginning of the century, Gdańsk was still by far the largest, with 70,000 inhabitants, followed by Warsaw (30,000), Kraków (28,000), Poznań and Lwów (20,000), Elbląg (18,000), Toruń (12,000) and Lublin (10,000). Of the other nine hundred or so townships throughout the Commonwealth, most had between five hundred and 2,000 inhabitants. In all, about a quarter of the population lived in towns. The Swedish army looted and torched the towns it entered, with the result that between 1650 and 1660 the urban population of the Commonwealth declined by up to 80 per cent.

The major towns had long been under pressure from private towns belonging to magnates or the Church, losing much of their business as agents for the produce of the country and as providers of finished goods to the locality. They were poorly represented and heavily taxed. After the wars, which destroyed much of Warsaw, Kraków, Poznań, Lublin and Wilno – the latter was put to fire and sword for seventeen days by Alexey in 1655 – they found it difficult to rebuild. Such investment as was forthcoming was lavished on the private towns by their solicitous owners. But these private towns could not replace the older ones in one crucial respect. They were functionally limited to the exploitation and the provision of essentials to a given area, and there was little scope for enterprise or investment by individual merchants or manufacturers. They never grew into centres of finance and credit which could generate their own wealth and industry, yet the older towns were in no position to carry on this function as before. Only the magnates, the Church and the crown were capable of promoting industrial development, but they were neither motivated nor equipped for the job.

Elective monarchs tended to regard the Commonwealth not as part of their patrimony, to be cared for and enriched on behalf of their descendants, but rather as a sinecure to be enjoyed and a means to enhance their own glory or further the cause of their dynasty. It was only when it had become clear to Zygmunt III that his son would succeed him that he began to care for the economy of the Commonwealth. In 1624 he set up new steelworks at Bobra and Samsonów, and a few years later modernised the royal mines. Władysław IV, who felt dynastically attached to Poland, took an active part in its industrial development, but even where the will existed, the means often did not, as the Commonwealth did not have a proper fiscal regime in place.

The greatest areas of economic activity were the landowning szlachta's home and export sales, which were exempt from taxation; the large Jewish community, which assessed, collected and paid its own taxes without outside supervision, with predictable results; and the greatest financial centre of the Commonwealth, the city of Gdańsk, which benefited from extensive immunities. In short, they were hardly taxed at all.

The main body of Treasury revenue was from a plethora of taxes inherited from medieval times which were unproductive and complicated to collect. The crown's income from royal lands and starosties was susceptible to venality on the part of administrators and beneficiaries. All special taxes or surcharges, as well as the rates at which existing taxes were assessed, had to be voted on a one-off basis by the national Sejm. The result was that in the first half of the century the Commonwealth's revenue was only slightly higher than that of Bavaria, and about one-tenth that of France. Any suggestion of reform, however, raised hackles throughout the political nation, and not only because it did not wish to be taxed.

By the 1650s almost everywhere in Europe the state, in the form of the court or of administrative institutions, was concentrating power, taking it over from regional institutions and elites, which were transformed in consequence into court or service nobility. In Brandenburg, in Prussia, in Denmark and in Sweden, assemblies and noble estates which had kept a check on the power of the state had gradually been forced to cede their rights to increasingly absolutist central authority. The Polish political nation had always been suspicious of the state and of any concentration of power, and it had been an article of faith for it to keep its own weak.

Any attempt by the crown to reinforce its authority and increase the power of the state would therefore lead to direct confrontation with the szlachta. And the chances of success were slight. There was no administrative body in the Commonwealth able to guarantee continuity and provide a new king with organs of power, and even the army had slipped away from under the crown's control as the hetmans treated it more and more as their private domain. Since the reigning monarch was only a temporary incumbent, loyalty to the crown did not necessarily mean loyalty to the king. Each one had to build up his following and his own power base. The convention of life tenure, which had crept into practice at the end of the sixteenth century, meant that an incoming monarch might have to wait for years before he could place men he trusted in important posts. As well as representing his only method of exerting control, the king's right of appointment was his main source of influence. With the rise of the oligarchy of magnates, however, it grew increasingly difficult for him to exercise this freely. Jan Kazimierz found it impossible to promote his ablest soldier, Stefan Czarniecki, to the rank of Field-Hetman when this fell vacant, because it was coveted by the powerful Jerzy Lubomirski.

To pass legislation, the king needed the support of his ministers and other senators who made up the royal council, the *Senatus Consulta*, and the assent of the Sejm. And since the members of the two chambers rarely saw eye to eye, this was not always forthcoming.

The Sejm was not only the sole legislative organ and the supreme court. It had taken over many of the prerogatives normally vested in the crown, such as the right to declare war, sign peace and contract alliances. It also audited the accounts of the treasurers and held the king and his ministers to account in almost every area. Yet it was, on its own, incapable of executive action, and therefore confined itself to a largely negative role. This malfunction in the constitution, often described as a disease, *morbus comitialis*, exercised political writers from the late sixteenth century onwards, but there was no simple solution.

A major rethink of the constitution was hardly likely without a strong community of interest and a sense of purpose on the part of the entire political nation, the szlachta. And by the mid-seventeenth century there was little hope of achieving either.

While they still paid lip service to the principle of equality by addressing each other as 'brother', the gap between the magnates and the poorest two-thirds of the szlachata, the *bene nati sed non possessionati*, had grown immense. The szlachta was also growing increasingly mongrelised. Legislation aimed at preventing the upward mobility of other classes was almost impossible to enforce, and plebeians continued to marry or assimilate into the szlachta with little difficulty. The king ennobled Polish and foreign soldiers, particularly Scots and Frenchmen. Any Jew who converted to Catholicism was automatically ennobled. The attendant differences of outlook were compounded by the sheer size of the Commonwealth. The fear of Tatar raids felt by someone who lived east of Lwów seemed overstated to an inhabitant of Wielkopolska; the Livonian's anxiety about Muscovite intentions was of little concern to a landowner from Mazovia; and a nobleman from Podolia felt more out of place in Gdańsk than he would in Istanbul. Increasingly, regional political viewpoints held by factions in the Sejm obstructed the passage of legislation of national benefit.

The political culture of the electorate and its deputies was not what it had been, and their level of education had declined considerably. The Jesuit colleges now confined themselves to inculcating into their pupils a religious mindset and enough Latin and Rhetoric to enable them to drone on for hours at political meetings. Foreign travel, the panacea of sixteenth-century Poles, became less common and its effects more dubious. Those who had gone abroad in the 1550s had returned with an education and a collection of books. Those who travelled in the 1650s were more likely to bring back pictures and venereal disease. Gradually, the whole exercise came to be seen as pointless and pernicious, while foreigners and their ways were increasingly viewed as suspect. Even Polish cities, being full of imported manners, were widely regarded as dens of wickedness and depravity – as well as being the preserve of moneyed plebeians.

The contrast between the purity of country life and the wickedness of the court and the city is a recurring theme in contemporary European thought and literature. In Poland the contrast was between the alleged perfection of the szlachta's way of life in the country and any other. While local sejmiks continued to be well and vociferously attended, royal elections, which entailed a journey to Warsaw, drew fewer and fewer voters as time went by – no more than 3,500 in 1648 and 5,000 in 1674.

The parliamentary process suffered as a result of all these factors, which made it easy to manipulate by a handful of magnates. The Lithuanian deputies in particular were often little more than placemen elected by docile sejmiks in the presence of the local magnate's armed gangs. The Lithuanian magnates were so powerful that they were indulged by successive kings, with the result that by the middle of the seventeenth century their position was unassailable. It then became virtually impossible to deny a small group of families all the offices they wanted. The pattern of increasing oligarchy developing in Poland was only a pale reflection of the situation in Lithuania. In Poland, certain families felt one of the offices to be their preserve, but they did not simultaneously covet the others. The Lubomirski family obtained the staff of Marshal four times and the baton of Hetman once. The Zamoyski managed three Chancellors and one Hetman, the Leszczyński three Chancellors, the Potocki four Hetmans. In Lithuania, the magnates had the whole country sewn up. Between 1500 and 1795 the Radziwiłł held the Marshalcy five times, the Chancellorship eight times, the baton of Hetman six times, the Palatinate of Wilno twelve times, and the second most important Palatinate in Lithuania, Troki, six times. Such people felt little compunction to respect the niceties of the Polish constitution, and all too often used it for their own ends.

The most infamous example of this occurred in Warsaw on the evening of 9 March 1652, as the Sejm agreed to prolong its statutory session in order to deal with pressing business. Władysław Siciński, the deputy for Troki in Lithuania, stood up and registered his personal objection to the prolongation, before walking out of the chamber. The other deputies and the Marshal, Andrzej Fredro, believed they could not prolong the session in the face of the categoric objection of one of their number. Since it was only on the last day of the session of a Sejm that legislation voted earlier actually became law, dissolution at this point effectively annulled all the decisions taken so far. Siciński was a client of the Field-Hetman of Lithuania, Janusz Radziwiłł, who was piqued with Jan Kazimierz for not giving him the senior baton and meant to punish him for it by disrupting the Sejm so that the King could not collect any taxes or pursue any policy until the next session. It was the first time that the old principle of unanimity had been invoked in this manner, but it was not to be the last.

In the late 1650s Jan Kazimierz prepared a project for constitutional reform, in the belief that the crisis of the Swedish wars might predispose the szlachta to accept a strengthening of state power, particularly as, since he had no heir, the interregnum after his death was bound to be critical and possibly dangerous. At the instigation of the Queen, he proposed that his successor should be elected in his lifetime, *vivente rege*.

This was a red rag to the szlachta. Its right to elect the king was a cornerstone of the constitution, and any election carried out during the lifetime of a reigning monarch smacked of manipulation. In this instance it meant, as the Queen fully intended, that the French candidate nominated by the court would win. The szlachta were suspicious of the Queen's influence, and the Habsburgs, who were alarmed at the idea of the Bourbons establishing themselves in Warsaw, did everything they could to whip up feeling against the proposals.

The project for parliamentary reform, which included earlier suggestions on voting by two-thirds majority, the removal of the sejmiks' control over the deputy they had elected, a permanent annual tax, as well as the project for electing a successor *vivente rege*, came up before the Sejm of 1658. It foundered on minor points. The court party continued to press the issue in the following years, without success. The Queen, who believed that if all else failed a coup might be staged, was placing Frenchmen in key posts in the army. At the same time, Marshal Jerzy Lubomirski, who was in league with the Habsburgs, began to threaten rebellion if the court party persisted with its planned reforms. Following an attempt to impeach him in the Sejm, he rallied part of the unpaid army and groups of discontented szlachta and in 1665 staged a rebellion in the manner of Zebrzydowski. The court party decided to fight it out, and their troops were routed at Mątwy in 1666.

Not long afterwards, Jerzy Lubomirski came and begged the King's pardon, which was duly granted. The whole affair had been just as pointless as the Zebrzydowski rebellion, and severely dented the prestige of the crown and of Jan Kazimierz himself.

Louise-Marie died in 1667, and with his principal moral support gone, the ailing King abdicated two years later. Shortly after, he left for France, where he ended his days as Abbot of St Germain-des-Prés.

The election which followed was the first at which serious disturbances took place. The two principal candidates were Philip Wilhelm, Prince of Neuburg, the Habsburg favourite, and Charles de Bourbon, duc de Longueville. The szlachta who assembled at Warsaw were in no mood for 'foreign autocrats', and overwhelmingly voted for a Polish alternative, Michał Korybut Wiśniowiecki, son of the fire-eating scourge of the Cossacks, Prince Jarema. The new King was in a difficult position. Resented by the disappointed pro-Habsburg magnates and despised by the former court party, who openly referred to him as '*le singe*', his only power base was the szlachta who had elected him. But their vote had been a protest against attempts to limit their freedom and against foreign interlopers rather than a vote of confidence in him. There was little he could do except reign.

Large Tatar *tchambouls* hunted unmolested as the Sejm ignored alarming reports reaching it from Hetman Jan Sobieski, who was doing his best to police the south-eastern marches. In August 1667 he challenged a combined Tatar and Cossack force of some 25,000 with an army of 14,000, more than half of it made up of his own household troops, and defeated them at Podhajce. But this victory only served to obscure a storm that was brewing as the Ottoman Porte prepared a new onslaught on Europe.

In 1672 Sultan Mehmet IV invaded at the head of a substantial army, and the Commonwealth was given a rude awakening when the seemingly impregnable fortress of Kamieniec Podolski fell to his assault. It had been defended by no more than two hundred infantry and a troop of horse, and most of its cannon had remained silent, since there were only four gunners. This level of neglect was symptomatic. There was no army with which to stem the progress of the Turkish host, and Poland could do nothing but sue for peace. The Sultan imposed the humiliating Treaty of Buczacz, which detached Kamieniec with the whole of Ukraine and Podolia from the Commonwealth, and demanded a yearly tribute. This stirred the Sejm to vote money for a new army, which provoked protest from the Porte, and another Ottoman army gathered under the Grand Vizir, Hussein Pasha of Silistria.

King Michał fell ill, and as he lay dying in Warsaw Castle, Hussein Pasha's janissaries prepared to cross the Dniester into a Poland which faced the prospect of a new election. The King expired on 10 November 1673, and on that very same evening Hetman Jan Sobieski drew up his troops outside the Turkish camp at Chocim. On the morrow he attacked and annihilated the Ottoman army in a brilliantly executed action, news of which travelled rapidly back to the capital. The principal candidates for the throne, Charles of Lorraine, François Louis de Bourbon, Prince de Conti, and James Stuart, Duke of York (the future James II of England), were eclipsed by the aura of glory surrounding the returning hero. The szlachta assembled on the election field voted overwhelmingly for Sobieski.

Jan Sobieski, who ascended the throne as Jan III in May 1674, was an energetic man of forty-five. From his close-cropped head and his jewelled fur cap to his soft yellow boots with their silver heels he was every inch the Sarmatian magnate, and he had all the virtues and vices that implied. Since his baptism of fire at Beresteczko in 1651 he had seen service against each of Poland's enemies in turn. Although he had commanded a 3,000-strong *tchamboul* of Tatar allies against the Swedes in 1656, it was the Tatars and the Turks who were his most constant and savage foes. His forebear Żółkiewski had been slain at Cecora, his elder brother had fallen in the massacre at Batoh; the crusade against the Infidel was part of his life. Yet he spoke Tatar and Turkish and loved the amenities of the East.

At the same time he built himself an Italianate palace and collected European works of art with discrimination. He was well read in Italian and French literature, and he was one of Poland's best letter-writers. He wrote to his French wife, Marie Casimire de la Grange d'Arquien, every day or two for twenty years, whether he was at home or on campaign, letters full of verve as well as gallantry, referring to himself as 'Céladon' and his wife as 'Astrée' or some other heroine of French literature. This Sarmatian *galant* was a curious mixture: he was pious, almost superstitiously so, and managed to combine this with a strong dose of cynicism. He was greedy and not always scrupulous in his private affairs, but faultlessly correct in public life. He was as ambitious and dynastically minded as most fellow magnates – there is a portrait of his son (who was not christened Konstanty for nothing) wearing Roman costume and leaning on a classical shield bearing the Sobieski arms, inscribed with the words *In hoc signo Vinces* ('In this sign you will conquer') – yet he was not ruthless in the pursuit of his aims.

Jan III was a fine soldier, combining personal bravery and dash with tactical skill and a good strategic sense. He was strong and agile, quite capable of spending days in the saddle and nights under the stars, in spite of the obesity which came with age. In politics too he lacked neither enterprise nor vision. He calculated that the way to win the necessary authority to deal with internal questions lay through a successful foreign policy, and he set about constructing one.

As the political nation had never conceived a vision of its international role, the Commonwealth had no active foreign policy, only a reactive one, and no system of alliances. This had not presented a problem while it was strong and its neighbours weak, but the values in this equation had altered fundamentally.

In the south and east, the Cossacks and Tatars, who had in the past been no more than a minor nuisance, could now combine with the Turks or with Muscovy to create a formidable threat. An even greater threat loomed in the north – Sweden. This had in the past been engaged in a struggle against Danish and Dutch dominance of the Baltic and against Poland and Muscovy over its eastern shores, but it had come out of the Thirty Years' War as a major player on the international scene.

Gustavus Adolphus had been drawn into the war in 1630 principally out of a need to defend Sweden's possessions on the eastern and southern shores of the Baltic, and had in the process occupied virtually the whole shoreline. Under his successor Charles X Gustavus, Sweden went on to champion the Protestant cause and to challenge Habsburg influence in Germany, thereby engaging the sympathy and support of France. It was largely because Zygmunt III had always been perceived in Sweden as an agent of Habsburg designs on the Baltic region that the Swedes had invaded Poland.

Another threat had arisen in the shape of Brandenburg. In 1600, this sparsely populated state planted on poor, sandy soil, with no mineral deposits, no coastline and an unmanageable river system, had been diplomatically irrelevant, and its ruling family, the Hohenzollern, carried little weight with the older courts of Europe. Their only other resources consisted in a collection of rich but small dynastic lands in the west, along the border with the Dutch Republic, and a fragile connection with the former lands of the Teutonic Order in the east.

The last Grand Master of the order had been a Hohenzollern cousin of the Elector of Brandenburg, and after its secularisation in 1520 he had continued to rule the province, now known as Ducal Prussia, as a vassal of the Polish crown. He was succeeded by his son and grandson, who both paid homage to the King of Poland on their succession. The Elector of Brandenburg obtained from the Polish crown the right of succession if the Prussian line of Hohenzollerns were to die out. When it did, in 1618, Zygmunt III was at war with Sweden, and a handsome subsidy from the Elector of Brandenburg, John Sigismund, eased the passage of the duchy into his line of the family. In 1641 John Sigismund's grandson Frederick William (who would be known as the Great Elector) knelt in homage before Władysław IV at Warsaw Castle on succeeding as ruler of Ducal Prussia. Sixteen years later, in return for military support against Sweden, he extorted from a desperate Jan Kazimierz the right to rule there as a sovereign prince. There was much resistance to this in the duchy itself, where the noble estates feared the loss of their rights and appealed to Warsaw for protection, but with Habsburg support Frederick William managed to have his right to rule as a sovereign in the duchy confirmed by the Treaty of Oliwa in 1660. The duchy was thereby detached from the Polish crown and the Commonwealth. And it was obvious that the rulers of Brandenburg-Prussia would never rest until they had joined up their dominions, and that would necessitate acquiring a swathe of Polish territory and cutting the Commonwealth off from the sea. They had exploited the possibilities offered by the Thirty Years' War and the Swedish invasion of Poland to acquire both territory and prestige, while the army they had built up meant that they were now sought after as allies.

The Polish Commonwealth's pool of potential allies was limited by the fact that its policy was fundamentally pacific and it had little to offer in the way of an army. The Habsburgs had expended much energy in the first half of the century to bring Poland into their orbit and use it as an ally against Sweden. From the 1640s France had taken an interest in Poland as a potential ally against the Habsburgs, but the Francophile court party had failed to bring this about. Three decades later, as Louis XIV engaged in his struggle with the Habsburgs, he again looked to Poland. And Jan III saw in this an opportunity, not just to reaffirm the power of the Commonwealth and gain the prestige necessary to carry out some fiscal reforms, but also to further his own dynastic aspirations.

In 1675 he signed the Treaty of Jaworów with France, which offered to finance an invasion of Ducal Prussia (which Jan III hoped would be given to his son as a hereditary vassal duchy) while her other ally, Sweden, invaded Brandenburg. France undertook to neutralise the Habsburgs and persuade the Ottoman Porte to give back Kamieniec and other lands ceded by the treaty of Buczacz. Sweden duly went into action against Brandenburg, but the Polish forces were not able to invade Prussia because Turkey not only refused to give back Kamieniec, but launched a new offensive into Poland. The large army which had been assembled was used not against Prussia but against the Turks, who were defeated at Żurawno in 1676. By the time this operation was complete, Sweden had made peace with Brandenburg, and the opportunity had passed.

In the following decade, the Sultan proclaimed a new *jihad* and a large Ottoman army advanced into Europe. It invaded the Habsburgs' Hungarian provinces and, in the summer of 1683, laid siege to Vienna. This provided a fresh opportunity to gain the support of France, which welcomed the Ottoman assault on the Habsburgs and would have rewarded Poland for conniving at their defeat. But the Commonwealth could not countenance the possibility of the Porte conquering a swathe of Central Europe and taking up a threatening position along the whole of its southern frontier.

As Grand Vizir Kara Mustapha approached Vienna Jan III signed a treaty with the Emperor, and the Sejm voted a levy of 36,000 troops in Poland and 12,000 in Lithuania (which never turned up, since Hetman Jan Sapieha had no intention of assisting the King). At the end of August the fifty-four-year-old King set out at the head of his army, at the beginning of September he met up with and took command of the allied troops from various parts of the Empire, and on 12 September he routed the Kara Mustapha under the walls of Vienna.

The Turks retired in disorder, but the campaign was by no means over, and Jan III pursued the retreating Turks into Hungary. The majority of Hungarians had gone over to the Ottoman camp for anti-Habsburg reasons, and the King saw an opportunity of detaching Hungary from Austria and creating a new ally for the Commonwealth. On 7 October he lost the first battle of his life, at Parkany. Although he defeated the Turks two days later, it proved difficult to conclude the campaign. Meanwhile, opposition to further prolongation of the war was mounting at home. Once again the King, now beginning to feel his age and suffering from gall-stones, had to abandon his plans.

'Future generations will wonder in astonishment,' King Jan lamented in the Senate in March 1688, 'that after such resounding victories, such international triumph and glory, we now face, alas, eternal shame and irreversible loss, for we now find ourselves without resources, helpless, and seemingly incapable of government.'

ELEVEN

The Reign of Anarchy

By the last quarter of the seventeenth century it was becoming obvious to all that the Polish-Lithuanian Commonwealth was a very different kind of political unit from all the surrounding states, and that it did not lend itself to the conduct of the kind of policies they were pursuing. Commentators referred to it as 'the Polish Anarchy'. It was also evident that this curious polity was an expression of a culture which was growing increasingly alien to that of the rest of Europe.

At one level, Polish society differed little from that of other countries, and fed on the same literary and cultural canon. There was nothing particularly exotic about magnates such as the Treasurer of the Crown Jan Andrzej Morsztyn (1620–93). A gifted writer, he effortlessly wrote short erotic poems and aphorisms, religious and lyrical verse, and made fine translations of Corneille and Tasso. Stanisław Herakliusz Lubomirski (1642–1702), son of the rebellious Marshal Jerzy Lubomirski, spent two years on a grand tour before starting on a political career which was to culminate in his appointment to the office of Marshal by Jan III in 1676. He was a brave soldier and a discriminating patron of the arts, and in 1668 he married Zofia Opalińska, a bluestocking with a passion for music and mathematics: together they covered every conceivable interest from engineering to astrology. He wrote Italianate comedies as well as some of the best seventeenth-century religious verse in Polish, dissertations on current affairs and a treatise on literary taste, and translated a number of foreign works.

These and other magnates patronised the arts and studded the towns and the countryside with palaces and churches in a synthesis of the Baroque style that owed much not only to Italy and Austria but also to France and the Netherlands.

If Renaissance architecture suited the style and thought of the Poles of the sixteenth century, the Baroque might have been invented for those of the seventeenth. It awakened a degree of sensual appreciation of form, ornament and luxury which found immediate satisfaction in and complemented the increasing contact with the East. This fed on war just as well as on peacetime trade. Ottoman armies believed in comfort and splendour, and as a result the booty could be spectacular. 'The tents and all the wagons have fallen into my hands, *et mille autres galanteries fort jolies et fort riches, mais fort riches*, and I haven't looked through all of it yet,' wrote a triumphant Jan III to his wife from the Turkish camp outside Vienna a few hours after the battle.

By the early 1600s the Polish cavalry had adopted most of the weapons used by the Turks as well as many of their tactics. The hetmans used the Turkish baton of command, and the horse-tails which denoted rank among the Turks were borne aloft behind them too. The Poles also dressed more and more like their foe, and even the Tatar habit of shaving the head was widely practised on campaign. So much so that on the eve of the Battle of Vienna the King had to order all Polish troops to wear a straw cockade so that their European allies should not take them for Turks, from whom they were all but indistinguishable. With Sobieski's accession to the throne, military fashion invaded the court and became institutionalised. This 'Sarmatian' costume became a symbol of healthy, straightforward patriotic Polishness, while French or German clothes were equated with foreign intrigue.

The Poles also had a feeling for the beauty of Islamic art, which was not generally appreciated in western Europe. Eastern hangings replaced Flemish tapestries and arms joined pictures on the walls of manor houses. At the Battle of Chocim, Jan Sobieski captured a silk embroidery studded with 'two thousand emeralds and rubies' from Hussein Pasha which he thought so beautiful that he wore it as a horsecloth for his coronation. A few years later he gave it as the richest gift he could think of to the Grand Duke of Tuscany, who put it away and wrote it down in his inventory as '*una cosa del barbaro lusso*'.

Turkish clothes suited Baroque architecture, and servants were dressed up accordingly. Wealthy szlachta often kept captive Tatars or janissaries at their courts, but they also dressed their Polish pages as Arabs and their bodyguards as Circassian warriors. This taste was carried so far that religious music was provided in Karol Radziwiłł's Baroque chapel at Nieśwież by a Jewish orchestra dressed as janissaries.

There had never been any sumptuary laws in Poland and the tendency to show off was unrestrained. Money still had no investment role in the minds of most Poles, and all surplus went into movable property of the most demonstrable kind. Inventories made on the death of members of the szlachta are illuminating. A poor gentleman would be found to possess a horse or two, fine caparisons and horsecloths, saddles, arms and armour, a small number of rich clothes, jewellery, perhaps some personal table-silver, a few furs and lengths of cloth, and little in the way of money. Inventories of country houses and castles reveal the same pattern. Jewellery, clothes, silver, saddlery, arms and armour, cannon, uniforms for the castle guard, furs, lengths of cloth, Turkish, Persian and Chinese hangings, banners, tents, horsecloths and rugs, Flemish tapestries and pictures are listed. Furniture hardly figures, except where it is made of silver.

The Polish magnate's coat was a tradable item, so stiff was it with gold thread. Every button was a jewel, the clasp at his throat and the aigrette on his fur cap were works of art. The French traveller Verdum noted that Jan III wore 200,000 thalers' worth of jewels on a normal day, and that on a great occasion his attire would be worth a considerable proportion of his (by no means negligible) weight in gold. Urszula Sieniawska, whose inheritance was being disputed by a number of relatives in 1640, left no fewer than 5,000 diamonds, rubies, emeralds and sapphires in her jewel case. Maryanna Stadnicka, wife of the Palatine of Bełz, left 8,760 pearls. In 1655, when they looted the Lubomirskis' Wiśnicz, the Swedes required no fewer than 150 carts to carry away the booty. Many collections were so vast that the looting made only a slight impression. The inventory of Żółkiew, one of the Sobieski family seats, drawn up after Peter the Great had personally looted it in 1707, still lists upwards of seven hundred oil paintings in the castle.

These castles were also full of people, on the principle that the more there were surrounding a man, the more important he was. Poor relatives and landless friends, the sons of less wealthy henchmen and clients of one sort or another would form a court around a magnate. On top of this, he would employ teachers for his children, musicians, whole corps de ballet, jesters and dwarfs, chaplains, secretaries, managers and other officers. After that came servants, stable staff, kitchen staff, falconers, huntsmen, organists, castrati, trumpeters, units of cavalry, infantry and artillery. The fashion for show attendants meant that there were dozens of *hajduks*, wearing Hungarian dress, *pajuks*, in Turkish janissary costume, and *laufers* in what looked like something out of Italian opera, covered in ostrich feathers. These attendants had no purpose beyond standing about or running before the master when he rode out. The numbers were impressive. When Rafał Leszczyński's wife died in 1635, he had to provide mourning dress for just over 2,000 servants – and neither cooks nor kitchenmaids were included, as they were not seen. Karol Radziwiłł's army alone amounted to 6,000 regular troops.

The heads of great houses took themselves seriously, and much of this splendour was dictated by a feeling of self-importance. When Karol Radziwiłł's intendant commented that he lived better than the King, the characteristic reply was: 'I live like a Radziwiłł – the King can do as he likes.' Every major event in the life of the family was treated with pomp, and ceremonies were constructed round it. When a child was born, the artillery fired salutes and occasional operas were staged. When the master returned from the wars, triumphal arches were erected and fireworks let off.

It was more than mere show – it was a style of behaviour which introduced ritual into every action and translated its significance into visible activity. Nowhere is this more obvious than in the practice of religion as it developed in the seventeenth century, partly under the influence of the taste of the faithful, partly as a result of the Church's continuing policy of bringing every aspect of the life of the Commonwealth within its own ambit, if not actually under its control.

Control was not something that could be effectively exerted over the likes of Karol Radziwiłł, who summed up his attitude in a letter to Anna Jabłonowska in 1764: 'I praise the Lord, believe not in the Devil, respect the law, know no king, because I am a nobleman with a free voice.' A man whose ideal was the cult of unbounded liberty did not take easily to having, for instance, his sexual freedom restricted by laws even more nebulous than those of the Common-wealth. The hold on society which the Church did have was based on a juxtaposition of life and ritual which succeeded in making religion into an integral part of every person's regular activities.

The leaders of the Counter-Reformation insisted on the insepara-
bility of the Church as an institution from the Commonwealth as
an institution, of piety from patriotism. They were largely successful
in that they bred the notion in the average Pole that the Catholic
Church 'belonged' to him in much the same way as the Commonwealth did. Churches were used for sejmiks and for the sessions
of local tribunals. National commemorations and holidays were
fused with religious feasts. The priesthood became for the poorer
nobility much what the civil service or army were in other
countries – the only noble profession and a refuge for upper-class
mediocrity.

Outward signs of the faith were encouraged in every way. The
cult of the Virgin and of the saints, which had died away during
the Reformation, made a triumphant comeback. Every town,
village, institution, guild and confraternity was provided with a
patron. Pictures of the Virgin before which miracles allegedly took
place were 'crowned' and declared to be miraculous. The solemn
coronation of the Black Madonna of Częstochowa took place on
8 September 1717 before 150,000 faithful. By 1772 there were a
staggering four hundred officially designated miraculous pictures
of the Virgin, each one a centre of pilgrimage and a recipient of
votive offerings of jewellery, money, tablets and symbolic limbs.

From the purely religious sphere, the ritual spread into every
other. When a man of substance died, a huge architectural folly, a
castrum doloris, would be erected in the church as a canopy for his
coffin, and this would be decorated with symbols of his office and
wealth, his portrait and coat of arms, and with elaborate inscrip-
tions in his honour. The ritual included the old Polish custom of
breaking up the dead man's symbols of office and, if he were the
last of his family, shattering his coat of arms. Neighbours, friends,
family, servants and soldiers would pay their last respects in more
or less theatrical ways, while congregations of monks and nuns

sang dirges and recited litanies. The funeral of Hetman Józef Potocki in 1751 took two weeks, for six days of which 120 pieces of cannon saluted continuously (using up a total of 4,700 measures of powder). Over a dozen senators, hundreds of relatives and entire regiments congregated in Stanisławów to pay their last respects in the church which was entirely draped in black damask, before a huge catafalque of crimson velvet dripping with gold tassels, decorated with lamps, candelabra, Potocki's portrait, captured standards, pyramids of weapons and other symbols of his office and achievements.

This Sarmatian lifestyle was a unique growth, produced by cross-pollination between Catholic high Baroque and Ottoman culture. Everything about it was theatrical, declamatory and buxom. It was inimical to the bourgeois ethic of thrift, investment, self-improvement and discipline which was beginning to dominate western Europe, and as a result it was condemned, even by Poles of later centuries. At its worst, sarmatism was absurd and destructive, encouraging as it did outrageous behaviour and an attitude that bred delusion. But it did permit what was possibly an irreconcilable collection of people to reach a kind of harmony. As Jan III's English physician Bernard Connor commented: 'It is certain had we in England but the third part of their liberty, we could not live together without cutting one another's throats.'

And it helps explain how the Commonwealth was able to go on functioning, in a kind of parallel world, along lines that defied logic. The delusional condition it created was an essential ingredient in the survival of a polity whose constitution had broken down and which should have imploded or been conquered by one of its increasingly powerful neighbours.

The election that followed the death of Jan III in 1696 was a fiasco. The principal candidates were the King's son Jakub; François Louis de Bourbon, Prince de Conti; and Frederick Augustus Wettin, Elector of Saxony. Jakub Sobieski was rapidly eliminated from the contest by the intervention of Saxon troops. On 27 June 1697 the szlachta assembled on the election field voted overwhelmingly for the Prince de Conti, and the Primate proclaimed him king. On the same evening a small group of malcontents elected Frederick Augustus, who marched into Poland at the head of a Saxon army. On 15 September, while the Prince de Conti was sailing into the Baltic, Frederick Augustus was crowned in Kraków by the Bishop of Kujavia, as Augustus II of Poland. At the end of the month the Prince de Conti came ashore only to discover that he had been pipped at the post. His supporters were not keen to start a civil war, so he re-embarked and sailed back to France. It was the first time that a deceased monarch's son had not been elected to succeed him; that the successful candidate had been debarred from the throne by military force; and that the new incumbent was also the ruler of another state.

The twenty-seven-year-old Augustus was nothing if not picturesque. Universally known as Augustus the Strong and described by one of his subjects as 'half bull, half cock', he could break horseshoes with one hand, shoot with astonishing accuracy, drink almost anyone under the table, and fornicate on a scale which would be unbelievable if he had not left platoons of bastards to prove it. He was not a stupid man, and he intended to turn the Commonwealth into a centralised monarchical state. Like Jan III, he saw war as the surest way to gain prestige and a free hand to carry out his plans.

In 1698 the Livonian nobleman Johann Patkul, who had been forced to flee his province by the occupying Swedes, turned up at the court of Augustus II with an appeal for help from the Livonian nobility. Although they wished to rejoin the Commonwealth, Augustus saw an opportunity of acquiring the province for himself. Soon after, he met Tsar Peter I (later known as Peter the Great), who was on his way back to Russia from western Europe, and in the course of an all-night drinking bout the two men planned a joint war against Sweden. Augustus suggested to his uncle King Christian V of Denmark that he join them and take Bremen and Werden from Sweden as a reward. In 1699 an agreement was signed between Peter I, Frederick IV of Denmark (who had succeeded his father Christian V) and Augustus II. Augustus was not allowed to enter into such treaties as King of Poland. It was therefore an alliance of Muscovy, Saxony and Denmark that went to war on Sweden the following year.

The allies had made a mistake in thinking that they could easily defeat the eighteen-year-old Swedish king, Charles XII. This callow youth was endowed with inhuman energy, reckless bravery and a faith in his own destiny that was soon echoed in the popular myth that he was invulnerable. He made short shrift of the Danes, beat off the Saxon army attempting to take Riga, and then turned on the Russians, whom he drubbed at the Battle of Narva. Augustus decided it was time to sue for peace.

Charles XII would have none of it and demanded that the Poles dethrone Augustus if they did not wish to be invaded. The Commonwealth was not technically at war with anyone, and the problem of how to deal with the situation was aggravated by profound internal divisions. In 1702 the Sapieha family placed Lithuania under Swedish protection, and in April Charles XII entered Wilno. The Lithuanian rivals of the Sapieha appealed to the Tsar, and Muscovite troops moved into the Grand Duchy in support. But Charles XII had already moved into Poland in pursuit of Augustus. Incensed by this invasion, the szlachta who assembled in a rump Sejm at Lublin in 1703 called for war with Sweden. The following year those loyal to Augustus II voted to ally with Muscovy against Sweden. At this point Charles XII met Stanisław Leszczyński, Palatine of Poznań, an intelligent man of twenty-seven for whom he developed a great esteem, and arranged for him to be elected king by some eight hundred szlachta assembled for the purpose. There were now two kings of Poland, neither of them with much of a following or an army, and they were being swept along by Peter I and Charles XII respectively in a *contredanse* which took them twin-stepping around the Commonwealth, until Charles had the idea of invading Saxony. There he finally pinned down Augustus and extorted his abdication of the Polish throne. Stanisław I was king.

Charles decided that the time had now come to take on Peter I. He laid his plans with Stanisław and with Ivan Mazepa (originally Jan Kołodyński), a former page to Jan Kazimierz who had served Peter I loyally as Ataman of the Cossacks on the Russian side of the Dnieper. Their independence was being eroded by Muscovite rule and they dreamt of reuniting Ukraine. An alliance against Russia was formed, on the basis of an independent future for Ukraine in alliance with Poland. But on 8 July 1709 Charles XII and Mazepa were routed by Peter at Poltava.

The war was over, and Augustus II re-ascended the Polish throne, a little wiser but incomparably worse off for the events of the last ten years. When he and Peter had planned the Northern War on that night in 1698, he had been the stronger partner. After ten years of bungling he was little more than the Tsar's client, dependent on his support and protection. There was no clear way out of the predicament for him or for the Commonwealth, as the power balance in eastern Europe had altered dramatically during those ten years.

Sweden had been wiped out as a significant power by the débâcle of Poltava. Turkey was decisively defeated (Hetman Feliks Potocki's victory at Podhajce in 1697 was the last Polish-Tatar battle), and by the Treaty of Karlowitz in January 1699 the Commonwealth regained Kamieniec and the whole of left-bank Ukraine. France, despairing of its potential allies in the east – Turkey, Sweden and

Poland – shifted its theatre of confrontation with the Habsburgs to Spain and Italy. Distracted by the War of the Spanish Succession, the Habsburgs had failed to take advantage of the recent Northern War.

Prussia on the other hand had taken full advantage of the opportunities on offer to strengthen its military and diplomatic standing. On 18 January 1701 Frederick III, Elector of Brandenburg and Duke of Prussia, had dubbed himself 'Frederick I, King in Prussia': he could not call himself King *of* Prussia, since Prussia was not a kingdom, or King of Brandenburg, since that was part of the Holy Roman Empire. The subterfuge caused much mirth in the courts of Europe.

In similar vein, in 1721 Peter I of Muscovy took the title of Emperor of All the Russias. Nobody laughed at this. The recent wars had shown that Russia was not only a growing power, but also that it was strategically unassailable. And Peter had made it clear that he would be playing an active part in the affairs of Europe by extending his sphere of influence westward, into Poland.

The Sejm of 1712 had reached deadlock on reforms proposed by Augustus II, whereupon he brought in troops from Saxony. This rallied the opposition, which in 1715 formed a confederation to resist him. Peter I offered to mediate. With some reluctance, the offer was accepted, and a Russian envoy arrived in Warsaw – accompanied by 18,000 troops who were to keep order. The ensuing Sejm of 1717 was known as the Dumb Sejm. It sat in a chamber surrounded by Russian soldiers, the deputies were forbidden to speak, and the Russian mediator forced his solution on it, couched in the Treaty of Warsaw.

This laid down, amongst other things, that Augustus II could keep no more than 1,200 Saxon Guards in Poland. The Polish army was fixed at a maximum of 18,000 men and the Lithuanian at 6,000, which was deemed sufficient since Moscow arrogated to itself the role of protector, and promised to leave a Russian force in the Commonwealth. Augustus II, who wanted these troops out at any cost, secretly offered to cede Peter some border provinces in exchange for a withdrawal. A lesser man might have accepted, but Peter refused and went on to publish Augustus's proposals with the degree of indignation befitting the protector of the Commonwealth's territorial integrity.

On 1 February 1733 Augustus II died of alcohol poisoning in Warsaw. His last words were: 'My whole life has been one uninterrupted sin. God have mercy on me.' He had hoped to ensure the succession of his son Augustus to the Polish throne, but this seemed unlikely since Stanisław Leszczyński, whose daughter had married Louis XV of France, was expected to stand for election and to win easily. Russia, Prussia and Austria signed an agreement to throw their combined strength behind the young Saxon, who had already promised to cede Livonia to Russia if elected.

The 13,000 who assembled for the election voted unanimously for Leszczyński, who had travelled to Warsaw incognito. In Paris Voltaire composed an ode of joy, but Russian troops were already on the move. On 5 October 20,000 of them assembled 1,000 szlachta outside Warsaw and forced them to elect Augustus of Saxony. Five days later France declared war on Austria and started the War of the Polish Succession. King Stanisław's supporters gathered in confederations all over the country and the city of Gdańsk raised a sizeable army on his behalf. Two years of sporadic fighting ensued, but France made peace, having got what she wanted from Austria in Italy. Stanisław was given the Duchy of Lorraine as a consolation prize by his son-in-law, and Augustus III ascended the Polish throne.

The Commonwealth had effectively ceased being a sovereign state in 1718 with the imposition of the Russian 'protectorate'. It had also virtually ceased to function as a political organism. The Sejm was not summoned between 1703 and 1710, the years of the Northern War, which meant that no legislation was passed and no state taxes could be levied. When the Sejm did sit again, it was hardly more effective. Of the eighteen sessions called under Augustus II, ten were broken up by the use of the veto. The King had tried to impose stronger government, but his policies were poorly thought out. He had an unfortunate conviction that a show of strength by the Saxon army was a necessary prelude to any change, and this had the effect of provoking resistance even in those who would otherwise have agreed with him. In the last years of his reign he did manage to gain the support of a group of magnates and szlachta, but their programme for reform was cut short by his death in 1733.

His son Augustus, Poland's new monarch, was obese and indolent: he would spend his days cutting out bits of paper with a pair of scissors or else sitting by the window taking potshots at stray dogs with a pistol. He also drank like a fish. Augustus III reigned for thirty years. He spent only twenty-four months of that time in Poland, feeling more at home in Saxony. Yet he was not as unpopular with the szlachta as might have been expected – he never made the slightest attempt to curtail their prerogatives and increase his own. Only one Sejm completed its session under his rule, the army dwindled to half its theoretical size, and all visible signs of nationwide administration disappeared.

This state of affairs favoured the magnates, or rather the dozen or so men who stood at the pinnacle of wealth and power, who had turned into something approaching sovereign princes. It was to the courts of the leading families and not to the royal court at Warsaw or Dresden that foreign powers sent envoys and money. The Potocki, Radziwiłł and similar families involved half of Europe in their affairs and their activities were monitored at Versailles and Potsdam, at Petersburg and Caserta. The marital intentions of the young Zofia Sieniawska were a case in point.

The only daughter of Adam Mikołaj Sieniawski, Hetman and Castellan of Kraków, and of Elżbieta Lubomirska, Zofia was a formidable heiress. In 1724 she married Stanisław Doenhoff, Palatine of Polotsk, no pauper and also the last of his line, who died four years later. Every family in Poland produced a suitor in the hope of coffering her fortune. Louis XV was quick to realise what was at stake, and the young widow was invited to Versailles, where she might be married to the Comte de Charolais, a Bourbon in search of a throne; Augustus II tried to monitor her suitors; the Duke of Holstein wanted her for himself; the Habsburgs threw their influence behind the Duke of Braganza, for whom they had royal ambitions; and St Petersburg sent ambassadors and money to influence her choice. The interest in the widow was well-founded. In 1731 she settled for the poorest of all her suitors, Prince August Czartoryski, turning his family into the most powerful in Poland over the next hundred years.

The power of these families rested on a combination of wealth and control of their lesser peers, and reflected a growing disparity between rich and poor. The figures for the Palatinate of Lublin provide an example of the dramatic change in the distribution of land over the previous two hundred years. In the 1550s, 54 per cent of all land owned by the szlachta was in holdings of under 1,500 hectares, but by the 1750s only 10 per cent was in such medium holdings. In the 1550s only 16 per cent was in estates of over 7,500 hectares, but by the 1750s over 50 per cent was accounted for by these. The large estates grew larger, the small ones smaller, with the result that by the mid-eighteenth century about a dozen families owned huge tracts of land, another three hundred or so possessed lands equivalent to those of the greatest English or German landlords, and as many as 120,000 szlachta families owned no land at all. The remainder owned small estates which provided little more than subsistence for the family and its dependants.

The ravages of war, outdated methods, lack of investment and the continuous downward trend in agricultural prices condemned these to a vicious circle. Between 1500 and 1800 average yields increased by 200 per cent in England and the Netherlands, by 100 per cent in France, and by only 25 per cent in Poland. Inventories dating from this period show that even in such well-ordered areas as Wielkopolska small estates were in a condition of decrepitude, with buildings falling down, implements worn out and livestock depleted.

The underlying problem was not limited to Poland, and affected the whole of Central Europe, where the old property relationship between landowning lords and tenant peasants proved a formidable obstacle to the adoption of more profitable capitalist solutions. This would have entailed emancipating and at the same time expropriating the peasants, who would then have been in a position to enter into regular contractual relations with the landowners. But the upheaval involved would have been ruinous to both parties. As a result, the only means open to the landowner of intensifying production was to exploit his tenants to the limit, and their only option was a passive participation in this process of their own enserfment.

There was technically no such thing as a serf in the Commonwealth. No peasant belonged to anyone; he was his master's subject only insofar as he had contracted to be in return for a house and/or rent-free land. Every peasant, however abject, was an independent entity enjoying the right to enter into any legal transaction. Since, however, the relevant organs of justice were controlled by the landowners, his rights often turned out to be academic. By the seventeenth century the landowners in effect exercised almost unlimited power over their tenantry. How far they were inclined or able to abuse this power varied greatly from area to area, depending on the morality of the master rather less than on the level of education and determination of the peasant. Unlike in Germany, Hungary and almost everywhere else in Europe, let alone Russia, there were no peasant revolts in Poland after the Middle Ages, and no organisation to track fugitives. Confrontation with the landlord took place in the courts, such as they were. But the peasant of the 1700s was caught in a poverty trap which impaired his ability to stand up for whatever theoretical rights he had, and he was a poor successor to his forebears.

The most pauperised segment of the population were the Jews, who had been profoundly traumatised by the massacres perpetrated by the Cossacks in 1648 and the Russians in the 1650s. Jewish communities found it difficult to revive economically in a climate of mercantile stagnation which also exacerbated conflicts with Christian merchants, while their institutions ceased to function properly. The palatines who supervised the finances of the *kahals* in their provinces had done so only sporadically during the decades of war and unrest, with the result that venality and nepotism became characteristic features of their affairs. When a royal commission did eventually look into the *kahal* finances, it was discovered that most of the communities were on the verge of bankruptcy as a result of massive embezzlement and eccentric banking operations with the Jesuits. The whole Jewish state within the state had to be wound up in 1764 as a result.

The overwhelmingly destitute masses of Polish Jewry lived in an increasingly hostile environment, and it was out of this that Hasidism was born. This was a mystical ecstatic cult, rejecting painful realities and offering a spiritual palliative that attracted vast numbers of the poorest Jews in the teeming provincial *shtetls* of the Commonwealth. It was founded in Podolia by Izrael ben Eliezer (1700–60), also known as Baal Shem Tov, a charismatic who preached that since God was everywhere He should be worshipped in every thing and every action, even in eating, drinking and dancing. The joyful ceremonies he encouraged appealed to the poorest Jews but drew the ire of orthodox rabbis. They had also had to contend with the heresy of Shabbetai Zevi, who had proclaimed himself Messiah in the 1660s, and acquired a sizeable following. It was the son of one of his disciples who caused the greatest ructions in the Jewish community. Jakub Frank (1726–91) in turn proclaimed himself Messiah and decreed that Poland was the Promised Land. His following grew rapidly. Orthodox rabbis invoked the law to curb the heresy, which turned it into a public issue. The Bishop of Lwów staged a public debate between Talmudic experts and the Frankists, with the Jesuits as adjudicators. To the delight of the Jesuits, Frank succeeded in confounding his accusers and then announced that he and his sect would convert to Catholicism. Frank was baptised in 1759 with the King himself standing godfather, and all the converts were ennobled.

These outbursts of fervour stemmed from the psychological and material Babylon from which there seemed to be no possibility of escape. The depressed *shtetls* and the stinking Jewish slums of the larger towns were an eyesore which struck all foreign travellers. Yet they were only the darkest spots on a grim landscape of decrepitude and poverty, a poverty made all the more stark by the occasional evidence of fabulous wealth, and by the quantity of new building on a spectacular scale.

A new kind of grand country residence came into existence, no longer defensive but outward-looking and palatial, often modelled on Versailles or one of the great residences of minor German sovereigns. Craftsmen such as Boule, Meissonier, Caffiéri and Riesener in Paris were flooded with orders from Poland. But this magnificence and patronage did not correspond to any deeper artistic or intellectual revival. These buildings were an incidental excrescence, not connected to any informed taste or vision. The Branicki Palace at Białystok contained a theatre with four hundred seats, equipped with one Polish and one French troupe of actors and a corps de ballet, but while the stables held two hundred horses, the library boasted no more than 170 books. Hetman Branicki was not the man to repair the constitution.

The szlachta still believed wholeheartedly in the principles on which the Polish constitution had been founded: personal freedom, representation, accountability, independence of the judiciary, and so on. They knew that the constitution was malfunctioning, but believed that, with some justification, to be the fault of the magnates and of high-handed behaviour by successive kings, who naturally tended to try to turn the Commonwealth into a centralised monarchy. All attempts at reform which issued from the crown or the Senatus Consulta included some measure that would strengthen the central authority, and that ensured their rejection by the szlachta. They had developed an almost obsessive fear of absolutism and an attendant defensiveness with respect to their gloried prerogatives. In the last decade of the seventeenth century and the first of the eighteenth, they had mooted the idea of holding a 'mounted Sejm', that is to say appearing at Warsaw in the ranks of the *levée en masse* in order to challenge the magnates of the Senate on a more equal footing, but this proved too difficult to arrange. Faced with even the slimmest threat to their rights and immunities, they wielded their weapon of last resort, the veto.

The single deputy's power to block the will of the Sejm by registering his objection derived from the principle that consensus must be reached for legislation to have real force. Its use to invalidate decisions reached by a majority was technically legal though contrary to the spirit of the law. It was first used in 1652, but was not invoked again for seventeen years, and not for another ten after that. It was not until the period between 1696 and 1733 that it became endemic to parliamentary life, and that was a feature of the level to which this had sunk.

Those who made use of the veto tended to be obscure deputies from Lithuania or Ukraine, usually acting on behalf of a local magnate or a foreign power. The device was so convenient to these that in 1667 Brandenburg and Sweden agreed to go to war if necessary 'in defence of Polish freedoms' (i.e. to stop the Poles from abolishing the veto), and over the next hundred years the same clause was contained in virtually every treaty made between the Commonwealth's neighbours.

While many lamented the abuse of the right of veto, they stood by the right of their fellows to exercise it, just as during the Reformation ardent Catholics had refused to allow the persecution of people guilty of sacrilege. It was first and foremost a question of liberty. The phenomenon of the veto, normally viewed as a baffling aberration and the ultimate symbol of the Commonwealth's political impotence, did serve a specific purpose, that of preventing it from becoming an absolutist monarchy, which it could easily have done in the period of instability and war at the end of the seventeenth and the beginning of the eighteenth centuries. As far as the szlachta was concerned, absence of government was preferable to arbitrary government. And many had come to see government as unnecessary anyway.

When the Commonwealth had imploded under the combined assault of the Cossacks, Tatars, Swedes, Brandenburgers and Muscovites in the 1650s, the szlachta had held regional sejmiks to deal with essential local issues. This form of administration turned out to be not only more efficient, but also more accountable and less costly than central government. As a result, local land sejmiks, *sejmiki ziemskie*, and law and order sejmiks, *sejmiki boni ordinis*, became favoured instruments of local administration, responsible for electing judges, officers of the law and commanders of the militia; collecting taxes, raising troops and nominating functionaries.

Since life could go on normally without a national Sejm, the szlachta felt justified in proclaiming its dispensability. People began to believe that anarchy, in its literal sense of 'no government', was something of an ideal state, particularly as it denied the crown and the magnates the instruments through which to pursue their sinister aim of curtailing the szlachta's liberties. This was particularly relevant in times of war and instability such as the first decades of the eighteenth century, when a central Sejm might invoke national emergency to bring in pernicious legislation.

The Commonwealth therefore continued in a state of suspended animation, with no central administration beyond that which could be paid for from the king's personal revenue, and no organ of government other than the Senatus Consulta, which had no writ. Its internal and external affairs were as much the business of Russia, and to a lesser extent of Prussia and Austria, as its own. The three powers looked on its territory more and more as a sort of no-man's-land. Russia moved her troops about it as though it were a training ground, while Prussian and Austrian armies took short cuts through it, in times of war even setting up depots and garrisons in convenient Polish towns.

TWELVE

Renewal

With the abeyance of Poland as an active political organism, its history becomes the story of the few men and women who still believed in its viability as a state and struggled to restore it. Their story cannot be told in terms of wars, treaties and statutes, only in terms of ideas and social mobilisation.

A desire for constitutional reform was never quite extinguished, and it was first translated into action by Stanisław Konarski (1700–73), a Piarist priest who had studied in Paris and Turin. With the backing of Bishop Andrzej Załuski in 1732 he began publishing all the legislation passed since the fourteenth century in a compendium entitled *Volumina Legum*, in the belief that the electorate must be acquainted with the constitution before it could be persuaded to reform it. In 1740 Konarski founded the Collegium Nobilium, a public school which removed young noblemen from their family background in order to imbue them with the ideals of the Enlightenment. Konarski's next move was to reform the twenty Piarist schools in the Commonwealth. The Jesuits perceived that this modernisation of rival establishments might relegate their own colleges, and they transformed these by bringing in good teachers and widening the curriculum.

Konarski's friend Bishop Załuski was an avid collector of books

189

and manuscripts, a taste he shared with his brother Józef, and in 1747 the two pooled their collections, bought a palace in Warsaw, and donated to the nation the first public reference library on the European mainland. Its original holding grew, aided by a Sejm decree obliging printers to donate the first copy of any book to designated public libraries, to over 500,000 volumes when it was looted by the Russians in 1795 (to become the basis of the Russian Imperial Library).

At the political level, the regeneration of the Polish state was led by another two brothers, the princes Michał and August Czartoryski, supported by their brother-in-law Stanisław Poniatowski and a small group of relatives. They were united by an urgent desire, not devoid of personal ambition, to, as they saw it, rescue the Commonwealth. They worked as a team and were generally referred to simply as 'the family', *Familia*. They built up a significant following and there was talk of August standing as a candidate at the royal election of 1733, but this was scotched by the appearance of Stanisław Leszczyński, whom the Familia supported. It was while they were holding Gdańsk for Leszczyński in the hopeless war of 1734 that August had a son, Adam Kazimierz. A medal was struck to announce that the young prince would be brought up with royal pretensions; he was the descendant of Władysław Jagiełło's brother, and therefore of royal blood.

Two years before the birth of Prince Adam Kazimierz, the Familia had produced another child, Stanisław Antoni Poniatowski. Although she could hardly entertain royal aspirations for him, his mother Konstancja Czartoryska did take great care with his upbringing, and he was sent abroad to complete his education. By the time he returned to Poland aged twenty, he had visited Vienna, Paris and London, was fluent in six languages, and had developed a wide range of tastes and interests. In 1755 he went to St Petersburg to stay with the British minister, Sir Charles Hanbury-Williams, with whom he had struck up an intimate friendship. Sir Charles introduced him to the twenty-six-year-old Sofia Augusta Friederika of Anhalt-Zerbst, Grand Duchess Catherine Alekseievna, and the two became lovers. This was to weigh heavily on events.

The Familia had been preparing to overthrow Augustus III, but they had to contend with the probability that a Saxon party led by the Mniszech family and a group of politically incoherent but stubborn defenders of the state of anarchy, including Hetman Branicki, Franciszek Potocki and Karol Radziwiłł, would oppose this. In 1762 a coup placed the Grand Duchess Catherine on the imperial throne, and the Familia began to count on Russian support for their plans. The following year Augustus III died, and there was nothing to stop them from putting their man on the throne. But he, Prince Adam Kazimierz, preferred books to politics. Meanwhile, the Empress Catherine let it be known that she would favour her ex-lover Poniatowski as King of Poland.

Poniatowski was duly elected on 7 September 1764, taking the name of Stanisław II Augustus. With this election a new era dawned in Poland. Winds of change were already whistling through the Convocation Sejm, sitting under the marshalcy of Adam Kazimierz Czartoryski. The Sejm was confederated, which meant that it could pass legislation by majority vote, and implemented a number of measures on the Familia's programme. Majority voting was made statutory for sejmiks, a small but important step towards abolishing the veto. Fiscal and military commissions were established. All proposals put forward by the fiscal commission were subject to approval by the Sejm, but with no right of veto. A national customs tariff was established, and a project for municipal reform was commissioned. In addition, the King put into action several ideas of his own. In 1765 he founded the Szkoła Rycerska, literally 'College of Chivalry', an academy for the training of military and administrative cadres.

In the following year, Chancellor Zamoyski laid before the Sejm his project for constitutional reform which included the abolition of the veto. This elicited an immediate response from St Petersburg and Berlin, both of which threatened war if it were not withdrawn and the Confederated Sejm not immediately dissolved. There was nothing for it but to comply. Alarmed at the renewal taking place in Poland, Catherine and Frederick decided to stir up the conservative anarchist elements and muddy the political waters. They seized on the fact that in Poland (as in every other country in Europe, including Russia and Prussia) members of religious minorities did not enjoy full civic rights. Russia demanded that all the Orthodox be granted the same rights to hold office as Catholics, and Prussia demanded the same for Lutherans.

The granting of such rights lay within the spirit of the King's and the Familia's programme. It was their conservative opponents who were against them. Yet the way in which the matter was raised turned the whole issue on its head. Russian troops moved in to support two confederations, one of Lutherans at Toruń, and one of Orthodox at Łuck. With Russia and Prussia firmly on one side, many patriots, whether conservative or progressive, ranged themselves on the other.

This left the King and his supporters with no room for manoeuvre. In October 1767 the Sejm assembled in a capital full of Russian troops and deliberated under the eye of the Russian ambassador, who sat in the visitors' gallery. A couple of bishops and the hetman objected strongly to the emancipation of the dissenters. They were dragged from their beds that night and packed off to Russia under military escort. The Sejm bowed to Russian demands, which included the acceptance of five 'eternal and invariable' principles which Catherine then solemnly vowed to protect in the name of Poland's liberties. These principles (the free election of kings; the rule of the veto; the right to renounce allegiance to the king; the szlachta's right exclusively to hold office and land; the landowner's power of life and death over his peasants) were an effective barricade against further reform.

On 29 February 1768 a confederation was formed in the little town of Bar in Ukraine by the brothers Józef and Kazimierz Pułaski and Adam Krasiński, Bishop of Kamieniec. It lacked leadership of serious calibre and its programme consisted of windy phrases about the faith and national freedom. The Russians put pressure on the King to declare himself against the confederation, but he prevaricated, not wishing to fan the flames. At this point, France intervened by sending money to the confederates and encouraging Turkey to declare war on Russia, which broke out in October 1768. The confederation was now joined by several magnates opposed to the King, including members of the Pac, Sapieha and Potocki families, and Karol Radziwiłł. In July 1770 France sent Colonel Dumouriez as military adviser to the confederates. A provisional government was set up and Dumouriez advised it to take a more decided position. People like Karol Radziwiłł needed little prompting, and in October 1770 the Confederation of Bar declared the dethronement of Stanisław Augustus.

The forces of the crown joined Russian troops under General Suvorov and defeated the confederates at the Battle of Lanckorona. Russian intervention provoked sympathy for the cause, and a guerrilla war started all over south-eastern Poland. On the night of 3 November 1771, a group of confederates surrounded the King's carriage in the middle of Warsaw and abducted him. The plan was as ill-executed as it was ill-conceived. The kidnappers lost their way, one of them changed his mind and allowed the King to escape, and by next morning Stanisław Augustus was back in his palace. But his authority was seriously undermined.

The confederates were gradually mopped up by the Russian

armies, with the last of them holding out at Częstochowa until 1772. The magnates who had joined the confederation went into exile, but over 5,000 captured szlachta were sent to Siberia, endowing the cause with an aura of martyrdom. Both Rousseau and Mably had lent their support to it, seeing in it an expression of pure patriotism and civic spirit.

For the Commonwealth, the Confederation of Bar could hardly have come at a worse moment. Under the ministry of Choiseul, France was straining to bring a Franco-Turkish-Austrian-Saxon alliance to bear against Russia and Prussia. Hence the French interest in the confederation. Russia merely wanted to keep Poland docile. But Frederick the Great of Prussia had already announced his intention of eating up various Polish provinces 'like an artichoke, leaf by leaf'. The sudden fall of Choiseul in 1770 brought an end to French schemes in the area. Frederick had already worked out a plan for weaning Austria away from France and binding her to Russia and Prussia – by dragging her into a tripartite despoliation of Poland. He had opened negotiations with Russia on the subject in 1771, and signed an agreement with her in February 1772. Both powers then approached Austria. The Empress Maria Teresa was at first reluctant, but then complied, and on 5 August 1772 the first partition of the Polish Commonwealth was agreed. Prussia took 36,000 square kilometres with 580,000 inhabitants; Austria 83,000 square kilometres with 2,650,000 inhabitants; and Russia 92,000 square kilometres with 1,300,000 inhabitants. Prussia's share was the most valuable, since it included the most developed areas, linked up the two halves of the Prussian realm, and gave her control of the Vistula, Poland's lifeline to the outside world. The balance of power in the area was dramatically altered, with Prussia enlarged by some 80 per cent and the Commonwealth, which had lost over a third of its population, reduced by a third.

The first partition of Poland, 1772

BALTIC SEA

EAST PRUSSIA

PRUSSIA

Gdańsk

Poznań

Warsaw

Wilno

Mińsk

Smolensk

RUSSIA

Brześć

Kraków

Lwów

Bar

Kiev

AUSTRIA

TURKEY

- - - Polish boundary
Territory occupied by Prussia
Territory occupied by Austria
Territory occupied by Russia

The partition caused alarm in many quarters. It also shocked public opinion throughout Europe. The Polish Commonwealth was in alliance with Russia and was not at war with either of the other two powers when the arrangement was made. Moreover Russia was the self-proclaimed guarantor of Polish independence and the protector of Polish territorial integrity. In the hope of correcting this unfavourable impression, Catherine and Frederick enlisted the pens of their clients among the French *philosophes* to project an image of Poland as an obscurantist backwater which had been crying out to be liberated by enlightened monarchs such as themselves. They also insisted that the treaties of partition be ratified by the Sejm.

An assemblage of malcontents, magnates who had prospered under the Saxon kings and szlachta whose estates were now within Russia or Austria were elected, in the presence of Russian and Prussian troops, to a confederated Sejm under the marshalcy of Adam Poniński. Even so, some of the deputies raised havoc in the chamber, obstructing the ratification. The King and the Familia resorted to stalling tactics, while pulling every available diplomatic string to exert pressure on the three powers. Alarmed by the Prussian predominance in the Baltic, England lodged a strong protest, but nobody was prepared to go further. Russia and Prussia threatened to seize even more territory, so the Sejm had no alternative but to ratify the treaties of partition, which it did on 30 September 1773. Prussia took the opportunity to foist a trade agreement on Poland which included draconian duties on Polish corn shipped down the Vistula.

The five 'eternal principles' dictated by Russia excluded all possibility of constitutional reform, and neither Russia nor Prussia allowed their interest in what was happening in Poland to wane. Nevertheless, the next twenty years were to see a complete transformation of the Commonwealth. From 1775 the country was ruled by a Permanent Council, which carried out far-reaching improvements. The army, which could not be increased, was modernised. The treasury began to function in a regular way. The police department enforced legislation, reorganised the administration of towns, and made its mark on everything from roads to prisons.

In 1776 the King commissioned Andrzej Zamoyski to codify the laws, and the result was a proto-constitution which took Polish law back to its roots and restated or reinterpreted it with reference to eighteenth-century conditions. It effectively affirmed royal power, made all officials answerable to the Sejm, placed the clergy and their finances under state supervision, shored up the rights of cities and of the peasants and, most controversially, deprived the landless szlachta of many of their legal immunities and political prerogatives. Its publication in 1778 induced sabre-rattling in the minor szlachta and apoplexy in the clergy. Zamoyski's collaborator Józef Wybicki was nearly hacked to pieces at a provincial sejmik. With feeling running high it was held back by the reformers until the Sejm of 1780, but even then it was thrown out. It was nevertheless an important document, accepted amongst progressives as the basis for future political reform.

An extraordinary renewal was taking place in public life, but unlike that of the Renaissance this was not a natural evolution, a process of ideas spreading gradually through print, by word of mouth, or by example. It was the result of a concerted effort, a war on obscurantism declared by a relatively small group whose aim was the social and political regeneration of the state, based on the re-education of society. In 1773 at the King's suggestion the Sejm established a Commission for National Education, in effect a ministry of education. It comprised a selection of enlightened aristocrats – Bishop Ignacy Massalski, Joachim Chreptowicz, Ignacy Potocki, Adam Kazimierz Czartoryski, Andrzej Zamoyski – and its first secretary was the French physiocrat Dupont de Nemours. It was endowed with a part of the wealth of the Jesuit order, abolished by the Pope in 1773, and was put in control of every school in Poland, regardless of which religious order or institution it belonged to. It laid down curricula, commissioned and published textbooks, and supervised standards and teachers. With its extensive powers and resources, the commission was able to tackle the reform of the Jagiellon University and that of Wilno.

This was accompanied by a remarkable resurgence of literary activity, the majority of it didactic. The inspiration came from abroad, and the luminaries were Voltaire, Rousseau, Diderot, d'Alembert and the Encyclopedists, whose political and social comment seemed particularly relevant to the Polish predicament.

But the majority of minor szlachta viewed this with suspicion marked by xenophobia. The sort of argument which would rage in Russia a hundred years later between Westerners and Slavophiles, between those who wished to bring the country into line with the rest of Europe and those who felt that foreign influences were corrupting the purity of the ethnic genius, now began to develop in Poland. While the progressives attempted to apply logic and reason, jingoism and ignorance came together in defence of such hallowed institutions as Polish dress and the veto.

In 1765 Stanisław Augustus had founded the weekly *Monitor*, modelled on Addison's *Spectator*, and then a National Theatre. The editor of *Monitor*, Franciszek Bohomolec, also played a pioneering role in this sphere, writing plays for performance in schools and at the National Theatre, plays which mostly served to convey a moral through satire on subjects like sarmatian obscurantism or the oppression of the lower orders.

This second Renaissance produced only one great poet, Ignacy Krasicki (1735–1801), Prince-Bishop of Warmia, a fief in which the spiritual incumbent was also the temporal ruler. A creature of the Enlightenment, Krasicki despised stupidity and ignorance, and wrote poetry and novels that satirised and ridiculed in beautiful, witty language. No other Polish poet of the age measures up to him, but he had many talented contemporaries, some of whom struck the first proto-Romantic notes of sentimental nationalism, which are also present in the *History of the Polish Nation* written in 1774 by Adam Naruszewicz, Bishop of Smolensk, at the behest of the King.

The thread that runs through the work of the writers of the day is the urgency they felt with regard to reviving the Polish state. An impressive array of enlightened magnates devoted their fortunes and their influence to the same cause, while less exalted figures, including many of the clergy, worked assiduously to further it.

The King himself was in the forefront of the changes. He was vain and pleasure-loving, but behind the languid frivolity lurked a strong sense of purpose and a profound love of his country. He had no personal wealth and no distinguished ancestry. He was widely despised as an upstart who had reached the throne via Catherine's bed, who preferred the company of women to that of hard-drinking men, and who rejected sarmatian manners for foreign dress and taste.

At the outset, he was supported by the Familia, but during the 1770s this turned into the mainstay of a powerful opposition, which forced him into greater dependence on Russian support. His only assets were his personal charm, his intelligence and his patience. He had been a deputy six times, and was therefore familiar with the workings of the Sejm and the attitudes that prevailed in it. He was also aware as no other elected monarch had been of the considerable influence and powers still at the disposal of the crown. Skilful and diplomatic, he was prepared to compromise and bide his time on one project in order to further another.

His was not so much a policy as a vision. From his youth, he dreamt of a total 're-creation of the Polish world', to use his own words, involving a return to the ideals of the Commonwealth on the one hand, and turning the sarmatian szlachta into a European nation on the other. His reading and his travels, particularly in England, had taught him the value of the state as an institution. When political reforms were cancelled out by the Russo-Prussian intervention of 1772, he concentrated on this aspect of his programme.

By the 1780s two generations had passed through the reformed schools and been exposed to the thought of the Enlightenment, and a new eighteenth-century version of the traditional political nation had emerged, leavened by significant numbers of artists, functionaries and tradesmen ennobled by the King.

The Convocation Sejm of 1764 had been revolutionary not only in its political attitudes – the speech by the chancellor which heralded so many political reforms also hectored the deputies that 'To sell raw materials and buy finished goods makes one poor; to buy raw materials and sell finished goods makes one rich.' During the 1730s and 1740s a number of magnates had already tried their hand at manufacturing. The Radziwiłł established glass foundries, a furniture factory, a cannon foundry and workshops producing cloth, carpets and articles of clothing at their seat of Nieśwież and other estates. The range reflects a lack of specialisation which meant that the products were often of poor quality. The same was true of the factories set up by Ludwik Plater at Krasław near Vitebsk, producing velvet, damask, carpets, carriages, swords and rifles. The Potocki factories at Brody and Buczacz specialised in high-quality carpets, kilims, tents, hangings, sashes and cloth. During the same period the bishopric of Kraków, which owned large areas of what would become the industrial heartland of Poland, built several new iron foundries.

In 1775 the Sejm repealed the law forbidding the szlachta to engage in commerce, and the next twenty years saw a remarkable development of mercantile and capitalist activity among the magnates and szlachta.

Between 1764 and 1768, a royal mint was established at Warsaw, the currency was stabilised, weights and measures were standardised, and a state postal service was founded. In 1771 a canal was dug connecting the Vistula to the Warta; in 1775 the King launched a project for one between the Bug and the Pripet; in 1767 Prince Michał Ogiński had begun digging a canal linking the Niemen and the Dnieper, thereby making it possible to navigate from the Baltic to the Black Sea, which opened up alternative markets for exports.

Much of the industrial activity went hand in hand with a resurgence in the decorative arts. In 1774 the King founded the Belweder ceramic factory which produced high-quality vases and tableware; the Czartoryskis started a porcelain factory at Korzec which employed up to 1,000 workers in the 1790s in the production of more functional items of quality under the supervision of experts brought from Sèvres, and the same was true of the new furniture centre of Kolbuszowa. But there was also a certain amount of purely industrial enterprise. The state built an ordnance factory outside Warsaw and a large cloth mill geared particularly to supplying the army. In 1767 a joint-stock wool-manufacturing company was floated. The treasurer of Lithuania, Antoni Tyzenhaus, launched a wide-ranging programme of industrialisation in Grodno on the King's behalf. The most business-minded of all the magnates, Antoni Protazy Potocki, established banks in major Polish cities, factories in various parts of the Commonwealth, and a trading house at Kherson from which he operated a merchant fleet on the Black Sea and the Mediterranean.

Much of the manufacturing was based on small towns or large estates; peasants were often used as cheap labour, so there was little attendant growth in the urban proletariat. The only exception was Warsaw, which grew from 30,000 inhabitants in 1764 to some 120,000 in 1792, and began to resemble contemporary European capitals, not least politically. It had a large and vociferous artisan class and an increasingly influential patriciate, including such figures as the mayor, Jan Dekert, and the banker and entrepreneur Piotr Fergusson Tepper, who were to play an important role in the last decades of the century.

The transformation of Polish society did not stop there. In 1760 Chancellor Andrzej Zamoyski had freed the peasants on his estates from all labour-rents and dues, and turned all tenancies into financial transactions. Other landowners followed suit, and some went further. Ścibor Marchocki turned his estate into a peasant cooperative, while Paweł Brzostowski founded the Peasant Commonwealth of Pawłów in 1769, a self-governing village with its own school, hospital and citizen's militia. The Polish world was indeed being recreated, as the King had wished.

His most evident and personal contribution to the process was, ironically, viewed after his death as evidence of his frivolity: his exorbitant patronage of the arts. It began conventionally enough. In his youth he had admired the architecture of France and shown interest in the excavations being carried out at Herculaneum. When he ascended the throne in 1764, Stanisław Augustus decided to rebuild the Royal Castle extensively, and commissioned Victor Louis, subsequently architect of the Palais-Royal, and several craftsmen to submit projects for the building, the interiors and the furniture. By 1767 he had run into political problems, and financial ones were not far behind, so the project was discontinued. When he resumed his building plans, the French style was abandoned in favour of the Italian, and this, combined with many English and French elements, was to be a characteristic feature of the architecture of the Stanislavian period. He did not allow financial considerations to stand in the way. The Royal Castle was turned into a fine representational seat for the monarch and the Sejm, and barracks, customs houses, and a variety of other civic buildings gave Warsaw the attributes of a modern city.

It was largely the King's patronage that turned Warsaw into an important musical centre once more, and this would bear fruit in the first decades of the next century. He was also instrumental in reviving painting in Poland. He employed Italians but also encouraged native talent by sending young men to study abroad or putting them to work alongside the foreigners. He spent fortunes on the arts, running up vast debts in a number of countries, but he was not merely a spendthrift aesthete. He believed in the educational role of the arts, and hoped to improve those exposed to them. He was also trying to put across a message and to leave a legacy.

Detailed correspondence between him and his artists reveals that he participated intimately in the process of creation. He gave an astonishing amount of thought to the thematic aspects of every building and painting he commissioned. While planning the Senators' Hall of the Royal Castle, he meant to turn it into a sort of Polish hall of fame, and spent years deciding which great figures of the past should be represented, which of them should be in oil, which in marble, which in bronze, and in what relationship to each other they should be placed.

As he confided to Adam Naruszewicz, he was building for the future, attempting to leave to posterity a statement on the Polish past which would serve to inspire generations to come. It was all part of his vision of a Poland regenerated intellectually and refurbished materially. There was to be a new university in Warsaw, a *Museum Polonicum*, an Academy of Sciences, and an Academy of Arts. Only a small part of his plans ever saw the light of day, yet he did succeed at the very last moment of the Commonwealth's life in recapitulating and holding up its merits and its achievements in a form which would make their memory endure.

THIRTEEN

Gentle Revolution

In spring 1787 Catherine the Great of Russia set off on an imperial progress through her southern dominions. As she drifted down the Dnieper greeted by crowds of subjects lined up along the banks by her minister Prince Potemkin, King Stanisław Augustus left Warsaw to greet her on the Polish stretch of the river. On 6 May the imperial galley tied up at Kaniów, and the King came aboard. With the formal greetings over, the two monarchs, who had last met as lovers nearly thirty years before, retired for a *tête-à-tête*.

They emerged after only half an hour, and the assembled courtiers and diplomats sensed all was not well. The Empress entertained the King lavishly, but declined to go ashore for a ball he had arranged in her honour. Stanisław Augustus was mortified, and not just because his feelings were hurt. He had come to Kaniów to propose an alliance in Russia's forthcoming war against Turkey. The Commonwealth would contribute a substantial army and at the same time fend off potential belligerent moves by Prussia and Sweden, in return for which it would acquire Moldavia and a Black Sea port. Apart from permitting the Commonwealth to raise and test an army, participation in such a war would have eased the tensions building up in Warsaw and strengthened the King's position. Catherine's rejection of the plan left him without a policy at a critical moment and played into the hands of his opponents.

While the King had bowed to the conditions imposed by Russia after the partition in 1772, many had refused to reconcile themselves to this state of affairs and his seemingly docile acceptance of it. By the late 1780s there was a growing feeling, particularly among the younger generations brought up on Rousseau's pre-Romantic ideas on the rights of nations, that the time had come to shrug off the protection and the restrictions imposed by Russia, which stood in the way of almost any attempt at reform or modernisation. A group of magnates, including some members of the Familia, Ignacy Potocki, Stanisław Małachowski, Michał Kazimierz Ogiński, Stanisław Potocki and malcontents such as Karol Radziwiłł, who called themselves 'Patriots', began to stir up opposition to the King's collaborationist policy.

Those who had believed in anarchy as a blessed state had seen their argument demolished by the partition. As they looked around, at states such as Russia and Prussia which expended two-thirds of their revenue on the army and appeared more and more to be driven by a philosophy of military success (even their monarchs wore uniform), most felt that Poland's only hope of survival lay in abandoning the glorious liberties of the Commonwealth and turning it into an efficient modern state with an adequate army.

Prussia, which had just entered into an alliance with England and Holland aimed at checking Russian expansion, made it clear that the Commonwealth could count on military support were it to sever its connection with St Petersburg. With Russia engaged in wars against Turkey and Sweden, and with Prussia making friendly overtures to Poland and striking hostile attitudes at Russia and Austria, it looked as though the menacing concert of the Commonwealth's neighbours had fallen into discord.

The Sejm which assembled in 1788 under the marshalcy of Stanisław Małachowski, which would be known as the Great Sejm, was dominated by the Patriots. It promptly voted an increase in the army, which was placed under the control of a Sejm commission. The conduct of foreign policy was vested in another such commission. In January 1789 the Sejm abolished the Permanent Council which had been ruling the country since 1775 and prolonged its own session indefinitely. In March it imposed a tax on income from land of 10 per cent for the szlachta and 20 for the Church, the first direct taxation ever to have been imposed on either.

The Patriots encountered little opposition. The King's supporters were in disarray. Conservative and pro-Russian members were intimidated by events, which had taken on an ominous significance in the light of the revolution which broke out in France in the summer of 1789. On the night of 25 November 1789 Warsaw was illuminated for the twenty-fifth anniversary of the coronation of Stanisław Augustus, which many feared might act as a provocation to the mob. While the rabble in the streets confined itself to abusive lampoons, a real revolution was being prepared in other quarters. In September 1789 the Sejm had appointed a commission under Ignacy Potocki to prepare a new constitution for the Commonwealth.

Debate on the question of reform had grown progressively more radical and was now dominated by two political thinkers of substance, Stanisław Staszic and Hugo Kołłątaj. Staszic (1755–1826) was a priest of plebeian origin who had been befriended by Józef Wybicki and promoted by Andrzej Zamoyski. He had travelled through Germany to Paris, where he became a friend of Buffon, whose *Histoire Naturelle* he translated and published in Poland, and thence to Rome, where he lost his faith. On his return to Poland he devoted himself to political writing. Later, in 1800, he would found the Society of Friends of Learning with a fortune he had built up in business, and in 1815 publish a seminal work on the geological formation of the Carpathian Mountains, while working on a verse translation of the *Iliad*.

Staszic was a republican who believed in the sovereignty of the Sejm, but realised that a nation surrounded by despotic states must have a strong executive, and he therefore argued for a hereditary monarchy. He saw the nation as a 'moral entity' consisting of all the citizens of the Commonwealth, whether they were szlachta or peasants, townspeople or Jews, and believed that all citizens should subject their individual will to its greater good.

Hugo Kołłątaj (1750–1812) was of a very different stamp. He had studied at the Jagiellon University and in Italy, where he became a priest, and subsequently worked on the Commission for National Education. He showed his organisational skills when he was given the task of reforming the Jagiellon University, whose Rector he became in 1782.

As the Great Sejm convened, he formed a political pressure group known as 'the Forge' with the aim of promoting reform of the whole system, or a 'gentle revolution', as he put it. In *A Few Anonymous Letters to Stanisław Małachowski* (1788) he addressed the Marshal and the assembling Sejm. 'What then is Poland?' he taunted them. 'It is a poor, useless machine which cannot be worked by one man alone, which will not be worked by all men together, and which can be stopped by a single person.' Like Staszic, he demanded a strong hereditary monarchy, the supremacy of the Sejm and the extension of the franchise. It was he who composed the memorandum presented to the King by the representatives of 141 towns, dressed in black like the États Généraux in Paris the previous year and led by Jan Dekert, on 2 December 1789. A commission was set up to devise a system of representation for the towns, and several hundred tradesmen were ennobled.

As soon as he realised the strength of the movement behind the Patriots, Stanisław Augustus shifted his position and began to work with them. He invited Ignacy Potocki, Kołłątaj and Małachowski to join him in drawing up a new constitution. They worked in secret, with the King's secretary Scipione Piattoli editing the drafts. When the final draft was ready a wider group of reformists was invited to discuss it before the final wording was agreed.

Their project entailed the abolition of so many traditional rights and liberties that it was bound to encounter fierce opposition in the Sejm. They therefore prepared what amounted to a parliamentary coup. The support of the people of Warsaw was assured by a municipal law of 18 April 1791 giving seats in the Sejm to twenty-two representatives of major towns. Another law passed at the same time disenfranchised landless szlachta.

A date was chosen when many deputies and senators would still be on their way back to the capital after the Easter recess, and as a result, on 3 May 1791 only 182 deputies were present in the chamber, a hundred of them in on the secret. Outside, purposely mustered crowds surrounded the Royal Castle expectantly. The proposed constitution was passed overwhelmingly, after which the King was carried shoulder-high by the populace to the church of St John, where the *Te Deum* was sung.

The document which became law on 3 May 1791 was a pragmatic compromise between the republicanism of Potocki, the radicalism of Kołłątaj and the English-style constitutional monarchism of the King. The opening clauses were purposely anodyne. Catholicism was enshrined as the religion of state, although every citizen was free to practise another without prejudice; the szlachta was declared to be the backbone of the nation; the peasantry was piously acknowledged as its lifeblood; all the privileges bestowed by Piast and Jagiellon kings remained inviolate. Hidden deeper in the thicket of print lay the substance. The throne was to be dynastically elective as it was under the Jagiellons, and since Stanisław Augustus had no legitimate children, Frederick Augustus of Saxony was designated as the founder of the new dynasty. The Sejm became the chief legislative and executive power in the Commonwealth, and voting was to be conducted by strict majority. Both the veto and the right of confederation were abolished. The government of the country was vested in the king and a royal council to be known as the Guardians of the National Laws. This was to include the Primate of Poland, five ministers and two secretaries, all appointed by the king for a period of two years. The king could direct policy, but no act of his was valid without the signature of at least one of the ministers, and they were answerable directly to the Sejm.

The constitution was hardly revolutionary in itself: it was the commissions and other organs it set up which were to carry through the real reforms. Under the slogan 'The King with the People, the People with the King', and aided by a barrage of propaganda emanating from Kołłątaj and his assistants there set to their work transforming the country. An economic constitution was to cover property relationships, the protection of labour, investment, the establishment of a national bank and the issue of a paper currency. Kołłątaj began work on plans to turn all labour-rents into money rents for the peasants, while the King and Piattoli began discussions with the elders of the Jewish community with a view to emancipating and integrating it.

The events in Poland were hailed far and wide. Political clubs in Paris voted to make Stanisław Augustus an honorary member. Condorcet and Thomas Paine acclaimed the constitution as a breakthrough, while Edmund Burke called it 'the most pure' public good ever bestowed upon mankind. For the same reasons, they alarmed Poland's neighbours. The Prussian minister Count Hertzberg was convinced that 'the Poles have given the *coup de grace* to the Prussian monarchy by voting a constitution much better than the English', and warned that the Poles would sooner or later regain not only the lands taken from them in the partition, but also Prussia.

The fall of the Bastille in Paris two years before had caused fear in St Petersburg, Potsdam and Vienna, and the fact that what was viewed by their rulers as a second beacon of revolution had ignited in Warsaw induced a state of panic. They felt threatened by the revolutionary presence in their midst, if only because a steady trickle of runaways from all three countries flowed into Poland in search of new freedoms.

A year before the passing of the constitution, in March 1790, Poland had signed a treaty with Prussia, where Frederick II had been succeeded by Frederick William II. The immediate object was to make common war on Austria, from which Poland intended to recapture Galicia (as the Austrians had named their slice of Poland), but it also guaranteed Prussian military support if Poland were attacked by her eastern neighbour. Prussia then demanded that Poland give up Gdańsk, which was already cut off from the rest of the country by a Prussian corridor, in return for which Polish traffic on the Vistula would be granted customs-free passage. England, which was behind the Polish–Prussian alliance, and whose fleet was expected in the Baltic in the autumn, urged Poland to agree, but there was opposition in the Sejm.

In February 1791 the Emperor Joseph II was succeeded by Leopold II, who took a conciliatory line towards Prussia, but the international situation nevertheless remained favourable to Poland. Leopold and his Chancellor Kaunitz both believed that the passing of the constitution, far from being a threat, would probably prevent revolution in Central Europe.

Before the constitution was a year old, however, the international situation changed once more. On 9 January 1792 Russia signed the Peace of Jassy with Turkey and began to pull troops back from the southern front. On 14 February, at the first general election since its passing, the sejmiks throughout Poland voted overwhelmingly to endorse the constitution, to the dismay of the disenfranchised landless szlachta and conservatives who mourned the liberties of the Commonwealth, and much to the fury of Catherine, who had paid out fortunes in bribes to persuade them to reject it. In March she began moving her troops towards Poland. At the beginning of the month the Emperor Leopold died and was succeeded by Francis II. In April, revolutionary France went to war against him and Prussia. A few days later, on 27 April, Catherine sought out a number of Polish conservatives such as Seweryn Rzewuski, Feliks Potocki and Ksawery Branicki, who formed a confederation in St Petersburg. It was not proclaimed until 14 May in the border town of Targowica, under the slogan of defence of Polish 'glorious freedoms' against the 'monarchical and democratic revolution of 3 May 1791'. Four days later the confederates crossed the border at the head of, or rather in the baggage of, 97,000 Russian troops.

Against these veterans of the Turkish wars, the Commonwealth could field only 45,000 untried recruits. Frederick William of Prussia, who had written to Stanisław Augustus in May 1791 professing his 'eagerness' to 'support the liberty and independence of Poland', refused the appeal for help in June 1792, and the Polish forces went into action on their own. One corps, under the King's nephew Józef Poniatowski, won a battle at Zieleńce, another under Tadeusz Kościuszko fought a fine rearguard action at Dubienka. But there was no real hope of stemming the Russian advance.

Stanisław Augustus tried to negotiate directly with Catherine, offering to bring Poland back within the Russian hegemony and to cede his throne to her grandson Constantine. Catherine demanded that he join the Confederation of Targowica. The King and his advisers, desperate to find a way out which could guarantee the integrity of the Commonwealth and the survival of the constitution, decided to bend to her will.

This act of humility was of little avail. In November, after the defeat of his armies by the French at Valmy, the King of Prussia demanded areas of Poland as compensation for his efforts to contain Revolutionary France. A second partition was agreed

The first partition of Poland, 1772

0   200 miles
0   300 km

BALTIC SEA

PRUSSIA
Gdańsk
EAST PRUSSIA
Poznań
Warsaw
Brześć
Wilno
Mińsk
Smolensk
RUSSIA
Kraków
Lwów
Bar
Kiev
AUSTRIA
TURKEY

- - - Polish boundary
Territory occupied by Prussia
Territory occupied by Austria
Territory occupied by Russia

The second partition of Poland, 1792

0   200 miles
0   300 km

BALTIC SEA

PRUSSIA
Gdańsk
Poznań
Warsaw
Brześć
Dubienka
Kraków
Lwów
Wilno
Mińsk
Smolensk
RUSSIA
Zieleńce
Kaniów
Kiev
Bar
AUSTRIA
TURKEY

- - - Polish boundary
Territory occupied by Prussia
Territory occupied by Russia

The third partition of Poland, 1794

0   200 miles
0   300 km

BALTIC SEA

PRUSSIA
Gdańsk
Poznań
Maciejowice
Warsaw
Brześć
Racławice
Kraków
Lwów
Wilno
Mińsk
Smolensk
RUSSIA
Kiev
AUSTRIA
TURKEY

- - - Polish boundary
Territory occupied by Prussia
Territory occupied by Austria
Territory occupied by Russia

212

between Russia and Prussia, and signed in Petersburg on 3 January 1793. Catherine helped herself to 250,000 square kilometres, and Frederick William to 58,000. The Commonwealth now consisted of no more than 212,000 square kilometres, with a population of four million. Wielkopolska and most of Małopolska, the ethnic and historic heartlands of Poland, had gone, leaving a strange elongated and uneconomic rump. Even this was to be no more than a buffer state with a puppet king and a Russian garrison.

As with the first partition, Catherine insisted that the arrangement be ratified by the Sejm, to be held at Grodno in Lithuania rather than in the potentially explosive Warsaw. At first Stanisław Augustus refused to cooperate, but he was eventually browbeaten and blackmailed into going, and as he left his capital all hope and will to fight deserted him.

The Russian ambassador carefully selected candidates for the Sejm and used everything from bribery to physical assault in order to ensure their election. But once they had assembled at Grodno, some proved less than cooperative, in spite of the presence of Russian troops in the chamber who would drag out recalcitrant deputies and beat them up. At one stage, a battery of guns was trained on the building. After three months of stubbornness, the Sejm bowed to the inevitable and ratified the treaties.

The King returned to Warsaw. But it was the Russian ambassador that governed and Russian troops who policed the country. There was little possibility for action by patriots and most of them went into voluntary exile, some to Vienna, Italy and Saxony, others to Paris. Kościuszko was hatching a plan for military action based on a French victory against Prussia and Austria. Kołłątaj and Ignacy Potocki were thinking in terms of a national rising by the masses.

Catherine was unconsciously creating the perfect conditions for a revolution. She started by reducing the Polish army to 12,000 and disbanding the rest. Some 30,000 able-bodied fighting men were made redundant, and these patriotic vagrants were drawn to Warsaw, creating the revolutionary mob on which every upheaval depends. The way in which Poland had been carved up virtually precluded what was left from supporting itself. Cities had been cut off from their agricultural hinterland and trading patterns disrupted. Economic activity came to a virtual standstill, and in 1793 the six largest Warsaw banks declared insolvency. The country had to support a 40,000-strong Russian garrison and pay stringent customs dues imposed by Prussia. Thousands of unemployed cluttered Warsaw. The army was the focal point of discontent. When, on 21 February 1794, the Russians ordered a further reduction and the arrest of people suspected of subversive activity, revolution became inevitable.

On 12 March General Madaliński ordered his brigade into the field and marched on Kraków. Émigrés flocked back to Poland, and on 23 March Kościuszko arrived in Kraków. The following day he proclaimed an Act of Insurrection. He assumed dictatorial powers, took command of the armed forces and called on the nation to rise, delegating the conduct of the administration to a Supreme National Council with emergency powers. When the Insurrection was over all power was to be handed back to the Sejm.

From Kraków Kościuszko marched north. At Racławice on 4 April he defeated a Russian army with a force of 4,000 regulars and 2,000 peasants armed with scythes. On 17 April the Warsaw cobbler Jan Kiliński raised the standard of revolt in the capital. After twenty-four hours of fighting the Russian troops abandoned the city, leaving 4,000 dead on the streets. On the night of 22 April the city of Wilno rose under the leadership of Colonel Jakub Jasiński, a fervent Jacobin, and several of the adherents of the Confederation of Targowica were lynched. But while Jasiński wrote to Kościuszko that he would prefer 'to hang a hundred people, and save six million', the dictator would have none of it. There had also been some lynchings in Warsaw, but Kościuszko put a stop to that when he reached the capital.

The Insurrection could hardly arouse optimism in the more settled sections of the population, and there remained uncertainty as to its real political nature. While the King remained in his castle, untouched by the mob and ostensibly recognised by the leaders of the Insurrection, a number of Jacobins waited in the wings to seize control. Kołłątaj, who had taken over the Treasury, implemented a number of revolutionary measures. He introduced graded taxation and issued paper currency as well as silver coinage, underwritten by confiscated Church property. Kościuszko's proclamation, issued at Połaniec on 7 May, granting freedom and ownership of land to all peasants who came forward to defend the motherland, was a provocation to landowners.

Some magnates declared for the Insurrection and the King donated all his table-silver to the cause, but the majority of the szlachta were cautious, and most made sure their peasants never received the message of the Połaniec manifesto. It was only in the cities that large numbers came forward, and in Warsaw the Jewish community formed up and equipped a special regiment of its own under the command of Colonel Berek Joselewicz, the first Jewish military formation since Biblical times.

Kościuszko, who had marched out to meet the advancing Prussian army under King Frederick William, was outnumbered and defeated at Szczekociny on 6 May. On 15 June the Prussians entered Kraków. In July a combined Russo-Prussian army of 40,000 besieged Warsaw, but Kościuszko used a combination of earthworks and artillery to repel it, and after two months of siege the allies withdrew. Wilno fell to the Russians in mid-August, but a week later the Insurrection broke out in Wielkopolska and a corps under General Dąbrowski set off from Warsaw in support. He defeated a Prussian army near Bydgoszcz, then marched into Prussia.

The situation became hopeless when Austrian forces joined those of Prussia and Russia. Having extracted a pledge of neutrality from Turkey, Catherine ordered Suvorov's army to move against Poland from the south-east. Kościuszko marched out to head him off, but was isolated from his supporting column and beaten at Maciejowice on 10 October. His defeat would have been no great blow in itself, but he was wounded and captured, along with other Polish generals.

The capture of Kościuszko induced political instability. The need for compromise badly affected the choice of his successor as commander-in-chief, which eventually fell on a Tomasz Wawrzecki. The Russians, who had been intending to retire to winter quarters, now decided to push home their advantage and on 4 November Suvorov attacked Warsaw. He had little difficulty in taking the east-bank suburb of Praga. Only four hundred of the 1,400 defenders survived, while the mainly Jewish population was butchered as a warning to Warsaw itself. The warning carried weight, and the army withdrew, allowing Warsaw to capitulate. On 16 November, Wawrzecki was surrounded and captured, and the Insurrection effectively came to an end.

Russian troops once again entered Warsaw, soon to be relieved by Prussians, as the three powers had decided to divide what was left of Poland between themselves and the capital fell to them. A new treaty of partition was signed in 1795, removing Poland from the map altogether. The King was bundled into a carriage and sent off to Grodno, where he was forced to abdicate, and the foreign diplomats accredited to the Polish court were ordered to leave. The Papal Nuncio, the British minister and the chargés d'affaires of Holland, Sweden and Saxony refused as a protest against the unceremonious liquidation of one of the states of Europe. Their embassies were also crammed with fugitives seeking asylum. It took the three powers more than two years to sort out the mess, and it was not until January 1797 that they were able to agree a treaty finally liquidating the debts of the King and the Commonwealth, after which they signed a protocol binding themselves to excise the name of Poland from all future documents, to remove any reference to it from diplomatic business and to strive by every means for its oblivion.

Mainly out of spite to the memory of his mother, Tsar Paul celebrated Catherine's death in 1797 by freeing Kościuszko and other Polish prisoners, and inviting the ailing Stanisław Augustus to St Petersburg. Over the next months the Tsar repeatedly discussed with him plans to resurrect the Polish Commonwealth, and when the King died on 12 February 1798 Paul gave him a state funeral, personally leading the mourning.

It was not, however, the cranky behaviour of Paul that ensured the survival of the Polish cause. Stanisław Staszic had written that 'Even a great nation may fall, but only a contemptible one can be destroyed,' and the Poles did not see themselves as contemptible. They needed only to brandish the political testament of the dying Commonwealth, the constitution of 3 May, to claim their right to the esteem of other nations. This was summed up, decades later, by Karl Marx:

With all its faults, this constitution seems to be the only act of freedom which Eastern Europe has undertaken in the midst of Prussian, Russian and Austrian barbarism. It was, moreover, initiated exclusively by the privileged classes, the nobility. The history of the world knows no other example of similar noble conduct by the nobility.

FOURTEEN

Armed Struggle

The dismemberment of the Commonwealth presents the historian of Poland with something of a dilemma: should he henceforth chart the progress of each of the orphan nations – the Lithuanians, Ukrainians, Belorussians, Jews, Germans and other minorities which inhabited its territory – or should he concentrate on the Poles? The latter would appear to be the sensible course, but it raises the immediate question: which Poles? Somewhere around 90 per cent of ethnic Poles were illiterate peasants with no national consciousness, while the Polish 'political nation' of the szlachta and the new educated middle class was made up of every nationality represented in the Commonwealth.

To most of the peasants, the question of which kingdom or empire they might be living in was irrelevant, and they would pray for the Austrian Emperor in church on Sunday as readily as for the King of Poland. Much the same went for the Jews, who had no reason to feel any reluctance to transfer their loyalty to new masters. The German minority had no difficulty in becoming faithful subjects of the King of Prussia or the Emperor of Austria, or even the Tsar of Russia. The Lithuanians, Belarusians and Ukrainians faced a less congenial future under Russian rule, since this was accompanied by a programme of cultural and religious assimilation. But while that made some retain bonds of loyalty to the Polish world of which they had been part, it led others to search for a new identity of their own.

The constitution of 3 May 1791 had been, as much as anything else, a kind of regenerative act of faith and a pledge of a new start for the Polish project. It would have gradually turned the multicultural Commonwealth into a more homogeneous multi-ethnic nation bound together by a set of shared political values. And although both constitution and country were swept away, the political class that had brought it into being remained faithful to that vision; as a result their struggle for the restoration of a Polish state was based not on Polish ethnicity, but on the entire population of the former Commonwealth.

This introduced tensions, not only between the Polish supporters of this project and ethnic groups such as the Lithuanians, Belarusians and Ukrainians, but also within these. Some in these groups embraced loyalty to their new masters, but others yearned for a national identity of their own, distinct from both the Polish and the Russian. While these tensions form an integral part of it, the history of Poland in the period when there was no sovereign Polish state must be the history of the efforts and struggles of those who saw themselves as the guardians of the ideals of the Commonwealth and its political testament – particularly as those struggles flowed from the events of 1792 and 1794.

Champions of the Polish cause were back in the field against the three powers before the ink had dried on the treaties of partition. In Paris Józef Wybicki was planning a rising in Poland in connection with a French attack on Austria. A secret confederation was formed in Kraków, and in 1796 Colonel Denisko assembled a force of 1,000 men in Moldavia under the covert protection of the Porte which he led into action against the Austrians. In 1797 a regular Polish army was formed under French aegis.

The thousands of Polish soldiers who had taken refuge in Revolutionary France after the collapse of Kościuszko's insurrection had been absorbed into the French army, but when it emerged that many of the prisoners taken by the French in the Italian campaign were Poles conscripted by the Austrians in Galicia, General Bonaparte decided to concentrate them in discrete units. In 1797 a Polish Legion was formed in Milan under the command of Jan Henryk Dąbrowski. The soldiers wore Polish uniforms, Italian epaulettes and French cockades, and marched to a song written by Józef Wybicki which would, in the twentieth century, become the Polish national anthem. In 1798 a second Polish Legion was formed in Italy under General Zajączek and in 1800 a third, the Legion of the Vistula, on the Danube under General Kniaziewicz.

The Poles who fought in these legions believed that after liberating northern Italy from Austrian rule they would march through Hungary into Galicia, from where they would launch an insurrection throughout Poland. But after the Treaties of Campo Formio (1797) and Lunéville (1801), in which France made peace with Austria and other members of the coalition, the legions became an inconvenient embarrassment. Dąbrowski's temporarily became the army of the new state of Lombardy, some of the Polish units were disbanded, others were scattered throughout the French army, and one contingent 6,000 strong was sent to subjugate the black rebellion in Saint Domingue. Many felt let down by Bonaparte, but this was not to be the end of the Polish Napoleonic dream.

Although the image of the legions fighting for Poland's freedom in faraway lands haunted the young, more pragmatic supporters of the cause applied themselves to diplomatic solutions. Chief among these was Prince Adam Czartoryski, son of Adam Kazimierz. After the 1794 Insurrection, in which he took part, he was sent to St Petersburg as a hostage for his family's good behaviour. There he befriended his contemporary the Grand Duke Alexander, an idealistic young man enthused by the ideas of the Enlightenment and eager to right what he saw as the wrong of the partition of Poland. When he ascended the throne in 1801, Alexander nominated a 'Committee for Public Salvation' consisting of five close advisers which was to transform Russia into a modern constitutional monarchy. Czartoryski was given the brief of foreign affairs, and also placed in charge of education in the former Polish territories, the eight Western Gubernias of the Empire.

Czartoryski encouraged Alexander's dislike of Prussia in the hope that sooner or later Russia might recover the parts of Poland taken by Prussia, add them to her own share, and recreate a Polish state more or less loosely tied to Russia. It was, however, Napoleon who beat Prussia, in 1806. After the battles of Jena and Auerstadt his armies entered Poznań, led by a Polish corps under General Dąbrowski. Napoleon allowed Dąbrowski to issue a call for insurrection, adding his taunt: 'I want to see whether the Poles deserve to be a nation.' While many were cautious, large numbers of volunteers did come forward. On 28 November Marshal Murat marched into Warsaw and a few weeks later Napoleon himself entered the capital, greeted with triumphal arches and delirious crowds.

He was convinced, if not that the Poles deserved to be a nation, that they could provide him with plenty of good soldiers. Poland was no more than a minor element in his schemes, and his most pressing imperative was to force Russia to join him in alliance against Britain. He achieved this during his meetings with Tsar Alexander at Tilsit in 1807, and one consequence was a compromise on Poland. The Prussian share of the second and third partitions of the Commonwealth was reconstituted as the Duchy of Warsaw, under Frederick Augustus of Saxony (the candidate proposed by the constitution of 3 May 1791).

The Duchy was in no sense a sovereign Polish state, but Polish patriots saw it as a basis for further development. Many of those hitherto wary of Napoleon's intentions agreed to serve in its government, including Małachowski and Stanisław Potocki, and the last King's nephew, Józef Poniatowski, became commander-in-chief and Minister for War. Małachowski wanted to convoke a sejm similar to that of 1792, but Napoleon was having none of it. Before leaving Warsaw he dictated a constitution which included a bicameral sejm based on a suffrage that included non-noble voters, but this had virtually no legislative powers. He also introduced the Code Napoléon, which effectively removed the peasants' disabilities and made all equal before the law.

Napoleon exploited the Duchy of Warsaw for his own ends, mainly financial and military. Property and land confiscated by Prussia in 1792 was now sold back to the duchy by France at exorbitant rates. The economy could hardly flourish while Napoleon's European blockade constricted the grain trade, and while the duchy was expected to pay for a standing army rising to 60,000 men. In addition, Napoleon required six regiments of foot and two of horse for his Spanish campaign, some 10,000 men in all serving as the Legion of the Vistula, as well as a regiment of Chevaux-Légers for the Imperial Guard. When the duchy went bankrupt, France lent money and collected the interest in cannon fodder.

The Duchy of Warsaw was invaded by Austria in 1809. Poniatowski counterattacked and went on to capture Kraków and Galicia. However, when peace was made between France and Austria at the Treaty of Schönbrunn, the Poles had to give up most of these conquests. The enlarged duchy was nevertheless a source of alarm in Russia, where it was viewed as a magnet which would, sooner or later, attract all the former Polish lands. Matters came to a head in 1812, during what Napoleon called his 'second Polish war'.

Napoleon's intention was not to conquer Russia but to cow

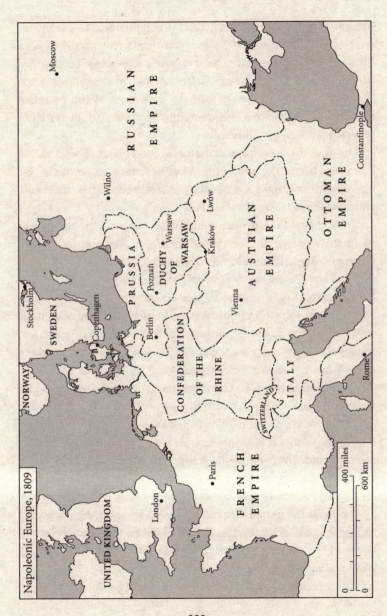

Napoleonic Europe, 1809

RUSSIAN EMPIRE

• Moscow

• Wilno

PRUSSIA

DUCHY OF WARSAW

Warsaw •

Lwów •

Poznań •

Kraków •

AUSTRIAN EMPIRE

OTTOMAN EMPIRE

Constantinople •

SWEDEN

Stockholm •

Copenhagen •

Berlin •

Vienna •

CONFEDERATION OF THE RHINE

SWITZERLAND

ITALY

Rome •

NORWAY

FRENCH EMPIRE

• Paris

UNITED KINGDOM

London •

400 miles

600 km

0

0

Alexander into submissive alliance. He was prepared to use the re-establishment of a strong Poland as a threat, but meant to keep his options open were Alexander to give in. So while he whipped up Polish hopes, he bypassed a Warsaw full of delegations from the provinces of the former Commonwealth. In Wilno he called the Lithuanians to arms, but refused to be drawn on the question of independence for Lithuania.

The war turned into a catastrophe for Poland. Some 96,000 Poles marched in the ranks of the Grande Armée, by far the largest non-French contingent. Countless others joined it in Lithuania and the eastern reaches of the former Commonwealth. They played a significant role in the operations. Polish lancers were the first to swim the Niemen and carry the French tricolour onto Russian territory: Colonel Umiński's dragoons were the first into Moscow; the Chevaux-Légers saved Napoleon's life from a pack of marauding Cossacks; the Legion of the Vistula defended the Berezina crossings. At least 72,000 never returned, and many more died of wounds or typhus in the following months. Yet they were the only contingent not to lose or abandon a single field-gun or standard to the enemy during the disastrous retreat.

As the remnants of the Grande Armée streamed westwards and Napoleon hurried to Paris, the Duchy of Warsaw was left defenceless. Dąbrowski's division followed the French army into Germany, but Poniatowski fell back on Kraków with 16,000 men. Alexander was not vindictive, and in the spring and summer of 1813, using those who had remained on the Russian side, he tried to persuade Poniatowski and his army to cast off their loyalty to Napoleon.

Poniatowski rejected Alexander's proposals and led his army off to join Napoleon in Saxony. On 19 October, the last day of the Battle of the Nations at Leipzig, the heavily wounded Prince died while trying to swim the river Elster when the French, whose retreat he was covering, blew the remaining bridge. The Poles continued to follow Napoleon. When he went into exile on the island of Elba, half of the symbolic guard he was allowed were Polish Chevaux-Légers.

Napoleon's attitude to Polish aspirations had been cynical from the start, and the whole episode had been of no benefit to the Polish cause. Yet the Napoleonic epos was important to the Poles. Since the relief of Vienna in 1683, military glory was something they could only read about. Between 1797 and 1815 they were able to demonstrate their bravery, loyalty and spirit on battlefields all over Europe. Feats of valour such as the charge of the Chevaux-Légers through the defile of Somo Sierra on 30 November 1808 (when a single squadron of 125 men cleared 9,000 entrenched infantry and four batteries from the defile, capturing ten standards and sixteen guns in the space of seven minutes at the cost of eighty-three dead) have gone down in legend. Countless other exploits earned them the respect of enemies, from the Peninsula, where the Spaniards of General Palafox spoke with awe of the '*infernales picadores*' (the Lancers of the Vistula), to the depths of Russia, where General Colbert of the Guard Cavalry ordered all French units to borrow the capes and caps of Polish lancers before going on picket duty, to keep Cossacks at a respectful distance.

These heroics provided a comforting mythology for generations with no state or army of their own, and Napoleon's image recurs in Polish art and literature well into the twentieth century as a focus for dreams of glory. The fall of Napoleon, which showed that even the greatest can be brought down by an alliance of lesser creatures, was a source of consolation to Poles who felt their cause had similarly been brought down by cynical collusion. The Romantic vision of Prometheus in chains could cover up a multitude of unpleasant realities.

At his abdication Napoleon committed his Polish troops to the clemency of the Tsar, and Alexander was neither vengeful nor blind to the opportunities of the Polish question. His paramount position in 1814 permitted him to entertain hopes that he would be able to reunite most of the territory of the former Commonwealth in a kingdom under his own sceptre, and he brought Czartoryski as one of his negotiators to the Congress of Vienna. But the Tsar's wishes were thwarted by Austria, Britain and France, which could not countenance Prussia being given swathes of Germany in compensation for those she would relinquish in Poland, nor indeed the huge westward expansion of Russian power attendant on the creation of a Russian-dominated Poland. The re-establishment of a fully independent Poland was mooted by Britain and France but never seriously considered, and for all his good intentions Alexander would never have been able to sell the idea at home, where opinion reacted to his Polish plans with indignation.

In the end, a Kingdom of Poland consisting of 127,000 square kilometres with a population of 3.3 million was carved out of all three partitions. In addition, Kraków and a tiny area around the city was turned into a republic. The Tsar of Russia was the King of Poland, and all three partitioning powers were the protectors of the Republic of Kraków. The remainder of the Polish lands held by Austria were administered separately, as the Kingdom of Galicia and Lodomeria, with the help of docile assemblies. The major share of the Polish lands retained by Prussia was given separate status as the Grand Duchy of Posen. All three partitioning monarchs made fulsome declarations pledging themselves to treat their Polish subjects with benevolence and to respect their institutions.

The new Polish state, usually referred to as the Congress Kingdom, was a curious entity. The constitution, drawn up by Czartoryski, was the most liberal in Central Europe. There was a bicameral Sejm of 128 deputies, seventy-seven of them elected by the szlachta and fifty-one by non-noble property owners, and sixty-four senators. It lacked any legislative powers, and its function was

The Congress Kingdom, 1815–31

primarily administrative, regulatory and judicial. Foreign policy and the police were both run from St Petersburg; Alexander's brother Constantine was installed in Warsaw as commander-in-chief of the Polish army; the former legionary General Zajączek was Alexander's viceroy; and the Russian Nikolai Novosiltsev was Alexander's commissioner in the government of the Kingdom.

There was something unnatural about the close association between huge, autocratic Russia and the tiny constitutional Congress Kingdom. It was perhaps inevitable that either Poland would act as a springboard for the liberalisation of Russia or that Russia would gradually swallow up and digest its small satellite. At first, the former seemed the more likely. Large sections of Russian society had come under foreign influence as a result of the Napoleonic wars and appeared open to change. As a consequence of absorbing so much Polish territory, by 1815 no less than 64 per cent of the nobility of the Romanov realm was of Polish descent, and since there were more literate Poles than Russians, more people within it could read and write Polish than Russian. The third largest city, Wilno, was entirely Polish in character and its university was the best in the Empire.

In his speech at the opening of the Polish Sejm in April 1818, Alexander held out a succulent carrot to the Poles. 'Live up to your duties,' he exhorted them. 'The results of your labours will show me whether I shall be able to abide by my intention of expanding the concessions I have already made to you.' But his enthusiasm for liberalism waned, while Novosiltsev, who had no time for Polish aspirations and did not like Czartoryski, did all he could to undermine Polish autonomy. He exploited the incipient conflicts between Alexander and Constantine, and between both of them and various Polish statesmen, promoting the view, which gained acceptance in Russia, that the Poles were not grateful for the favours they had been granted. When, in 1820, the Sejm began to openly debate political issues and stood up in defence of the constitution, which had been infringed by Alexander and his officers, he dissolved it. When he opened the next session, in 1825, he insisted that its deliberations be held in camera and excluded all those deputies he deemed subversive.

The violence done to the territory of the Commonwealth between 1792 and 1815, and the succession of governments to which its various parts had been subjected in the same period, had surprisingly little impact on the life of the nation. The frontiers themselves figured only as administrative impediments in the minds of most Poles, who referred to them as 'the Austrian cordon' or 'the Prussian cordon'. A Pole travelling from Warsaw to Poznań or Wilno in the 1820s crossed into a different country, but as far as he or his hosts were concerned, he was still travelling around his own.

Similarly, people who had fought on opposing sides sat together in the Sejm and Senate. Alexander's viceroy in Poland had started out as a Jacobin, fought in Kościuszko's army in 1794, had commanded a Polish Legion in Italy, and been wounded fighting for Napoleon at Borodino. Adam Czartoryski, who had also fought with Kościuszko, was one of the pillars of the Congress Kingdom, although his father had presided over the provisional government set up by Napoleon in 1812. Stanisław Potocki, a prominent Patriot in the 1780s and a minister in the Duchy of Warsaw, was now Minister of Education. Even the chief censor appointed in 1819, Józef Kalasanty Szaniawski, had been a Jacobin in 1794.

In a sense, the Commonwealth continued to exist in defiance of political boundaries, and its traditions were carefully nurtured. The University of Wilno flourished under the direction of Adam Czartoryski and took over as the centre of academic life. New institutions such as the Krzemieniec High School, founded by Tadeusz Czacki, provided Polish education to a high standard. The Załuski library had been looted by the Russians, but in 1811 Stanisław Zamoyski opened his considerable library in Warsaw to the public. The Czartoryski historical museum at Puławy recorded past glories, while its archive served historians. In 1817, the year the Austrian authorities founded a German university at Lemberg (as they had renamed Lwów), Józef Ossoliński opened a Polish archive and library in the city, the Ossolineum. In 1829 Edward Raczyński did the same in Poznań, which was also endowed with a museum by the Mielżyński family. Adam Tytus Działyński founded the Poznań

Society of Friends of Learning, which began publishing manuscript sources in the 1840s from his library at Kórnik, which he had opened to the public in 1828. Everything, from old coins to folk songs, was collected, documented and studied.

The literary revival of the late eighteenth century continued to flourish with a new generation of poets. The same was true of the musical scene, which gave birth to the genius of Fryderyk Chopin. The architects fostered by Stanisław Augustus came to maturity at the beginning of the century and over the next three decades embellished Warsaw and dotted the countryside with elegant neo-classical houses. As a result, the Warsaw of the 1820s was an imposing and vibrant city, very much the capital of a Polish world still defined by the boundaries of the defunct Commonwealth.

But the post-Napoleonic generation was not temperamentally suited to compromise. There was much heated discussion among students, particularly at the University of Wilno, where secret societies burgeoned. It was all fairly harmless, but the Russian secret police has never been known to consider any discussion harmless, and when, in 1821, Major Walerian Łukasiński founded a Patriotic Society in Warsaw, it began to investigate further.

In 1823 the Professor of History at Wilno, Joachim Lelewel, was sacked and a number of students arrested. Other arrests followed, including that of a young poet, Adam Mickiewicz, a former student, now a teacher in Kowno, and the author of an *Ode to Youth* whose allusive phrases the censor could not understand but did not like. The university was further chastened by the removal of its curator Adam Czartoryski, which followed the dismissal of Stanisław Potocki from the ministry of education. These measures had the effect of irritating the young and many hitherto content with the status quo. Discussion and conspiracy spread to the army and after the failure of the Decembrist coup of 1825 in Russia, which sought to place Constantine on the imperial throne, investigations led the

Russian police back to Warsaw. As the new Tsar Nicholas clamped down on freethinking in Russia, his lieutenants in Poland began ferreting about in earnest.

They arrested a number of ringleaders of conspiratorial groups, and Novosiltsev demanded, at Nicholas's behest, that these be dealt with in accordance with Russian criminal procedure. The Polish government demurred on constitutional grounds and the men were tried by a tribunal appointed by the Sejm. Since their actions could not be construed as criminal under Polish law the case against them was dismissed in 1829. In his fury, Nicholas actually had the members of the tribunal arrested before countermanding their verdict and imposing his own sentences on the prisoners.

The government in Warsaw found itself in an untenable position, losing authority at home and undermined by its Russian patrons. This played into the hands of revolutionary elements, and tension mounted throughout the early months of 1830. News of the July Revolution in France and the subsequent upheaval in Belgium in September brought matters to a head. Nicholas announced his intention of sending an expeditionary force made up principally of Polish troops to crush the revolution in Belgium, and mobilisation was decreed on 19 November 1830.

FIFTEEN

Insurgency

On the night of 29 November 1830 a group of officer cadets broke into the Belvedere Palace to assassinate Grand Duke Constantine while another attacked a nearby Russian cavalry barracks. Everything went wrong. The Russians were alerted in time and the Grand Duke escaped the knives of the assassins. An attack on the Arsenal was more successful, with fatal consequences. Armed gangs roamed the streets lynching Russians and Polish collaborators, and, by mistake, two of the best Polish generals.

The Polish authorities moved swiftly to bring the situation under control and avoid confrontation with Russia. Prince Franciszek Ksawery Drucki-Lubecki, the Minister of Finance, took the initiative of coopting Czartoryski and other figures of standing to join him in a National Council. In an attempt to keep the army together and restore order the popular General Chłopicki was proclaimed Dictator on 5 December. He hoped to be able to deal with the whole matter as an internal Polish problem. He granted Constantine safe-conduct out of Warsaw, along with his court, his troops, even his police spies and political prisoners, and he despatched Lubecki to St Petersburg to negotiate.

But the Tsar refused to receive the Prince, and on 7 January 1831 sent him a note demanding unconditional surrender as a precondition to any negotiations. This inflamed patriotic fervour throughout the country. Talk of accommodation was branded as defeatist, and, seeing no other way out, Chłopicki resigned. The Sejm acknowledged a state of insurrection, and under pressure from below, on 25 January 1831 burnt its bridges by voting the dethronement of Nicholas as King of Poland. A new government was formed under Czartoryski with Michał Radziwiłł as commander-in-chief. The Kingdom of Poland had seceded from Russia.

In February a force of 115,000 Russian troops under General Diebitsch marched into Poland. The Polish army, consisting of 30,000 men, blocked his advance successfully at Grochów on 25 February. At the end of March General Jan Skrzynecki sallied forth and routed the Russian corps separately in the three battles of Wawer, Dębe Wielkie and Iganie, obliging Diebitsch to withdraw eastwards. The position of the Russian forces was parlous, with Diebitsch isolated and the Guard Corps on its way to reinforce him easy for the Poles to intercept. General Dwernicki had been sent with a small force to Volhynia to raise a revolt there, while Generals Chłapowski and Giełgud marched into Lithuania with the same intention. The Poles were well set to win the campaign. They called up reserves of 80,000, and with the Lithuanian and other contingents, they could count on up to 200,000 in total. The Russian forces in Poland numbered some 250,000, but the Polish soldier was more motivated and the officer corps more experienced. The insurrection also attracted valuable volunteers from abroad. Hundreds of Napoleonic officers took part, including General Ramorino, the son of Marshal Lannes (Marshal Grouchy wanted to come, but insisted on too high a rank). The next largest contingent were Germans, who also supplied over a hundred military surgeons, and there were volunteers from Hungary, Italy and Britain.

But none of those standing at the helm approved of the rising or believed in its chances of success. Czartoryski was convinced that the only solution was a diplomatic one. He sent missions to London, Paris and Vienna in order to secure support and finance, and to offer the throne of Poland to a Habsburg archduke or a member of the British royal family in return for assistance. The commander-in-chief, General Jan Skrzynecki, felt that the less blood was spilled before negotiations were resumed the better. He therefore dragged his heels and failed to intercept the Guard Corps. When this joined up with Diebitsch's army, he was attacked and defeated on 26 May at Ostrołęka. Diebitsch died of the cholera epidemic raging in the Russian army, but Skrzynecki failed to exploit the situation. General Paskevich took over command of the Russian forces and prepared for a new advance.

In Paris, King Louis-Philippe made sonorous speeches hinting at French military support, and there was a moment when it looked as though Czartoryski's diplomatic efforts might yield fruit. Events in Poland aroused strong international sympathy and engaged the poetic fancy. In Germany, this gave rise to a genre of *Polenlieder*. In America, Nathan Parker Willis wrote odes to Poland, while in England the young Tennyson wrote what he termed 'a beautiful poem on Poland, hundreds of lines long' (which was used by his housemaid to light the fire). In France, Delavigne, Béranger, Musset, Vigny, Lamartine and Hugo glorified the Poles' struggle in verse. On 23 May 1831 the Aldermen and Council of New York made a strong declaration of support, while Boston offered standards for the Polish regiments. In Paris, James Fenimore Cooper started a Polish-American Committee to gather funds for the rising.

Given time, some of this feeling might have been brought to bear. But the lack of political determination at the top allowed Paskevich to seize the initiative. He marched westwards, bypassing Warsaw to the north, and swept round to attack it from its least defensible western side. Instead of delivering a flank attack on the moving Russian columns, Skrzynecki sent two army corps off in different directions to create diversions. On 6 September 1831 Paskevich attacked Warsaw. After two days of determined but costly fighting, the new commander General Krukowiecki capitulated and withdrew with the rest of his forces. The Poles still had some 70,000 troops in the field but these were dispersed around the country, and continued resistance seemed pointless. On 5 October the main army crossed the border into Prussia to avoid capture by the Russians, while other units sought refuge behind the Austrian cordon, followed by most of the political leadership.

Nicholas abolished the constitution of the Kingdom and closed down the universities of Wilno and Warsaw, along with the Warsaw Polytechnic, the Krzemieniec High School, the Society of Friends of Learning and other educational establishments. In exchange, Warsaw was endowed with a citadel from which Nicholas promised to bombard the city to rubble if there was any more trouble. General Paskevich was named Prince of Warsaw, and Russian generals and officials were given estates confiscated from Polish families.

Ten people, with Adam Czartoryski at the head of the list, were condemned to death by decapitation, and a further 350 to hanging (most of them had already left the country). While a generous amnesty was trumpeted to the world, 10,000 officers were sent off to hard labour or service as simple soldiers in Russian regiments in the Caucasus. Over eight hundred 'orphans' (children whose fathers had been killed or gone into exile) were taken from their mothers and given to Russian infantry regiments to bring up. In the Kingdom, countless families of minor szlachta were degraded and 3,176 had their estates confiscated. In the province of Podolia, 5,000 families of minor szlachta were dispossessed of everything, reduced to peasant status and transported to the Caucasus. A few years later 40,000 families of szlachta from Lithuania and Volhynia were conveyed to Siberia. Prince Roman Sanguszko, who was of Rurik's royal blood and might have qualified for some respect, was sentenced to hard labour for life in Siberia and made to walk there chained to a gang of convicts. When his mother, a friend and former lady-in-waiting to the Empress, begged for leniency, she was told she could go too.

The fate of the exiles was less lurid but no more enviable. Some 8,000 senior officers, political figures, writers and artists found themselves consigned to a life of hopeless anticipation. Theirs was supposed to be a tactical withdrawal. To keep themselves in shape, many of the soldiers took service in the new Belgian army, and the French tried to pack as many as they could into a Foreign Legion created for the purpose. Others converged on Paris, which became a focal point of Polish political and cultural life. It was there, amid bitterness and mutual recrimination, that the next moves in the struggle to recapture Poland were planned and discussed.

Two principal groupings emerged: the Czartoryski party and the Polish Democratic Society. The first pinned its hopes on diplomacy. Adam Czartoryski, referred to even by his political opponents as the *de facto* king of Poland, lobbied British Members of Parliament and French Deputies, wrote memoranda and petitions, and maintained unofficial diplomatic relations with the Vatican and the Porte. He set up a network with offices in several capitals which sprang into frenetic activity whenever a crisis loomed in Europe.

The Democratic Society, whose nerve centre, the Centralizacja, was based at Versailles, was committed to starting a mass rising in Poland at the earliest possible moment. It also built up strong links with similar movements in other countries, such as Giuseppe Mazzini's Young Italy; like the French in the 1790s, the Poles had begun to see themselves as universal champions of freedom, obliged to assist sister nations in their struggles, and thousands of them conspired, fought and died for the causes of others.

In 1837 the Russians uncovered the network the Centralizacja had carefully organised throughout the Kingdom and Lithuania, and cut a swathe through it with shootings, hangings and deportations to Siberia. The Democrats then shifted their activities to the less perilous Austrian and Prussian sectors, where they agitated throughout the 1840s, often playing on anti-manor sentiments in order to gain support among the politically passive peasantry.

A peasant rising was planned in both Galicia and Poznania for 22 February 1846. But premature action alerted the Austrian authorities, which reacted with speed and perfidy. They appealed to the Galician peasantry, explaining that the Polish lords were plotting a rising which would enslave them and offering cash for every 'conspirator' brought in dead or alive. There followed three days of mob violence in which bands of peasants attacked some seven hundred country houses, killing about a thousand people, few of them conspirators. On 4 March Austrian and Russian troops crushed the Socialist Republic which had meanwhile been proclaimed in Kraków and abolished the free status of the city, which was incorporated into the Austrian Empire. In Poznania the Prussian authorities arrested the entire leadership before the planned local rising had time to break out.

The revolutionary ardour of the Poles revived in the 'Springtime of the Nations' of 1848. In February of that year the Paris mob overthrew the regime of Louis-Philippe; three weeks later the barricades went up in Vienna and Berlin; by the summer there was hardly a state in Europe that had not been affected by disturbances. Poles were involved in all of these, as well as in events taking place in Poland itself.

Kraków and Lwów rose and proclaimed provisional revolutionary committees designated by the Versailles Centralizacja, which presented a list of demands for autonomy and the emancipation of the peasants. In the desperate straits in which it found itself the Austrian government had no option but to accept the *fait accompli*.

The Berlin mob had released from prison all the Polish conspirators arrested in 1846, and they went to Poznań to take control of the National Committee which had already formed there. The Berlin government was prepared to concede almost anything to weather the storm and therefore sanctioned the committee, promising 'national reorganisation' of the Grand Duchy of Posen along Polish lines. Attention then switched to Frankfurt, where the all-German Parliament assembled in a mood of pan-European liberalism. The fear that Tsar Nicholas would send in his troops to restore order in Central Europe prompted much talk of a common crusade to liberate Russian Poland and roll back the boundaries of tsarist autocracy.

Poles from all over Europe flocked to Poznania. Even Adam Czartoryski arrived from Paris, greeted along the way like a future king. In Poznania the National Committee had by now some 20,000 men under arms, commanded by Ludwik Mierosławski, and proceeded with a programme of local reforms.

In the early summer the mood in Germany and in the Frankfurt Parliament began to veer away from internationalist liberalism, and deputies representing the German population of Poznania, Silesia and Pomerania began to voice anti-Polish sentiments. As the liberal ardour spent itself, the Berlin government began to contain the crisis. It promised to abide by its plan of 'national reorganisation' in Poznania, but insisted the Polish militias be disbanded. The National Committee tried to negotiate, but when Prussian forces attacked one of the Polish units the Poles fought back. They won two pitched battles against the Prussian army, at Miłosław and Sokołowo, but were eventually bombarded into surrender with heavy artillery. Talk of reorganisation and autonomy was dropped, and in the end the Frankfurt Parliament voted to incorporate the Grand Duchy of Posen into Germany. As Friedrich Engels noted wryly: 'Our enthusiasm for the Poles changed into shrapnel and caustic.'

In November, the Austrian army bombarded Kraków and then Lwów into submission. The 'Springtime of the Nations' had turned into another bleak winter for Polish patriots; far from benefiting their cause in any way, it had actually had the effect of liquidating the remaining privileges in the Republic of Kraków and the Grand Duchy of Posen.

The Poles had been among the first on the barricades of Vienna and Berlin; they fought in the Dresden rising; a Polish legion formed by the poet Adam Mickiewicz in Lombardy fought at Rome, Genoa, Milan and Florence; Mierosławski commanded the anti-Bourbon forces in Sicily and then the German revolutionaries in Baden; General Chrzanowski commanded the Piedmontese forces at Novara. Wherever there were Russians, Prussians, Austrians or their allies to be fought, there were Poles in the ranks. Their greatest contribution was to the Hungarian cause. General Bem, who had saved the day for the Poles at Ostrołęka in 1831, commanded the revolutionary forces in Vienna in 1848 and then Lajos Kossuth's army in Transylvania. General Dembiński was the commander-in-chief of the Hungarian forces. They and hundreds of Polish officers fought to the bloody end at Temesvar, while Czartoryski backed the Hungarians with diplomatic and material resources.

All this only served to associate the Polish cause with revolution in the European mind, and Europe was frightened by revolution. The outbreak of the Crimean War in 1853 should have been a godsend to the Poles, combining as it did both of the nations most sympathetic to their cause against the arch-enemy Russia. The former British Foreign Secretary and future Prime Minister Lord Palmerston knew Czartoryski and had often made sympathetic pronouncements on the Polish question. Napoleon III inherited sympathy for the Polish cause with his political pedigree, and his Foreign Minister was Count Walewski, the half-Polish natural son of the first Napoleon. The Poles began to dream of a Franco-British expeditionary force landing in Lithuania, but Palmerston and Napoleon III buried the Polish issue in order to buy Austrian and Prussian neutrality in the conflict, and only allowed Polish units to be raised under the Turkish flag to fight the common enemy in the Caucasus and the Crimea.

The Russian defeat in the Crimea and the death of Tsar Nicholas in 1855 did, however, have an immediate effect on conditions in Poland itself. The new Tsar, Alexander II, visited Warsaw and expressed himself open to suggestions for reform, but warned against political illusion: '*Point de rêveries, messieurs, point de rêveries!*' It was an idle taunt. Any attempt at improvement by the Poles was virtually bound to be seen in St Petersburg as '*rêveries*', as the next few years were to demonstrate.

With cautious optimism, the Warsaw banker and industrialist Leopold Kronenberg and Andrzej Zamoyski of the Agricultural Society initiated a discussion of possible reforms. It was the area tackled by Zamoyski that absorbed most attention – the question of the peasants. By the late 1850s more than half of all peasant tenancies had been transformed into money-rents, mainly by voluntary commutation on the part of the landlord. But most small estates still operated on the old labour-rent system. In 1858 the Russian government asked the Agricultural Society to prepare a land reform project. Since discussions were going on in Russia on the subject of the emancipation of serfs, the matter began to assume starkly political overtones. It was a question of whether the Polish peasant would thank the Tsar or his Polish masters for his emancipation.

The Agricultural Society eventually settled on a project which commuted all labour-rents to money-rents with assured tenancy, to be followed by a conversion of tenancies into freeholds by negotiation between landlord and tenant. The country followed the course of the discussion and by 1860 the Agricultural Society had come to be regarded as the *de facto* Sejm, its meetings reported even by the London *Times*. It was soon caught between the admonitions of St Petersburg and the increasingly strident demands of the Warsaw radicals. St Petersburg's strong man in this instance was not a Russian but a Pole, Aleksander Wielopolski, an intelligent, urbane aristocrat who had supported the 1830 rising but had since come to see the pointlessness of such heroics.

In 1860 Wielopolski came up with a plan acceptable to the Tsar which was, in essence, a cautious return to the principles of the Congress Kingdom of the 1820s. Russia would concede a measure of administrative reform in the government of the Kingdom and permit the creation of consultative bodies; the clampdown on education would be eased and the peasant question would be solved by Wielopolski, who in 1862 became head of the civil government. In replication of earlier arrangements, Alexander's brother Constantine was sent to Poland as viceroy. For his part, Wielopolski undertook to maintain order and keep Polish political ambitions under control.

This would not be easy. Wielopolski was disliked for his arrogance and apparent subservience to Russia. His rival Andrzej Zamoyski was a man of lesser intelligence but greater popularity who was beginning to be propelled by pressures from below. When summoned by Grand Duke Constantine he refused to collaborate, preferring to remain in opposition. The promise of liberalisation had acted like a tonic on the more radical elements of the population. Meetings were held, discussions raged in word and print on every aspect of reform, emancipation and autonomy, and the conclusion was drawn more often than not that any accommodation with Russia was impossible. The police listened, people were investigated, and the cells of the Citadel began to fill up with hundreds, then thousands.

On 25 February 1861, a meeting commemorating the 1830 rising was dispersed by police. Two days later a religious procession was fired on, leaving five dead. On 8 April a similar demonstration resulted in over a hundred deaths. Disturbances recurred in Warsaw and other cities in a climate of mutual provocation. Martial law was decreed and on 15 October Russian troops broke into a couple of Warsaw churches in which demonstrators had sought sanctuary, and some 1,500 were carted off to the Citadel. All churches and synagogues in the country closed in protest, leading to the arrest of bishops, priests and rabbis.

A group of radicals known as 'Reds' had founded a secret Warsaw City Committee, and this set up a countrywide provisional government to coordinate a mass rising in 1862. The military weakness of Russia demonstrated by the Crimean War, as well as the recent successes of Garibaldi in Italy, suggested that it might succeed. While liberals saw a Polish Cavour in Czartoryski, radicals saw a Polish Garibaldi in Mierosławski, who was a friend of Prince Napoleon, nephew of the Emperor of the French. The military commander appointed by the City Committee, Jarosław Dąbrowski, made contact with officers, both Russian and Polish, throughout the Russian army in order to cripple the military response at the moment of outbreak. Plans were well advanced when, in the summer of 1862, the Russian police got wind of the preparations and arrested many of the officers, including Dąbrowski.

Meanwhile, Wielopolski was trying to impose his own solution to the peasant question, which was similar to Zamoyski's proposals of 1859. By now, however, Zamoyski and the Agricultural Society had shifted their position. In an attempt to outbid the Reds they pressed for more radical measures. Zamoyski was summoned to St Petersburg where he was given a reprimand by the Tsar and sent into exile. The Agricultural Society was abolished and Kronenberg's City Deputation dissolved. It was now the turn of the moderates, known as the 'Whites', to go underground and start plotting.

The Poles had learnt a great deal from their experiences and displayed remarkable professionalism in the art of subversive organisation. The City Committee became the Central National Committee under the chairmanship of Stefan Bobrowski. It had five ministries: a diplomatic service which travelled widely and freely on forged documents, gaining admittance to European chancelleries as well as Russian émigrés' garrets; a treasury which collected donations from sympathisers and 'taxes' from the luke-warm, and even floated an international loan; a quartermastership which purchased and smuggled arms and supplies; a department of the interior which formulated policy on emancipation of the peasants and the Jews; and a department of justice complete with its own 'stiletto police'. The intelligence department had men in every branch of the Russian army and civil service. The fighters trained and operated clandestinely in Warsaw under the noses of the Russian army encamped not only in the Citadel but in the squares and streets. The Russian General Berg, who had been instructed by the Grand Duke Constantine to investigate the conspiracy, reported back after some weeks that he had discovered 'only one thing, namely that I don't belong to it'. As an afterthought, he added: 'And neither does Your Imperial Highness.'

Wielopolski still hoped to avert insurrection. He brought forward the annual selective conscription into the Russian army and excluded landowners and settled peasants from the lists. By concen-trating the draft of more than 30,000 on the educated young and the cities he calculated that the majority of the conspirators would be caught in the net, while those who purposely avoided it would reveal their identity. In the event, the majority slipped away from home as the draft drew near. On 22 January 1863 the National Committee proclaimed the insurrection, and that night small units attacked Russian garrisons around the country.

The rising was doomed to failure. The insurgents numbered no more than about 20,000 ill-equipped men dispersed in bands of between fifty and five hundred. Their numbers grew periodically, and in all some 100,000 people would fight over the next eighteen months, but they were no match for the 300,000 Russian regulars concentrated against them. By virtue of good reconnaissance, timing, and an ability to melt away into the countryside, they managed to harass the Russian forces, cut supply lines, and occasionally defeat a column on the march, but they could not capture a town or take on a full division in pitched battle, as they had no artillery. Only in the remoter areas of Sandomierz, Podlasie and Kielce was it possible for units of more than 2,000 men to survive in the open. Nor was there any continuity of command. Ludwik Mierosławski, who was to take control, was defeated while moving in from Poznania. Marian Langiewicz did manage to assume overall command, but was soon defeated and forced to withdraw to Galicia.

World opinion was strongly pro-Polish, and while newspapers ranted against Russian injustice, young men flocked to Poland, from Ireland, England, France, Germany and, most of all, Italy. Garibaldi's friend Francesco Nullo was one of several redshirts who fought and died in Poland. Remarkably, the largest non-Polish contingent was Russian.

Foreign governments were less eager to help. Bismarck made it clear that he would help Russia if the need arose. Austria turned a blind eye to the activity going on along its border, which was the only entry point for supplies. On 17 April 1863 Britain, France and Austria made a joint *démarche* in St Petersburg protesting at Russia's violation of the Vienna settlement of 1815. Privately,

Napoleon III and his ministers intimated that they would send arms and eventually troops, urging the Poles to hold on. It was largely as a result of this that the Whites, who were in close touch with their political siblings in Paris, decided in February to join the insurrection officially and to make a bid for control of the movement.

This changed hands more than once over the next months, and in October 1863 came to rest in those of Romuald Traugutt, a Lithuanian landowner. He was a devout, almost ascetic thirty-five-year-old father of two who had reached the rank of colonel in the Russian army and seen service in the Crimean War. He reorganised the National Committee and the military command, and it was largely owing to his leadership that the insurrection revived in the autumn of 1863 and expanded its area of operations.

It had been said that the boundaries of the putative future Poland would draw themselves with the blood of insurgents. Predictably, they did not stretch very far into Ukraine, where only groups of Polish szlachta came out. In Belorussia, they included much of the old Commonwealth, with not only the peasants, but also the Jews of towns such as Pińsk joining the cause. In Lithuania and even southern Livonia, they corresponded to the borders of 1772, with mass participation by all classes. It was a slap in the face to the Russian policy carried on in these areas since the first partition.

On 2 March 1864 the Tsar pulled the carpet from under the feet of the insurrectionary government by decreeing the emancipation of the peasants with full possession of land. In April Traugutt was arrested. Sporadic fighting went on for another six months, but the uprising was over. The Tsar issued a ukase changing the name of the Kingdom of Poland to the 'Vistula Province'. All Polish institutions were abolished, and a period of intense repression began. General Muravyov, known in Russia as 'Hangman' Muravyov, scoured the Western Gubernias for signs of dissent and carried out a thorough purge. Brutality was meted out on a hitherto unknown scale, the path to Siberia was trodden by chain gangs numbering tens of thousands of young people who would never return, and the nation went into mourning.

It went into mourning not only for the failure of the insurrection, but for the whole tradition of insurgency. The 1863 rising was an uncommon achievement – it was no mean feat for 100,000 intellectuals, noblemen, workers and peasants to keep Europe's largest military machine tied down for eighteen months. It had also proved that the szlachta were not alone, and the very last engagement was fought by a detachment of peasants. Nevertheless it was the end of an era in Polish history.

SIXTEEN

The Polish Question

The 'Polish Question' haunted nineteenth-century diplomacy like an uneasy conscience, inducing as much discomfort in Poland's friends as in its enemies. Britain made many a diplomatic *démarche* on behalf of the Poles; Turkey never let an opportunity pass to show its disapproval of the partitions; the French Chamber of Deputies opened every session after 1830 with a solemn declaration of its wish for a free Poland. Yet they were all only too keen to bury the issue under a few pious phrases whenever it began to threaten the stability of Europe.

But as the tide of support for the Polish cause ebbed in the chancelleries it surged in other quarters. It was characteristic that a Polish commemorative meeting held in London in 1841 should have had as its principal speaker a black man from Haiti. As Engels pointed out, every workers' movement of the nineteenth century only ventured beyond its own sphere of interests to make a gesture or a pronouncement on the Polish Question. In 1848 the Paris mob marched on the Hôtel de Ville to cries of '*Vive la Pologne!*', and their sentiment was echoed by the Chartists in England, the Berlin workers who carried Mierosławski shoulder-high out of the Moabit jail, and by every Italian activist from Mazzini to Garibaldi. It was not gimmickry that put the slogan 'For Your Freedom and

Ours' on the Polish standards in 1831; the Polish nation was the founder member of the *internationale* of peoples arrayed against the Holy Alliance of monarchs.

In the resolution he submitted to the Central Council of the First International, Karl Marx explained that the Poles' struggle for freedom was carried on in the common interest, as without an independent Poland the whole of Europe was threatened by Russian autocracy, and what happened in Poland had an immediate and crucial bearing on the course of events elsewhere. In 1792 the Russian armies which Catherine had hoped to use against Revolutionary France were deployed instead in Poland. The same happened in 1830. As Lafayette explained to the French Chamber: 'The war had been prepared against us . . . Poland was to form the vanguard: the vanguard has turned against the main body of the army.' Had Poland regained her independence it would have been more difficult for Austria to maintain its hegemony in northern Italy, for Russia to expand its influence in the Balkans, and for Prussia to establish its ascendancy in Germany. At the same time, a Poland carved up between the three powers sealed their cooperation with the enduring bond of complicity and mutual self-interest which was the greatest impediment to change of any kind.

And the exclusion of Poles from active public life at home gave rise to a tribe of wanderers who had an impact elsewhere. Their presence was most noticeable in wars and revolutions. They fought in the French colonial wars and in the Spanish civil wars; they fought for Garibaldi and for the Paris Commune; they fought in the northern and southern hemispheres, and on both sides of the Atlantic. The Shah of Persia had two Polish regiments in his Imperial Guard. In America, the first officer to die for the Union in 1860 was a Captain Blandowski. Another 4,000 Poles fought for the Union, many in the 58th New York Infantry or Colonel

Krzyżanowski's United States Rifles, while a further 1,000 fought in the Confederate Army. It was in Ottoman service that such men found a lasting refuge, as staff officers, artillerymen, engineers, cartographers and surgeons. Poles could rise to high positions, provided they embraced Islam, which many did.

Typical is Aleksander Iliński, a wealthy nobleman who fought in the 1830 insurrection and then went into exile. He took service in the Polish legion organised by General Bem in the Portuguese army, then fought in the Spanish Civil War (developing a sideline as a successful bullfighter), and for the French in Algeria, winning the Légion d'Honneur in the process, followed by service in Afghanistan, India and China. In 1848 he was at General Bem's side in Hungary, whence he made his way to Turkey. He converted to Islam and fought in the Crimean War as General Iskinder Pasha. He later became Turkish governor of Baghdad before dying in Istanbul in 1861.

Such a wide dispersal of the nation's human resources raised the possibility of its extinction, particularly as the Polish nation had never been based on ethnic, territorial, religious or political affinities. When the state ceased to exist the diverse elements that made it up might have been expected to fly off like so many satellites deprived of the centre of their orbit. Yet, instead of disintegrating into its component parts, a Polish nation survived, albeit in a somewhat changed, and forever changing, form. 'Polishness' had become a condition which defined itself.

But given that the Commonwealth had excluded over nine-tenths of the population from active participation, those who wished to promote the Polish national project needed to win over a sizeable proportion of the others. And they had to give it new form: to an age that viewed an efficient centralised state as desirable, the Commonwealth, like the recently defunct Holy Roman Empire, appeared anachronistic and deeply flawed. Its greatest achievement, a minimalist, multi-cultural democracy, was not one that appeared viable to the nineteenth-century mind. If the Polish patriots were to entice the passive and the peasants to embrace their cause, they would have to come up with a better project.

In this they were greatly aided by the incompetence of the occupying powers, particularly Russia. For while it would be too much to say that the new nation was forged in the struggle, the successive risings punctuated a process of thought and self-discovery which might otherwise have turned into meaningless waffle. They also tested theories and destroyed illusions.

The experience of 1794 made it clear that there was little national consciousness among the peasants. The military activity of 1797–1815 did involve greater numbers, at least a quarter of a million men, in a way that mixed aristocrats with peasants and initiated a significant number of people from the lower orders to the cult of the national cause. The events of 1830–31 showed up a divergence of interest in different social groups, which the risings of 1846 and 1848 were intended to remove by radicalising the issue. In the event, these two risings showed up the pointlessness of amateurs taking on empires with little more than slogans for ammunition. The rising of 1863 was marked by greater professionalism and tactical sense, as well as by large-scale participation of peasants, workers, Lithuanians, Belorussians and Jews, but it also revealed that warfare had taken a giant technological step forward.

Each of these struggles highlighted various implications of the Polish predicament, and their increasingly ruthless repression committed more people to participation in activities which they might have originally viewed as futile or even irresponsible. The minor szlachta, traditionally the most reactionary element in the population, were progressively turned into revolutionary extremists. By dispossessing landowners who were involved often very indirectly in resistance, the occupying powers forced the most docile members of the community into violent opposition. By penalising members of the aristocracy they forced even this into some measure of resistance. Families which in the 1820s saw their interest as lying in allegiance to St Petersburg or Vienna were otherwise convinced by the image of Prince Sanguszko walking to Siberia in a chain gang and by the Galician butchery of 1846. The old szlachta solidarity of shared privilege turned into one of shared wrong, and this embraced anyone who identified with Poland, opening up a new channel of inter-class dialogue. And this dialogue concerned two principal issues: where they had gone wrong, and how they should go about constructing a programme for the future.

The Czartoryski faction, the political descendant of the Familia and the Patriots of the Great Sejm, held that the constitution of 3 May would have cured the ailing Commonwealth. They believed that Poland's eclipse was not the result of internal failure but the consequence of a breakdown in the proper functioning of diplomacy. Their efforts after 1831 were directed at convincing European statesmen of the desirability of restoring Poland to Europe in the interests of the balance of power.

The socialist elements among the émigrés were influenced by the works of the historian Joachim Lelewel, leader of the Patriotic Society and a member of the insurrectionary government in 1831. Lelewel had developed a theory that the social and political structure of ancient Slav societies in the pre-Christian era had been based on peasant communities. It was a vision of rural democracy later favoured by Russian historians and it held a strong attraction for many on the left of the political spectrum. According to Lelewel the constitution of 3 May was a piece of Western liberalism alien to the spirit of Polish society.

The manifesto of the Polish Democratic Society, published at Poitiers in 1836, rejected the liberal idea of giving the peasants their land – i.e. turning them into mini-capitalists. 'The question of property is the question of our age,' it proclaimed, in the conviction that 'The land and its fruits are common to all.' It therefore concluded that 'Private property must be transformed into common property.' The majority of the Democrats were minor szlachta who had lost everything. Offended by the prosperity and materialism they encountered in London and Paris, they yearned for revolution, spiritual as much as political.

The English section of the Democratic Society, founded at Portsmouth in 1834, gave rise the following year to a Community of the Polish People whose manifesto, written by Stanisław Worcell, a former member of the wealthy szlachta and son of a senator, contained the phrase: 'Property is the root of all evil.' It established settlements in Portsmouth and on the island of Jersey, agricultural communes consisting of peasants and penitent gentry who sought regeneration through work. Though most émigrés did not go to such extremes, they did live out theories and beliefs, in damp London basements and freezing Paris garrets, or in Tsarist chain gangs or Austrian gaols.

With the Poles divided between three empires and scattered in exile, the printed word assumed enormous significance, and the fact that this was an age rich in literary talent ensured that the men setting up communes in Portsmouth and Jersey were not cut off from their fellows who had remained in Poland to farm their estates.

The first traces of Romanticism in Polish literature appear in the 1790s. The heart began to rule the mind just as the ravished motherland was being enslaved; the Polish Romantic heart could beat for no other unattainable object of love. The poets of the day wrote of the expiring Commonwealth as lovers. Their successors sang the praises of her vanished accomplishments and would go on to give spiritual meaning to their own lives.

The greatest poet of the age, Adam Mickiewicz (1798–1855), was a case in point. A student at Wilno University, Mickiewicz had started out writing lyrical works. In 1822 he published *Ballads and Romances*, which earned him critical acclaim, and in the following year *Grażyna* and part of *Forefathers' Eve*. The first is a tale of self-sacrifice and honour culled from historical folklore, the second a dramatic work based on the pagan Lithuanian custom of invoking the dead on All Souls' Eve, which presents a series of tortured souls recounting their errors and sufferings. In the same year Mickiewicz was imprisoned. He was exiled to St Petersburg, and in 1825 to Odessa, where he wrote *Crimean Sonnets*. In Odessa he shared a mistress with the chief of police for southern Russia, who secured him a transfer back to Moscow. There he made friends with a number of Russian writers including Pushkin and came to understand, and to fear more than ever, the nature of the Russian state. It was in 1828 that he published, in *Konrad Wallenrod*, his first overtly political poem.

This historical tale about a Lithuanian child captured by the Teutonic Knights and brought up as one of them, rising to the Grand Mastership of the Order and then leading its armies to defeat at the hands of his own people, explores the idea of patriotic action through collaboration with the enemy. In the third part of *Forefathers' Eve* (1832), Mickiewicz touched on the whole range of moral and ethical problems confronting the Poles in captivity, and on the questions of good and evil in political life.

In 1834 he published *Pan Tadeusz*, a mock-heroic evocation of country life in Lithuania. Written in Paris at a time when Mickiewicz had already condemned the values of the Commonwealth and was leaning heavily towards the left of émigré politics, it could hardly be more telling. As they searched for answers to present problems, such men could not avoid hankering for the past. The quest for the lost state of innocence, present in Polish literature from the sixteenth century, was becoming inextricably confused with the quest of the lost motherland, or rather, the state of being that had vanished with it. For the émigrés in particular, Arcadia became indistinguishable from Poland.

At the same time, Mickiewicz concerned himself with the plight of all those, languishing in prison or exile, who suffered for their cause in an apparently indifferent world. In *The Books of the Polish Nation* (1832) he suggested that Poland had been crucified in the cause of righteousness. The crucifixion would expiate the political sins of the world and lead to resurrection. This messianic image gave hope. Christ too had cried out on the Cross and had been answered with silence, but by His death He had conquered death itself. Through their sacrifice the Poles would conquer persecution.

Few were naïve enough to take this literally, but at some level of the subconscious the messianic vision was a healing balm for every suffering Polish soul, which instinctively rejected a reality that excluded its aspirations. Nor were they exceptional in this: both Mazzini and the French historian Jules Michelet also developed visions of Italy and France respectively redeeming the world through their own crucifixion. It was not so much a question of escapism, as a search for a deeper truth.

The philosopher Bronisław Trentowski (1808–69), a pupil of Hegel, evolved a national philosophy of action and attempted to produce a practical programme for the 'regeneration' of Poland. Very close to him was the remarkable figure of Józef Maria Hoene-Wroński (1776–1853). Bafflingly, he fought for Kościuszko at Maciejowice, served on Suvorov's staff and in Dąbrowski's legions within the space of four years. He settled in France, where in 1804 he had a vision of 'the absolute', and published a vast corpus of work, some of it purely mathematical, but most of it devoted to restructuring the relationship between science and life. He tried to elaborate a system of history in which the fate of Poland played a seminal part.

In 1848 Mickiewicz went to Rome to raise a Polish legion,

whose uniform was marked by a large cross. While it battled against the Austrians in Lombardy, he returned to Paris to edit the international socialist periodical *La Tribune des Peuples*. A devout if at times rebellious Christian, Mickiewicz kept trying to arrive at a synthesis of Christian Socialism and to construct a programme of action which fitted the historical moment.

By the late 1840s the thinking of people such as Mickiewicz and his colleague the poet Juliusz Słowacki (1809–49) was going round in diminishing circles, becoming almost pathological. This was inherent in the conundrum of their predicament, and partly the result of poverty and personal misery. Słowacki dying of tuberculosis in Paris and the poverty-stricken Mickiewicz supporting seven children and a wife who had lost her senses could not be expected to take anything but an embittered view.

More aristocratic Poles grouped around the Czartoryski faction, which functioned like a kind of court in the magnificent Hôtel Lambert in Paris, and those artists who, like Chopin, were able to find a place in the mainstream of European culture and social life, were spared such extremes of suffering, and were therefore able to take a more balanced position. Of the three major Romantic poets Zygmunt Krasiński (1812–59) stood out in this respect. He was christened Napoleon Stanisław Zygmunt by his father, a general in the Grande Armée, but the first of these names was dropped as the general became a prominent reactionary in the Congress Kingdom and a trusted servant of the Tsar. The boy's life at school was marred by the unpopularity of his father, and he was eventually sent to complete his studies in Geneva. It was there that the outbreak of the 1830 rising found him. He was painfully torn between the desire to join his fellows in the rising and obedience to his father in St Petersburg, who forbade it.

While most Poles viewed the situation in terms of national oppression, and socialists as a struggle between revolution and reaction, Krasiński saw it in a different light. To him, the political status quo amounted to a dishonest and morally indefensible inversion of reality, which turned Russia into the guardian of legitimacy and lent Prussia a civilising mission to oppress Poland. The three powers had, by sleight of hand, turned the Polish cause into a revolutionary one, and the Austrian chancellor Metternich tried to convince the world that the Polish cause 'does not declare war on the monarchies which possess Polish territory, it declares war on all existing institutions and proclaims the destruction of all the common foundations which form the basis of society'.

To Krasiński, the Russian system was, as he put it in a letter to Pope Pius IX, 'a huge merciless machine, working by night and by day, crushing thousands of hearts and minds every minute . . . the irreconcilable enemy of all spiritual independence'. It was the bureaucratic apparatus of the police state that was the real enemy of European civilisation, and it was all the more dangerous for masquerading as its champion, since it perversely encouraged and strengthened the forces of revolution, which were equally destructive. He saw Poland as the only possible counterbalance to both. 'To make Poland a free, constitutional, moderate state would be to save her, and with her the world,' he explained in a letter to Louis-Philippe's minister François Guizot. 'It would at one stroke kill all the wild hopes of the Tsars and the destructive hopes of the demagogues, whose very real power is based on the profound and hideous injustice of the present European system.'

He was, ultimately, arguing the cause of the anti-statist values of the Commonwealth. In a remarkable play he wrote at this time, *The Undivine Comedy*, he foresaw that the current belief in the state over the individual would lead to greater repression and finally revolution, a revolution that would throw up demagogic tyrants. The character of the tyrant in his play is grimly prophetic of Stalin and Hitler.

If Krasiński's perception was cooler than that of his peers, he lacked the conviction that sustained Mickiewicz to his bitter end, brought on by cholera in Turkey in 1855 while attempting to raise a Jewish force for the liberation of Palestine. Krasiński could see no promise in any programme. He too went through a phase of messianic exaltation: 'Where there is pain, there is life, there is resurrection,' he wrote to Słowacki. Ultimately, the poets and the philosophers had to admit that there was no answer to the Polish Question – no political answer and no spiritual answer. It remained a question of faith and hope. The only thing the Poles could do was to cling to their Polishness. Not their patriotism or their political hopes for the resurrection of Poland, but quite simply the state of mind of Polishness. As Krasiński exclaimed in his last major poem, *The Dawn*: 'you are no longer just my country; a place, a home, a way of life; the death of a state or its birth; but a Faith – a Law!'

SEVENTEEN

Captivity

Although the territory of the Commonwealth had been repeatedly cut and pasted since 1772, with almost every part of it coming under the domination of more than one of its neighbours, and in the case of the area around Warsaw under all three and the French as well, an immaterial but nevertheless real Polish world remained in existence throughout the period of partition. And at some level, most people who thought of themselves as Poles identified with that, not with the state they paid taxes to. Yet they were obliged to accommodate themselves to that state, and most were naturally inclined to do so, as it is the prosaic activities such as eating, working and breeding rather than spiritual issues that preoccupy men's minds for most of the time.

It was the inability of the three powers to provide a congenial framework for ordinary life and accommodate minimal cultural aspirations that kept their Polish provinces in an explosive condition. During a century when states such as Britain and France were able to control and exploit vast and populous colonies, the three greatest powers of the European mainland devoted incomparably greater resources in troops, funds and gigantic bureaucracies to policing a small, thinly populated and easily accessible country in their midst, with lamentable results. The only thing that made

Poland a difficult country to colonise was that the legacy of the Commonwealth did not include a native civil service or police force. The entire apparatus of social control had to be imported, with the result that authority never lost its alien garb.

It was Prussia that gained most in real terms from the partitions, and it should have had little trouble in digesting its share.

The lands of partitioned Poland, c.1860

Frontiers of Polish Commonwealth c. 1772
Frontiers of three partitioning powers
Boundary between the Congress Kingdom and Western Gubernias
Old Polish Basin
Dąbrova Basin
Galician Basin
Textile centres
Coal mining centres
Railways

SWEDEN

BALTIC SEA

RUSSIAN

To Petersburg

EAST PRUSSIA

Danzig

Wilno

PRUSSIA

WEST PRUSSIA

Minsk

To Berlin

GRAND DUCHY OF Posen POSEN

KINGDOM OF POLAND

WESTERN

GUBERNIAS

Białystok

Warsaw

Brest Litovsk

EMPIRE

Łódź

Żyrardów

Breslau

Radom

Kielce

Lublin

Kiev

Kraków

GALICIA

Lemberg

To Vienna

AUSTRIAN

EMPIRE

0   300 miles
0   400 km

TURKEY

Odessa

This was not large, it was hemmed in on three sides by Prussian lands, and it contained a significant number of people of German origin. The area that had fallen to Prussia in the first partition had been integrated into the Prussian kingdom, while Wielkopolska with the city of Poznań was defined in 1815 as the Duchy of Posen, a semi-autonomous province with its own (largely symbolic) representative bodies and a viceroy in the shape of Antoni Radziwiłł. The Prussian administration was heavy-handed, but on the whole conciliatory towards local Polish elites.

This changed in 1830, as many young men crossed the border into the Kingdom to take part in the insurrection (including about 1,000 from the Prussian army). When units of the Polish army sought refuge on Prussian territory in 1831, they were warmly greeted by Germans and Poles alike, but the Prussian army ill-treated the disarmed soldiers and either handed them back to the Russians or encouraged them to leave for France or Britain. The rising in the Kingdom had alarmed the Prussian authorities and the province lost some of its autonomy, along with its viceroy, and assimilation replaced conciliation as the underlying policy. But repressive measures associated with this were relaxed after the accession of Frederick William IV in 1840.

In 1848, however, the Germans of Poznania began to feel threatened by Polish aspirations, and their fears, couched in strident calls for the 'defence of Germandom', met with a response from the nascent nationalism in Germany. The Poles were branded as 'a nation of lesser cultural content' by one speaker at the Frankfurt Parliament, and henceforth the emphasis was shifted onto a policy of Germanisation (*Germanisierung*). All remaining vestiges of autonomy in the Polish provinces were dismantled. Poles nevertheless took the majority of the thirty Poznanian seats in the Prussian Landtag.

The 1863 insurrection only confirmed the Prussian authorities in their view of the Poles as dangerous troublemakers. This was borne out further during the Franco-Prussian war of 1870. Although tens of thousands of Polish recruits fought in the Prussian ranks, the population staged pro-French demonstrations and failed to celebrate Prussia's victory.

The unification of Germany and the promotion of the Prussian kings to the status of German emperors in 1871 placed the Poles in a curious and unenviable situation: from being foreign subjects of the King of Prussia they were suddenly transformed into members of an ethnic minority in an emphatically German Germany. At the same time, the incorporation of the former Polish provinces into the empire meant that Polish deputies were returned to the German Reichstag, in which they took some 5 per cent of the seats, giving them a far greater degree of representation than in the Prussian Landtag. What had been a marginal colonial question now became an internal issue of the empire.

When Bismarck declared his *Kulturkampf* – the war on Catholic and regionalist tendencies in the empire – Polish deputies found new allies in the Catholics of Bavaria and Westphalia. The equation of Catholicism with 'foreignness' prompted Catholic Germans living in Poznania and Pomerania to identify with the Poles. Similarly, Pomeranian peasants who had never asked themselves whether they were Poles or Germans but knew that they were Catholics declared themselves to be Polish, since this had become synonymous with being Catholic.

The original Prussian analysis had been that once the Polish nobility and clergy had been emasculated, the peasant masses would turn into loyal Germans. In fact, while the parish clergy and the smaller landowners were nationalist, the Church hierarchy and the aristocracy had on the whole accommodated themselves to the reality of Prussian rule and were only obliged to change their stance under German pressure. The Archbishop of Poznań and Gniezno,

Mieczysław Ledóchowski, was fairly typical in his pro-German attitude, which made him unpopular with the Polish patriots and most parish priests. He did not protest too vigorously when, in 1872, Bismarck placed Catholic schools under German state supervision. But when priests who would not bow to all the new prescriptions were persecuted, he found himself obliged to make a stand. He was imprisoned as a result, in 1874, and turned into a national hero overnight. After this, Polish nationalists and the Catholic Church made a common front. Efforts by the authorities to arrest recalcitrant priests were thwarted by gangs of angry peasants. It was a formidable alliance, and it managed to blunt the main thrust of German colonial policy, which was aimed at the Polish language.

At the beginning of Prussian rule, Polish remained the language of instruction in the Polish schools of Poznania. In the 1870s it was gradually displaced by German, and in 1874 the use of Polish textbooks was forbidden. In 1876 German became the exclusive administrative language, and no other was countenanced in anything from a law court to a post office. In 1887 the study of Polish as a second language was abolished throughout the educational system. In 1900, the law that Polish be replaced by German even in religious education produced widespread school strikes. Instances of German police marching into churches to prevent children from praying in Polish, which were widely reported abroad, were counter-productive in more ways than one. Parish priests played a crucial role in the preservation of the language by holding clandestine classes, and this in turn endowed it with a degree of sanctity.

The clergy also helped the peasants in other ways, giving advice and information on everything from agriculture to taxation, and it was they who introduced the cooperative movement into Poznania in 1871. In 1886 Bismarck made a speech announcing a campaign to buy out Polish landowners, in which he suggested that they would be happier spending the cash at the roulette tables of Monte Carlo than farming their estates. A Colonisation Commission was set up with a capital of 100 million marks to finance this operation. The Polish landowners fought back by establishing their own Land Bank to bail out those in difficulty. In Pomerania the Prussian Junkers outpaced Poles in the battle for possession of land, but in Poznania the Poles held their own and even gained ground.

This was no mean achievement, as these provinces supported an intensive and competitive agricultural industry: by 1895 over 40 per cent of all farms had some machinery. This competitiveness created redundancy among the rural population (still 60 per cent of the whole), which led to large-scale emigration, particularly to the United States. Early emigrants set off in groups, often led by a priest, and established discrete settlements such as that founded in 1854 at Panna Maria in Texas, and later ones at Częstochowa, Polonia and Kościuszko in Texas, New Pozen in Nebraska, and others in Virginia and Wisconsin. This form of emigration merely relieved the pressure on land at home. But from the 1870s onwards new waves of emigration brought greater benefits. The later emigrants went primarily in search of work, and they found this in the industrial and mining centres of Pennsylvania, New Jersey, Michigan and Illinois. As well as setting aside part of their salary to support Polish priests and build their own churches, they also regularly sent money back to their families at home. Alternatively, a landless peasant could return home after twenty years in the Chicago canneries with enough capital in his pocket to buy a comfortable smallholding.

The year 1890 marked the end of the Bismarck era. The new Chancellor Leo von Caprivi made concessions to the Poles in return for their votes in the Reichstag. But this change of mood was not to last. In 1894 three Junkers founded the Deutscher Ostmark Verein, an organisation dedicated to promoting German interests in the east. It played on German phobias, invoking pseudo-scientific theories of Slav inferiority and fecundity, and received support from ruling circles. When visiting Marienburg Kaiser Wilhelm II called on the spirit of the dead Teutonic Knights to 'join the fight against Polish impudence and Sarmatian effrontery'.

The whole panoply of cultural, economic and political repression was once more brought to bear against the Poles. Government investment and officials poured into Poznania – the province had more of both than any other in the Reich. Officials and policemen who chose to retire there were given higher pensions. The Colonisation Commission bought up tracts of land and gave them to German colonists. Place names were replaced by German ones. In 1898 a series of special laws turned the Poles into second-class citizens.

As the pressure mounted, the Poles grew increasingly efficient and inventive. When it became illegal for them to buy land they set up cooperatives and, in 1897, a Land Purchase Bank, which bought the land and leased it back to them. When a law of 1904 forbade Poles to build houses on their land the peasant Michał Drzymała started a worldwide *cause célèbre* by setting up home in a circus caravan. It was a measure of the ingenious resilience of Poles of all classes that the government was finally obliged in 1908 to pass a stark expropriation law permitting compulsory purchase of Polish land by Germans.

What industry there had been in Poznania had all been in German hands, but in the 1870s the Poles began to take over. Hipolit Cegielski started a factory making agricultural machinery, then founded sugar refineries, and eventually built up a huge industrial complex in Poznań. Others followed suit. The need to help the Polish farmer impelled Poles into the cattle and grain markets, to cut out German and Jewish middlemen. Competition reached such a pitch that in the first decade of the twentieth century both sides began boycotting each other's businesses and shops, and since the majority of the market was Polish, the Germans lost out. Although the draconian legislation continued, they could not win the battle for the province.

The German-speaking population of Poznań fell between 1860 and 1890 from 41 to 34 per cent, and in Danzig (Gdańsk) from 75 to 72 per cent. In rural areas the drop was much sharper. Far from smothering the Polish element, the German tactics had hardened it, and indeed furnished it with allies. Attempts to enlist the Kashubians (a small Baltic people native to Pomerania) and the Mazurians (the natives of the southern part of East Prussia) as Germans were a fiasco, and in the 1890s both areas returned Polish deputies to the Reichstag. In 1903 Upper Silesia, which had been cut off from the Polish state since the fourteenth century, also returned a Pole, Wojciech Korfanty.

The Jewish inhabitants of the former Polish lands which fell under Prussian and then German rule were not, unless they had assimilated and identified with the Polish cause, subjected to the same rigours. Most transferred their loyalty from the Polish to the Prussian king with little reluctance. They came across discrimination on the part of the smaller established Jewish colonies of the major German cities, and some social exclusion. But as the century wore on and they attempted to play a more active part in their adopted state, they came up against a range of restrictions, particularly in the public sphere, and were barred, amongst other things, from being teachers and army officers.

As an authoritarian, militaristic Lutheran state, Prussia could have been expected to make a mess of ruling its Polish dominions. Austria, the only Catholic one of the three powers, should have had little trouble in absorbing hers. But the partitions had coincided with the reforms of Joseph II, which introduced regulation, enforced by a rigid bureaucracy, into every sphere of life, and this offended a society used to the minimalist administration of the Commonwealth. It also introduced comparably astronomical levels of taxation.

A representative assembly was set up in Lwów (now Lemberg) in 1817, but it was hampered by an army of administrators. These administrators also encouraged antagonism between the Poles and the Ukrainian and Jewish inhabitants, who between them made up about half of the population of 3.5 million. The Jews suffered cruelly as a result of mass conscription into the Austrian army, as this forced them to sin by wearing uniforms that mixed wool with cotton and to eat non-kosher food. Reforms in peasant–landlord relations hardly improved the status of the peasant and managed to bind both parties in a complicated system of fiscal and legal obligations which soured relations between them.

In 1841 a group of wealthy landowners led by Leon Sapieha founded a Land Credit Society, followed in 1844 by a Savings Bank and a Technical Academy, and in 1845 by a Galician Economic Association, but when at his instigation the Lemberg Assembly asked Vienna for permission to explore the possibility of reforming manor–cottage relations, it met with refusal. The Austrian chancellor Metternich was not inclined to allow cooperation between the Polish elites and the peasants. Austrian policy was revealed in all its cunning in 1846, when the Governor of Galicia, Count Stadion, incited the peasants against their landlords. That year even the unthreatening Lemberg Assembly was abolished. In 1848 Austria granted personal freedom and the possession of land to the peasants, and at the same time began to foster a national movement among the Ukrainians of eastern Galicia to undermine Polish influence there.

Martial law imposed after the disturbances of 1848 remained in force until 1854. The appointment of a Polish governor, Agenor Gołuchowski, was little more than a piece of window-dressing, since he was a loyalist trusted in Vienna. But things began to change in 1859. Austrian defeats in Italy signalled the beginning of a protracted crisis that would transform the structure of the Habsburg monarchy. Taking advantage of the situation, the Poles carried out their own reforms and by 1864 they had forced Austria to grant autonomy, with their own Sejm, a Polish viceroy to represent the emperor, and the right to send deputies to the Reichsrat in Vienna, in which they held some 15 per cent of the seats. Polish became the official language of Galicia, and education was left in the hands of the Lemberg Sejm. The addition of the former Republic of Kraków, abolished by Austria in 1846, added substance to the province and enriched it culturally.

For the next fifty years the inhabitants of Galicia were allowed to rule themselves. They also supplied more than their fair share of ministers and even prime ministers – Alfred Potocki, Kazimierz Badeni, Agenor Gołuchowski junior, Julian Dunajewski and others – to the Vienna cabinet. The wealthy szlachta of Galicia were supported by an influential conservative intelligentsia, and together they managed to keep more radical elements under control. They operated within the bounds imposed, concentrating their patriotic efforts on areas such as education.

In economic terms, Galicia was the most backward of the Polish lands. Great estates continued to operate on traditional lines, while tiny farms barely supported large peasant families. This caused unrest and led, in 1895, to the foundation of a Peasant Party, which brought about a strike of farm workers in 1902. It also caused waves of emigration to the United States, which eased conditions in the villages (the money sent back by the emigrants in the early 1900s has been calculated as $50 million per annum). The large

Jewish population was particularly vulnerable, and many of the shtetls in which they lived were sinks of poverty. The establishment of industries was hampered by competition from the Austrian empire's well-established industrial province of Bohemia. The only exceptions were coalmining and oil drilling. Oil was struck at Borysław in 1850, and by 1910 Galicia was the largest single producer in the world, with 5 per cent of the world market. But this was as nothing to the development achieved in the Russian partition.

Russia's Polish problem was more extensive and more crucial to its own internal affairs than was the case with either of the other two powers, and it offered a wider range of solutions. One was to incorporate all the Polish lands into the empire outright. Another was to leave them as a semi-autonomous unit which could be kept loyal by the promise that at some stage in the future a war against Prussia or Austria would lead to the recovery of Poznania and Galicia.

Russia tried both of these alternately. The lands of the Commonwealth taken by Russia were originally divided up into two categories: the large strip of Lithuanian, Belorussian and Ukrainian lands were incorporated into Russia as the Western Gubernias, while the rest, the Kingdom of Poland, was treated as a separate administrative and political entity. Between 1815 and 1830, and to a lesser extent between 1855 and 1863, Russia delegated its administration to the Poles themselves. For the rest of the century it ruled the area directly, with varying degrees of harshness. There were moments when the Western Gubernias were shunted closer to the Kingdom administratively, and others when the Kingdom itself was abolished and turned into a province of the Russian empire. This lack of consistency served Russian interests poorly. And in economic terms, the Kingdom on the whole profited from arrangements meant to disadvantage it.

The transformation of the Congress Kingdom from a predominantly agricultural economy began after 1815. Stanisław Staszic, who had been appointed Director of the Department of Industry in 1816, encouraged the development of mining and reactivated the production of steel in the Old Polish Basin around Kielce. He built the first zinc mills and the first steel-rolling mill, and organised a Mining Corps run on semi-military lines with a remarkable system of compensation and pensions. The production of iron, copper and zinc increased. Coalmining, which began to use steam power for pumping, doubled its output between 1824 and 1836. The 1830s and 1840s saw continued development in spite of political problems and a new smelting centre was developed in the Dąbrowa Basin, whose Huta Bankowa was one of the largest steelworks in the world.

The process was masterminded by Franciszek Ksawery Drucki-Lubecki. In 1821 he took over the Treasury, which became the leading entrepreneur. He sought to build up Poland's economy in such a way as to make it industrially self-sufficient. His efforts were cut short by the 1830 insurrection, but some of his creations, such as the Bank of Poland established in 1828, carried on his programme. He brought new ideas to the Polish economic scene, including direct intervention, credit and protection. In 1825 he set up the Land Credit Society, which enabled private estates to clear debts and fund improvements or new ventures. Chief among these were sheep-rearing, distilling and the production of sugar-beet which, with the building of the first sugar refinery in 1826, opened up an important new avenue of agricultural industry.

The most spectacular product of Lubecki's policies was the Polish textile industry. In 1821 the government assisted the establishment of a weaving centre in the village of Łódź. By 1830 Łódź had over 4,000 inhabitants and a number of steam-powered spinning machines. The production of wool tripled between 1823 and 1829, and the production of cotton quintupled between 1825 and 1830. Łódź exported to Russia and even China, and by 1845, when it was linked by rail to Warsaw, it had become the principal supplier of the Russian market. By then Łódź had 20,000 inhabitants, although it was now in competition with new textile centres at Białystok and Żyrardów, started in 1833. Between 1865 and 1879 the number of power looms in Łódź increased twenty-fold. The value of production of cotton rose from five million roubles in 1869 to 25 million in 1889. By 1900 Łódź had 300,000 inhabitants and over 1,000 factories.

This industrial revolution was unspectacular by European standards, yet the pace was breathtaking. The number of steam engines in use increased twenty-five times between 1853 and 1888. Overall industrial production increased by over six times between 1864 and 1885. Centres such as Łódź, Warsaw (which reached over half a million inhabitants in the 1880s) and the Dąbrowa Basin employed a workforce which doubled over the twenty years after 1860 to some 150,000. Fortunes were made and lost in the speculative ventures to which the boom gave rise. Foreign capital, often brought in by entrepreneurs who came to settle, flooded in from France, Germany, England, Belgium and Italy, accounting for up to 40 per cent of the entire industrial capital. A new class of Polish tycoons sprang up, mostly from the Jewish population of the cities. Families like the Kronenbergs, Rotwands, Wawelbergs and Epszteins amassed wealth, became assimilated into Polish society and married into the aristocracy.

These developments were closely connected to Russian policy. Between 1819 and 1822 the Kingdom was part of the same customs area as Russia. In 1831 a tariff barrier was imposed between the two states. These tariffs were imposed and lifted several times, often for political reasons, creating enormous problems for Polish industry. In the 1870s Russia switched to protectionist policies, within which the Kingdom was included, and this created the conditions for the Polish boom of the next decades. Three-quarters of the cotton produced in Łódź in the 1880s was exported to Russia. The metallurgical industry of Warsaw and the Old Polish Basin increased its output by over thirty times in the last quarter of the century, largely as a result of the expansion of railways in the Russian Empire. The Lilpop railcar and rail factory in Warsaw was the largest in the whole empire and grew fat on the spread of the Russian network. By the 1890s Russia accounted for 90 per cent of Poland's trade, a huge captive market.

In the late 1890s Russia began her own industrial revolution, which meant that engineers and technicians trained in Poland found new scope for their skills. Hundreds of these men invaded the empire to build bridges, lay tracks and manage mines and factories from the Urals to Manchuria, some building up vast fortunes in the process. After digging tunnels for the Trans-Siberian railway, Alfons Kozieł-Poklewski went on to become one of the richest men in the Russian Empire, owning goldmines, diamond mines, steel mills, distilleries and a string of other concerns. Even some of those who had been exiled to Siberia for revolutionary activity ended up building sizeable fortunes in cities such as Tomsk and Irkutsk. At the economic level, the colonial relationship was reversed and favoured the Poles rather than Russians.

This was not so in agriculture, which, being the economic base of the szlachta, was subject to political considerations. It also involved the peasants and their relationship with the szlachta, which had a direct bearing on their ability to mobilise the masses in support of the Polish cause. The manner in which peasant emancipation was introduced in 1864 was almost entirely shaped by such considerations. The decree was rich in phrases such as 'the lords who have oppressed you', which were supposed to give the peasants the impression that it was the Tsar who was liberating them from the szlachta. The idea was to drive a wedge between the szlachta and the peasant, and to ruin the minor szlachta, perceived as the most patriotic section of society.

There were five areas which the decree tackled: the abolition of labour-rents; the commutation of money-rents into freehold possession of land; the distribution of land to landless peasants; grazing and wood-gathering rights on manorial land; and finally the setting up of peasant councils under tsarist administration which would put an end to landowners' influence over village affairs.

The consequences were not long in making themselves felt. The landless peasants were given too little land to survive on. The compensation to the landlords was paid out not in cash as in Russia, but in negotiable bonds which immediately plummeted in value. Thousands of small landowners had to sell up and move to the towns. Large estates were hardly affected. Their owners had mostly switched to money-rents long before, they had capital reserves to employ farmhands and bribe local officials, and they could afford to fight in the courts over pastures and grazing rights.

The richer peasants bought out the hitherto landless who had been given plots too small to survive on. While land in peasant ownership increased by nearly 10 per cent in the next twenty-five years, the number of landless peasants increased by 400 per cent during the same period. The doubling of the population in the second half of the century only aggravated the land hunger.

The economic ruin of thousands of szlachta families did not have the hoped-for consequences. Many of those who remained in the country assimilated with the richer yeoman-peasants, strengthening defiance in the villages. Those who drifted to the cities brought their values and their patriotism into the middle classes into which they married.

Russian policies were similarly counter-productive when it came
to matters of religion. The partitions had pulled the Polish province
of the Church to pieces. Six dioceses found themselves in Austrian
Poland, under the primacy of the Metropolitan of Lwów. Warmia
(Ermland) and Wrocław (Breslau) were directly affiliated to Rome.
The rest of the dioceses incorporated into Prussia were placed
under the administration of the Protestant Church of Prussia. The
dioceses of the Western Gubernias were subordinated to the Metropolitan of Mogilev, while those of the Kingdom were placed under
the newly created Archbishopric of Warsaw. After 1830 there was
not even a nominal Primate.

The Papacy, intent on preserving its diminishing temporal
status, was wary of antagonising the partitioning powers, and went
so far as to condemn the uprisings of 1794 and 1830. It was in no
position to protect the Polish hierarchy in the lands of the former
Commonwealth. The Josephine reforms had subjected the clergy
of Austria to the state, and this was extended to Galicia. Prussia
gradually confiscated Church property in the course of the century
and took over the appointment of bishops, but stopped short of
the kind of measures adopted by Russia.

In 1801 the Polish Church was subjected to a secular administrative body in St Petersburg. After 1831 half of the convents and
monasteries on former Polish territory were closed down. After 1864
all Church property was confiscated and monastic orders disbanded.
The clergy were forbidden to write to Rome. Seminaries and other
Church institutions were placed under a police inspectorate, and
sermons had to be passed by the censor. In 1870 the government
decreed that the Catholic liturgy was henceforth to be said in
Russian. Recalcitrant priests were flogged or deported to Siberia
and peasants were terrorised by the police, but there was such
determined resistance that the authorities relented and in 1882
signed a Concordat with Rome, which laid down the conditions

under which the faith could be practised. But this did not herald any fundamental change of attitude. When the young Nicholas II visited Warsaw in 1897, he gave orders for the building of a vast Orthodox church dedicated to St Alexander in the middle of its largest central square.

Russian policy towards the Uniates was even more draconian. In 1773, after the first partition, Catherine II sent troops into the villages to convert them to the Orthodox faith. The persecution abated after her death, but Nicholas took up the crusade for Orthodoxy with a vengeance. Between 1826 and 1838 a huge operation was mounted which has been likened to Stalin's purges. Uniate peasants were ordered to abjure their faith, and children were mutilated and butchered before their mothers if they refused. Where even this failed, massacres and deportations ensued. A further such campaign was carried out in the 1870s. These crusades failed to stamp out the Uniates, who would hold undercover services in woods or across the border in Galicia. Instead of inspiring loyalty to St Petersburg, it made them look to Poland and to Austria as havens of toleration, and contributed to the rise of Ukrainian nationalism.

Whether they were Ukrainians or Poles, the peasants tended to identify first and foremost with religion and language. It followed that they remained loyal to their Church, and not always just for religious reasons: throughout the nineteenth century the village priest was the peasant's adviser and support in the struggle against oppression and injustice. They also resented state interference in education, particularly when it came to language.

The educational system in the Western Gubernias had been Russified after 1831. After 1864 a set of new edicts forbade the use of Polish in printed form, even on shop fronts and hoardings, while written Polish was forbidden in official correspondence. At one stage it even became illegal to give Polish Christian names at baptism.

Legislation in the Kingdom was less harsh. Nevertheless, in 1869 the Warsaw Main School, founded in 1862 as a substitute for the university, abolished in 1831, was shut down and in turn replaced by a Russian university. In 1885 Russian was substituted for Polish as the teaching language, even in elementary schools. Children were not allowed to address each other in anything but Russian within the precincts of the school.

As the tsarist government clamped down, secret classes were organised to teach Polish and history as well as religious instruction. A 'flying university' operated lectures and exams for hundreds of students at secret locations. According to Russian sources, clandestine education at some level involved one-third of the entire population of the Kingdom by 1901. Conspiracy, illegal presses and the smuggling of books once again became part of the everyday experience of Polish society.

Poles lived out the nineteenth century in a continuously changing state of dislocation: life went on, children were born, money was made and lost, in a physical environment that would have been familiar to any contemporary in England, France or Germany, but one that was sporadically shaken by the intrusion of brutality from above and subversion from below, most of it irrational and groundless, necessitating changes of outlook and positioning with regard to the system and within society. The attendant strain, mental, emotional and psychological, marked Polish society all the more as it refused to accept this state of affairs, and continually tried to regain control of its destiny, by rational means, through word, print and, where possible, action.

EIGHTEEN

Nation-Building

The commander of the Paris Commune in its final stages was the Polish émigré Jarosław Dąbrowski, who had been the first military leader of the 1863 rising. As French government troops closed in on the communards, he rallied a group of sailors and led them in a heroic but suicidal attack. In another part of the city, another Polish émigré, Florian Trawiński, was surreptitiously draining paraffin from the barrels placed all over the Louvre by the Commune for the purpose of burning it down. Dąbrowski's body lay in state at the Hôtel de Ville before being buried with full honours, and to this day he has streets named after him in every Polish town. Trawiński was subsequently appointed a director of the Louvre, awarded the Légion d'Honneur and ended up as Secrétaire Général des Musées de France.

By then, few in Poland would have felt any hesitation in deciding which of these two acts was of greater value. The self-evident point-lessness of all the revolutionary effort of 1848 and the failure of the 1863 insurrection provided powerful arguments to those opposed to armed struggle, and by that time a strong reaction had set in against romantic gesture and useless sacrifice.

This was underpinned intellectually from the mid-1860s by a group of historians at Kraków's Jagiellon University who suggested that the Commonwealth's downfall had not been a martyrdom of the innocent, but the deserved collapse of a state which had ceased to function because of the blindness of its citizens and the inefficiency of its political institutions. They saw the tradition of insurrection in the same light. It followed from this that the road to independence lay not through insurrection but through self-improvement and societal progress.

This was not a new thought. In 1841, Karol Marcinkowski, a returned political émigré, set up a Society for Scientific Assistance in Poznań whose purpose was to provide grants for young Poles to go and study at the best universities of Germany. Two years later he established the Poznań Bazaar, a managerial school. He preached self-improvement and education to all classes, stressing that everyone could make a difference to their predicament.

Under the influence of people such as Marcinkowski, and with the active participation of parish clergy, the Polish inhabitants of Poznania had implemented a programme of 'organic work' through which to carry on the struggle for national survival; they would stand up to the Germans by keeping their houses cleaner, tending their livestock and crops with greater care, working harder and educating themselves and their children. But it was not until the latter part of the century that such ideas achieved the status of theory.

The works of Auguste Comte, John Stuart Mill and Charles Darwin appeared to many to hold special relevance to the situation in Poland, and under their influence the Romantic concept of the nation as spirit gradually gave way to one of the nation as an organism. The high priest of this Positivist Movement (as it became known) was Aleksander Świętochowski, fittingly not a poet but a journalist. Throughout the 1880s he edited the Warsaw weekly *Prawda* (Truth), one of a range of periodicals which spawned a horde of essayists and publicists who criticised old habits of thought, questioned sacred values, and dwelt on the material aspects of everyday life. The ingredients of the new literature were to be, according to the writer Eliza Orzeszkowa, 'a burgher, a banker, a factory-owner, a merchant, tails and top hats, machines, surgeons' instruments, locomotives'. Next to the periodical, the principal pulpit for these views was the stage.

The dramatic works of Mickiewicz, Słowacki and Krasiński were not written for the stage, since there had been no theatre in which they could be performed. As they were taken up with ethical or political argument and relied heavily on symbolism, they took a fantastical, disembodied form unique in European drama. The new theatres which did spring up in the 1860s, in Poznań, Lwów, Kraków and later Warsaw, encouraged a more realistic dramatic tradition and dwelt on everyday matters.

The novel and the short story were not far behind. It was Eliza Orzeszkowa (1841–1910) who broke the tradition of the Romantic historical novel and developed it as an instrument of social investigation and ethical polemic. She was a spirited woman from Lithuania who had taken an active part in the 1863 insurrection before settling down to a life of writing. An ardent feminist, she was also concerned with breaking down the barriers of social constraint in the interests of other groups caught in the trap of poverty or prejudice, most notably the Jews. Another woman, Gabriela Zapolska (1857–1921), wrote novels and plays which dwelt more specifically on the exploitation of women by society. The most talented woman writer of the period was Maria Konopnicka (1842–1910), who separated from her husband after ten years of marriage in order to devote herself to writing.

The frequent imprisonment or exile of the menfolk in a family left women in positions of responsibility for its survival, and their participation in conspiratorial and even guerrilla activity tended to place them on an equal footing with men. As a result, they were voicing views and demands on the subject of sexual equality and freedom that were not heard in England or France until the next century.

One of the most formative writers where young men were concerned was the Nobel Prize winner Henryk Sienkiewicz (1846–1916). Ostensibly a Positivist dedicated to the diagnosis and cure of social ills, Sienkiewicz also displayed a Romantic nationalism not entirely in keeping with the current ideology. He indulged this by writing a trilogy – *With Fire and Sword*, *The Deluge* and *Pan Wołodyjowski* – a historical adventure covering the Cossack Mutiny, the Swedish Wars and the Turkish war of the mid-seventeenth century, written to comfort and to boost the morale of the Poles. It met with huge success and heavily influenced how the Poles of the next generations would see themselves and their national destiny.

A more typical figure and the best Polish novelist of the nineteenth century was Aleksander Głowacki (1847–1912), who wrote under the pen name of Bolesław Prus. He was a member of the minor szlachta, but his penniless father was a functionary and his education was cut short for lack of money. He was wounded during the insurrection of 1863 and spent some time in prison after it. As a young man he had been fascinated by mathematics and the natural sciences, which he had studied at Warsaw's Main School before being obliged to earn his living as a contributor of humorous pieces to periodicals. He went on to write two of the greatest novels in the Polish canon, exploring the major questions, existential as well as national, facing Polish society with a degree of scepticism that inspired reflection.

Positivism and the programme of organic work which accompanied it produced impressive results. Everything from hygiene to education was affected. People with brains were encouraged to use them to pursue specific goals rather than waste them on planning hopeless risings. It is largely thanks to this that Poland did not disappear from the intellectual map of Europe along with its frontiers.

Compared with other European nations, the Poles contributed little to the scientific advances of the nineteenth century. Ignacy Łukasiewicz succeeded in distilling crude oil in Galicia and built the first kerosene lamp in 1853; Zygmunt Wróblewski and Karol Olszewski of the Jagiellon University were the first to achieve the liquefaction of oxygen; in 1898 Maria Skłodowska-Curie discovered Polonium and went on to pioneer research into radiation; the organic chemist Jakub Natanson, the biochemist Marceli Nencki and others added in various ways to the sum of human knowledge. Science was a politically neutral sphere.

The arts, on the other hand, were profoundly marked by their subjection to the national cause or to that of social progress. When disaster overtook the Commonwealth, artists began to render not the present but the past, often in idealised form. This gave rise to a tradition of patriotic genre painting – lancers on picket duty, Husaria at the charge and other scenes which implied the glories of the past. After the death of the Romantic poets, this function of painting took on extra significance. It was indulged with greater abandon by artists such as Artur Grottger (1837–67), who covered the 1863 insurrection in a series of symbolic scenes, and Jan Matejko (1838–93), best known for monumental canvases of great moments in Polish history which embalmed for all time the myths and heroes of a bygone age. Others concentrated on subjects, such as peasants or Jews, which raised social and national issues. This set them apart not only from the Romantic historicists, but also from those who swam in the mainstream of European art and embraced trends such as Impressionism.

Every generation contributed new writers, some of whom, such as the novelist Stefan Żeromski (1864–1925), carried the political debate forward, scouring every aspect of life and evaluating everything from the historical past to social institutions, philanthropic initiatives and cooperative ventures. Another, Władysław Reymont (1867–1925), the son of a village organist, was in turn a tailor's apprentice, a monk, a clerk and several other things before he became a writer and won the Nobel Prize. His *Promised Land* (1899), a Zola-esque novel set in the rapidly expanding industrial centre of Łódź, provides his verdict on the Positivist faith in regeneration through material progress:

> Villages were abandoned, forests were felled, the earth was deprived of its treasures, rivers dried up, people were born – all for that 'Promised Land', for that polyp which sucked them in, crushed and chewed up people and things, the sky and the earth, giving in exchange useless millions to a few and hunger and hard work to the masses.

These writers would be followed by waves of others adhering to new literary and stylistic canons. But whatever angle they came at it from, they all contributed to a sustained process of nation-building, if only by bringing together and enlarging a thinking readership that spanned not only the Russian, German and Austro-Hungarian empires, but also western Europe, the United States and South America. And this readership could ill afford to waste time on past glories or sophisticated new trends, as the question of what kind of a Polish world they wanted to recreate was taking on real urgency.

What most of them understood by the term 'Poland' was the territory of the Commonwealth and the community of peoples it embraced. But while much effort had gone into bringing the other orphan peoples of the Commonwealth into the cause, with some success, as the 1863 insurrection had demonstrated, these were now being drawn in other directions by new national movements.

The Lithuanians were a case in point. They had their own language, their own culture and a long history, but in the thirteenth century their rulers had extended their sway over vast areas of Belorussia and Ukraine to create a Grand Duchy of Lithuania in which the ethnic Lithuanians were a minority. That minority diminished as Lithuanian lords embraced first Russian and then Polish culture: the last grand duke who spoke Lithuanian died in the year Columbus discovered the new world.

A Lithuanian national revival began in the first half of the nineteenth century, and although its supporters made common cause with Polish patriots at first, there was an inherent conflict. The failure of the 1863 insurrection, which demonstrated to them that there was nothing to be gained from alliance with the Poles, marked a parting of the ways. In its search for distinctiveness, Lithuanian nationalism began to define itself against Poland and Polish culture, and particularly against the inclusive culture of the Commonwealth.

It also, perversely, laid claim to the heritage of the whole Grand Duchy of Lithuania, the majority of whose population was Belarusian or Ukrainian, and whose elites were overwhelmingly Polish. This brought it into conflict not only with the Polish inhabitants, but also with the budding Belarusian nationalist movement, which also laid claim to the whole Grand Duchy. The city of Wilno, now Russian Vilna, was a microcosm of the problem: its population was overwhelmingly Polish and only 2 per cent spoke Lithuanian, yet it was claimed, on historical grounds, by the Lithuanians as well as the Belarusians, who brushed aside Polish claims, and ignored the fact that one-third of its population was Jewish.

Similar problems bedeviled the nascent Ukrainian national movement, which was in competition with both Polish and Russian influences, both of which exerted cultural and religious magnetic fields. Its claim to the legacy of Kievan Rus was disputed by Russian nationalists, who dismissed Ukrainian as a dialect of Russian. The

RIGHT: King Zygmunt III. Contemporary portrait by an unknown artist.

BELOW: Władysław IV taking the surrender of the Muscovite army outside Smolensk in September 1633.

LEFT: The Lubomirski stronghold of Winicz, built by Matteo Trapola between 1615 and 1621.

ABOVE: Łukasz Opaliński, Grand Marshal of the Crown, by an unknown artist.

LEFT: The body armour of a soldier of the winged cavalry, the *husaria*, with the cross and a medallion with the Virgin on the breast.

ABOVE: A provincial sejmik taking place in a church. Pen-and-ink drawing by Jean Pierre Norblin de la Gourdaine.

RIGHT: Wooden Church of St Joseph, Baborów (c.1700), a typical baroque village church.

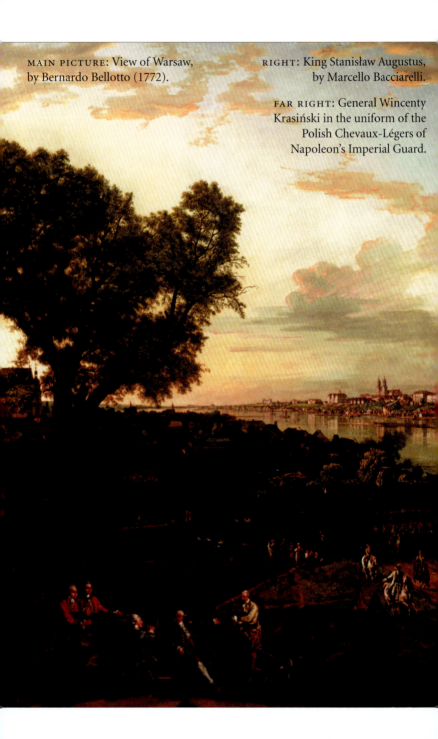

MAIN PICTURE: View of Warsaw, by Bernardo Bellotto (1772).

RIGHT: King Stanisław Augustus, by Marcello Bacciarelli.

FAR RIGHT: General Wincenty Krasiński in the uniform of the Polish Chevaux-Légers of Napoleon's Imperial Guard.

A fighter in the 1863 insurrection, photographed in Kraków before crossing into Russian-occupied Poland.

Józef Piłsudski, photographed in 1915 in the uniform of his Legions.

ABOVE: The pilots of 303 Polish Squadron, the top-scoring unit in the Battle of Britain, photographed at RAF Northolt in 1941.

RIGHT: General Władysław Sikorski, photographed in Washington in 1943.

A Solidarność rally, May 1989.

Lech Wałęsa with Pope John Paul II.

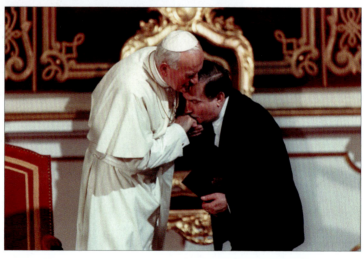

majority of the surviving leading families descended from Kievan times had associated with Poland centuries before, depriving the national movement of its natural leaders.

The birth of modern Ukrainian nationalism was also marked by a visceral anti-Semitism whose roots can be traced to the end of the sixteenth century, when large numbers of Jews settled in the area, mainly as agents of Polish estates, innkeepers and traders. This would be compounded in the last decade of the nineteenth century by manipulation on the part of tsarist authorities eager to channel Ukrainian energies into anti-Semitic pogroms.

The Jews were the one orphan people of the Commonwealth who had no national pretensions. Russia, which had not previously admitted Jews, designated the old Polish frontier of 1772 as an easternmost pale beyond which those she had acquired by the partition could not settle or even travel. Although they transferred their loyalty promptly, and showed it by remaining faithful to the Tsar throughout the French invasion of 1812, the Jews were heavily discriminated against. Nicholas I brought in further restrictions and subjected them to military service, often with forced conversion to Orthodox Christianity. His successor Alexander II (1855–81) relaxed many of their disabilities, and allowed them to move around the whole of Russia freely. But following his assassination the Jews were blamed for everything from Russia's failures to carrying out ritual murders of Christian children, and became victims of officially sanctioned pogroms. In 1882 they were confined to the pale of settlement once more and were subjected to further restrictions. Hundreds of thousands of the poorest Jews, who could not fit into the area of the pale, moved westwards into Poland. Most of these 'Litwaks', as they were known, were destitute. They were as unwelcome to their brethren in Poland as they were to the Poles, and they nourished a new anti-Semitism.

This, and the rise of a modern Darwinian strain of nationalism among the other peoples of the former Commonwealth, placed Polish patriots on the horns of a dilemma, suggesting as they did that not only the model of the Commonwealth but even an updated state-based multiculturalism were unworkable. The best way forward appeared to be to follow other European states in taking the ethnic core and the language as the bases of the nation. But this meant rejecting the inclusiveness and toleration of the Commonwealth in favour of an exclusive ethnocentric conformism that would lead inevitably to intolerance and the need to somehow remove the foreign bodies within such a nation. It was this dilemma that would shape the political countenance of the new Polish nation.

The first political parties of modern Poland sprang from the peasant cooperatives and self-help groups which burgeoned in Galicia in the 1870s. The earliest were the Peasant Party (1893), the People's Party (1895) and the Polish People's Party (1903). The workers of the cities had also organised themselves into unions and in 1882 a socialist workers' party, Proletariat, was founded by Ludwik Waryński. This suffered a setback in 1884, when the Russian police arrested the leadership. Waryński was sentenced to sixteen years' hard labour, four of his colleagues were hanged, others were imprisoned or exiled. The remnants of the party were brought together by Stanisław Mendelson and transformed in 1892 into the Polish Socialist Party (PPS).

In the following year another group of socialists led by Róża Luksemburg and Julian Marchlewski founded the Social Democratic Party of the Kingdom of Poland (SDKP), which rejected nationalism. This soon began to disintegrate, but was revived in 1900 by Feliks Dzierżyński, who added Lithuania to the name (SDKPiL). Although it grew to an impressive size, this party would play a greater part on the Russian than the Polish political scene ('Bloody Feliks' became the first head of the Cheka, forebear of the NKVD and KGB). The PPS on the other hand quickly gained in influence in all three partitions.

In 1894 it started publishing a clandestine organ, *The Worker*. Its editor, Józef Piłsudski (1867–1935), was a gifted conspirator whose early life reads like a novel. He had spent five years in Siberia for helping to supply Lenin's brother Alexander Ulyanov with explosives for a bomb which was thrown at the Tsar in 1887. He was twice sprung from Russian jails by colleagues. After escaping in 1900 from a prison hospital in St Petersburg, where he had got himself transferred by faking madness, he dodged from Tallin to Riga, thence to Kiev (where he managed to compile and publish an edition of *The Worker*) and Lwów, then to London, from where he entered Russia again on forged papers. He was deft at moving the presses of *The Worker* from one hiding place to another, and he also made it interesting reading, with the result that by 1899 the illegal paper had a circulation of 100,000. Since he used it as a platform for his own views, it helped him to win the leadership of the PPS.

Polish socialism was heavily marked by the national issue. The first manifesto of the PPS proclaimed the goal of an independent Poland within its 1772 frontiers, as a homeland to all the nations living within them. It was in effect a call for the restoration of the Commonwealth, and therefore of Polish hegemony, which was to ignore the nationalist aspirations of many Lithuanians, Belarusians and Ukrainians.

It was also to ignore the five million Jews living within the area, who, thanks to the mass migrations from the Western Gubernias, now made up 14.6 per cent of the population of the Kingdom. Many did not even speak Polish. They had no reason to hanker after Polish independence, and they joined the Zionist movement founded in Basel in 1897 or, more often, the Jewish Socialist Union, the Bund, founded the same year in Wilno, which in 1898 allied itself with the Russian Social Democratic Party, turning its back on the PPS and the cause of Polish independence.

There was no conservative political organisation to balance all these movements, since most conservatives acquiesced in the status quo and refrained from subversive politics. The socialist and peasant parties were challenged by an entirely new element in Polish political life. The Polish League, founded in Geneva in 1887, was renamed the National League ten years later, and eventually became the National Democratic Party. Neither conservative nor revolutionary, it rejected passive acquiescence and castigated the Positivists, but believed in realistic resistance. Its membership included the bourgeoisie, the *déclassé* szlachta and some sections of the peasantry. It was less aristocratic than the PPS and less romantic in its outlook. It was dominated by Roman Dmowski (1864–1939), whose political philosophy was practical, logical and implacable.

In 1903 he published *Thoughts of a Modern Pole*, in which he criticised traditional Polish values, arguing against such concepts as multiculturalism and toleration, and for a more ethnically based concept of the nation. He favoured a 'healthy national egoism' which could embrace all those prepared to sign up to the project and assimilate. Minorities, whether based on religion or ethnic differences, should be regarded as alien bodies within the nation.

In the National League Dmowski intended to create an all-Polish pressure group, an underground political apparatus which could unite like-minded people into a disciplined and ideologically homogeneous force. In 1899 the League founded a Society for National Education, and it gradually extended its influence over cultural associations and other political groupings, including peasant parties and factory workers' unions. His methods were as unlike those of Piłsudski as his outlook.

Piłsudski, at heart an heir to the Democrats, had always believed in active subversion, and in 1904 he set up terrorist commandos known as *Bojówki* to carry out acts of sabotage and diversion. The outbreak of the Russo-Japanese war in the same year was a bugle call to him. The humiliating defeats suffered by Russia delighted the Poles, but also made them anxious, as thousands of young Polish conscripts were being killed in the East. Piłsudski went to Tokyo with a series of proposals. He suggested the creation of a Polish Legion out of Russian prisoners of Polish origin, and offered the Japanese a guerrilla war in Poland to tie down Russian troops. In return, he wanted the Japanese to demand the establishment of an independent Poland at the peace negotiations. The Japanese were wary of getting involved.

On 13 October 1904 the PPS organised a massive demonstration in Warsaw. When the police shot at the crowd, Piłsudski's armed squads returned fire. The fighting squads of the PPS then launched a campaign of attacks on tsarist officials. While hostilities escalated in the Kingdom, Russia itself heaved with unrest. In the new year, in the wake of the bloody clashes on the streets of St Petersburg, the PPS proclaimed a general strike which lasted for two months and involved some 400,000 workers all over the Kingdom, despite severe retaliatory measures by tsarist troops.

In May 1905 the Russian fleet was disastrously defeated by the Japanese at Tsushima, bringing discontent to a head, and the crew of the battleship *Potemkin* mutinied on the Black Sea. In June barricades went up in Łódź and workers held off troops and police for three days. In October the Tsar issued a manifesto promising the Kingdom a constitution, but during the demonstration held to celebrate, troops opened fire on the crowds, and on 11 November a state of siege was declared. In December revolution broke out in Moscow and on 22 December the PPS called for a rising of all the workers in the Kingdom.

Events in Poland were dominated by a struggle for control

between the Socialists and the National Democrats. During the June 1905 unrest in Łódź, when the PPS had called for action and the National Democrat-controlled Workers' Union had opposed it, there were clashes between the two and even bloodshed. When the Imperial Manifesto turned the Russian Empire into a constitutional monarchy and announced elections to the Russian parliament, the Duma, the National Democrats were keen to take advantage, while the PPS boycotted the elections on the grounds that they endorsed Russian government in Poland.

At the first elections to the Duma the National Democrats gained thirty-four seats out of a total of fifty-five which went to Poles (who held around 10 per cent of the whole). Dmowski assumed that this would carry some weight, but he was mistaken. In the first twelve months of the new order, 2,010 people were killed by the army and police, and over a period of three years the governor of Warsaw, Georgii Skallon, signed over 1,000 'political' death sentences. Dmowski's attempts at bargaining with the government came to nothing, while opponents in Poland denounced him for selling out. Nevertheless, he continued building up the Polish lobby in the Duma. In *Germany, Russia and the Polish Question* (1908) he argued that Germany was the greater threat to Poland and that Poland must side with Russia in any conflict between the two.

The PPS found itself in trouble when the dust had settled after the events of 1905. It had failed to bring about armed insurrection and was left protesting out in the cold. It was riven with dissension and in 1907 split into two different camps. Piłsudski managed to keep control of the larger, and his thinking prevailed. This too was becoming dominated by the approaching war, and it was diametrically opposed to Dmowski's.

Piłsudski had established a paramilitary training school in Kraków, and by the summer of 1906, some 750 people were operating all over the Kingdom in five-man squads. During that year they killed or wounded nearly 1,000 Tsarist officials and officers, and carried out raids on prisons, tax offices and mail trains, the most spectacular being the hold-up at Bezdany of the train carrying the Kingdom's taxes to Russia in September 1908. In the same year the *Bojówki* were replaced by the Union of Active Struggle, an apolitical Polish 'army' founded by three members of the PPS: Kazimierz Sosnkowski, Marian Kukiel and Władysław Sikorski. With the unofficial approval of the Austrian authorities, sporting clubs sprang up all over Galicia, followed by Riflemen's Unions in Kraków and Lwów. In 1912 Piłsudski reorganised these on military lines, and by June 1914 he had nearly 12,000 men ready to take the field. When war broke out he took up arms in the Polish cause. On 2 August 1914 one of his cavalry patrols marched into the Kingdom, followed four days later by a battalion of riflemen. They briefly occupied the town of Kielce in the name of Poland before being forced to withdraw by Russian troops.

On 27 August the Austrians agreed to recognise Piłsudski's force and organised it in two Polish Legions with their own uniforms and colours under the command of Austrian army officers of Polish nationality. These quickly grew to a strength of 20,000 men and over the next two years created something of a legend. Officers were addressed as 'citizen', and the almost mystically revered and loved Piłsudski was simply 'the Commander'. Piłsudski was careful to emphasise that they were not Austrian troops, nor even allies of the Central Powers.

All three powers were keen to engage the sympathy of the Poles in general, and desperate to ensure the loyalty of their own Polish subjects in particular (between 1914 and 1918 millions of Poles were drafted by all three, and some 450,000 died and 900,000 were wounded fighting in the Russian, Prussian and Austrian armies). A proclamation by the Russian Grand Duke Nicholas on 15 August 1914 promised autonomy for the Kingdom, to which captured parts of Galicia and Poznania would be joined, but the details were left vague. Dmowski pressed for the formation of a Polish army in Russia, but the authorities were reticent.

By August 1915 the whole area of the Kingdom had fallen to the Germans, but they were undecided as to its future. Various schemes were passed back and forth between Berlin and Vienna, culminating in a proclamation by the two emperors on 5 November 1916, which promised to set up a semi-autonomous Kingdom of Poland made up of areas conquered from Russia. The Germans needed cannon fodder, and the main purpose of the proposed kingdom was to provide the vehicle for the recruitment of an army, the *Polnische Wehrmacht*. They soon realised that they could not do without Piłsudski.

Piłsudski had already achieved much of what he had set out to do, by demonstrating that Poland represented a military as well as a moral force, and had no intention of being used to further German plans. He agreed to join the Council of State of the new kingdom as head of the military department, but insisted on explicit guarantees that its forces would not be German 'colonial troops' as he put it, and would never be used against the British or the French. The Germans were not prepared to accept this, so Piłsudski resigned. In July 1917 he was arrested. Of the Polish units already raised, most refused to swear the required oath and were disbanded. The men swelled the ranks of the Polish Military Organisation (POW), an underground network set up across the entire area of the Commonwealth by Piłsudski in the previous two years, a silent army which awaited his signal.

Dmowski had left Poland in 1915 and concentrated his efforts on promoting the Polish cause in France and Britain. A number of his colleagues had been engaged in this from the beginning, most notably the writer Henryk Sienkiewicz until his death in 1916, and the pianist and composer Ignacy Jan Paderewski, who had been remarkably successful in the United States. It was largely as a result of his agitation that President Woodrow Wilson made his declaration to the US Senate on 22 January 1917 that 'Statesmen everywhere are agreed that there should be a united, independent, and autonomous Poland.'

In June 1917 France sanctioned the formation of an allied Polish army on French soil. In September France recognised Dmowski's National Committee in Paris as a provisional government of the future Poland. Britain, Italy and America followed suit. Thus by the autumn of 1917 there was a Polish government and a Polish army recognised as co-belligerents, if not formal allies, of the Entente, as the Western allies were generally known.

They could only do this because their ally Russia had been shaken by revolution, and Alexander Kerensky's government had agreed to the principle of an independent Poland. But October brought the Bolsheviks to power. The Russian front collapsed, and the German army was able to occupy the whole area of the Commonwealth. In March 1918 the Bolsheviks signed the Treaty of Brest-Litovsk, sanctioning this state of affairs.

As a protest against this new peace, General Haller led the Second Brigade of the Legions, the last Polish unit fighting for Austria, across the front to join up with Polish units which had left the disintegrating Russian army. Over the next two years units such as these bobbed about on the swell of the Russian Civil War in a desperate effort to maintain their fighting potential for the day they could be used in the Polish cause. They were often defeated or disbanded, and sometimes forced to serve 'White' Russian generals at the behest of the Entente. General Haller made his way to Paris and took command of the Polish army being formed there.

The German Kingdom of Poland still had no king, and was ruled by a Regency Council made up of Poles. But even as revolution toppled first the Habsburg and then the Hohenzollern thrones, the Germans and Austrians did not desist from their imperial machinations. The Germans had for some time been fostering the formation of a small ethnic Lithuanian state as a German satellite. They were also encouraging Belorussian nationalists to form a state of their own. Austria was contemplating a Habsburg Kingdom of Ukraine. On 1 November 1918 Ukrainian flags were hoisted on the public buildings of Lwów and regiments of the Austrian army recruited in Ukraine took over the city. Piłsudski's POW units and the mainly Polish inhabitants fought back and regained control, but they were besieged within a small area. The newly established Lithuania claimed Wilno and areas of the former Grand Duchy, which brought it into conflict with Belorussian nationalists.

On 7 November 1918 the socialist Ignacy Daszyński proclaimed a provisional Polish government in Lublin. On 10 November, the day before the Armistice in the west, Piłsudski was freed from his German jail and arrived in Warsaw. He was met at the station by Zdzisław Lubomirski and Archbishop Aleksander Kakowski, who handed over to him the powers of the Regency Council. All over the country his POW and ex-legionaries disarmed German troops and took control. Piłsudski proclaimed to the world that 'The Polish state has arisen from the will of the whole nation.'

The leaders of the Entente were not best pleased. They had assumed that it was up to them to grant independence to Poland. They had a provisional government in Paris ready to be installed, and they mistrusted Piłsudski. And if he had triumphed in Poland, the final shape and status of the resurrected state would depend largely on the peace negotiations about to open in Paris and the willingness of the Entente to supply everything from the food the country so badly needed to arms with which to defend itself. A compromise was quickly reached, and Paderewski arrived in Poland to take his place as Prime Minister in a coalition government, with Piłsudski as head of state and commander-in-chief.

Elections were held in January 1919 in the area of the former Congress Kingdom and Galicia, and as they could not take place in the former German provinces on account of fighting between Poles and Germans, eighteen deputies to the last imperial Reichstag were given seats in the 340-strong Polish Sejm. Six months later, elections were held there too, along with other areas, bringing the Sejm up to a strength of 432. This embarked on the laborious process of putting in place a state administration, leaving Piłsudski and Paderewski to deal with the country's frontiers, none of which had yet been fixed.

Poland's frontier with Germany depended entirely on the decisions reached by the Entente, and these were subject to every consideration except that of Polish reasons of state. It was only in Silesia, where an uprising against the Germans by the population proved effective, that the Poles were able to break this rule. Prussia and Pomerania were awarded to Germany, and Gdańsk was left as a free city under League of Nations administration, linked to Poland by a thin corridor through German territory. In the south-west, the new Czecho-Slovak state invaded the coal-rich area around Cieszyn (Teschen), in which Poles outnumbered Czechs by more than two to one, with the unofficial sanction of France. Poland's frontiers with Russia, on the other hand, depended not on words uttered at Paris, but on actions in the field.

Piłsudski was convinced that a small, ethnically defined Poland would not survive long beside a Russia which possessed Belorussia and Ukraine. He also felt a strong emotional and ideological attachment to the principles of the Commonwealth, and meant to adapt them to the circumstances by creating a federal union of Poland, Lithuania and Ukraine.

But the dialogue with the Lithuanians and the Ukrainians began only after shots had been exchanged. It proved impossible to reach agreement with the Lithuanians, who were suspicious of Poland.

There was more common ground with the Ukrainians, and negotiations started after the fighting over Lwów had ceased. But no solution to the problems of Ukraine, Belorussia and Lithuania could be adopted without reference to events in Russia.

In August 1918 the Bolsheviks had declared all the treaties of partition null and void – which did not mean that they were willing to see Poland reborn within its 1772 frontiers. Throughout 1918 and 1919 they were too busy fending off White offensives to bother much about the Polish frontier. Piłsudski too was worried by the successes of the Whites. Their leader, General Denikin, made it clear that he envisaged only one Russia – great and indivisible. Piłsudski certainly did not wish to see him established in Moscow with Allied backing, for then not only Poland's eastern frontier but her sovereign status would be dependent on deals made between Moscow and Paris. Piłsudski therefore refrained from any military activity against the Bolsheviks which might help the Whites, and even made a secret pact with Lenin, in spite of urgent appeals from London and Paris that he should support Denikin.

When the Whites had been defeated, in the winter of 1919, the Bolsheviks began to prepare for exporting the revolution through Poland to Germany. Piłsudski decided that this was the moment to implement his own plans. The Bolsheviks had already flooded into Ukraine, ousting the nationalist forces of Ataman Symon Petliura from Kiev. Petliura was forced to fall back westwards, and to seek Polish protection. Piłsudski signed an alliance with him, and in April 1920 he launched an offensive into Ukraine. On 7 May Polish and Ukrainian forces marched into Kiev.

Piłsudski hoped that Petliura would raise a Ukrainian army capable of holding the area. This would permit Polish troops to be transferred north, to face an alarming Russian concentration there. Progress was slow and Petliura's army grew to little more than 30,000 before the Russian attack came in the north. Polish forces in the area managed to contain it along the Berezina, but on 5 June the Cavalry Army of Budionny broke through to the south of Kiev, precipitating a chaotic Polish-Ukrainian withdrawal. On 4 July the five Russian army groups in the north launched a second offensive, and over the next six weeks the two Russian prongs, under Mikhail Tukhachevsky and Aleksandr Yegorov, advanced inexorably into Poland.

The Bolsheviks announced the overthrow of the bourgeois order and successfully agitated among workers all over Europe to block supplies being shipped to Poland. Western governments were unhelpful. The British Prime Minister Lloyd George's attitude was

The Polish Republic

- - - Frontier of Poland 1772
/// Poland 1921–1939
▨ Free city of Danzig

0   200 miles
0   300 km

that 'The Poles have quarrelled with all their neighbours and they are a menace to the peace of Europe.' On 12 August the Red Army reached the defences of Warsaw and the city's fall seemed imminent. But on 15 August Piłsudski launched a daring flank attack which all but annihilated Tukhachevsky's forces. After another Polish victory on the Niemen, the Russian front collapsed. Polish troops reoccupied large areas of Belorussia, Podolia and Volhynia before an armistice was signed on 16 October.

Pressure from the Entente and the fact that the Ukrainian national movement had proved too weak forced Piłsudski to abandon his federalist dreams. The peace negotiations which followed, in the Latvian capital Riga, were conducted by the peasant leader Jan Dąbski and Stanisław Grabski, a National Democrat, neither of whom was interested in reviving the Commonwealth.

The result was a compromise. The Poland that emerged occupied an area of 388,600 square kilometres and included large Belorussian, Ukrainian, German and Jewish minorities, but excluded over two million ethnic Poles who were left outside its boundaries. So was the city of Wilno, but Piłsudski could not countenance this, and he sanctioned a supposedly mutinous military operation by one of his generals, who seized the city for Poland.

Poland was an independent state once more, the sixth largest in Europe by population. Welcoming its return to the map of Europe, the Polish-born English novelist Joseph Conrad singled out what he saw as his nation's greatest achievement during a century of captivity: 'Under a destructive pressure, of which Western Europe can have no notion, applied by forces that were not only crushing but corrupting, we have preserved our sanity.'

NINETEEN

The Polish Republic

Suspicion of central authority had been a constant of Polish political life from the earliest times. During the period of partition, it had morphed into more or less active and patriotically motivated civil disobedience and subversion aimed at the occupying authorities. With the recovery of independence in 1918, the state had to be accommodated among the most sacred elements of a Pole's life, and this did not come naturally. For too long virtue had lain in opposition. This marked the attitude of the peasant to the policeman as much as it did that of the general to his government.

Creating the structures of the new state was not going to be easy. A hundred years of living within one or other of three entirely different cultures had marked mentalities and behaviour. Those brought up in a Prussian mould found it difficult to work with those of more urbane Habsburg habits, let alone with those schooled in the Byzantine inefficiency of the tsarist bureaucracy. The same was true of those who had any experience of parliamentary practice: whether they had sat in the Russian Duma or the German Reichstag they had generally blocked and opposed. This augured ill for the political life of the new Polish state.

The provisional Sejm which assembled on 10 February 1919

was dominated by parties of the right under Wojciech Korfanty, with the centre taken by peasant parties led by Wincenty Witos' Polish People's Party (PSL Piast) and the left by three socialist parties. The largest party had less than a quarter of the seats, and the very first sessions led to further splintering, but this was not as dangerous as it might have been, as the Sejm had conferred extensive executive powers on Piłsudski for the duration of the war, and its most important task was to prepare a constitution for the new state.

The constitution adopted on 17 March 1921 was based on that of the French Third Republic: it consisted of a Sejm of 444 deputies elected by universal suffrage of both sexes and proportional representation, a Senate of 111 seats, and a president elected by both chambers for a term of seven years.

Neither president nor Senate had extensive powers, most of which were in the hands of the Sejm. But this was crippled by the impossibility of achieving stable majorities or durable coalitions. The principal currents of Polish politics had been defined from the start not by ideology but by group interest: conservative-minded peasants hungry for land had nothing in common with conservative-minded landowners, and left-wing industrial workers who wanted low food prices would not combine with left-wing peasants who wanted the reverse. Proportional representation favoured minority parties and single-interest groups, while the demographics of Poland gave rise to ethnically based parties with specific agendas.

The first elections held under the new constitution, in November 1922, saw a turnout of 68 per cent and returned no fewer than thirty-one parties to the Sejm. Not one had more than 20 per cent of the seats, and most of the major parties had no more than about 10. They coalesced into clubs, but these often fell apart in the very process of building coalitions. The large number of single-interest parties meant that coalitions or even clubs were likely to fracture over a particular piece of legislation. The chamber contained thirty-five members representing Jewish parties, twenty-five representing Ukrainian interests, seventeen the German and eleven the Belorussian minority. Their voting patterns were erratic, but their number could exert a disproportionate effect.

The sense of instability was only enhanced when the first President of the Republic, Gabriel Narutowicz, was assassinated by a lunatic on 16 December 1922, two days after his inauguration. Four days later the Sejm and Senate voted in his successor, Stanisław Wojciechowski, while General Władysław Sikorski, who had been appointed Prime Minister, stabilised the situation. But instability continued to dog the Sejm, with budgets failing to be passed and governments coming unstuck over minor issues – no fewer than fourteen cabinets fell in the space of seven years.

The self-perpetuating dissension which enveloped parliamentary politics provoked disgust, and, with time, a chorus calling for 'strong government'. Only one man in Poland enjoyed the sort of public esteem and personal authority needed to provide this: Józef Piłsudski. In the early 1920s Piłsudski withdrew into sullen retirement on his small estate of Sulejówek, whence he exerted a muted but pervasive influence through his writings, his Sibylline pronouncements on various matters, and his very absence from public life. He had a strong following in the armed forces and was respected by people on the right and the left of the political spectrum, by the most chauvinist Poles and by the Jewish minority.

On 10 May 1926 Wincenty Witos formed the latest in a succession of cabinets too weak to rule effectively. Two days later Piłsudski marched on Warsaw at the head of a few battalions of troops, and demanded its resignation. Witos was ready to comply, but President Wojciechowski urged him to stand firm and called out the army. Some units dragged their feet, others backed Piłsudski, as did the entire left, with the result that railwaymen refused to move regiments loyal to the government. After three days' street fighting Wojciechowski and Witos resigned.

The Sejm offered the presidency to Piłsudski, but he declined and put forward the name of an eminent scientist and one-time member of the PPS, Ignacy Mościcki, who was duly elected. Changes introduced into parliamentary procedure had the effect of marginalising the Sejm and strengthening the role of the president, who henceforth appointed the government. Piłsudski himself briefly served as prime minister, and then handed over to Kazimierz Bartel, a respected politician of the People's Party.

Piłsudski had no policy beyond 'cleaning up the mess' of parliamentary bickering, and took little interest in the day-to-day affairs of government. He was more interested in the army, which he saw as the key to Poland's survival and a repository of its chivalric values, and the only formal title he accepted was that of Marshal. He hovered on the sidelines, part-dictator, part-monarch, his role ill defined, his influence paramount. By these means he managed to conserve his popularity: he was at once accessible and aloof, and while he was the linchpin on which the whole regime was hung, he was not too closely associated with any programme or policy to forfeit his essentially non-party appeal. If his manner, which grew increasingly surly, and his methods, which became more peremptory, were deplored by many, his purpose could be faulted by few. He was a national hero embalmed in the legend of his life of struggle for the freedom of Poland, embodying rebellion as well as authority.

At the next elections, in March 1928, the Non-Party Bloc of Cooperation with the Government (BBWR), created by Piłsudski as a surrogate party through which to support his policies, came out with almost 30 per cent of the vote, while his greatest enemies, the National Democrats, were soundly beaten. But Piłsudski was disappointed that his Bloc had failed to gain a more substantial majority, and what little respect he had for parliamentary procedures evaporated.

A life of conspiratorial activity had taught Piłsudski to use trusted men to carry out his plans and to obviate institutional channels. He gathered round him a bevy of trusties from the PPS, the Bojówki, the Legions or the POW. They were men like Walery Sławek, honourable, naïve, devoted, with no political ideas of his own and few talents; and Edward Śmigły-Rydz, a soldier and patriot with the soul of a second-in-command. They were the levers through which the Marshal exerted power. He treated all parliamentarians with mounting scorn and attempted to intimidate the opposition in the Sejm by various means, including packing the chamber with army officers on one occasion, and when this did not work he ignored it.

This was not as unpopular as might have been expected: in Poland, as elsewhere in Europe, many committed democrats found the parliamentary process wanting and reached the conclusion that 'strong government' of one sort or another was needed to deal with the acute problems of the day. Others, spiritual heirs of the nineteenth-century Democrats, found parliamentary politics too humdrum, and lurched to the left out of a romantic longing for upheaval.

The opposition grew increasingly truculent, and in 1929 a new centre-left coalition of 183 deputies (known as the *Centrolew*) called for reform to strengthen the powers of the Sejm. At a meeting in Kraków the following year its members spoke out in defence of democracy and criticised the government and the President in strident terms. President Mościcki responded by dissolving the Sejm, nominating Piłsudski Prime Minister, and arresting eighteen deputies. The elections held in November 1930 were marred by intimidation, arrests, confiscation of leaflets and vote-rigging. The BBWR received 46.8 per cent of the vote, which was somehow translated into 56 per cent of the seats.

Piłsuski and his henchmen backed up their increasingly authoritarian rule with a barrack-room ideology of 'cleaning up' political life which earned the regime the sobriquet *Sanacja* ('sanitisation'). Opposition leaders such as Witos, arrested in 1930, were put on trial on charges of conspiracy, and the freedom of the press was gradually restricted. Following the death, on 12 May 1935, of Piłsudski, the ruling clique tightened its grip.

A new constitution was passed, by sleight of hand, when many opposition deputies were absent from the chamber, in April 1935. It reduced the Sejm to a more manageable 208 deputies elected from 104 constituencies, which cut out small parties that had thrived on proportional representation. Its powers were curtailed and those of the president extended, enabling him to legislate by decree, but it was not President Mościcki who ruled. The camarilla put in place by Piłsudski remained in control, dominated by the *éminence grise* of Marshal Śmigły-Rydz, head of the armed forces.

Most of the opposition boycotted the elections of September 1935, and turnout fell to 45.9 per cent, but this did not affect the situation. The government founded the Camp of National Unity (OZN), which sucked in frustrated National Democrats as well as malcontents from smaller parties. The only weapons left to the opposition were strikes and demonstrations, but these were put down with force.

In 1936 a group of concerned constitutionalists, including Wicenty Witos, General Józef Haller, General and ex-Prime Minister Władysław Sikorski and Ignacy Jan Paderewski, met at the latter's home near Morges in Switzerland and founded the Morges Front in an attempt to build a respectable centre-right opposition. There was little they could do, as opposition at home melted away in the face of intimidation and a certain conformism took hold – at the 1938 elections turnout was back to over 67 per cent, and the OZN captured 80 per cent of the vote.

European politics of the 1920s and 1930s present an unedifying picture of confrontation, fed by class hatred and racism, thuggish behaviour and riots, and constitutional crises leading to military coups. In Poland, the twenty years of the Republic witnessed a breakdown of parliamentary procedures and the emergence of intimidation as a tool of governance; but neither public life nor politics sank to the levels seen in most neighbouring countries, let alone in France, Spain and Italy. Poland may not have resembled a democracy, but it was not a dictatorship, and dissent flourished despite the *Sanacja* regime.

This was partly due to the human fabric of the country. The peacemakers of 1918 had attempted to create nation-states in Central Europe, but the communities embraced by the Commonwealth were so interwoven that merely contracting its frontiers did not produce a homogeneous Polish state. The Republic was about half the size of the Commonwealth in 1772, yet in 1920 only 69 per cent of the population of 27 million were Poles: 17 per cent were Belarusians or Ukrainians, nearly 10 were Jews, and 2.5 were Germans.

The Polish 'nation' of the Commonwealth had been open to all nationalities, but when Poland was resurrected as a nation-state in 1918, it could only be based on the linguistic, cultural and religious tradition of the dominant group. Minorities were not actively discriminated against, but it was difficult for a member of one of them to gain high office in the army or the civil service. This was partly because many came from poor backgrounds and backward parts of the country, and it was easier, for cultural reasons, for a member of the German or Jewish minority than for a Ukrainian.

The Ukrainians who inhabited the east and south-east of the country were treated as second-class citizens by local administrators and police, and with suspicion by the central authorities. After 1926 Piłsudski launched a programme of local cultural autonomy in the hope of engaging the loyalty of the population to the Polish state. But this was undermined by the Soviets, who launched cross-border raids which targeted Poles and Ukrainians loyal to Poland.

In 1930 a Ukrainian nationalist organisation, Orhanizatsiia Ukrainskykh Natsionalistiv (OUN), founded in Vienna in 1929 and funded from Germany, began a campaign of terrorism and sabotage. Meaning to polarise attitudes, it concentrated on murdering Ukrainians who sought accommodation within Poland and Poles sympathetic to the Ukrainian cause. The authorities responded with a brutal ten-week pacification during which troops combed the area, burning down restive villages and publicly flogging real or suspected terrorists. In June 1934 an OUN activist assassinated the Minister of the Interior, Colonel Bronisław Pieracki, in Warsaw. The government responded by setting up an 'isolation camp' for subversive and undesirable elements at Bereza Kartuska near Brześć.

The extremists were undermined by an agreement in the same year between the government and the principal Ukrainian party (UNDO), whose original hostility to the Polish state had been tempered by Stalin's genocidal activities across the border in Soviet-occupied Ukraine. Calm returned to the countryside until 1939, when many of the extremists would re-emerge as a German fifth column. Meanwhile, the camp at Bereza Kartuska filled up with other enemies of the regime.

Relations with the German minority were more decorous but no more cordial. The *Volksdeutsche* resented having been marooned in a foreign country and felt no loyalty to Poland. With the rise of Nazism in Germany, they became increasingly strident in their denunciation of the Versailles settlement, demanding the return to the Reich of large areas of Poznania and of the Free City of Danzig. But even this hostility did not pose the same problems as did the Jewish minority.

Up to 1772 the Commonwealth had sheltered some four-fifths of the world's Jews, who fitted more or less comfortably into its political, economic and cultural framework. This symbiosis disintegrated when, under the new conditions created by foreign rule, the Jews came into direct economic competition with the *déclassé* szlachta, the urban proletariat and the budding Polish middle class. This was aggravated by the influx, in the 1880s and 1890s, of some 800,000 Jews from the Western Gubernias into the Kingdom, where they were seen as Russian interlopers.

Numerous Jews assimilated into Polish society, but the community as a whole did not identify with Polish aspirations. While many were active in the PPS and fought in Piłsudski's Legions, many more supported the Bund. Most were hostile to the National Democratic movement, which openly proclaimed that those not prepared to assimilate completely should be encouraged to emigrate, and whose members often gave vent to anti-Semitic feelings.

The collapse of law and order in November 1918 had produced a rash of anti-Jewish outrages in country areas and in towns such as Lwów and Pińsk. Further violence and reprisals took place in the wake of military operations between the Poles and the Bolsheviks, since numerous socialist Jews had welcomed or even joined the Red Army. Like much of European society at the time, many of the clergy did not distinguish between Jews and Bolsheviks, and parish priests encouraged anti-Semitic feelings. Hostility towards the Jews was inadvertently heightened by American and British Jewish pressure groups at the Paris peace talks of 1919. It was at their insistence that states such as Poland were made to sign 'Minority Treaties', which subjected their treatment of their Jewish citizens to international scrutiny. In Poland, with its long tradition of toleration, this was seen as an insult.

The census of 1931 revealed that there were 3,113,900 Jews in

Poland, representing 9.8 per cent of the entire population. They made up over 30 per cent of the population of Warsaw, a fairly standard figure for most of the larger cities, with exceptions such as Białystok's 43. In smaller towns the proportion was often much higher, reaching 60, 70 and in a handful of cases over 90 per cent of the population. As the majority wore black gabardines, side-locks and beards, and spoke Yiddish rather than Polish, they were conspicuous. They also stood out by their economic relationship to the rest of the population.

The occupational breakdown of the 1931 census reveals that only 0.6 per cent of those engaged in agriculture were Jews. They made up 62 per cent of all those making a living from trade, and the figure for the town of Pińsk was 95. Their fortunes fluctuated dramatically during the economically unstable twenties and thirties. Every time a new peasant cooperative was founded or a village combined to sell its produce direct to the buyer, the livelihood of several Jewish families vanished. By 1936 at least a million Jews in Poland were losing their source of subsistence, and by 1939 just over that number were entirely dependent for their survival on relief from Jewish agencies in the United States.

Polish representatives to the League of Nations urgently pressed for the lifting of restrictions on immigration into Palestine and the United States. The desire to be rid of the Jews may have gone hand in hand with concern for their plight, but it was not entirely racially motivated: the same representatives also appealed to the League to facilitate large-scale emigration of poor Polish peasants.

While the majority of Jews in Poland were caught in a poverty trap, they never managed to dispel the envy surrounding the community as a whole. In 1931, 46 per cent of lawyers and nearly 50 of doctors were Jews, who were also disproportionately successful at getting into universities. An anti-Semitic campaign began in the mid-1930s at the University of Lwów, spreading to other universities

and technical colleges, which resulted in some cases in the introduction of admission quotas based on percentages of the population.

The National Democrats, denied power for so long, had largely
lost their sense of identity as well as much of their membership.
In an attempt at gaining the support of disgruntled elements, they
began to play the card of anti-Semitism, but they were outdone
in this by small openly fascist parties, the most notorious of which,
Falanga, carried out assaults on Jewish shops and synagogues.
Violence of this kind was not uncommon, but the overwhelming
majority of popular disturbances were the result not so much of
racial hatred as of economic factors. Law and order were precarious,
and the police force (whose inspector-general was a Jew) was
about half the size of that in Britain and France in relation to the
respective populations.

Relations between Poles and Jews varied enormously; they were
far more complex than, and rarely as bad as, is usually made out.
There was certainly a great deal of low-level but deeply ingrained
anti-Semitism in some areas of Polish society. Yet at no point did
the sort of biological anti-Semitism of the Nazi or anti-Dreyfusard
variety catch on in Poland. The points at issue were political,
cultural and economic, and they have to be viewed in the context
of the situation confronting the population as a whole.

Along with four legal systems, the Republic inherited six different
currencies, three railway networks, and three administrative and
fiscal systems. There were huge discrepancies between the agri-
culturally advanced Poznania, the primitive rural economy of
Mazovia and the industrially developed Silesia. Galicia, the grain-
basket of the Habsburg Empire, and the Kingdom, which had been
the industrial centre of the Russian Empire, were cut off from their
respective markets. The area had been ravaged by six years of war.
Four and a half million hectares of agricultural land had been
devastated, two and a half million hectares of forest felled, and

over four million head of livestock removed by the Germans alone. According to Vernon Kellogg of the American Food Mission, one-third of the population were on the point of starvation in 1919.

Nearly 64 per cent of the population lived off the land, and most could not support themelves. The political solution to this problem was land reform, introduced in 1925, whereby 200,000 hectares were distributed each year to landless peasants at the cost of large estates. But this only aggravated the problem of production, by multiplying the number of tiny, inefficient farms. In 1939 there was still only one tractor for every 8,400 hectares of arable land, and yields were as much as 50 per cent lower than in neighbouring Germany.

The solution was massive industrialisation, but this was made no easier by the fact that in 1918 the retreating German army had carried out a gigantic operation quaintly termed 'the de-industrialisation of Poland', which left no factory, railway station or bridge standing, and no piece of machinery in place. The state came into being with vast debts to the Allies (for equipping and arming the Blue Army and supplying armaments between 1918 and 1920), and the obligation of making war reparations on behalf of those parts of the country which had been Austrian or German during the Great War. Poland was not the only country rebuilding its economy, and therefore it had to compete for credits. Foreign capital saw the new country as an uncertain investment.

The result was a bumpy start. In December 1918 the US dollar bought 9.8 Polish marks; in December 1923 it bought five million. At that point Prime Minister Władysław Grabski managed to balance the budget and to stabilise the situation with the intro-duction of the złoty. Nevertheless, foreign capital continued to elude Poland, while Germany waged a tariff war against it. It was not until 1929 that production reached the pre-1914 levels, only to sink to an all-time low in 1932.

In spite of a host of teething troubles and extremely unfavourable conditions, the Republic achieved a modest measure of economic success. By the end of its twenty-year existence it was the eighth largest producer of steel in the world, and the ninth of pig iron. It exported over 12 million tonnes of coal, 1½ million tonnes of crude oil, 100,000 tonnes of textiles, and 140,000 tonnes of yarn, and was developing a world-class chemical industry. Per capita income reached the same levels as in Spain and Portugal.

Since the Free City of Danzig was dominated by its predominantly German population, which yearned for incorporation into Germany, Poland built its own port. The dredging of the new harbour was started in 1924, in the fishing village of Gdynia. By 1938 Gdynia was the busiest port in the Baltic, with 12,900 ships docking annually. A Polish merchant marine of over eighty ships was built up, as well as a small but well-equipped navy.

The building of the economy had been hampered by the need to create a whole state apparatus from scratch, including administrative buildings, law courts, schools, museums, theatres and so on, and by the obligation to maintain an army. It was made all the more difficult by the hopeful assumptions of every social group in the euphoria attendant on the recovery of independence. In 1918, even before the fighting was over, the first Polish government passed decrees on social insurance and an eight-hour working day. In 1920 the government launched a health insurance scheme, and in 1924 an unemployment insurance act. The 1930s saw the building of remarkable state housing schemes for the low-paid, and by the middle of the decade Poland had the highest levels of social security in the world.

Over the twenty years of independence illiteracy was almost halved. By 1939 the six universities of Kraków, Warsaw, Lwów, Wilno, Poznań and Lublin contained 48,000 students, almost a third of them women, while a further twenty-seven technical colleges provided higher education for many more. The standards achieved in the Polish educational system during the 1930s compared very favourably with those of other countries, particularly in the humanities and pure science.

Retrospectively, it appears that the overriding problem faced by Polish society in its new role as a sovereign nation was one of identity. There might be a Sapieha foreign minister, a Zamoyski presidential candidate, a Potocki ambassador and members of szlachta families in every officers' mess, but it was not their values that triumphed in the new Poland. Nor did those of the nineteenth-century intelligentsia. Piłsudski and Dmowski had already been superseded by the movements they had created. The higher echelons of government and of the administration were largely filled by new men of disparate origins who had been tempered in the furnace of conspiracy, jail, and struggle for independence. They were united by their common experiences and service in the army, which played a major role in forging a new national consciousness. It was not just Ukrainians and Jews who felt out of place. Many members of the landed classes, the old intelligentsia, and particularly artists, became alienated. In the grotesque poem *Herrings in Tomato Sauce*, written in 1936, Konstanty Ildefons Gałczyński (1905–53) brings back to life Władysław the Short, the king who had struggled to reunite the fragmented country in the thirteenth century: 'Well, you wanted your Poland, now you've got it!' he is told. The sentiment expressed spoke for many.

The 1920s and 1930s witnessed an explosion of literary and artistic talent of a very high order. Liberated from the need to serve the national cause, writers and artists felt free to express themselves in ways that on the whole found little recognition in the reigning zeitgeist of the Sanacja regime. And while they enjoyed a following in the vibrant artistic milieus of Warsaw and other major cities, many found it difficult to associate themselves with the realities of the resurrected Poland. Musicians too found the promised land disappointingly philistine.

The long-yearned-for independence had been under threat ever since it was achieved in 1918. The Versailles settlement had created a situation in Central Europe which was uncomfortable for all parties. Germany could not help feeling a grudge against Poland, and the Poles could not help feeling one against every one of their neighbours, all of whom felt the same way towards the Poles. The powers which had helped restore Poland to the map were reluctant to commit themselves to her survival, and while all formally guaranteed the 1919 Franco-German border, only France did the same with respect to Germany's eastern border with Poland. Since the Western powers demonstrated at the Locarno Conference in 1925 that they would do anything to avoid involvement in another war, Central European states had to fend for themselves. Another war seemed likely, and all but the most sanguine or ill-informed realised that Poland did not stand a chance on her own.

With all the wisdom of hindsight, it is hard to suggest a foreign policy that might have saved Poland. Between 1932 and 1939 foreign policy was conducted by Colonel Józef Beck, who saw clearly that in the diplomatic game Poland had nothing to offer a potential ally. In 1932 he signed a non-aggression pact with the Soviet Union. This elicited an aggressive response from Germany, which demanded the Free City of Danzig. When Hitler came to power in 1933 Piłsudski considered a Franco-Polish pre-emptive strike on Germany. But Hitler stepped in with conciliatory offers and in January 1934 Poland and Germany signed a ten-year non-aggression pact. Hitler was keen to meet Piłsudski and discuss plans for a German drive into the Baltic countries in conjunction with a Polish drive to the Black Sea. But this was not a realistic option for Poland.

After the *Anschluss* with Austria in the spring of 1938 it became obvious that the West would be of no practical assistance to Poland.

Beck could not turn to the Soviet Union for a military alliance, since no Pole who knew his history could consider allowing Russian troops onto Polish soil, even if they came as allies. The only hope was to placate Germany in the hope of staving off aggression and of eliciting a convincing promise of military support from Britain and France, who were naturally anxious to keep Poland out of Germany's orbit.

In October 1938, after the German seizure of the Sudetenland, the Poles reoccupied the Zaolzie (the part of Cieszyn which the Czechs had annexed in 1918). It was intended partly as a show of force and partly as a strategic measure to strengthen Poland's southern flank against German attack – a consideration which also prompted a Polish ultimatum to Lithuania to open diplomatic relations and declare her intentions. These moves had little practical effect beyond creating the impression that Poland was a bully little better than Germany or Italy.

On 22 March 1939 the German government delivered an ultimatum to Poland demanding Danzig and the strip of Polish territory dividing East Prussia from the rest of Germany, the so-called 'Polish Corridor'. The ultimatum was rejected. On 31 March Great Britain offered an unconditional guarantee of Polish territorial integrity, and a few weeks later a military alliance was signed by Britain, France and Poland.

There followed three months of uneasy calm. Optimists saw this as a sign that the situation had been contained and peace assured. In fact Germany was using the time to make final preparations. Hitler put pressure on Romania to rescind her defensive military alliance with Poland, and started negotiating with Stalin. In August, the foreign ministers of the two states, Joachim von Ribbentrop and Viacheslav Molotov, signed a secret protocol detailing a new partition of Poland.

On the evening of 31 August 1939 a dozen German convicts

were dressed in Polish uniforms and ordered to attack a German radio station in Gleiwitz in Upper Silesia. Early next morning, as the world awoke to the remarkable news that Poland had attacked the Third Reich, the Wehrmacht invaded Poland in defence of the threatened Fatherland. Two days later, on 3 September, Great Britain and France declared war on Germany. Two weeks after that, on 17 September, when it had become clear that they would do nothing further to help their ally, the Soviet Union also invaded Poland.

What followed was no ordinary war. It was a concerted and sustained effort by Germany and Russia to destroy not only the Polish state, but the Polish nation itself. And although full-blown military operations would end in 1945, it would not be over for Poland until September 1989, almost exactly fifty years after it began.

TWENTY

War

A new chapter in the history of warfare opened as Hitler launched his Blitzkrieg against Poland. On 1 September some 1.5 million German troops invaded from three sides: East Prussia in the north, Germany in the west, and Slovakia in the south. They were supported by 2,700 tanks, of which the Polish army boasted barely three hundred, and 1,900 aircraft, which quickly wrested control of the skies from the 392 planes of the Polish air force. The Polish defences were pierced by eight German spearheads, while the Luftwaffe bombed roads, railways, bridges and cities. The German units raced ahead without pausing, outflanking those Polish units which stood their ground.

The Poles had approximately one million men under arms, but since mobilisation had been delayed at the request of Britain and France in an attempt to reach a last-minute solution to the crisis, a large proportion of them were nowhere near the front line, and most units went into action a third below strength. This, combined with an inflexible plan of defence, meant that the full potential of the Polish army, navy and air force could not be brought to bear. The chaos induced by the relentless bombing was aggravated by soldiers trying to reach their units and by the activities of a German fifth column. By 6 September the Polish command had lost control of the situation; by 10 September the Germans had overrun most of northern and western Poland; on 14 September Warsaw was encircled.

Once the first shock had worn off, Polish commanders reacted with determination. The Pomeranian and Poznanian army groups under General Tadeusz Kutrzeba held off the Germans in a two-day battle at Kutno. They then fell back on the Vistula and Bzura rivers, whence, reinforced by other units, they launched a counter-attack which threw the Germans back and won a breathing space for other retreating Polish units. In order to avoid encirclement, the Polish command had ordered a withdrawal to the region of Lwów, where a new line of defence was being organised, pivoting on the frontiers with supposedly neutral Russia and friendly Romania. In the more rural expanses of eastern Poland, where tanks and heavy artillery would be of less value, the Polish army would be able to face the Germans on a more equal footing. But on 17 September Russian armies invaded from the east, and it was revealed that Romania had, under German pressure, renounced its military alliance with Poland. Continued defence of this corner of Poland was impossible. The government, the general staff and those units within reach of it crossed the Romanian border in order to continue the fight from abroad, taking with them Poland's gold reserves. Warsaw, besieged since 14 September, capitulated two weeks later; the garrison on the Hel peninsula off Gdańsk held out till 2 October; General Kleeberg's Polesie Defence Group surrendered at Kock on 5 October after a week of fighting on two fronts against Germans and Russians. Smaller units continued to fight in various parts of the country until the spring of 1940, when their remnants went underground.

The September campaign is usually portrayed as a courageous fiasco and characterised by the image of lancers charging tanks. It is difficult to understand why. In September 1939 no European army could hope to stand up to the Wehrmacht, with its crushing superiority in both tactics and firepower. It had been agreed with the British and French staffs that in the event of aggression, Poland was to pin it down for a period of two weeks, time enough to allow the French to throw ninety divisions, 2,500 tanks and 1,400 planes across the virtually undefended Rhine. But the French did not move, while the RAF confined itself to dropping leaflets on German cities. In the event, the Poles tied down the Germans for over three weeks, and would have managed to keep going longer had the Russians not invaded (which it is now known they would not have done if the French had attacked Germany). For all its inadequacy, the Polish army acquitted itself valiantly, taking a greater toll of German men and equipment than the Franco-British effort of 1940. The Germans lost roughly 45,000 men dead and wounded, three hundred planes and 993 tanks and armoured cars. But the cost to Poland was nearly 200,000 dead and wounded.

That figure covers only military casualties, and does not include the tens of thousands of civilians killed in bombing raids or mown down by marauding aircraft intent on spreading panic. Nor does it include the thousands of landowners, priests, teachers, doctors, policemen and others who, along with their families, were murdered by the advancing German army as a prelude to the ethnic cleansing of the part of western Poland that was to become the German province of Warthegau.

In October the country was divided between its captors. The larger Soviet zone was incorporated into the Soviet Union and over the next months about 1,700,000 of its inhabitants were transported to labour camps in Siberia or the far north of Russia. The Germans incorporated Pomerania, Silesia and Poznania into the Reich, while the remainder of their conquests was designated as the *Generalgouvernement*. This was a colony, ruled from the Royal Castle in Kraków by Hitler's lawyer friend Hans Frank. He announced that

the concept of Poland would be erased from the human mind, and
that those Poles who were not exterminated would survive only as
slaves within the new German Empire.

The process began at once. Here too, priests, landowners,
teachers, lawyers and other persons of education or influence were
summarily shot or sent to a concentration camp at Oświęcim,
renamed Auschwitz, in a process that aimed to decapitate Polish
society and leave a leaderless and compliant workforce.

The Nazi-Soviet partition of Poland, 1939

People were shunted about in a vast programme of rearrangement whose logic is difficult to follow. Over the next five years about 750,000 Germans were imported into the areas that had been incorporated into the Reich: 400,000 Poles from the same areas were resettled in the *Generalgouvernement*, while a further 330,000 were shot. In all, some two million Poles were moved out of the Reich into the *Generalgouvernement*, while 2.8 million were taken from the *Generalgouvernement* to the Reich as slave labour. Supposedly Aryan-looking children were kidnapped, as many as 200,000 of them, to be brought up as Germans. Some 2,000 concentration camps of one sort or another were set up on Polish soil, in which people from all over Europe were incarcerated alongside Poles.

Poland's Jewish population was singled out for special treatment. In small towns and villages, Jews were rounded up and shot by the Wehrmacht or special police units following in its wake, and in some cases burnt to death in their wooden synagogues. In larger cities, they were made to wear yellow stars on their clothes and herded into designated areas known as ghettos. In May 1940 the Jewish ghetto of Łódź was sealed, and the same happened in Warsaw and other cities. From 1942, the people trapped in these ghettos were transported to camps set up at Treblinka, Majdanek, Sobibór, Bełżec, Auschwitz-Birkenau and elsewhere, for extermination. In all, 2.7 million Polish citizens of Jewish origin were murdered.

Normal life became impossible. Schools were closed down, as were theatres, the press and other amenities, and all institutions that could not be made to serve the German war effort were abolished. Conditions under which people lived defy concise description. The occupation was not only unspeakably harsh, it was also unsettlingly haphazard, as a number of different German military, police and civilian agencies operated independently of each other, creating a climate of confusion and uncertainty that kept people in a state of permanent fear. This had a corrosive effect on society, and while there was no collaboration as such, the Germans could always find people ready to spy or denounce. Yet the overwhelming majority of the nation continued to resist, actively and passively, as though the defeat had only been a setback.

In the last days of September 1939 President Mościcki, who was interned after he crossed the Romanian frontier with what was left of his government, appointed Władysław Raczkiewicz, former President of the Senate, as his successor. On 30 September Raczkiewicz formed a government in Paris under the premiership of General Władysław Sikorski, who also became commander-in-chief of the Polish armed forces. A National Council consisting of senior representatives of all the major parties was convened under the symbolic presidency of Ignacy Paderewski and the chairmanship of Stanisław Mikołajczyk, leader of the People's Party. This government was recognised by the Allies and proceeded to re-form the Polish armed forces with escapees filtering through from eastern Europe and émigré Polish volunteers from France and the United States.

By June 1940 these numbered 84,500 men in four infantry divisions and two brigades, an armoured brigade, an air force consisting of 9,000 men, and a navy of 1,400. A Polish brigade took part in the ill-fated battle for Narvik; two divisions, two brigades and 150 pilots fought in the French campaign of June 1940. Three-quarters of the land forces were lost in the fall of France, but the remnants followed the government to Britain, where they began to organise anew.

They were joined there by other forces that had survived the Polish campaign, such as the three destroyers and two submarines that had slipped out of the Baltic to join the Royal Navy, and by thousands of men and women who made their way there by various routes. By 1945 there would be 220,000 men in the Polish armed forces serving alongside the British. The Polish air force, which accounted for 7.5 per cent of all German aircraft destroyed in the Battle of Britain in the summer of 1940, grew to ten fighter and four bomber squadrons which, until the arrival of the USAAF, represented 25 per cent of the Allied bomber force. The Polish Air Force flew a total of 102,486 sorties, lost 1,973 men, and shot down 745 German planes and 190 V-1 rockets. The Polish naval ensign flew on some sixty vessels, including two cruisers, nine destroyers and five submarines, which were involved in 665 actions at sea. The land forces took part in the defence of Britain, the campaigns in North Africa and Italy, the Arnhem operation, the invasion of France and the liberation of Holland.

Perhaps the greatest Polish contributions to the Allied war effort were less easily quantifiable. One was the huge volume of intelligence provided by agents scattered all over Europe by the fortunes of war, deportations and slave labour schemes, which placed them in vital positions throughout Germany. The other was the work done by the Polish army throughout the 1930s on monitoring the use by the Germans of the 'Enigma' encrypting machine and their construction of the 'bombe' that could be used to decipher the encrypted orders, which, when handed over to the British and developed at Bletchley Park, allowed the Allies to intercept and read all orders issuing from the German high command by the beginning of 1940.

The struggle also went on inside Poland. The day before the fall of Warsaw on 28 September, a group of senior officers established a resistance command which assumed authority over units operating throughout the country and built up its own under the name Union of Armed Struggle (ZWZ). It was some time before this subsumed the 150-odd resistance groups that had sprung up spontaneously all over the country. The ZWZ was then transformed into the Home Army, Armia Krajowa (AK), directly subordinated to the commander-in-chief in London. By 1944 the AK numbered well over 300,000 men and women, which made it the largest resistance movement in occupied Europe, and the most active, losing 100,000 killed in action over the next four years.

Open resistance and assassinations of German personnel provoked such massive reprisals on the civilian population that they were abandoned in favour of more covert action. As well as derailing trains, blowing bridges and cutting communications, AK operations embraced the wholesale sabotage of German military materiel – engines, view-finding and navigation equipment for tanks, guns and planes – at source in the factories which produced them.

The life of the nation was lived in hiding. The government was represented by the Delegatura, an executive based in Warsaw with its own consultative committee drawn from all parties. The Delegatura was the political master of the AK and controlled everything in Poland from underground law courts to the flying universities and clandestine schools, much as the City Committee had done in 1863.

For a period of six years, education at every level was carried on secretly. Bombs were manufactured, plays were staged and books were published under the noses of the Germans, and an active clandestine press kept people informed. These activities were carried out with an efficiency and a wit that sometimes obscure the difficulties and dangers involved. Torture, concentration camp and death awaited anyone on whom German suspicion fell, and many thousands paid the price.

One area in which the German reign of terror was devastatingly successful was in dividing and estranging the various ethnic groups inhabiting Poland, and particularly in segregating Poles of Jewish descent and sealing them off from the rest of society prior to exterminating them. This was achieved mainly by regulations that did not obtain in any other country occupied by the Germans.

In Poland, anyone caught assisting or sheltering a Jew faced an automatic death penalty not just for himself, but for his entire family. Faced with this, even most philo-Semitic Poles were reluctant to get involved. The same penalty applied to anyone failing to report that someone else living in the same house was sheltering a Jew. This meant that someone who noticed that another occupant in his apartment block was hiding one was powerfully tempted to save himself and his family by reporting the fact rather than run the risk of death by waiting until some other inhabitant of the block did so. But there were other factors at work as well.

Not unlike the Jews themselves, many Poles responded to repeated and relentless failure and misfortune by developing an exclusive sense of grievance, and a paranoid, inward-looking sense of the uniqueness of their predicament, accompanied by an inability to view events and processes otherwise than in a strictly personalised manner. This allowed them to watch the Jewish tragedy unfold around them without seeing it, or indeed seeing it merely as an element in a scenario in which they, the Poles, were the chief victims. And there were plenty of anti-Semites who regarded the German extirpation of Jews from Polish society with indifference, or even as a favourable development.

At the same time, countless Poles did risk their lives to hide Jews and provide them with false papers. The clergy saved thousands of Jews, mostly children, by concealing them in schools or orphanages attached to monasteries and convents. In 1942 the AK set up a special commission of assistance, codenamed Żegota, which was responsible for saving the lives of some 10,000 Jews.

Such operations were made all the more difficult and hazardous by splits and conflicts within the resistance movement itself. Followers of the extreme right in politics had formed the National

Armed Forces (NSZ), which remained independent of the AK, and which took a different line on this and other issues. An even greater source of difficulty for the AK and the Delegatura was the People's Army (AL), affiliated to a recently founded Polish Workers' Party and ultimately to Moscow.

The Polish Communist Party had never been a significant force on the political scene. In the mid-1930s its leadership was imprisoned, and the bulk of the activists sought refuge in Russia, where in 1938 Stalin liquidated the higher echelons and dispatched the rest to the Gulag. The only senior Polish communists to avoid this fate were those, like Władysław Gomułka and Marceli Nowotko, who were safe inside Polish jails.

In the spring of 1941, Stalin began seeking out those surviviing Polish communists. In December 1941 he instructed Nowotko to start a Polish workers' party, which he did, in January 1942, but he was assassinated less than a year later. In 1943, Gomułka, who had been organising underground units in south-eastern Poland, became leader of the party, and it was under his leadership that the People's Army built its own structures as an alternative to those of the Polish government, which Stalin meant to unseat.

After the fall of France in June 1940, Poland became Britain's only effective ally and helped ward off the danger of a German invasion and keep the convoy routes open. But they had lost the war in Europe, and there was no prospect of Britain ever being in a position to help Poland regain her independence.

On 22 June 1941 Hitler launched Operation Barbarossa against Russia, and as the Soviet armies disintegrated under the impact, Stalin was forced into the Allied camp. He negotiated an alliance with Britain and, on 30 July, another with Poland, under the terms of which all Polish citizens imprisoned in Russia were to be released and formed up into a Polish Army which would fight alongside the Red Army.

This alliance was undermined by severe tensions: although

Russia repudiated the Ribbentrop–Molotov pact of 1939, it stopped short of recognising Poland's pre-war frontier. Polish prisoners were released grudgingly and some were re-arrested. The new army, forming in Uzbekistan under the command of General Władysław Anders, was exposed to provocations and attempted infiltration by communists. As time passed, Anders grew uneasy about the fate of some of his colleagues. He had drawn up lists of officers he knew had been captured by the Soviets in 1939, but few of these came forward: as many as 20,000 were unaccounted for. Sikorski took the matter up with Stalin, and was fobbed off with a promise to investigate. Meanwhile, General Anders' army was being harassed and even had its food rations withheld. The two years he had spent in Soviet prisons had taught him to fear the worst, and, against the wishes of Sikorski, who wanted to keep it on the eastern front, he decided to take his army and its horde of Polish waifs and strays, some 110,000 in all, out of the Soviet Union to Iran, where the British needed it.

On 11 April 1943 German radio announced that mass graves had been discovered in the forest of Katyn near Smolensk containing the bodies of 4,231 Polish officers, each with his hands tied behind his back and a bullet in his head. The first sample of names given (they all had their documents and uniforms) tallied with those on the list made out by Anders in 1941. The officers had been killed by the Russian NKVD in the spring of 1940, but the Russians accused the Germans of the massacre. The Polish government demanded an investigation by the International Red Cross, whereupon, on 26 April, Russia accused it of bad faith and collaboration with the Germans, and broke off diplomatic relations.

The inhabitants of Warsaw heard of the Katyn massacre one week before SS Brigadeführer Jurgen Stroop launched the operation to slaughter the remaining inhabitants of the Warsaw ghetto, who had staged a last-minute desperate resistance. The whole area was reduced to rubble over the next three weeks as the Jewish fighters defied the German onslaught. The ruins were still smouldering when, in June 1943, the commander of the AK, General Stefan Rowecki, was arrested in Warsaw by the Gestapo. On 5 July, the plane in which General Sikorski was travelling back to London from the Middle East, where he had been inspecting Anders' Second Polish Corps, crashed on take-off from Gibraltar, killing all its passengers. This string of disasters highlighted the hopelessness of Poland's position.

Until Hitler invaded Russia, Poland had been Britain's only effective ally. When Russia joined the Allies in June 1941, it was relegated to third place in a coalition which was still at that stage dominated by Britain. With the entry into the war of the United States in December 1941, Poland took fourth place in an alliance increasingly dominated by America. After the Russian victory at Stalingrad in February 1943, Stalin's position in the Allied camp became unassailable, and he used it to undermine the Polish government, denouncing it as a clique with no following in the country. At the same time he began recruiting his own Polish army out of those Poles he had failed to release two years previously.

Stalin declared the Polish-Russian frontier of 1939 unsatisfactory, arguing that it should be moved westward to correspond to the areas in which Poles constituted an overall majority, and adroitly seized on the 'Curzon Line', a ceasefire line pulled out of a hat by British diplomats in 1920. Terrified by the possibility, however remote, that Stalin might make a separate peace with Hitler, Roosevelt and Churchill gave their assent and tried to persuade the Polish government to accept this frontier. Sikorski was succeeded as prime minister by Stanisław Mikołajczyk, and as commander-in-chief by General Kazimierz Sosnkowski.

Mikołajczyk wanted to negotiate directly, but Stalin became

increasingly evasive; the Tehran Conference of November 1943 had convinced him that he need fear nothing from Churchill or Roosevelt. There was no good reason for him to tie his hands on an issue on which he now perceived he would have both entirely free. Time was on his side, not on that of the Poles. In January 1944 the Red Army crossed the 1939 Polish–Russian frontier in pursuit of the retreating Wehrmacht. Soon Stalin would have his divisions in Poland, while those of the Polish government were in Britain and Italy. He even had the 80,000 men of the First Polish Army commanded by General Zygmunt Berling, an ex-legionary who had been imprisoned in 1939 and persuaded to remain in Russia. Ironically, the Polish government's one remaining asset in Poland, the AK, turned out to be a political liability. Its long-awaited show of force was reduced to a peripheral episode of pointless heroism which profited only Stalin.

The AK command had been preparing a rising in support of Allied operations. After the British and American advance through Italy into Austria, the Polish Second Army Corps of General Anders was to race ahead into Poland from the south, while a special independent parachute brigade waited in England to be dropped in to support the rising. But the Soviet armies advanced faster than those of the Allies. In the event, Poland would be liberated by the Red Army, while Anders battled from Monte Cassino to Ancona and Bologna, and the parachute brigade was destined to meet its effective end in the battle for Arnhem.

The underground authorities in Poland therefore had to face the fact that they would be liberated by allies who did not recognise them. As they prepared to conduct military operations against the Germans, they realised that they would simultaneously have to make a political stand against the Soviets. The AK's amended plan, code named 'Tempest', was to conduct operations in the German rear in support of the advancing Soviet troops. AK units were to make contact with Red Army commanders and combine further operations. It was an attempt to bridge on the battlefield the chasm which had opened at the political level.

In April 1944 the AK's 6,000-strong 27th Division helped the Red Army capture Lwów. In July the 5,000-strong local AK units similarly assisted in the battle for Wilno. In both cases, the Red Army and AK units cooperated, but two days after the celebratory bear-hugs and handshakes, the AK officers were arrested or shot, and their men pressed into Berling's army. Discouraging as this was, the AK command clung to the hope that the Soviets might behave differently once they crossed the Curzon Line into territory which they formally recognised as Polish. These hopes were dashed when, after the joint liberation of Lublin at the end of July, the AK units taking part met with a similar fate.

In June Stalin had told Churchill that he would only consider negotiating with the Polish government if certain changes were made within it. Roosevelt suggested that he discuss these directly with Mikołajczyk. Under strong Allied pressure, Stalin agreed. Mikołajczyk flew to Moscow on 26 July, but by this time his position was weakened further. Stalin had collected a number of his client Poles into a 'Union of Polish Patriots', and on 20 July a group of these, under the leadership of an erstwhile member of the PPS, Edward Osóbka-Morawski, constituted themselves as the Polish Liberation Committee. A week later they issued a manifesto composed earlier in Moscow, and began acting as a provisional government in liberated areas, taking their seat at Lublin on 1 August.

The AK command had little room for manoeuvre. The Red Army crossed the Bug on 20 July, and on the following day news broke of the bomb plot against Hitler. On 23 July the German administration began to evacuate its offices in Warsaw, while columns of German settlers, stray soldiers and camp followers clogged roads leading west. On 27 July Soviet units crossed the Vistula to the south, and the sound of Russian guns could be heard in Warsaw. On 29 July Moscow Radio broadcast a message from Molotov to the inhabitants of Warsaw, calling on them to rise against the Germans. 'There is not a moment to lose,' it urged. The AK command were only too aware of this, and they were caught on the horns of an impossible dilemma.

An uprising in Warsaw was a terrifying prospect. The AK would probably be wiped out and the civilian population was bound to suffer. If they did not rise, the Soviets would brand them as Nazi sympathisers. They also knew that it would be hard to restrain their men, who had waited five years for the moment they could openly fight the Germans. Units of the communist-controlled People's Army were preparing to go into action, and this would provoke a general free-for-all which nobody would be able to control.

The Delegatura consulted their superiors in London, who advised against a rising, warning that the Allies would be unable to support it in any way, but left the final decision up to them. The Delegatura left it to the military. After a meeting of senior officers, the commander of the AK, General Tadeusz Bór-Komorowski, made his decision. With the advance units of the Red Army only twelve kilometres from Warsaw, and the thud of their guns rattling the windows, he gave the order to start on the following day.

At 5 p.m. on 1 August 1944 units of the AK went into action. Their initial aim was to clear the enemy from the city and seize arms. This might have been feasible in the volatile atmosphere of the last days of July, but by 1 August the Wehrmacht had reinforced its outposts throughout the city and was moving fresh Panzer divisions across the Vistula.

The AK units failed to take a number of their primary objectives, or to expel the Germans from a crucial east–west axis running between the Old Town and the city centre. Over the next couple of days they extended the area under their control, but failed to take the airport, the main railway station, or any of the Vistula bridges. By 6 August they had fought to a standstill, and from then on could only defend themselves. This they did for a total of sixty-three days.

The Germans mobilised a special force to deal with the rising under the command of General von dem Bach. It included the SS Viking Panzer division, an assortment of military police battalions, a brigade composed of German convicts, the SS Azerbaijan battalion and several units of Russian prisoners-of-war drafted into the 'Russian National Liberation Army' (RONA).

Over the next weeks the Korpsgruppe von dem Bach pushed the AK back, house by house, slaughtering the civilian inhabitants as they went. Following their capture of the Wola quarter, they indulged in a butchery of the civilian population which shocked even the German command. The Luftwaffe dive-bombed Polish-held areas, while long-range artillery pounded them. Conditions were indescribable. Short of ammunition, medical supplies, food and even water, the soldiers of the AK fought on with ingenuity (the German high command reported that the fighting was as hard as at Stalingrad, and casualty figures of 17,000 dead and only 9,000 wounded testify to the care taken with every bullet). They managed to capture several tanks and a quantity of other weapons, but they desperately needed air-drops of arms, ammunition and medical supplies and a Soviet advance against the Germans if they were going to regain the initiative.

An attempt to drop arms was made on the night of 4 August, but the price paid was enormous. The planes flew a round trip of 2,500 kilometres from northern Italy, and of the 196 sorties by British, Polish and South African crews over the next few days only forty-two made it to Warsaw. Churchill suggested a shuttle operation and requested landing facilities on Soviet airfields for the RAF and USAAF, but Stalin refused.

A couple of days after the outbreak of the rising, Moscow Radio denounced it as a conspiracy against the Soviet Union. Stalin told Mikołajczyk, who was still in Moscow, that 'The Soviet command dissociates itself from the Warsaw adventure and cannot take any responsibility for it.' The Soviet armies facing Warsaw ceased fighting and stood idle for the next six weeks.

On 20 August Churchill and Roosevelt sent a joint appeal couched in the strongest terms, to which Stalin replied that since the Poles had started the business they must bear the consequences, and described the AK as 'a handful of power-seeking criminals'. He invoked a number of technical reasons why his armies did not go to the aid of Warsaw, but while there were certainly military difficulties involved, the real reason was political. It would have been madness for him to interfere while the Germans were liquidating the very elements that would be hostile to his purpose of turning Poland into a Soviet satellite.

After increasingly forceful demands from Churchill and Roosevelt, Stalin eventually agreed to a shuttle operation. On 13 September his own air force appeared over Warsaw to drop supplies. Soviet forces at last occupied Praga, the east-bank suburb of Warsaw, and on 16 September Berling's Polish troops attempted to cross the Vistula. On 18 September 107 B-17 Flying Fortresses of the USAAF carried out the first shuttle drop, but by then the Polish-held areas of the city had shrunk so far that most of the canisters fell into German hands.

The AK held the Old Town to the north, the city centre, and the large residential district of Mokotów to the south, as well as several smaller pockets. Communication between these was poor, while the large and well-armed units which had congregated in the countryside outside the city could not break through the ring of Germans surrounding their comrades within.

The Germans began by liquidating resistance in the western suburbs of Wola and Ochota before concentrating on reducing the stronghold of the Old Town. It was here that some of the fiercest fighting took place, at very close quarters. After four weeks of dogged resistance, the command of the group defending the Old Town decided to evacuate. On the night of 1 September the remnants of this force, over 4,000 men, climbed down into the city sewers, carrying as many of their wounded as they could. The long trek waist-deep in filth was not made any easier by the Germans pouring poison gas down manholes, but eventually most of the men emerged in the city centre.

This continued to hold out, but towards the end of September the other pockets of resistance were reduced one by one. There seemed to be little point in prolonging the agony, and on 2 October General Bór-Komorowski signed the capitulation. Churchill and Roosevelt had stressed that the soldiers of the AK were regular Allied troops, and the Germans treated them accordingly. The civilian population, however, were herded into cattle trucks and sent to concentration camps or forced labour in Germany.

They left behind 250,000 dead, buried in the ruins. As soon as they had gone, Hitler's personal instructions went into effect: squads of SS demolition experts, Vernichtungskommando, moved in and proceeded to dynamite every building left standing. By the time the Red Army entered Warsaw in January 1945, there was nobody and nothing to liberate, except for stray dogs and rats. A huge desert of rubble remained as a monument to the city which suffered more than any other in the whole war.

In the last hours before the capitulation tens of thousands of people had slipped out, making for the safety of the countryside. Among them were several thousand soldiers of the AK, its new commander, General Leopold Okulicki, and the entire Delegatura. The fall of Warsaw was not to be the end of the struggle for the AK, which still had units throughout the country. Yet its role was effectively at an end.

Five years of meticulous planning, ingenuity and heroism had yielded impressive results in the field of intelligence-gathering, and accounted for some 150,000 German military personnel. But neither the Tempest operations nor the Warsaw Uprising gave the organisation a chance to show its full potential. And they had proved politically disastrous as well. Far from strengthening Mikołajczyk's bargaining position, the Warsaw Uprising had turned him into a supplicant.

During talks which took place in Moscow in October, Stalin demanded that Mikołajczyk accept his proposed frontier in the east, in return for which Poland would be compensated with former German territory up to the river Oder. He also wanted Mikołajczyk to dissolve the Polish government and come to Poland to head a provisional government made up of men from the Lublin committee. Pressed by Churchill and Roosevelt, the Polish Prime Minister felt obliged, against his better judgement, to demonstrate his goodwill by accepting this compromise. In January 1945 General Okulicki dissolved the AK and released its soldiers from their oath of loyalty to the London government.

Stalin had no intention of sticking to this compromise. Despite strong objections from Churchill and Roosevelt at the Yalta Conference in February and at Potsdam in July, he went on to appoint an interim government consisting of twenty-one ministers of whom sixteen were his men, with Edward Osóbka-Morawski as premier and Mikołajczyk as his deputy. The Allies formally recognised this and withdrew recognition from the Polish government, the majority of whose ministers had rejected the compromise agreed to by Mikołajczyk. They protested at the Allies' high-handed behaviour and continued to function in London in defiance of these arrangements. The majority of its soldiers and hundreds of thousands of civilians who found themselves in the west remained loyal to the government and refused to return to Poland. The wisdom of their decision would soon become apparent.

Behind the Red Army came Stalin's secret police, the NKVD, and with it the new Polish security services, the Urząd Bezpieczeństwa (UB). They were concerned primarily with rooting out of Polish society every element deemed unsympathetic to the Soviet Union, and in the first place that meant former members of the AK.

In March, sixteen men, including General Okulicki and all the members of the former Delegatura, were invited by Stalin's plenipotentiary in Poland, the NKVD General Ivanov, for talks at Pruszków outside Warsaw. There they were seized and flown to Moscow where they were put on trial for collaborating with the Nazis, and given sentences of up to ten years. Tens of thousands of AK members, former officers, political workers and landowners were interrogated, tortured, and often murdered: as many as 16,000 people are thought to have died in this way.

Although the AK had been dissolved, many of its members remained on their guard, while units of the right-wing NSZ and the newly founded Freedom and Independence (WiN) engaged in active self-defence. By 1946 this militant underground numbered as many as 80,000 men, who were, ironically, much better armed than the AK had ever been, thanks to the passage of the Russo-German front through the country. As the NKVD and UB intensified their activities, this self-defence grew into a guerrilla war which would cost the lives of some 30,000 Poles and 1,000 Soviet soldiers over the next two years.

By the middle of 1946 the new Citizens' Militia (MO) was twice as strong in numbers as the pre-war Polish police, and the internal security forces numbered as many again. While the Polish and Soviet troops dealt with the militant underground, these attended to the rest of the population. Although its prime objective was the annihilation of what was left of the landed gentry and the intelligentsia, there was nobody so insignificant that he or she did not qualify for the attentions of the UB, attentions which were both meticulous and brutal. Recently vacated German concentration camps were reactivated and filled up.

The new order was imposed ruthlessly. The decisions of the political men on the ground and those of their colleagues of the police could be highly arbitrary. Anything could be 'nationalised' – not only estates, factories, smallholdings, livestock, pictures and other valuables, but the humblest personal possessions. In addition, units of the Red Army stationed all over Poland not only lived off the land, but engaged in regular plundering expeditions.

All this took place in an atmosphere of uncertainty and confusion. Over six million Germans either fled or were evicted, mostly from parts of Germany which had been allocated to Poland under an agreement between Stalin and the Western Allies. Their place was being taken by Poles flooding in from every quarter, 2.2 million returning from slave labour and concentration camps in Germany, 1.5 million ousted from former Polish territory taken over by the Soviet Union.

It was only after more than a year of careful preparation and positioning that elections were held, in January 1947. The strongest contestant was Mikołajczyk's Polish People's Party (PSL). The second largest party was the new PPS. Its old leadership having remained in exile or in hiding, it was led by a pre-war activist and survivor of Auschwitz, Józef Cyrankiewicz. The party favoured by Stalin, the Polish Workers' Party (PPR), led by Władysław Gomułka, had only 65,000 members in December 1945, just over one-tenth of the membership of the PSL. In the event, however, the PSL would be awarded only 10.3 per cent of the vote.

One million people were disqualified from voting by bureaucratic sleight-of-hand, and thousands more were arrested on the day or beaten up on the way to the polling stations, which were heavily staffed with members of the security services; 128 activists of the PSL were murdered, 149 of its candidates were arrested, 174 were disqualified and only twenty-eight were elected, of whom fourteen were subsequently disqualified. Fearing for his life, Mikołajczyk escaped to the West.

A provisional constitution adopted in February 1947 established a Council of State with almost unlimited legislative and executive powers, which were exercised by the leadership of the PPR. Operations against the remnants of the underground were intensified, a campaign of harassment was launched against the Church and all pretence at conciliation and social democratic window-dressing was dropped.

In August 1948 Władysław Gomułka, secretary of the PPR and deputy premier, the principal advocate of 'a Polish road to socialism', was accused of 'nationalist deviation' and sacked from his post, which was filled by Bolesław Bierut, a staunch Stalinist. In December 1948 the remaining deputies of the PPS were forced to merge with the PPR in the new PZPR (Polish United Workers' Party), which henceforth became *the* Party. The remains of the PSL were amalgamated into the ZSL (United People's Party), which was only nominally independent of the PZPR.

There followed, in 1950, a purge of 'alien elements' in the PPS and the PPR, and a witch-hunt in the army. Those who had served in Polish forces abroad and returned to offer their services to the new state were mostly shot. The Russian Marshal Rokossovsky was put in charge of the army, which was staffed throughout by Russian officers.

The purge was carried through to trade unions, local organisations and the street. Stalinist verbiage about 'foreign agents' and 'enemy espionage' invaded everything from a quarrel between two Party bosses to a police report on petty pilfering or a wayside robbery. A brief affair with a former member of the AK was pretext enough for a girl to be interrogated, tortured and imprisoned for years. The prisons were bursting, and new concentration camps at Mielęcin and Jaworzno filled up with some 30,000 workers who had dared to strike. Peasants were forced to join Soviet-style collective farms. In 1951 Gomułka and others who had fallen from grace were imprisoned.

By then, Poland had been hermetically sealed off from the outside world, and not just by the three hundred kilometres of barbed-wire entanglements and 1,200 watchtowers surrounding it. In February 1947 leaders of the ruling parties of the Soviet-occupied countries of Central Europe met and set up an 'information bureau', the Cominform, ostensibly a vehicle for friendly cooperation. Although it was supposedly an inter-party body, it was in effect an inter-government one, and an instrument through which Stalin could exert pressure. In February 1948 a coup in Prague turned Czechoslovakia into a Soviet dependency, and the same happened in Budapest later that year. The Berlin blockade in June and the transformation of the Soviet zone of occupation in Germany into another Soviet satellite the following year finally drew the Iron Curtain across Europe. In 1952 a Soviet-style constitution, personally edited by Stalin, was imposed on the country, which was officially renamed the People's Republic of Poland.

The People's Republic of Poland

BALTIC SEA

Gdynia
Kaliningrad
Gdańsk
Vilna
Szczecin
GDR
Bydgoszcz
Białystok
Berlin
Poznań
Warsaw
USSR
Legnica
Łódź
Wrocław
Radom
Opole
Kielce
Lublin
Prague
Katowice
Sandomierz
Kraków
Lvov
CZECHOSLOVAKIA

——— Polish frontier in 1939
///// Polish frontier 1945
—··— "Curzon Line"

0   100 miles
0   200 km

TWENTY-ONE

The Cost of Victory

It is a grim irony that although it had been a member of the victorious alliance, Poland was the ultimate loser of the Second World War. It lost its independence and almost half its territory – in defence of which the war had been declared. According to the Bureau of War Reparations, it also lost 38 per cent of its national assets, a gigantic proportion when compared with the figures for France and Britain: 1.5 and 0.8 per cent respectively. These assets included the majority of its cultural heritage, as museums, libraries, palaces and churches had gone up in smoke. But the real losses were far greater than that, and the consequences more lasting.

Nearly six million Polish citizens had been killed, a proportion of one in five. The proportion among the educated elites was far higher: nearly one in three for Catholic priests and doctors, and over one in two for lawyers. A further half a million of Poland's citizens had been crippled for life and a million children had been orphaned. The surviving population was suffering from severe malnutrition, while tuberculosis and other diseases raged on an epidemic scale. Another half a million Polish citizens, including a high proportion of the intelligentsia, most of the political and military leadership, and many of the best writers and artists, had been scattered around the world, never to return. In all, post-war Poland had 30 per cent fewer inhabitants than the Poland of 1939. But these figures give only a pale picture of the real harm done to Polish society: the Second World War destroyed not only people, buildings and works of art. It ripped apart a fragile yet functioning multi-racial and multi-cultural community still living out the consensual compact that had lain at the heart of the Commonwealth.

There had been no lack of suppressed tensions before 1939 between the ethnic Poles and the various minorities, and indeed between some of the minorities, but there had been remarkably little violence, and this had been limited to fringe groups of the kind that exist in any society. Toleration, albeit sometimes grudging, was the norm. It was inevitable that these tensions would be aroused by the advent of war, and that not only the German minority would openly declare for Germany against Poland and their Polish neighbours. Ukrainian nationalists in south-eastern Poland greeted both the Germans and the Soviets with open arms, while further north many Lithuanians, Belorussians and communist Jews received the invading Soviets as liberators.

These fissures were exacerbated by the elimination or removal of local elites, the closing down of schools and other communal institutions, the brutalisation which is the constant companion of war and the banditry that thrives under wartime occupation. Communities were further torn part by the massive deportations carried out by both occupying powers.

Both Nazi Germany and Soviet Russia were determined to destroy Polish society. They therefore imported onto the multi-ethnic and socially diverse territory of Poland methods of racial, social and political manipulation they had developed in their own countries. It was these that tipped the realities of the war in occupied Poland into a circle of hell far below that reached in any other country.

The Germans' first priority was to decapitate Polish society through the removal of all political, intellectual, spiritual and social leadership. The second was to divide it up into its racial components. All Polish citizens of German origin were classified as Germans and granted commensurate privileges. Polish citizens with German-sounding names who looked the part were encouraged to declare themselves to be *Volksdeutsch* and claim the same privileges. The Jews were segregated and destined for extermination. Ukrainian and Belorussian nationalists were encouraged to come forward and define themselves against their Polish neighbours.

When, in 1941, the Germans moved into the eastern areas of Poland hitherto under Soviet occupation, they used the same techniques to implement ethnic cleansing, thereby unleashing not only an orgy of horror, but also a self-perpetuating spiral of hatred and violence. What made their behaviour so deeply destructive in the long run was that in these areas the Germans were generally admired and considered to be more advanced and civilised than the Poles, and certainly than the Russians, and this lent them an authority that passed a civilising mantle to any local they chose to employ.

In the *Generalgouvernement*, the Germans generally removed all Jews from the community and took them to special camps for extermination. East of the Ribbentrop–Molotov line, they played on residual anti-Semitic feelings among the peasants and got locals to do the dirty work for them. The well documented case of Jedwabne, a Polish village occupied by the Soviets in 1939, provides a useful example. The invading Soviets had been warmly greeted by young Jewish communists, some of whom were then involved in the provisional administration and the 'Sovietisation' of the area. All Polish landowners, priests, teachers, doctors, policemen, postal and state functionaries had been murdered or deported by the Soviets, along with many humbler pillars of the community. When the Germans came, they encouraged the remaining inhabitants to take their revenge on the entire Jewish community, who were duly rounded up in a barn and burnt to death.

The picture was even uglier in south-eastern Poland. Soviet occupation had completely decapitated civil society, making it easier for extremists and criminals to operate, leading to a great deal of low-level violence between the Polish and Ukrainian communities. When the Germans crossed the Ribbentrop–Molotov line in 1941, Ukrainian nationalist activists came out into the open. The Germans armed them and gave them the task of murdering all the Jews in the area, which they carried out with enthusiasm. The lesson they learnt from this was that the easiest way of dealing with undesirable elements in their midst was to wipe them out, and they turned their weapons on their Polish neighbours.

In 1942, OUN, which had now superseded the more tractable UNDO, created the Ukrayinska Povstanska Armiya (UPA), which set about cleansing Volhynia, where Poles and Ukrainians had hitherto cohabited amicably. Over the next year it would kill up to 60,000 Poles, mostly peasants living in out-of-the-way villages, in bestial ways refined on the Jews. They also liquidated Ukrainians with communist or Polish sympathies.

Young Poles who managed to survive ganged up in partisan units and fought back, some even joining the German police special battalions in order to get hold of arms. Soon a regular civil war was raging between the Ukrainians and Poles of the area, tacitly encouraged by the Germans, who preferred to see both groups butchering each other than engaging in partisan warfare against them. The battle lines were often unclear. Both communities spoke each other's language fluently, and since some bands on both sides often posed as partisans of the opposing side in order to winkle out alien elements, they sometimes ended up murdering their own kith. German policy changed after the defeat at Stalingrad, and they began recruiting Ukrainians into the SS Galizien Division, whose principal task was to act against Polish partisans and self-defence groups in Galicia.

By this stage, OUN had moved on to dreams of an independent Ukraine and saw neither the weakening Germans, nor the seemingly exhausted Russians, but the Poles as the main enemy. The Polish–Ukrainian fighting carried on throughout 1943 and intensified in 1944 as deserters from SS Galizien brought manpower, arms and German military skills to one side, and the AK attempted (with limited success) to organise the disparate Polish units into a more coherent force on the other.

At this point, the Soviets entered the fray once more. Both Stalin and his Polish communist acolytes had shed their earlier internationalism and saw the future in terms of discrete ethnic political units. Stalin's preferred means of achieving this was mass resettlement.

In September 1944, after it had been occupied by the Soviets, a huge operation was put in train to remove all Poles and Jews from territory east of the new Polish frontier and resettle them in Poland, and to uproot all Ukrainians living to the west of it and transplant them to Soviet Ukraine. Virtually the entire population of the city of Lwów would eventually be moved into the ruins of the former German city of Breslau (now Wrocław). In all some 780,000 Poles and Jews were moved in this way, a trip which sometimes involved weeks in cattle trucks which were shunted onto sidings and repeatedly redirected before they were allowed to spill their human loads in some depopulated area. Those who did not register for 'repatriation', feeling no great national loyalty and wishing only to remain where they had always lived, were harassed by the NKVD or attacked by UPA fighters. Similar arrangements with regard to Lithuania and Belorussia yielded comparable numbers, most of whom were resettled in Pomerania or the areas newly acquired from Germany. Not surprisingly, since the area taken over by the Soviet Union amounted to 47 per cent of Poland's pre-war territory, the 1,500,000-odd resettled in Poland did not account for the whole Polish population of the area, and at least as many remained behind.

The same went for the Ukrainians and Lemkos (a small Ruthene nation inhabiting the eastern Carpathians) whose homeland was to remain in the new Poland. According to arrangements made by Stalin, they should have been resettled in Soviet Ukraine, but they had no wish to go, and they were supported in this by fighters of the UPA and the remnants of the SS Galizien division, which had been forced out of Soviet Ukraine and were now operating in south-eastern Poland. Attempts to implement Stalin's plans led to a running battle beginning in late 1945 between them and NKVD and Polish army units under Russian command, in the course of which half a million Ukrainians and Lemkos were deported and some 4,000 killed. But the action was by no means conclusive, and early in 1947 the Polish army launched Operation Vistula to deal with UPA and the remaining Lemkos. As the Soviet Ukraine no longer wanted them, some 150,000 of these were resettled, family by family, in distant parts of Poland. The UPA was defeated and forced to withdraw into Soviet Ukraine, where it went underground.

The massive scale on which people were being shunted about and resettled, a process which normally involved brutality at the outset, followed by rape and pillage by bandits of one sort or another along the way, and hostility from the host community at the other end, had a profoundly traumatic effect on all those involved. Communities which had been uprooted and split up lost their sense of identity and disintegrated into embattled family groups. Resettled on farms or in houses that had belonged to others who had been murdered or deported, they felt no empathy with the alien landscape and no real sense of ownership, only a fear of potential consequences. With no local leadership of any kind (surviving landowners were not allowed to come within fifty kilometres of their former estates) and a constant prey to lawless militia, soldiers and criminal gangs, they did not constitute communities, only masses of fearful families and individuals.

As they tried to rebuild their lives against a background of civil war and political terror, all felt an overwhelming sense of powerlessness, which bred resentment and even hatred of any 'other', along with a desire for revenge for all the wrongs they had suffered. Anyone living through those times witnessed hideous acts of revenge in the final stages of the war. Wartime informers and representatives of the new order were tortured to death by former AK soldiers. AK soldiers were subjected to all the refinements of Soviet interrogation by UB operatives. *Volksdeutch* families fleeing west before the Red Army were murdered in horrible ways, often burned alive, by Polish peasants and Jews who had come out of hiding or German captivity. One of the ugliest and most eloquent examples of the degree to which humanity had been degraded occurred in the town of Kielce on 4 July 1946.

Some 300,000 Polish Jews survived the war, and their return home from concentration camp, hiding or deportation in the Soviet Union was often traumatic. When they had been removed by the Germans, their houses had usually been occupied by the poorer, and often criminal, elements of the local community, and their reappearance met with resentment and sometimes violence. They encountered the same fear and suspicion as all other displaced groups, and in their case resentment was heavily tinged with the anti-Semitism prevalent in provincial towns such as Kielce.

On 3 July a nine-year-old boy who had gone to visit relatives in the country for a couple of days without telling his parents reappeared and in order to avoid punishment told them that he had been kidnapped, pointing out a house in which he had supposedly been held. This happened to be the home of several Jewish families. The parents reported the matter to the militia, which sent three armed patrols to investigate. The militia's appearance outside the house drew a crowd of onlookers, and rumours began to circulate that Jews were kidnapping Polish children. When the militia entered the building they began confiscating arms, and for reasons unknown shot a couple of the inhabitants. They then evacuated the house and the inhabitants found themselves pushed out into the street, where a by now threatening crowd was howling abuse. A detachment of a hundred soldiers had turned up to control the crowd, but stood by idly, along with the militia, while the crowd attacked the Jews. The head of the Jewish community was shot by one of the soldiers when he tried to get help from the militia head-quarters only a hundred metres away, where the local commander and his Soviet superior ignored the events. Wild rumours flew around town, and more Jews and their homes were attacked. By the end of the day, over forty Jews and two Christians had been killed. News of this, along with instances of aggressive anti-Semitism elsewhere, caused many of Poland's surviving Jews to opt for emigration.

The creators of the People's Republic of Poland liked to stress that it was a truly Polish state and to represent it as a kind of socialist reincarnation of the Piast kingdom. The Poland of 1952 was certainly more ethnically and religiously homogeneous than it had been at any point since the days of the Piast dynasty. But the process that had led to this had not given rise to a new Polish society, only to a profoundly damaged mass of individuals, many of them reduced to a feral day-to-day existence. And those in power did nothing to bring anything resembling a normal human society into being.

All the active elements which had survived the war, such as the Church and various social organisations, and including even the nationalist right-wing parties and members of the aristocracy, readily involved themselves in the process of rebuilding the country. This manifested itself as much in the spirit of piety with which the shards of its cultural heritage were rescued and the meticulous rebuilding of historical city centres as in the recreation of pre-war social and cultural institutions. But it soon became clear that those in power had no intention of allowing Polish society to reconstitute itself: a new social order was to be imposed from above, along lines dictated by the Central Committee of the Party, enforced by its own cadres and Party-directed organisations such as the Association of Polish Youth (ZMP), the trade unions, cooperatives, and so on. Not only were groups or organisations outside the ambit of the Party harassed and censored, their access to both information and publication was severely limited. Even where they were permitted to publish papers or periodicals, they were only allowed miserly allocations of paper. The same was true of independent publishers, which withered before being eliminated in 1947. All information and the possibility of disseminating it was gradually brought under the sole control of the Party.

The Sejm, theoretically the expression of the will of the people, was entirely dominated by the Party, since the Party decided whose names appeared on the list of candidates. So while the Sejm nominated the Council of State, the Council of Ministers, the legislature and the holders of all major offices, it was the Party that dictated the choice. For the purposes of window-dressing, a small group of Catholic deputies was allowed to stand and be elected, but while they were listened to during debates, in which they served as a kind of bad conscience, they were otherwise ignored.

Many young men and women had joined the Party hoping to change the world, and after it had consolidated its grip on power in 1947 many more signed up, since this represented the only possibility of achieving anything. But, having eliminated all opposition, and securely hemmed in behind the Iron Curtain by socialist neighbours, the Party embarked, at the end of 1948, on a purge of its ranks, ostensibly to weed out 'nationalists' and 'deviationists'. The white-collar element were adept at keeping their heads down, while factory-floor idealists could be tripped up only too easily. As a result, the purge removed significant numbers of its blue-collar members. By the early 1950s the Party, whose membership never rose much above 1.3 million, or 5 per cent of the population, during this period, was in large measure made up of bureaucrats of one sort or another. By 1955 only one in five workers belonged.

By contrast, over 90 per cent of them belonged to the Catholic Church. This had come through the war morally enhanced by its uncompromising stand against the Germans. Thousands of priests had been sent to concentration camps or shot, and no trace of collaboration tainted the hierarchy's reputation. It was led by redoubtable cardinals such as Adam Stefan Sapieha, Archbishop of Kraków, Augustyn Hlond, Archbishop of Gniezno, and Stefan Wyszyński, who succeeded him as Archbishop of Gniezno and Primate of Poland.

As soon as it had consolidated its power, the Party set about undermining this alien body within the new order. In 1949 the Church's property was nationalised and its charitable institutions taken over by the state. Religious instruction was forbidden in schools and chaplains were banned from prisons and hospitals. In 1953 a number of priests were put on trial charged with spying for the United States, receiving sentences of death or imprisonment. Later that year Primate Stefan Wyszyński himself was imprisoned.

Another element which did not fit the socialist model were the peasants, who still made up over half of the population. In 1944 their support had been assured by grants of land taken from confiscated estates: over a million families acquired land in this way. But within a couple of years many of them were forced into collective farms on the Russian model, of which there were 10,000 by 1954, mostly in the territories transferred from Germany to Poland in 1945. The remaining private farmers were squeezed by the imposition of compulsory quotas which they had to deliver at fixed prices, usually below the cost of production. Force was used to collect the quotas and a newly imposed land tax from the unwilling farmers, and tens of thousands of them were imprisoned. In these conditions, agriculture lagged in productivity and the countryside became increasingly pauperised.

Similar techniques were employed to eliminate small traders, private businesses and manufactures, and self-employed artisans. They were heavily taxed, starved of raw materials and excluded from markets. This was perverse, since they provided a valuable resource in the dire post-war economic climate.

The advancing Germans had done extensive damage in 1939, and when they retreated they dynamited everything they could. In the wake of the advancing Soviet armies came special units whose job it was to dismantle and remove anything that could prove useful back in the Soviet Union, including entire telephone exchanges and tramway installations, thereby reducing the country's infrastructure to nothing.

The fact that it was necessary to start from scratch favoured the socialist penchant for a command economy based on central planning. A three-year plan (1947–49) was followed by a six-year plan (1950–55). The State Economic Planning Commission issued rigid directives which turned out to be unworkable in local conditions of which the planners were entirely ignorant. The commission did not encourage initiative or even questioning by factory managers, so there was little these could do except muddle along by cooking figures and bribing inspectors. Since it was known that factory managers concealed their real resources so as not to be caught out under-fulfilling the quotas they were set, the planners found themselves ignoring reports and estimating the possibilities themselves. The whole process of economic planning, from investment to costs and prices, was therefore carried out at a largely theoretical level and was as often as not based on guesswork. Since each factory hinged on the performance of a dozen others, and since a further dozen depended on its own performance, and since each of these had preordained supplies, capacity and output all calculated from figures which bore scant relation to reality, the results were often ludicrous.

Much of the planning defied common sense. New factories were built hundreds of miles away from existing industrial centres, coalfields or manpower pools. The planners had a weakness for monumental projects that would be seen and smelt for miles around. This went hand in hand with ideological dictates: the Stalinist city and steelworks of Nowa Huta were purposely located as a counterbalance to Catholic, traditionalist and academic Kraków.

The results were low productivity in factories, which were inefficiently managed, on collective and state farms, where low motivation and under-investment undermined attempts at raising yields, and particularly in coalmines, where the authorities resorted to using forced labour of military conscripts in an effort to boost output. The scale of growth was nevertheless impressive, and the economy emerged rapidly from the ashes of war. But the cost was borne entirely by the people, in low wages, long working hours and poor conditions, and high prices of everything from food to shoes and clothing.

It was no coincidence that the six-year plan, which ended in 1955, brought Poland's economy into line with the Russian cycle of five-year plans. The pattern of Poland's industrialisation had been dictated by the Soviet Union, which wanted the economies of its satellites to mesh with its own and which had forced Poland and the others to refuse Marshall Aid in 1947. All the members of the Soviet bloc were bound together into the Comecon by a set of rigid trade treaties which made them interdependent and worked in Russia's favour. In addition, some $US5 billion-worth of coal from the fields acquired from Germany was given to the Soviet Union between 1946 and 1955 as war reparations, at a time when coal was virtually Poland's only means of acquiring foreign currency.

It was Soviet demands too that burdened the Polish economy with the obligation to maintain a huge army and police apparatus, and to pay the keep of the Russian armies stationed in Poland. The economy was viewed as one of the fronts on which the battle for socialism was being fought, and when a machine broke down or productivity fell, it was blamed on 'imperialist saboteurs', agents of the London government or 'hooligans'. Miners, factory workers and collective-farm workers were continually bombarded with paranoid propaganda representing the Soviet bloc as a peace-loving brotherhood of nations threatened by capitalist warmongering and aggression, and the conflicts in China and Korea were made to loom large in their everyday work.

The sort of industrialisation that was implemented in post-war Poland usually has the effect of drawing people from the country-side into the towns, where they soon turn into a rootless proletariat. In Poland the process was so rapid and on such a large scale that it backfired. By 1970 no less than 63 per cent of the entire blue-collar workforce had come from the country. In 1968, 22.3 per cent of industrial workers, 28 of construction workers and 31.7 of transport workers still lived in the country and commuted to work, while 10 per cent of industrial and building workers and 15 of transport workers were also part-time farmers. Instead of creating a socialist urban proletariat, the rapid industrialisation had the effect of ruralising the workers of the cities. This helped keep them within the ambit of the Church, which was stronger in rural parishes than in the cities, particularly the new industrial centres, where there were no churches.

Trade unions were set up to control the workers, which they did on the one hand through a programme of elaborate rituals ranging from May Day parades to banner-waving rallies and ceremonial deliveries of finished products, and on the other by meticulous monitoring of their attitudes, friendships, private vices and opinions. The personnel manager in any factory was an officer of the UB, and Party members in the workforce were expected to inform on their comrades. Workers accused of 'crimes' that were difficult to disprove were also blackmailed into spying on their colleagues.

In addition, the Ministry of Public Safety had paid informers everywhere – over 70,000 of them by 1954. By that date the register of 'criminal and suspicious elements' in the population contained nearly six million files, covering one in three of the adult population. The criminal justice system was geared not so much to delivering justice as to protecting the social, economic and political order, and as a result there were some 35,000 political prisoners behind bars by the mid-1950s. These were mostly people whose outlook, education, independence of mind and leadership potential classified them as elements to be weeded out so that those left at liberty could be more easily manipulated and moulded.

Since the essential precondition for creating the desired new socialist citizen was the elimination of the family unit as a formative influence, women were obliged to work and to place their children in crêches, where the process of indoctrination began. It was followed up in nursery, primary and secondary schools. Textbooks, particularly on history, were rewritten and new subjects, mostly dealing with Marxism or the history of Russian communism, found their way onto the curriculum. The children were obliged to join the Scouts or the Pioneers, and later the Union of Polish Youth (ZMP), which ensured that they were fully occupied outside school hours, and took them off to summer camps or winter sports during the holidays. These organisations fed them with a stream of propaganda, taught them to distrust their parents, and inculcated socialist principles and the virtues of collective action. The process of indoctrination did not end with school. An Institute of Social Sciences turned out new cadres of teachers and experts who subjected every field of study and endeavour to Marxist theory.

Censorship was omnipresent, and even some of the works of classic authors such as Mickiewicz and Słowacki were banned. Translations of books from 'imperialist languages' such as English were halted, and the market was flooded with translations of Russian socialist literature. Adults had to endure lectures and courses so that they too might understand the class struggle and Marxist economic theory, and everyone was expected to belong to at least one progressive organisation, such as the Polish Women's League or the Polish–Soviet Friendship Society.

Culture played a major part in the process. Outside a handful of showcase examples, what was left of Poland's heritage, particularly the built environment, was wilfully neglected or destroyed, including tens of thousands of country houses.

In 1947 the Party's Central Committee issued guidelines on which themes should be addressed in art and literature, denouncing the 'anachronistic ideal of falsely interpreted "artistic freedom"', and in the following year called for a new literature and art of Socialist Realism. The members of the Writers' Union were taken on factory visits while their weekly organ *New Culture* hectored them on Marxist theory. Painters and sculptors were encouraged to turn out representations of workers wielding hammers, soldiers marching forward with their jaws resolutely stuck out towards the new socialist dawn, or steelworkers holding a discussion on the Korean War during their lunch break. Musicians were not exempt. Andrzej Panufnik, prize-winning composer and conductor of the Warsaw Philharmonic Orchestra, was twice nominated as State Laureate and even awarded the Order of the Banner of Labour for his works. But in 1952 his new *Heroic Overture* was labelled 'formalistic', 'decadent' and 'alien to the great socialist era'. Party activists demanded that the scores be burnt and his music was banned from performance for the next thirty years.

TWENTY-TWO

Trial and Error

The announcement of Stalin's death, on 5 March 1953, stunned more than it relieved, and the degree to which his system had been implanted in Poland can be gauged from the fact that many Poles actually wept. Katowice was promptly renamed Stalinogród as a mark of respect and subservience while the Party waited nervously to see which way the wind would blow. After a few months, the signals from Moscow were that a general 'thaw' could take place. As a result, writers who had not published for years appeared in print, journalists discussed taboo subjects and economists went so far as to question Marxist-Leninist theories.

A few months later, Colonel Józef Światło, deputy chief of the UB's Tenth Department, in charge of keeping tabs on the Party itself, defected and began a series of broadcasts on Western radio. Even senior Party members were astonished to hear to what extent every aspect of Polish life had been dictated by Moscow. Gomułka and others were quietly released from prison, the Ministry of Public Safety was abolished, and the security services lowered their profile. Party Secretary Bierut admitted that 'mistakes' had been made and that there had been a 'tendency to widen the field of activity of the security services', but he wavered.

He was in the unenviable position of having to gauge which

way Moscow would move next and he therefore zig-zagged between thaw and repression, personally favouring the latter. There were many traditional Stalinists like him in the Party. Their reaction to the Światło revelations was not that the system had to be cleaned up, but that security ought to be tightened in such a manner as to prevent a repetition of the scandal. They were comforted when, partly as a reaction to West Germany's accession to NATO in the previous year, the Warsaw Pact, signed on 14 May 1955, bound all the Soviet satellites to Moscow more firmly than ever.

In February 1956 Nikita Khrushchev made his famous speech to the Twentieth Congress of the Communist Party of the Soviet Union denouncing Stalin's rule. Bierut, who was in attendance, died, purportedly of a heart attack. The Party was in disarray. Khrushchev came to Warsaw to attend the plenary session of the Party's Central Committee, which was to elect a new First Secretary, and he suggested Edward Ochab, who was duly chosen. Ochab proceeded to announce a programme of liberalisation, a partial amnesty for political prisoners, and the arrest of the chief procurator and several high-ranking persons in the UB. He committed the Party to rectifying recent 'errors and distortions'. But this was a dangerous course, as the summer months were to show.

Back in December 1955 the 15,000 workers of the former Cegielski and now Stalin works in Poznań had discovered that bureaucratic venality had cheated them of a percentage of their salary. They remonstrated with their management, took the matter up at District Party level, and finally sent delegates to Warsaw, without effect. On 28 June 1956, during the International Trade Fair in Poznań, they staged a demonstration. They demanded that Prime Minister Cyrankiewicz come to talk to them. When he refused, they attacked a police station in which they seized arms, and went on to demolish a radio-jamming station and the Poznań headquarters of the UB. The authorities responded by sending in tanks, and the riots came to a bloody end two days later. The civilian death toll stood at seventy.

'Imperialist agents' were blamed, and reactionaries within the Party argued that such outbreaks were the inevitable consequence of relaxing discipline. While the Party continued its programme of decentralising the economy and democratising itself, a faction of Stalinist diehards, the so-called Natolin group, called on their allies in Moscow. As the Eighth Plenary Session of the Party opened on 19 October 1956, a delegation headed by Khrushchev flew in unannounced and Russian troops stationed in Poland began to move on Warsaw. Crisis loomed as the government called out the army, and even distributed arms to the car workers of Żerań. The situation was assuming international dimensions.

Although the Polish armed forces in the West had been gradually disbanded after 1946, despite efforts to keep at least a skeleton Polish Legion in existence, the London government still upheld its claim. It was supported by a highly active emigration, which constituted a kind of Polish state in exile. As the Cold War set in, the United States began to show an interest in Polish affairs once again. In 1952 the CIA founded Radio Free Europe to broadcast straight news and cultural programmes to the whole Soviet-dominated region. It cooperated with the London Poles, and parachuted agents into Poland to liaise with people on the ground. While the fighting underground had been defeated by 1948, many of its former members were still at large, and armed attacks as well as more common acts of resistance such as defacing propaganda posters and painting slogans were recorded as late as 1955.

Władysław Gomułka managed to convince Khrushchev that he could contain the situation. As the Soviet units returned to base, Gomułka told a rally in Warsaw on 24 October that 'The Party, united in the working class and the nation, will lead Poland on a new road to socialism.' It was to be socialism with a human face and a Polish garb. Cardinal Wyszyński was released and the Church was allowed to resume its normal activities in return for a pledge of allegiance to the regime. Marshal Rokossovsky and hundreds of Russian officers were dismissed from the Polish army and sent home. A quarter of a million Poles stranded in the Soviet Union were allowed to emigrate to Poland. Commercial treaties were re-negotiated on more favourable terms and the Soviet Union was to pay for the upkeep of its troops stationed in Poland. But none of the fundamentals had changed.

On 30 October the Hungarian Prime Minister Imre Nagy announced a return to democracy, and five days later the Soviet army invaded his country in defence of 'Leninist principles of equality among nations'. The warning for Poland was clear.

Gomułka was finding it difficult to contain the revolution which had brought him to power. A purge of Stalinists was being carried out in the ranks of the Party, factory workers in Silesia were sacking their bosses and collective farms were being dissolved spon-taneously by those working on them. Associations and periodicals suppressed in 1948 revived, opening up debate on every subject. The collecting of funds, medical supplies and blood on behalf of the Hungarian freedom fighters was a major embarrassment to the Polish government, which found itself obliged to take a different line from the Soviet Union in a United Nations vote on the issue. On 10 December the Soviet consulate in Szczecin was stormed by angry workers.

Even reformers in the Party had to admit that the time had come to close ranks and safeguard its interests. A few months earlier Gomułka had praised the workers of Poznań for having taught the Party 'a painful lesson', but he had never abandoned his old authoritarian views. By the middle of 1957 the striking tram-drivers of Łódź were branded with the more traditional epithet of 'hooligans', and 1,500 miners in the Katowice area were fired in the interests of 'discipline'. Following the elections of 1957, during which Gomułka posed as the saviour of Poland, he began a crackdown on revisionists in the Party. In 1959 General Mieczysław Moczar, a member of the Natolin group and hero of the Stalinist 'partisans', was placed in command of the security services.

A new campaign of petty persecution was launched against the Church. The government had already tried repression, which had merely turned priests into martyrs. It had tried subversion, by encouraging a movement of 'patriotic priests' who were to reconcile the teachings of Marx with those of Christ, which, after some initial success, had turned into a fiasco. Thereafter it followed the course of pettifogging obstructionism and judicial harassment, while seducing the young into rival activities. Practising Catholics were banned from holding office within the Party. The security services infiltrated the Church, spying on priests who might reveal foibles so they could be turned into agents and informers. Crosses were removed from schools and hospitals, and a ban was imposed on the building of new churches.

Despite this the Church's position in national life went from strength to strength. Faced with the injustice, falsehood and drabness of socialist reality, people of all classes sought solace, truth and beauty in the Catholic faith. As the countryside had been methodically denuded of social elites, the parish priest was the one educated man to whom people could turn. In the hideous industrial quarters of the cities workers looked to the parish priest for comfort and guidance, and resisted with force when the militia tried to tear down crosses erected on plots where they hoped to build new churches.

The Catholic University of Lublin was the one free seat of learning. For a long time the Catholic periodical *Znak* and the weekly *Tygodnik Powszechny*, both published in Kraków, were the only papers to maintain any editorial freedom. They brought together priests and laymen, who formed the Club of the Catholic Intelligentsia (KIK), a discussion group which grew into a youth organisation offering an alternative to Party-sponsored associations.

After the 'thaw' of 1956 the universities once more became centres of learning, and cultural life revived. Increased contact with the outside world – through trade, travel, cultural exchange and the broadcasts of such services as Radio Free Europe – expanded horizons and raised hopes of a return to normal relations with the outside world. But such contacts had a depressing side, as they revealed that the outside world viewed Poland in negative terms.

One of the more bitter aspects of Poland's post-war experience was that it had come out of the conflict not only as the greatest loser, but with its reputation seriously tarnished. The pre-war Polish state and its government were generally viewed as backward and authoritarian. The Western love affair with communism and the Soviet Union meant that Poles were also seen as ideologically suspect. The Polish war effort was dismissed as futile and its leadership as inept. Catholicism was not in fashion in Western intellectual circles, and nor were the kind of values the Poles had fought for. In addition, the Polish nation stood accused, particularly by the intellectuals and Jews of France and America, of anti-Semitism on a scale to rival that of the Germans. The fact that the extermination camps had been sited on Polish territory (because over four-fifths of those to be exterminated lived in that part of Europe and it was conveniently free from interference by the RAF) was held up as evidence of Polish collaboration in the Holocaust.

This lack of empathy from outside meant that Polish society had to come to terms with its predicament on its own, and this had a profound influence on the development of literature and the arts. The war had scythed through the established writers of the 1930s, and those who were not killed were scattered – to London, Paris, New York, Buenos Aires or Tel Aviv. Their writings, published by independent émigré presses, nevertheless found their way back to Poland, where they played a part in a remarkable literary flowering whose best-known figures were the poets Tadeusz Różewicz, Zbigniew Herbert and Czesław Miłosz, the novelists Jerzy Andrzejewski, Stanisław Dygat, Jarosław Iwaszkiewicz and Tadeusz Konwicki, the playwright Sławomir Mrożek, the writer Stefan Kisielewski and the philosopher Leszek Kołakowski. This was run close by a similar flowering in film-making, whose greatest exponent was Andrzej Wajda, which explored Polish realities in subtle but penetrating ways.

The holiday did not last long, and in 1958 a clampdown began. Books were banned and periodicals shut down. Censorship was imposed more ruthlessly than ever, with the censor's office deciding how many copies of each book could be printed and how many performances of a play could be staged. Writers who did not conform were harassed and arrested. And while they responded by retreating into allusion and other subterfuges to evade the censor – or, in the case of Stanisław Lem, into the realms of science fiction – the state's manipulation of language reached Orwellian proportions, for different reasons.

In 1965 two young Party activists, Jacek Kuroń and Karol Modzelewski, wrote an open letter demanding a complete overhaul of the political machine and a return to the basic values of socialism. They were immediately arrested and sent to prison, but others, most notably their colleague Adam Michnik, carried on the discussion, in universities and youth organisations. While Gomułka grew more reactionary, a faction within the Party viewed him as soft and incompetent. General Moczar, now Minister of the Interior, was biding his time.

The Church had been preparing to mark a thousand years of Christianity in Poland in 1966, and as part of this preparation, in November 1965 the Polish bishops sent an open letter to their

German counterparts calling for mutual forgiveness and reconciliation between the two nations. Gomułka had already launched a rival programme of celebrations to mark the millennium of the Polish state, to provide an excuse for the disruption of the Church's celebrations by police and 'worker activists'. Now Moczar's faction seized on the bishops' letter and accused them of encouraging 'German revanchism' and undermining the Polish state.

The Six-Day War between Israel and the Arab states in 1967 raised the political temperature. The Soviet Union and her satellites backed the Arabs, but most Poles were on the side of Israel and greeted its successes with delight, partly as a slap in the face to Russia, partly because they could identify with the Israelis, many of whom were of Polish origin. The deputy Konstanty Łubieński cast one of the only two votes ever registered against the government in the Sejm on its condemnation of Israel, one of many open manifestations of sympathy for the embattled state. Gomułka responded by declaring that Poles could only have one motherland and denounced Israeli sympathisers as 'Zionists'.

In January 1968 Mickiewicz's *Forefathers' Eve* was playing in Warsaw to houses filled with students who cheered the anti-Russian references in the play. The authorities took the absurd step of banning it. The demonstrations which ensued at Warsaw University were dispersed with unwarranted brutality by the militia, supported by its Volunteer Reserve (ORMO). Over a thousand students were arrested and thousands more expelled. A small demonstration on their behalf elicited similar overreaction, with hundreds of ORMO's 'sociopolitical activists' doing their utmost to turn it into a pitched battle. The Catholic members of the Sejm protested and the bishops' conference issued a condemnation. The student protest had spread to other parts of the country and other organisations, and demands for democratic processes and freedom of the press were voiced openly. The press gave lurid accounts of massive disturbances barely contained by the forces of order, and on 11 March blamed them on 'Zionist agents' taking their orders from Germany.

According to Moczar's partisans, a huge conspiracy was afoot, and Gomułka called for the Party to be purged of 'revisionists, lackeys of imperialism, Zionists and reactionaries'. This impressive umbrella reflected the fact that while he was principally concerned with ridding it of intellectuals and revisionists, Moczar, who was more in tune with the virulent anti-Semitism of his Russian colleagues, saw the whole thing as a Jewish conspiracy. He pointed out the Jewish origins of some of the student ringleaders, and indeed of some high-ranking Party officials. On 13 March a number of senior officials were dismissed for Zionism.

Moczar's partisans played heavily on the fact that during the first years after the war some of the best Party jobs had gone to people of Jewish origin. The envy of the lower ranks did the rest, and a purge began as Party members sniffed at each other's pedigrees. Among the most vociferous of the anti-Zionists were those like Edward Gierek, Secretary of the Silesian Committee of the Party, new men hungry for power. At a lower level, disgruntled workers and peasants were more than happy to express their hatred of intellectuals of every kind by calling them 'bloodsucking Jews', a random linkage that would resurface more than once in the future. Hundreds of Party officials and people in senior posts were sacked for 'Zionism'.

Gomułka was no longer in control, but hung on in the hope that the witch-hunt would deflect the discontent with his own leadership. He decided to grant exit visas to those 'Zionists' who wished to emigrate, and over the next few months up to 15,000 Polish Jews availed themselves of these, including a couple of hundred former employees of the Ministry of the Interior and the secret services. Gomułka's Jewish wife was not among them, nor were some highly placed Jews who had managed to sidestep the attack, nor was Adam Michnik, who was in gaol.

Gomułka's position was nonetheless tenuous, and he had to reach out for Soviet support. He secured it with the participation by 26,000 Polish troops in the invasion of Czechoslovakia in August of that year. But this did nothing to enhance his popularity within the Party and in the country at large – on 8 September a former AK officer, Ryszard Siwiec, burned himself to death before Gomułka and a huge crowd in the country's largest stadium in protest.

People were also far from enthusiastic about the effects of Gomułka's economic policy. He had tried to decentralise the economy, but it had proved impossible to shrug off the old habits of central planning. As wages slumped and working conditions declined, absenteeism and careless work crippled production. The private sector in agriculture was starved of investment; socialist principle demanded that it should be eventually phased out, although it was responsible for 80 per cent of all production. Terrified of the country becoming a debtor, Gomułka resisted imports, including those of grain and animal feed. The result was a fall in the quantity of livestock, and following two bad harvests in 1969 and 1970, a severe shortage of meat.

The cost of living had risen throughout the 1960s, while wages lagged far behind. The sudden increase by an average of 30 per cent in the price of food announced on 13 December 1970 produced an instant reaction. The following day workers at the Lenin shipyard in Gdańsk went on strike and marched in protest to the local Party headquarters. Militia and Interior Ministry forces had been placed on full alert two days before, and those guarding the building opened fire on the strikers, who burnt it down. Similar confrontations took place in nearby Gdynia and in Szczecin, and on the following day tanks moved in, supported by 27,000 troops. The fighting spread to Elbląg and other coastal cities, and on 17 December the whole area was sealed off by the army. By the end of the first four days, forty-one people had been killed, over 1,000 injured and 3,200 detained.

On 19 December an emergency session of the Politburo assembled without Gomułka, who had suffered a stroke, and voted to replace him with Edward Gierek. Gierek managed to impress the workers with his apparent goodwill, but it was not until he rescinded all the price rises that the strikes abated. He admitted that the episode was 'a painful reminder that the Party must never lose touch with the working class and the nation', and many believed in his sincerity. But the next ten years of his rule were to transform this lack of contact into an unbridgeable chasm. The unimaginative traditionalist communists of Gomułka's generation were replaced by a new breed of apparatchiks who fancied themselves as modern managers and socialist captains of industry, and felt a concomitant contempt for the grimy peasants and workers.

Gierek entertained ambitious plans for an 'economic leap forward', to be achieved by massive borrowing from the West which was to be repaid through the improved extraction of raw materials and the export of goods produced in new factories built with foreign capital. The spirit of *détente* favoured his scheme, and money poured in from Western banks only too happy to lend. Companies such as Fiat and Coca-Cola eagerly signed contracts to start production in Poland.

Initial results were dramatic: production rose sharply and the Polish economy began to grow at a faster rate than any other bar Japan's. New roads were built, railways were modernised and modern apartment blocks sprang up around every city. The standard of living went up, and its cost went down. Private cars, dishwashers and trips abroad came within the reach of the average citizen. Gierek was out to buy popularity, so the peasants were relieved of the compulsory delivery quotas, and national insurance was extended to cover them. The price of food was frozen at the 1965 level in order to win the hearts of the workers.

It was not long before cracks began to appear in Gierek's economic structure. The new factories were finished behind schedule, while their products proved to be of inferior quality and difficult to sell in the West. The foreign debt spiralled. The only answer was to increase exports of coal and other raw materials, and to divert consumer goods originally intended for the home market to exports. The consequences were felt immediately, through shortages of staple items. As Gierek juggled with figures, he forgot the lessons of history. In 1975 he raised the prices of 'luxury' consumer goods, and on 24 June 1976 the price of food by an average of 60 per cent. On the following day strikes broke out in Radom, Warsaw and around the country. The price rises were quickly withdrawn, but the motorised detachments of the Citizens' Militia (ZOMO) went into action, arresting and beating the striking workers. People were dismissed from their jobs by the hundred, and sentences of up to ten years were handed out.

The crisis brought to the surface a basketful of problems which had been obscured by Gierek's economic fireworks. His plans were based on an assumption of technical competence on the part of the Party cadres, but while membership had risen to a record three million, quality had not. The new men lacked the commitment to socialist ideals of those they replaced, and brought neither a sense of realism nor managerial ability in its stead. Rather than curing the ills endemic to socialist economies, they added to them, as corruption came in on the tail of incompetence. It was corruption on a vast scale, spreading through every branch of the system in the most flagrant manner, giving birth to a vast kleptocracy that bred resentment throughout society.

Gierek had leapt at every opportunity of credit and cooperation offered by the spirit of *détente*, and balanced this by increasingly servile behaviour towards the Soviet Union. Polish capital and personnel were committed to Soviet development projects; Polish goods produced from dollar investments were sold on for useless rubles; and the level of 'fraternal aid' to 'liberation movements' in Angola and elsewhere in the Third World rose sharply. While he flew off on official visits to France, Germany and the United States and hosted their presidents in Warsaw, Gierek also had to go to Moscow and, in 1975, play host to a none-too-happy Soviet premier Alexei Kosygin.

The Soviets wanted tangible tribute, in the form of a series of amendments to the Polish constitution. Poland was to be constitutionally committed to socialism, to the 'leading role' of the Party and, most important, to a 'fraternal alliance' with the Soviet Union. In addition to being larded with references to the Great October Revolution (which had brought the Bolsheviks to power in Russia in 1917), the constitution was also to contain an insidious clause which made civil rights dependent on 'the fulfilment of civic duty', but this was dropped as a result of public protest and the vehement intervention of the Church.

The breadth of the public response and the fact that Gierek felt obliged to give in were twin symptoms of a radically altered relationship between Poland's government and its people. It was not that the authorities had grown soft or neglected their defences – the budget of the Interior Ministry remained larger than those of the ministries of culture, health and education put together. It was simply that society had grown more assertive and politically more mature.

The early 1970s had seen an exponential increase in the numbers of predominantly young Poles travelling to western Europe and the United States in order to learn a language and earn enough money to buy a car or a flat on their return. Members of the post-war emigration and their children began visiting Poland in similarly growing numbers. This great movement of people broke down the barriers built up by decades of isolation, and opened permanent channels of communication. Polish thought and culture evolved in a semaphoric concert of individuals scattered throughout the world, transmitted through émigré journals and publishing houses of which the Paris monthly *Kultura* and the imprint Instytut Literacki were the most distinguished. These contacts were to prove of vital importance over the next years.

In the summer of 1975 the conference on Security and Cooperation in Europe meeting at Helsinki reached a number of agreements which were ostensibly a triumph for Soviet diplomacy. The division of Europe into a Soviet and a Western sphere of interest was tacitly recognised and accepted by both sides, which amounted to a betrayal by the West of all the nations under Soviet domination. But the third basket of agreements extended human rights to the citizens of all thirty-five signatory states, and obligated those states to respect them. This would play a part in the Soviet Union's undoing.

There had been plenty of dissident activity since 1968, and radical discussion involved large numbers of people, both at personal level and in *samizdat* or émigré publications smuggled into Poland. By the middle of the 1970s political programmes were beginning to take shape. But it was not until after Helsinki that a new sense of strategy emerged.

The first sign of this was the formation of the Workers' Defence Committee (KOR) in September 1976 by a group which included former AK officers, lawyers, writers and young dissidents. This provided workers with legal advice, sent observers to their trials, and informed the public on their treatment through its *Information Bulletin*. It also collected money to help pay fines and to assist their families. The committee gradually extended its activities to cover all cases of human rights violations, and mercilessly heckled the authorities on points of law. As it was entirely open, invoking the relevant clauses of the Helsinki agreements, the authorities could not simply silence it by arresting its members and banning it. This did not stop them from harassing active supporters – with searches of their homes, confiscations of property, dismissal from work or expulsion from university, short detention on technical grounds and severe beatings by supposed hooligans, and, occasionally, murder. But all of this was meticulously documented and reported to the Helsinki monitoring organs and to the world. KOR was joined in March 1977 by the Movement for the Defence of Human and Civil Rights (ROPCiO), and in May by a Students' Solidarity Committee in Kraków, both of which helped to collate the evidence against the Polish authorities and their doings.

Periodicals of every kind and underground presses began pouring forth a torrent of literature. In the same year a Flying University began operating in Warsaw, and discussion clubs burgeoned. The police arrested individuals, raided premises and confiscated materials, but the dissidents were well organised and protected by the sympathy and cooperation of the public. They were also given tacit support and facilities by the Church, which played an active part in defending human rights and helping sacked workers.

Gierek could ill-afford to crack down. He had official talks with the Primate, Cardinal Wyszyński, in 1976; in 1977 he visited France, Italy and India, and he hosted Jimmy Carter, Willy Brandt, King Baudouin of Belgium, Helmut Schmidt and the Shah of Iran in Warsaw. He needed to appear statesmanlike in order to stave off economic nemesis. The world recession was hurting the overstretched and incompetently managed Polish economy. The terminal condition of Polish industry spelt chaos, the desperate condition of Polish agriculture threatened crisis. The election, on 16 October 1978, of the Cardinal Archbishop of Kraków Karol Wojtyła to the Holy See meant that the crisis could, when it came, no longer be confined.

TWENTY-THREE

Papal Power

To the Poles the election of Pope John Paul II was not only a solace in their misery, as well as a great national honour, it was also the final breach in the wall behind which they had been kept since 1945. The pontiff's visit to his homeland in June 1979 not only reaffirmed their belief in their spiritual and cultural values, it was a catalyst that set in motion a process that would not cease until 1989.

The Pope travelled around the country holding a number of open-air masses attended by hundreds of thousands, and in one case over a million people. The militia looked on sheepishly as those who had come together realised the strength implicit in their number and spoke to each other with a new-found confidence and sense of solidarity. The Pope's homilies dwelt on the need to respect and demand respect for the innate dignity of man, and while the message was couched in religious terms, its relevance to the situation in Poland was lost neither on the listening crowds nor on the authorities. In Kraków, he told a vast crowd 'never to lose hope, give way to discouragement, or give up'.

While those who had pondered his teachings began to think of themselves as a community and to consider how to take responsibility for its future, Gierek was foundering in an economic morass.

370

In July 1980 he again made the mistake of attempting to balance the books by drastic rises in the price of food. A rash of strikes broke out in response, but this time their tenor and their strategy were entirely new.

At dawn on 14 August 1980 a previously dismissed electrical fitter climbed into the Lenin shipyard in Gdańsk to lead a strike over the illegal dismissal of a fellow worker, Anna Walentynowicz. His name was Lech Wałęsa. A participant in the 1970 strikes, he had learned that workers out in the open were no match for tanks, and in years of discussion with KOR and underground workers' cells he had forged a strategy and defined goals. Instead of marching out onto the streets, he occupied the shipyard and demanded that representatives of the government come to listen to the strikers.

At a meeting of the Politburo on 28 August, Gierek admitted that he did not know what to do and offered his resignation. Representatives were despatched to Gdańsk and to Szczecin, where a similar sit-in was being staged, in the hope of dividing the workers. But the leaders of KOR, KIK and ROPCiO, and dozens of prominent dissidents, such as Michnik, Kuroń, the historian Bronisław Geremek and the journalist Tadeusz Mazowiecki, had homed in on Gdańsk, to advise the inter-factory strike committee which had been formed to coordinate the strikes breaking out in various parts of the country.

The government was left with no option, and on 31 August signed an agreement with the workers. This was no mere settlement of wage claims or disputes over working conditions. It was a whole package involving the establishment of free trade unions, freedom of information, access to the media and civil rights. Historically, it was a seminal event. It was the first authentic workers' revolution in European history, and it showed up the 'dictatorship of the proletariat' for what it was, puncturing the fiction that had entranced so many and destroyed so many others since 1917.

On 17 September delegates representing some three million members met in Gdańsk to establish the form the new trade unions should take, and, on the advice of the lawyer Jan Olszewski and the historian Karol Modzelewski, who argued that smaller local unions would be easier for the authorities to infiltrate and manipulate, opted for a single nationwide union, to be called NSZZ Solidarność (Independent Self-Governing Trade Union Solidarity). Wałęsa was elected chairman of the national coordinating committee. The aspirations of most of the union's members and activists were limited to working conditions and a return to a purer and more authentic form of socialism. But that is not how they were viewed in Warsaw or Moscow.

Gierek had suffered a heart attack five days after the signature of the Gdańsk accords, and his place was taken by Stanisław Kania, who promised to combat 'anti-socialist forces' and to strengthen ties with the Soviet Union. Two days earlier, the Russian Politburo had instructed its Polish colleagues to prepare a 'counter-attack' and created a special group, which included the former Commissar for Foreign Affairs Andrei Gromyko and the KGB chief Yurii Andropov, to monitor the situation in Poland. They urged Kania and his Minister of Defence General Wojciech Jaruzelski to deal with the situation, and on 22 October the latter gave instructions for the preparation of a plan for the imposition of martial law. The Kremlin gave him to understand that he could count on Russian, East German and Czech army units. The United States was distracted by the Iran hostage crisis, and weakened by the fact that Jimmy Carter's presidency was in its last months. Carter was nevertheless alarmed enough by the situation to send Brezhnev a strongly worded telegram on 3 December.

It is unlikely that this had any effect on Soviet thinking, as the military option remained on the agenda. The German and Czech borders were closed and the Soviet press agency TASS announced that Soviet military manoeuvres would be taking place on Polish territory. On 5 December the Polish Party leadership and the ministers of defence and the interior flew to Moscow for talks.

Solidarność continued to grow as new unions, of journalists, publishers, teachers, students, peasants and other groups, sprang up and affiliated themselves, and by the end of the year it had over nine million members, representing 30 per cent of the adult population. This inevitably altered its profile and its motivation.

The Party's evident helplessness in the face of genuine people power had encouraged individuals at every level of society and in every walk of life to think and do the hitherto unthinkable. Knowledge and information on every subject from politics to ecology was disseminated through a rash of independent publications. People openly talked about and debated taboo subjects, and teachers began to tell their pupils the real story of the Second World War and the truth about Katyn and the Warsaw Uprising. Writers pulled out of their bottom drawers things they had never conceived of publishing; film-makers set about making films they had only dreamt of making; émigrés returned, some, like the Nobel laureate Czesław Miłosz, in triumph. A mood of deep exhilaration reigned, particularly among the young, even though the political situation remained ominous and the economic conditions catastrophic.

The harvest of Gierek's economic policy was a bitter one. The foreign debt reached giddy heights while the machinery bought with borrowed currency either fell to pieces or ground to a halt for lack of spare parts. What trimming Gierek had attempted in the late 1970s had resulted in skimping at the last moment, so that many projects suffered in the finishing stages, while a scale of pollution unknown elsewhere in Europe added to the misery of the population. By 1979 over 75 per cent of export revenue went to service the foreign debt. An inflexible freeze on foreign spending ruined what little chance there was of muddling through, and hit the health service severely. By the summer of 1981 there were widespread shortages of drugs, and no syringes with which to administer them. Malnutrition and diseases connected with dirt and deprivation reached epidemic proportions.

The cost of living rose by some 15 per cent in the first six months of 1981, and many everyday products were only available on the black market or in government foreign-currency shops. Even factories resorted to barter in order to obtain essential materials and supplies. Tens of thousands of people emigrated, and while many found work in the West, the helpless were gathered in refugee camps in Austria and West Germany. The situation was developing into a world crisis as the West waited to see whether the Soviet Union, which was chastened by its disastrous invasion of Afghanistan, would dare resort to its usual measure of invading a disobedient ally.

In Poland, the authorities employed delaying tactics with regard to Solidarność, while trying to disrupt its activities. Protest meetings were brutally attacked by ZOMO units, which did everything they could to provoke violence in the hope of being able to turn the issue into one of law and order. The government delayed passing the laws which would permit the trade union to function legally, thereby undermining the Gdańsk accords. As Solidarność staged nationwide strikes on 27 and 30 March to force its hand, Polish television broadcast images of Soviet troops conducting exercises. Tension mounted as President Ronald Reagan, who had assumed office two months earlier, issued a warning to Moscow not to intervene.

The situation in Poland was beginning to polarise along political lines. In February, Solidarność had issued a programme which made it clear that it believed economic improvement could not be achieved without political change and called for 'a complete renewal of the country'. That same month, General Jaruzelski had taken over as Prime Minister, and in March he authorised procedures for the imposition of martial law.

The Communist Party of the Soviet Union sent its Polish counterpart a letter in which it criticised it for giving in to counter-revolution, and the Kremlin urged it to act. But the PZPR was in no condition to play a leading role. Its Congress, which opened on 14 July 1981, revealed deep divisions between hard-liners and revisionists. The dominant atmosphere was one of fear and hesitancy, and people continued to leave the Party in large numbers.

There could hardly have been a greater contrast between this and the first National Congress held by Solidarność at Oliwa near Gdańsk in September 1981. The Congress constituted the first democratically elected national assembly since the pre-war Sejm, which lent its deliberations gravity. While Wałęsa and the moderates attempted to pin the discussion down to matters concerning the union itself and the Gdańsk accords, many of the delegates, frustrated and incensed by the government's bad faith, raised issues of principle that went far beyond these confines.

There were calls for the foundation of a political party to represent the workers and for free elections. As the Soviet Baltic fleet held the largest exercise since the Second World War, on 8 September the Congress passed a motion to issue a statement of sympathy and support to all the downtrodden peoples of the Soviet bloc and to encourage them to start free trade unions. TASS called the Congress 'an anti-socialist and anti-Soviet orgy', and the Polish Politburo accused Solidarność of violating the Gdańsk accords.

The Soviet leadership was nearing the limits of its tolerance. Yet the Soviet Union was diplomatically isolated as a result of its invasion of Afghanistan, and economically dependent on the West. The scale of the popular movement in Poland, its charismatic leader's immense popularity throughout the world, the high profile of the Polish Pope on the international scene and the determined attitude of the British Prime Minister Margaret Thatcher and President Ronald Reagan meant that an invasion might end in catastrophe for the Soviet Union.

Conveniently for Moscow, Jaruzelski was prepared to do almost anything to avoid one. After Kania's resignation in October, he took overall control and began preparations for a clampdown, which began on the night of 12 December 1981. At 11.30 p.m. the telephone network went dead, followed by radio and television transmissions. In a complex operation carried out with remarkable efficiency, almost the entire leadership of Solidarność were arrested. Thousands of people were dragged from their beds and ferried to prisons and concentration camps, while tanks patrolled the snow-covered streets and ZOMO stormtroopers were deployed at potential trouble spots. Factories, mines and the railway network were occupied and placed under military command. A curfew was imposed and travel was forbidden. At six in the morning of 13 December the national anthem was played on television and Jaruzelski declared that he had imposed martial law as the country had been on the edge of a precipice.

The workers were unprepared, and while there was a wave of strikes and sit-ins on 14 December, there was little resistance when the troops moved in. The Wujek mine in Silesia was the scene of an underground sit-in which ended on 16 December with ZOMO firing on and killing nine of the surrendering miners. Their colleagues in the Piast mine held out longer, but the last nine hundred came to the surface on 28 December. Although a few Solidarność leaders remained in hiding and mounted a campaign of underground opposition, the movement was ostensibly crushed. In all, some 5,000 of its members were detained, while another 150,000 were hauled in for 'preventive and cautionary talks'.

On 22 December Jaruzelski told the Politburo that they had won the first battle, but that they still had a campaign to fight and a war to win, which would take ten years. He was right about the battle. There was some low-level protest, with slogans daubed on walls and fliers distributed in the streets. Many writers and actors boycotted the state media. Strikes and demonstrations were staged on the national day of 3 May 1982, but they were put down brutally and effectively. People who did not submit lost their jobs and were subjected to pressures of one sort or another. On the anniversary of the signing of the Gdańsk accords there were demonstrations in over sixty towns, but these were dispersed. Over 5,000 people were arrested, and at least three people killed and hundreds wounded in the process, demonstrating the pointlessness of this kind of action. In December 1982, a year after its imposition, martial law was suspended, and six months later, lifted. By then a number of special powers had been brought in that made it unnecessary.

Jaruzelski's attempts at normalising the situation were less successful. He tried to garner support for the government by creating a Patriotic Movement for National Regeneration and an official trade union, which people were pressured to join. But neither carried much credibility.

The United States had imposed stringent trade sanctions, and other Western countries followed suit. This hit Jaruzelski's attempts at reviving the economy. Plans and reform programmes were announced, but nothing came of them. The złoty was devalued twice, in 1983 and 1985, and inflation rose to around 70 per cent.

Those Solidarność leaders who had slipped through the net on 13 December 1981 had organised an underground leadership, and gradually dissident life resumed in time-honoured ways. Radio Solidarność went on the air from clandestine studios, and underground presses went into action all over the country. They would publish at least 1,700 different papers and periodicals and about 1,800 books, often in large print runs, between 1982 and 1985. Literary and artistic activity flourished, often under the umbrella of the Church, which provided venues, facilities, means of communication and even cash. It also provided a vital link with individuals and organisations abroad which were sending aid of every kind and materials such as paper and printers' ink and machines.

Most of those detained, including Wałęsa, had been released by the beginning of 1983, and in July of that year a general amnesty was announced. Those, like Jacek Kuroń and Adam Michnik, held on charges of attempting to overthrow the state, were not brought to trial. But this did not reflect any change of attitude. Soon after being released, Wałęsa was accused of fraud and tax evasion, and he was harassed by the police. When he was awarded the Nobel Peace Prize in October of that year, he was forbidden to collect it and the Polish government sent a note of protest to the Norwegian government.

The security services had been expanded, and by 1983 employed more people than they had in Stalinist times. In November 1985 up to a hundred senior academics were dismissed in a purge of the educational system. Lesser mortals were bullied, beaten up or murdered. The security services also vastly expanded their pool of collaborators, putting pressure on people who had been caught committing some minor offence, or who simply had a past, to spy and report.

Life under these conditions became unbearable for many, and increasing numbers escaped to the West, in stolen planes, in boats and a multitude of other means. The suicide rate rose by nearly 40 per cent.

In June 1983 the Pope paid a second visit to his homeland. He reproved Jaruzelski, and at an open-air mass outside Katowice he told a crowd more than one million strong that to form a trade union was a fundamental human right. The security services responded with a campaign of low-level harassment of the Church.

Crucifixes were removed from public places and priests roughly handled. Several were murdered. Only in one case was the murder pinned on the security services, and on 27 December 1984 three militiamen were tried for killing Father Jerzy Popiełuszko.

That it should have come to this was a symptom of changes taking place outside Poland. Jaruzelski had done everything to bring Poland back under the control of Moscow, and to normalise the situation, a process he hoped would be concluded with elections to the Sejm in October 1985 and the release of all political prisoners the following year. But by then things had moved on in Russia, in an unexpected direction.

Leonid Brezhnev, on whose behalf Jaruzelski had conducted his clampdown, had died in November 1982. He had been succeeded by the KGB chief Yurii Andropov and then, briefly, by the hard-line Konstantin Chernenko. But in March 1985 the reins of power in the Kremlin were taken up by Mikhail Gorbachev, who, faced with a collapsing economy, a losing position in the arms race and a vigorous anti-Soviet alliance led by Ronald Reagan, initiated a twin policy of *glasnost* (openness) and *perestroika* (reorganisation).

In short, Jaruzelski's boss had gone soft, and this undermined his own position in Poland. He had always justified his actions by presenting them as the lesser of two evils, since they supposedly prevented a Soviet invasion and serious bloodshed. But with reforms being implemented in Russia, the bottom dropped out of this argument and with it the only pillar of his legitimacy.

Jaruzelski, now head of state, controlled not only the army, but also, through his Interior Minister General Czesław Kiszczak, the security apparatus. He had elbowed aside the Party in 1981 in order to carry out his clampdown and ruled through a Military Council of National Defence (WRON) while the Party set about purging unreliable and revisionist elements and reordering its ranks. But the Party had been so thoroughly demoralised that it was in no position to reassume its 'leading role', even if Jaruzelski had allowed it to.

A new government had been formed in 1985 under the economist Zbigniew Messner, a man with a low Party profile, but his efforts at curing the country's economic ills got nowhere. By 1987 the foreign debt had gone up to $37.6 billion. A mood of despondency enveloped the country, and a vast economic migration of three-quarters of a million joined the political refugees. The state of health of the nation reached alarming levels, and population growth halved over the period 1980–89. People took to black-marketeering and petty trading on a gigantic scale for survival. Ironically, the near-collapse of the economy stimulated the growth of small private enterprises, which by the end of the decade accounted for over 20 per cent of GDP.

Although still outlawed, Solidarność continued to exist as a force. Its old leadership had come together and, under the influence of moderates such as Kuroń and Michnik, issued repeated calls for dialogue, calls which were supported by the Church and by foreign governments. But it also occasionally showed its teeth. When price rises were announced in 1986, it threatened a nationwide strike, and the proposals were withdrawn. Jaruzelski's attempt to ignore the movement's existence was beginning to look foolish. Every foreign statesman visiting Poland, including US Vice President George Bush, trod the path to Wałęsa's home and consulted him on whether or not to ease sanctions.

The Pope's third visit to his native land, in June 1987, was almost as important as his first, and it was by far the most political. The militia were unable to prevent a sea of Solidarność placards waving above the heads of the crowds at his open-air masses, which were televised and watched by the whole nation. The Pope talked to Wałęsa and had several discussions with a more attentive Jaruzelski. But the General still baulked at the idea of talking to Wałęsa. Instead, he attempted to engage Polish society on his own terms, by holding a referendum on proposed economic initiatives, which was a failure, and announcing, in October 1987, the formation of a new Consultative Council.

Wałęsa had pre-empted him by setting up, in September of the same year, an Interim Council, with regional committees, to formulate a new consensus, and Bronisław Geremek suggested dialogue with reform-minded members of the Party.

The volume of public protest was rising steadily, and a new generation of activists within Solidarność pressed for more determined action. Austerity measures introduced in February 1988 provoked widespread strikes, which were put down with the use of force. In response, Solidarność threatened Jaruzelski with a general strike to take place on 1 September.

On 26 August General Kiszczak announced that he had been authorised to hold consultative talks with opposition groups. A meeting with Wałęsa and Bishop Dąbrowski took place five days later, and it was agreed that 'round table' talks would be held in October. Wałęsa called off the strikes. A new government was formed under Mieczysław Rakowski including a few independent figures, and preparatory talks began.

But while the round table was ready by the prescribed date, the talks did not start. There was disagreement about who should take part and about the scope of the talks. Wałęsa and the Church representatives wanted them to cover not only economic issues, but constitutional ones as well. Fresh dates were set and then cancelled as the two sides argued over procedure and the issues at stake, but the talks did finally begin, on 6 February 1989. Fifty-seven people convened at the round table, presided over by Kiszczak, with many more meeting in subcommittees dealing with subjects such as the economy, agriculture, political reform and so on. At the opening session, Kiszczak announced that the final goal of the talks was to bring about 'non-confrontational elections', which raised many questions. In private, he was heard to comment that he and his comrades were putting a noose around their own necks.

The Party may have been in disarray, but its two million members included the security services and most of the army, and there were plenty who would be prepared to fight for their positions. And for all his liberal talk, nobody could be sure how Gorbachev would react to fundamental change in Poland, the cornerstone of Soviet Russia's military system. The opposition negotiators therefore trod warily, allowing generous terms for the capitulation of the nomenklatura.

The talks ended on 5 April, in a spirit of unexpectedly harmonious agreement. Solidarity and the Church recovered their legal status, the right of free association and freedom of speech were guaranteed, as was the independence of the judiciary. Most important were the constitutional changes: the office of president was revived and a bicameral parliament was established. Elections were to be held in June.

As a concession to the PZPR, 65 per cent of the seats in the lower house were to be reserved for its members, with opposition candidates permitted to contest the remaining 35 per cent. The elections to the new Senate were to be unrestricted. The next elections, to be held in 1993, were to be entirely free. General Kiszczak declared that the agreement 'closed a chapter in our history and opened a new one'.

The elections were held in two rounds. The first, on 4 June, proved a fiasco for the Party. Solidarność won ninety-nine out of the one hundred seats in the Senate, with the remaining one going to a non-Party businessman. In the Sejm, its candidates won outright in all but one of the open seats, while thirty-three of the Party's nominees standing for seats reserved for the Party, including General Kiszczak and Prime Minister Rakowski, failed to get the

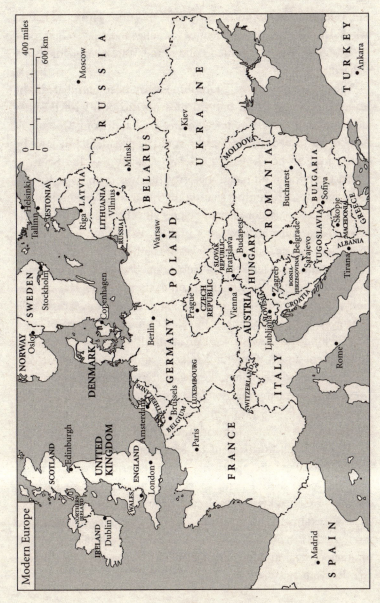

Modern Europe

400 miles

600 km

NORWAY
Oslo
SWEDEN
Stockholm
DENMARK
Copenhagen
Helsinki
Tallinn
ESTONIA
Riga LATVIA
LITHUANIA
Vilnius
RUSSIA
Minsk
BELARUS
RUSSIA
Moscow

SCOTLAND
Edinburgh
UNITED
KINGDOM
NORTHERN
IRELAND
IRELAND
Dublin
ENGLAND
WALES
London
NETHERLANDS
Amsterdam
Brussels
BELGIUM
LUXEMBOURG
GERMANY
Berlin
POLAND
Warsaw
Kiev
UKRAINE

FRANCE
Paris
SWITZERLAND
Prague
CZECH
REPUBLIC
Vienna
AUSTRIA
SLOVAK
REPUBLIC
Bratislava
Budapest
HUNGARY
SLOVENIA
Ljubljana
Zagreb
CROATIA
BOSNIA
HERZEGOVINA
Sarajevo
YUGOSLAVIA
Belgrade
MOLDOVA
ROMANIA
Bucharest
BULGARIA
Sofiya
MACEDONIA
Skopje
Tirana
ALBANIA
GREECE

ITALY
Rome
SPAIN
Madrid

TURKEY
Ankara

minimum number of votes required. A mortified Jaruzelski had to ask Wałęsa whether he would agree to change the rules so that some of these could be rerun at the second round. Wałęsa magnanimously obliged.

The entire communist establishment had been humiliated. The leadership of the PZPR had no idea how to deal with the new situation, and there was no guidance on hand from Moscow. It had been assumed that Jaruzelski would be president, but since he would have to be elected by the two chambers of the Sejm, in which the opposition had a majority, this was open to question.

Despite its resounding victory, the opposition was hesitant. It had conducted a vigorous campaign, with the support of people of all ages and from all walks of life, yet the turnout had been no more than 62 per cent. Such a level of apathy in the electorate was the consequence of ten years of frustration, of a fatalistic conviction that nothing would ever change, and of the psychological exhaustion resulting from years of poor living conditions, stress, food shortages and poor health. It dictated caution and restraint.

In behind-the-scenes discussions Jaruzelski proposed a coalition government under General Kiszczak, and Wałęsa put forward Tadeusz Mazowiecki. Michnik suggested the compromise of 'your president, our prime minister' as a basis for agreement, and this was taken up by US President George Bush, who was on a long-scheduled visit to Poland and addressed both chambers of the Sejm on 10 July. Jacek Kuroń went on television to explain that it was essential to allow the presidency to go to Jaruzelski, in order to reassure Russia about Poland's position within the Warsaw Pact. On 19 July the General was duly elected, by one vote. On 12 September Mazowiecki named his government, which included five ministers from the PZPR, including Kiszczak as Minister of the Interior and another general as Minister of Defence, to reassure the Kremlin that its security system was safe.

TWENTY-FOUR

The Third Republic

It is a historical given that the recovery of independence brings with it problems those struggling to achieve it had never foreseen or even believed possible. In Poland's case, the usual problems were aggravated by the scale of the violence done to the country and the people over the preceding half-century, and above all by the psychological damage inflicted by decades of untruth and moral manipulation.

The government headed by Tadeusz Mazowiecki, often referred to as the contractual government, applied itself with remarkable determination to the immediate problems facing the country. The Finance Minister Leszek Balcerowicz employed shock therapy to bring inflation under control and introduced a package of reforms which in effect created a free market. The Minister of Labour and Social Affairs Jacek Kuroń energetically tackled the social costs of the previous decade. The Foreign Minister, Krzysztof Skubiszewski, set about repositioning Poland with regard to its neighbours and preparing for its admittance into the Council of Europe. The government did not neglect purely political issues, amending the constitution in December 1989, replacing the Citizens' Militia with a state police force, and establishing fully independent organs of local government. But it was soon overtaken by events.

On 9 November the Berlin Wall came down. The collapse of communist power in East Germany precipitated the 'velvet revolution' in Czechoslovakia and similar upheavals in Hungary, Bulgaria and Romania, effectively bringing to an end the Soviet hegemony imposed on the area in 1945. As if in recognition of this, at the end of January 1990 Poland's Communist Party (PZPR) dissolved itself.

Yet, while it was the Poles who had been the first to breach the Soviet system, Mazowiecki's contractual government was wedded to the compromise which had brought it to power, and still contained former members of the PZPR, including the Interior Minister General Kiszczak, the Sejm contained an overwhelming majority of them, and the President was General Jaruzelski. Moreover, since there had been no spectacular overthrow of the existing regime, as in the German Democratic Republic, Czechoslvakia or Romania, the old security apparatus was still in place. Mazowiecki and his team therefore trod warily, fearful of overstepping their self-imposed bounds. They carried on with their economic reforms, eschewing radical political change in favour of stability.

Their fears were not entirely groundless. While the PZPR had dissolved itself, it had immediately re-formed as the Social-Democratic Party of Poland (SdRP), and this was a force to be reckoned with, if only on account of its huge financial clout. The PZPR had owned thirty-six limited companies created out of state assets, which passed to the SdRP, along with huge state funds abroad (there had been no formal delineation between the Party and the state), and control of the financial mechanisms which handled the repayment of Polish foreign debt before 1989. The ranks of the new state police were filled with former militiamen, who remained under the command of people who belonged to the communist camp. The same went for the army, the legislature and the media. The militia reserve, ORMO, had also been dissolved, but it formed itself into an association and remained an ominous presence.

Mazowiecki's fears were magnified by a sense of powerlessness. His government was hamstrung by the fact that the entire administrative *apparat* was still in place. His ministers were at the mercy of the personnel of their ministries. And, with the ministries of defence and the interior in communist hands, a process of burning, shredding or rewriting of secret service files in order to obscure and reinvent the past was being implemented on a massive scale.

Mazowiecki and the former opposition elites, led by Adam Michnik and the independent newspaper *Gazeta Wyborcza*, clung to the spirit of the round table, hoping that magnanimity would lead to reconciliation, and made it clear that a 'thick line' would be drawn under the past. This sent the message to the former members that they had nothing to fear, and to the man in the street that the government had allowed itself to be drawn into the communist camp – a reasonable suspicion, since a majority of its members were renegades from the old apparat. While they argued for stability and gradual change, a disenchanted electorate clamoured for a clean break with the past and for social justice. And while Mazowiecki represented himself and his colleagues as the only legitimate opposition to communism, many disputed this and called for free elections.

Leading this chorus were the Confederation for an Independent Poland (KPN), formed by Leszek Moczulski as far back as 1979, and the Christian National Union (ZChN) founded by the veteran anti-communist and political prisoner Wiesław Chrzanowski. But in May 1990 the cry was taken up with stridency by the twins Jarosław and Lech Kaczyński, head of the Bureau of National Security, who called for 'acceleration' and 'decommunisation' under the leadership of Lech Wałęsa, demanding immediate elections, at least for the post of president.

Over the next months the hitherto united front of all those who had fought for the overthrow of communist rule disintegrated, to the accompaniment of name-calling and mutual recrimination. New parties and groupings sprang up, based not on ideology or specific political programmes, but on personal factors. Mazowiecki's decision to stand as a candidate against Wałęsa when Jaruzelski agreed to step down was at least in part dictated by emotional reactions. The level of debate between them and their supporters in the run-up to the elections so disgusted the voters that in the first round, on 25 November 1990, in which turnout was no more than 60.6 per cent, the outsider Stan Tymiński, a former emigrant to Canada who claimed to have made a fortune and promised to make every Pole a millionaire, took second place after Wałęsa, knocking Mazowiecki out of the race. This placed Mazowiecki's supporters in the unhappy position of having to vote for their rival in the second round, in which Wałęsa won, with 74 per cent of an even lower turnout.

The election campaign had brought to the fore the worst aspects of Polish politics. The debate had been personal rather than political throughout, and all sides had resorted to populism and xenophobia. In a grotesque echo of 1968, people denounced each other as 'cosmopolitans' or 'Jews', epithets which bore little relation to racial origins, but were meant to suggest lack of patriotism and communist atavisms.

When Wałęsa was sworn in, on 22 December 1990, he was handed the pre-war presidential insignia and seal of office by the president of Poland in exile, who had flown in from London to bestow on this first freely elected president the legitimacy handed down consecutively by the last one. But this symbolic reconnection and legitimation did not presage a new harmony. Wałęsa appointed as prime minister Jan Bielecki, a non-partisan liberal whose main concern was the economy and the preparation of the first free parliamentary elections. He kept on Balcerowicz as Finance Minister and Skubiszewski in foreign affairs, which provided continuity in those vital areas. But endless disagreements about technicalities delayed the elections until the autumn of 1991, which allowed time for frequent confrontations between a Sejm still made up mainly of former communists and Wałęsa, goaded on by the head of his chancellery, Jarosław Kaczyński.

In preparation for the elections, new groupings and parties were formed from fractions of disintegrating ones, against an uncertain international background: after a failed coup in Moscow that summer, Lithuania, Latvia, Estonia and Ukraine declared their independence from Russia. Comecon was formally dissolved in June 1991, and the Warsaw Pact soon after that, but there were still large numbers of Russian troops based in Poland. At the same time, the opportunity provided by the first free elections precipitated a free-for-all, with over a hundred parties contesting them.

The result of the elections, held on 27 October 1991, was predictably inconclusive. The party which came out on top, Mazowiecki's Democratic Union (UD), won no more than 12.3 per cent of the vote, and only seven of the twenty-nine parties represented in the Sejm took more than 5. An ominous sign was that the PZPR, restyled as the SdRP and now as the Alliance of the Democratic Left (SLD), came second, with 12 per cent of the vote.

It took nearly two months for a centre-right coalition to be cobbled together and to form a government, under Jan Olszewski. And although this had a genuine mandate, it found itself paralysed in various areas by the post-communists who still infested the administration and all state services, and who had become emboldened by the lack of any attempt to hold them to account for past crimes, as well as by the electoral success of their party. It also came under vicious attack from the post-communist controlled media and from Michnik's *Gazeta Wyborcza*, whose staff and contributors vented their bitterness on their erstwhile colleagues.

A burning issue was whether people who had committed crimes against the Polish nation under the communist regime should be called to account. Popular feeling demanded it, reinforced by the knowledge that many were making careers for themselves, and that even those members of the former security services who had retired or been dismissed were getting higher pensions than ordinary citizens. But many of the former post-Solidarność camp were opposed to raking over the past, on the grounds that it would divide the nation. The issue was soon personalised, and rather than focusing on those who had murdered AK members or perpetrated serious crimes, attention was shifted onto the altogether more interesting subject of who among living public figures might have worked for the secret services as informers. Ministers who had access to secret service files leaked gobbets of unverifiable information, and even Wałęsa was accused of having been an informer. The issue brought down Olszewski's government in a welter of accusations and recriminations, and after lengthy negotiations, a new centre-right coalition was formed under the premiership of Hanna Suchocka, the first woman to hold the post.

Her government was buffeted by the consequences of a world recession, which produced unemployment of up to 20 per cent in some areas, giving rise to strikes and, at the beginning of 1993, the rise of a peasant organisation called Self-Defence, under the leadership of Andrzej Lepper. While the governmwnt struggled with the economy, discussion in the Sejm and outside was dominated by such questions as the role of the Church in political life and the unresolved issue of calling to account the criminals and informers of the communist era. Wałęsa, who had lost his way politically and squandered much of his authority by making absurd off-the-cuff statements, was growing increasingly dictatorial, and weaved about supporting the government one day and opposing it the next. Public anger mounted, and at the end of May 1993 Suchocka's government fell.

Wałęsa dissolved the Sejm and called an election, to take place in September. In emulation of Piłsudski, he created a Non-Party Bloc of Support for Reform, but this only won 5.4 per cent of the vote. The highest scorer, with 20.4 per cent, was the post-communist SLD, followed by the Polish People's Party (PSL). The despised former communist government spokesman Jerzy Urban reappeared on television, clutching a bottle of champagne and sticking out his tongue at the viewers – and at the whole post-Solidarność camp.

There followed four years of post-communist rule, first under the laconic PSL leader Waldemar Pawlak, then SLD's Józef Oleksy, followed by Włodzimierz Cimoszewicz. Emboldened by their party's victory at the polls, creatures of the communist regime who still staffed ministries and state enterprises at every level inaugurated an orgy of corruption, facilitated by the start of a far-reaching privatisation of the state sector. Earlier privatisations and private–public partnerships had provided golden opportunities for the old nomenklatura, but the programme of wholesale privatisation that began in 1994 offered far richer pickings. Friends or clients were placed on the boards of privatised businesses, usually for a financial consideration, while other businesses were sold off to them at grossly undervalued rates. Fortunes were also made on insider trading in the course of privatisation by those close enough to the politicians and heads of enterprises. A number of politicians also became involved with organised crime, which burgeoned in the prevailing climate.

Such levels of corruption shocked the electorate, as did the disclosure, in December 1995, that Prime Minister Oleksy was still on the payroll of the Russian secret service as an active agent. But the post-communists were competent and, in contrast to the post-Solidarność governments, did not ceaselessly quarrel amongst themselves, as a result of which things did get done. President Wałęsa's attempts to call them to order took the form of often poorly planned attacks that ended in conflicts which he usually lost, further undermining his authority.

At the next presidential elections, in November 1995, Wałęsa lost to the SLD candidate Aleksander Kwaśniewski, winning 48.3 per cent of the vote to the latter's 51.7. Kwaśniewski was a former PZPR ideologue singled out in the 1980s as a rising star, but it was not this that won him the presidency. His comparatively youthful looks, the image of a smartly suited, tennis-playing, cosmopolitan new man he projected, and not least his conveniently media-friendly wife, contrasted with those of the garrulous, slightly crude and provincial Wałęsa, and appealed to the soap-opera-conditioned middle electorate.

Kwaśniewski was also a cunning politician with a gift for achieving his goals, and he cut a statesmanlike figure that permitted him to distance himself from the growing stink of corruption (although he was heavily implicated). He pushed through the new constitution, a compromise which inspired little enthusiasm on either side of the political spectrum, in May 1997, and vigorously promoted the process of Poland's accession to the European Union and to NATO.

Eager to avoid a repetition of the defeat they suffered in 1993, largely as a result of their lack of a unified voice, the post-Solidarność parties prepared for the parliamentary elections of

September 1997 by coalescing in a Solidarność Election Campaign (AWS). This duly won the elections, polling 33.8 per cent of the vote, and formed a government under Jerzy Buzek, who was to be the only premier to remain in office for a full parliamentary term.

Buzek's party was little more than an uneasy alliance, and it had to form a coalition with the Union of Freedom (UW), which was to prove a shaky partner. He faced the challenge of having to bring the country into line with European norms as part of the process of preparing for EU membership and to implement a series of reforms in the health service, education, pensions, the civil service and local government, which infringed interests and were bound to cause hardship. His government was bedevilled by strikes and demonstrations organised, ironically, by the very trade union movement that had brought him to power. While Buzek did manage to carry through a number of sensible reforms, his government was unloved. The only member who achieved a measure of popularity was the Minister of Justice Lech Kaczyński, whose tough line on crime was seen to produce results.

The presidential elections of October 2000 were another triumph for the post-communists, with Kwaśniewski winning in the first round with nearly 54 per cent of the vote, and Wałęsa failing to win a single percentage point. As the next parliamentary elections drew near, the disintegrating AWS alliance splintered. In the centre the Union of Freedom was replaced by the Citizens' Platform (PO). On the right, a new party, the League of Polish Families (LPR), grew out of a number of traditionalist Catholic and nationalist groupings, and in the centre-right the Kaczyński brothers formed the Law and Justice party (PiS). But these new parties failed to stem the triumphant progress of the post-communists, who won over 40 per cent of the vote at the elections in September 2001. An alarming development was that the rabble-rousing Lepper's

Self-Defence party won over 10 per cent of the vote, and the League of Polish Families nearly 8.

A new government was formed under Leszek Miller, a man of the old order who had already been implicated in a number of shady financial deals during the previous spell of post-communist rule. He was perhaps a fitting figurehead for a time when a nation-wide opinion poll revealed that no more than 28 per cent of the country's inhabitants were satisfied with their lives and only 9 with their country. Levels of criminality had reached unprecedented heights, with the number of reported crimes more than doubling since 1990, and with organised crime reaching impressive proportions. Miller himself was mixed up in two corruption scandals, one relating to the media, the other to an oil company, and stepped down in May 2004. He was replaced by Marek Belka, who presided over the final stages of a regime that became synonymous with corruption and criminality. Its activities brought back on the agenda the question of calling people to account for crimes against the Polish people, and meant that the next election campaign would be fought on moral and ideological ground.

This signalled the end for the post-communist parties, with the SLD getting just over 11 and the PSL under 7 per cent of the vote. The winner was the Kaczyński twins' Law and Justice party, closely followed by the Citizens' Platform, and since they had campaigned on a similar ticket and had vowed to support each other after the elections, the fact that they had polled more than 50 per cent of the vote between them suggested that the country might expect four years of stable centre-right government.

The two parties began negotiations on a coalition, but strains appeared as the concurrent presidential elections loomed. When Lech Kaczyński beat the PO leader Donald Tusk, with 54 per cent of the vote to 45, the latter's ill-concealed disappointment and his rival's triumphalism aggravated disagreements on minor points of policy between the two parties. The Kaczyńskis formed a minority government under Kazimierz Marcinkiewicz, with the tacit support of the populist Self-Defence, which had polled 15 per cent of the vote. Over the next months, PiS brought Lepper and the leader of the League of Polish Families into the coalition, thus isolating and offending the Citizens' Platform, which it treated as a political rival. The move also alienated many within PiS, resulting in the protest resignation of Foreign Minister Stefan Meller and undermining its cohesion.

The inclusion of such elements in the coalition skewed the PiS programme to a populist left in matters concerning agriculture and local government and to an extreme traditionalist Catholic stand on the family, education and other areas of social policy. This only compounded a process of decline in the quality of its politics as Marcinkiewicz was shunted aside to make way for Jarosław Kaczyński, who became prime minister in July 2006, creating the bizarre situation of twin brothers holding the two highest offices in the land.

While the PiS government did achieve some notable success in curbing crime and corruption, it failed to tackle many other issues, and expended its energies on picking unnecessary quarrels with the opposition and creating a febrile atmosphere which drove people to take extreme positions. The issue of answerability for past crimes, or rather accusations of collaboration with the communist regime, was used as a political weapon to destroy rivals. The constant vicious infighting at the top created a mood of exasperation in the country at large, encouraging many younger people to escape by finding work abroad, contributing to an economic emigration of well over a million, despite the existence of jobs at home.

The Kaczyński brothers gave the impression of being increasingly embattled against various real or imaginary foes, and in a mood of mounting paranoia saw traitors in their own ranks, dismissing a number of their ablest ministers, such as the Defence Minister Radosław Sikorski. The coalition eventually fell apart in August 2007, leading to fresh elections in October.

A real sense of crisis could be felt during the run-up, and for the first time since 1989 a large number of younger voters took the trouble to take part. The result was a resounding victory for Donald Tusk's Citizens' Platform, which took over 41 per cent of the vote, and PiS, which, although it was knocked into second place, increased its share of the vote to over 32 per cent, while the left scraped just over 13 and the People's Party less than 9. Lepper's Self-Defence and the League of Polish Families, with just over 1 per cent each, failed to reach the threshold for representation.

These elections represent something of a watershed in the history of the Third Republic. The hundred-plus parties which had contested the elections of 1991 had been reduced over the intervening years to no more than half a dozen, the dozens represented in the Sejm to no more than four. The demagogues, single-issue politicians and post-communists who had preyed on an inexperienced electorate had finally been voted out of the picture. At no stage during that time was the democratic process ever questioned, even by extremists, and the process of parliamentary democracy had firmly established itself at the centre of Polish life in a way it had not in the 1920s. Yet serious flaws can be detected in the mechanisms of Poland's democracy, most of them inherent in its origins.

In Poland, democracy was not imposed on a neutral country; it was won by the efforts of the oppositionists of 1947, the striking workers of Poznań in 1956, the students of 1968, the dockyard workers of 1970, the Radom workers of 1976, by the activists of

KIK, KOR, ROPCiO, by Solidarność and all those, inside the country and out, who struggled for the overthrow of Soviet domination. They included left-wing workers who were traditionalist Catholics, right-wing but populist and egalitarian peasants, intellectuals of every orientation, and traditional middle-class conservatives. Most of them had been conditioned by the communist world in which they had been brought up to reject such fundamentals of democracy as property rights, the rule of law and personal answerability. That upbringing had also inspired in them a subversive attitude to the state and all organs of authority.

While the political class that emerged triumphant in 1989 represented a wide spectrum of opinion and beliefs, it thought of itself as being on the 'right', since it had fought against the communists, and believed itself to be united because it had stood shoulder to shoulder against them. The run-up to the first free elections in 1991 shattered this fictitious political unity and sense of solidarity as over a hundred parties joined the campaign. These were not based on coherent political manifestos; they were merely groups of like-minded people focused on personalities or single issues.

The political thinking and strategies of the post-Solidarność camp had been forged in protest and subversion, which they had underpinned with moral arguments. Those arguments became irrelevant when the oppressive regime had been overthrown and the time came to build a new Poland, and they did not have any ready substitutes. As they struggled to reposition themselves in the new reality, the various leaders became locked in an acerbic debate on what kind of Poland they should rebuild, conducted in moral, and therefore often extremist terms. This, as well as their subversive skills, invalidated them as politicians.

By contrast, the post-communists were pragmatic and efficient. They were not communists, not even socialists by conviction;

they had joined the Party for opportunistic career reasons and been groomed to govern. Just as they were about to inherit the kingdom, in the late 1980s, it fell apart, leaving them stranded. With their managerial training and some experience of power, they were a natural governing class; their sense of discipline, connections and access to cash allowed them to form a successful political force.

All this created misunderstandings and contradictions. Supposedly right-wing governments carried through social-democratic programmes, thereby alienating not only their coalition partners but also their constituencies. As no genuine left-wing party emerged, those who would naturally vote socialist were confused, and often found themselves supporting parties which enacted capitalist policies. The post-communist SLD favoured the free market and was supported by middle-class conservatives who wanted order and stability. The ostensibly far-right PiS was supported by the poor, whom it seduced by its nationalistic, populist and socialist slogans.

At the time of writing, the Sejm was dominated by two allegedly right-wing parties, differentiated less by their policies than by their style and rhetoric. As both were formed by a coming together of earlier parties and splinter groups, they lacked a proper statement of their policy fundamentals, not to mention the internal democratic mechanisms regulating choice of leader, internal discipline, formulation of policy and so on. They were ultimately defined by the personality of their leaders, and it was a matter for conjecture whether they would exist at all under their current names in five years' time.

In contrast to the less than glorious trajectory of Poland's political development since 1989, her foreign policy has been surprisingly intelligent and consistent. This was a vital element in the re-establishment of the Polish state, considering both the Poles' former dominance in the east and the lack of any settlement with Germany after 1945, not to mention the problem of developing a new relationship with Russia.

Given the history of relations between the two over the past five centuries, the re-emergence of an independent Poland could not be viewed in Russia as anything but a challenge, one that raised a great many questions and posed huge problems for the ailing Soviet Union. Particularly as, in this area at least, Polish political thought had progressed radically over the preceding decades.

The question of how Poles should regard the areas of the former Commonwealth lying beyond Poland's boundaries had been exercising minds since 1795. But it was the events of 1918–21 and the horrors of the Second World War that turned the issue into a moral one for thinking Poles. The consequence was a wide-ranging discussion on the whole question of what a future Poland's attitude to Russia, Lithuania, Belarus and Ukraine should be. This discussion was carried on during the 1970s and 1980s, in word and print, in smoke-filled rooms and over the radio waves, both within Poland and in émigré circles, particularly in London and Paris, where the periodical *Kultura*, edited by Jerzy Gedroyc, led the debate. It was in many ways the kind of reassessment that former colonial powers were forced to make during the 1950s and 1960s, and it had three fundamental consequences. The first was that the Poles came to accept the necessity of taking territorial disputes and assumed wrongs such as the Volhynian ethnic cleansing of 1943 out of the argument. The second was that they grew used to treating the other nations as equals and their aspirations as legitimate. The third was an acceptance that the only way forward was through cooperation, at any cost.

Within weeks of its formation in September 1989, the contractual government's Foreign Minister Krzysztof Skubiszewski opened up relations with the Soviet republics of Lithuania, Belarus and

Ukraine, as if they were sovereign states. Within a year he was signing bilateral agreements with Ukraine, ignoring a clamour there for a Polish apology for Operation Vistula and one in Poland for a Ukrainian apology for the Volhynian cleansing. Relations with Belarus were circumscribed by its closeness to Russia, while those with Lithuania were complicated by the vociferous Polish minority there, which demanded territorial revision or at least special minority status. In response, Skubiszewski declared that Poland would never seek to revise her frontier with Lithuania and did not consider Poles resident in that country to be anything other than Lithuanian citizens. This attitude to minorities beyond its frontiers was in stark contrast to the irredentism displayed by other states in the area, notably Hungary, Slovakia and Serbia. But relations with Lithuania remained tense, partly because from the start Lithuanian nationalism had defined itself in opposition to Poland, and partly because Russia was loath to relinquish its grip on the area.

Poland's relations with the Soviet Union were bound to be strained. There were large bodies of Russian troops stationed in Poland (they would not leave until the autumn of 1993), and Russia was still hoping to keep the country within its sphere of interest. Both sides trod carefully; Poland refrained from bringing up the question of the troops and the Soviets made a formal admission that the Katyn massacre had indeed been perpetrated by the NKVD, a gesture greatly appreciated in Poland.

The break-up of the Soviet Union in 1991 marked a turning point. Poland was the first country to recognise Ukraine's declaration of independence, and the second to recognise Lithuania. Matters were more complicated with respect to Belarus, which identified strongly with Russia, and where nationalists claimed large areas of the former Grand Duchy of Lithuania.

Earlier, in February 1990, Wałęsa had met presidents Vaclav

Havel of Czechoslovakia and Jozsef Antall of Hungary at Vyšehrad, in Prague, where they reached a tripartite agreement to provide a framework for united action and regional security. Poland proposed that they seek entry into the European Union jointly, but this was rejected by Czechoslovakia, which, being economically fitter, was hoping to be admitted earlier on its own. Poland also wanted the Vyšehrad group, as it became known, to act as a bridge to Europe for countries such as Lithuania, but this initiative was turned down too.

Although it was not always successful, Polish diplomacy in the 1990s was remarkably inspired, sophisticated and consistent, despite the frequent changes of government, and was largely responsible for the peaceful resolution of painful problems in the whole region, which might otherwise easily have developed as they did in the Balkans.

Another area in which demons from the past had to be confronted was the issue of Polish–Jewish relations over the course of the twentieth century. In May 1991, during a visit to Israel, Wałęsa made a public apology on behalf of every Pole who had ever harmed a Jew. More important, Polish historians initiated a sensitive and objective discussion of the subject, which forced the whole of society to reconsider their view of the past. An important element in this was their uncoupling of acts of violence perpetrated on Jews by Poles from the harm done by Jews to Poles, which had the effect of disabling the tit-for-tat arguments hitherto used by both sides to blame and justify. This went hand in hand with a revival of interest in Jewish culture and its place in Poland's past.

Polish diplomacy faced a no less delicate subject as it opened relations with Germany. In 1945 Poland had acquired, by Stalin's writ and the Western Allies' acquiescence, a huge swathe of former German territory, and those who had been ousted from it joined

German nationalists in a chorus demanding its return. Alarm bells began ringing in Warsaw in 1990, when the West German Chancellor Helmut Kohl showed reluctance to ratify the existing border and Poland was not invited to take part in the 'two plus four' talks (the two Germanies and the four wartime allies America, Britain, France and Russia) on the proposed unification of Germany. Poland demanded formal ratification of its western border, reminding all concerned that, when signing agreements with Lithuania, Belarus and Ukraine, it had declared its unconditional recognition of existing borders and its refusal to encourage claims by minorities either within those countries or ousted from them. This put moral pressure on Germany, and, with the support of the United States, which was already viewing Poland as a strategic partner for the future, the existing borders were confirmed.

Poland submitted an application for EU membership in 1994, and was formally admitted on 1 May 2004. A more significant date for many Poles was 12 March 1999, when the country joined NATO, along with Hungary and the Czech Republic, as this act finally cancelled out the Yalta Agreement by placing Poland firmly outside the Russian sphere of influence.

Poland took NATO membership seriously and offered large contingents for every one of its operations, including, crucially, that in Iraq, where the Polish special force GROM played a vital role, capturing the oil terminal of Basra in an advance operation. This earned the country recognition in Washington, where in January 2003 President George W. Bush told his Polish counterpart Aleksander Kwaśniewski that Poland was America's best friend in Europe – but not in Paris, where President Chirac described its behaviour as 'infantile'.

Relations with both of Poland's major neighbours subsequently took a turn for the worse, and echoes from an ugly past reverberated across the region. In 2004 a demand for compensation for those expelled from former German areas annexed to Poland in 1945 resurfaced as a political issue in Germany, the Poles countered by raking up German atrocities in Poland, and public opinion in both countries took over from common sense. While diplomatic relations remained cordial, politicians on both sides could not resist getting involved. When, in September 2005, the German Chancellor Gerhard Schroeder signed an agreement with Russia to reroute a gas pipeline which was to have gone through Poland under the Baltic Sea, there was talk of the Ribbentrop–Molotov pact.

Gas had become Russia's new weapon, and she did not hesitate to use it as a reminder of her power and her interest in the area by cutting off the supply to Ukraine in February 2004. Poland continued to take a keen interest in Ukraine, despite a resurgence of anti-Polish nationalism there, and when the interference of Moscow and electoral fraud robbed Viktor Yushchenko of victory in the Ukrainian presidential election of November 2004, precipitating the so-called Orange Revolution, thousands of Poles, including Wałęsa and other leading figures, went to Kiev to support him. And it was Poland's President Aleksander Kwaśniewski who played the decisive role in defusing the crisis and negotiating a settlement.

This had an immediate effect on Polish–Russian relations. Having previously revealed secret documents and admitted the truth about crimes committed against the Polish people in Stalin's day, various Russian agencies now began to backtrack and to take the Stalinist line on subjects such as Russia's involvement in the Warsaw Uprising of 1944. In the autumn of 2005, a new Russian national day was instituted, 4 November, the date the Poles were ejected from the Kremlin in 1612, and the following day Russia banned the import of Polish meat on grounds of hygiene. Poland involved the EU in the trade issues, and in 2006 Prime Minister Marcinkiewicz suggested a European joint energy security pact in the face of renewed Russian threats to use gas supply as a weapon of coercion.

By then, Poland had developed a close relationship with the United States, which had come to view it, along with the Czech Republic, as part of its global security system. By calling for the admission of Ukraine and Georgia to NATO and building up links with Moldavia and Azerbaijan, Poland was also turning itself into the diplomatic pivot of NATO in the region. This placed it in the front line of America's confrontation with Russia, but, ironically, probably made it more secure. Russia remained wedded to an old-fashioned sense of greatness, one that would be affronted by a confident sovereign Poland, whether it was in alliance with the United States or not.

Polish society has certainly not shown itself to be devoid of patriotism and a wish to enhance its international standing, but it has also, like other European societies, shown a greater interest in economic development. And in this it achieved a remarkable degree of success.

The transformation from a Soviet centrally planned command economy to a free-market one was bound to be slow and painful, and it was made more so by the catastrophic condition of the Polish economy in 1989. The new government inherited vast debts, a burdensome welfare system that could not cope with the demands placed on it, and inflation of 586 per cent. The Soviet-era flagship industries such as steel and shipbuilding were not only unable to pull the economy out of the crisis, they were haemorrhaging money.

The bold moves made by Balcerowicz in the first months convinced the outside world that Poland was serious, and in 1990 the IMF granted a credit of $700 million and the World Bank $1.5 billion. A number of state enterprises were privatised and a stock exchange was opened in Warsaw at the beginning of 1991 (in the redundant former Party headquarters). In March of that year nearly half of Poland's foreign debt was cancelled. In the following year all state farms were sold off, and the first signs of improvement were visible, despite the difficult conditions created by the world recession. Industrial output rose in 1992 by 4 per cent and agricultural production by 12. In 1993, GDP grew by 3.8 per cent, half of it accounted for by the private sector. Inflation was down to 35 per cent and the people of Poland were accustoming themselves to personal income tax and VAT.

By 1995, when the złoty lost four zeros and the exchange rate was floated, GDP had reached 7 per cent growth. The break-up and privatisation of the large state enterprises were under way, and while a complicated regulatory and tax system discouraged it, foreign investment began to flow in – $33 billion over the next five years. The economy was damaged by the crisis in Russia in the late 1990s, weighed down by unemployment hovering between 15 and 20 per cent, and by the lack of firm direction and the difficulty of voting budgets attendant on weak coalition governments. Yet by the end of the decade inflation had fallen to 10 per cent and the złoty was rising steadily against the dollar and the euro. By then the private sector accounted for over three-quarters of GDP, and when, in 2002, inflation was brought down to 3 per cent, the country's economy could be said to have come out of the woods.

Structural problems remained, and economic life was hidebound by overregulation and arcane practices left over from the past, which meshed with newly introduced EU regulation to create an expensive and time-consuming business environment. Although average income increased in real terms by 22 per cent between 1995 and 2000, large sections of the population, particularly the elderly and rural communities, did not benefit from the fruits of the changes, and continued to live in relative poverty. Yet the Polish economy was more broadly based than that in most post-communist countries, and a large middle class was beginning to emerge.

The whole process was beset by profound psychological and social problems. The overwhelming majority of those brought up before 1989 found it difficult to grasp that capitalism is not some kind of new doctrine but merely an extension of the rights to freedom and property. This had the effect of turning purely economic problems into political ones. That is why no government was willing or bold enough to return property confiscated by the communists or to compensate the owners. Aside from the dubious moral message this sent out, it meant that large tracts of central Warsaw were not developed and much investment was arrested. More importantly, this inability to grasp realities revealed the degree to which life under Soviet communism moulded the psyche and rendered people incapable of logical thought and action. This affected political and social discourse, which was regularly distorted by a tendency to direct it onto a supposedly moral plane which usually reverted to an ideological and fundamentally communist one.

At the same time, Polish society was being exposed through the media to Western consumerist culture and offered a bewildering variety of choice, which led to a splintering of the old solidarities based on shared deprivation, both moral and material. While some segments of society became caught up in a scramble for money and the attributes of a Western lifestyle, others retreated into angry nationalism or a Sunday-school Catholicism epitomised by the bigoted and xenophobic Radio Marya.

The cultural and educational scene which had been dominated by acknowledged masters and role models gave way to a free-for-all, with new private schools and universities showing up venerable institutions such as the Jagiellon University, and minor television personalities garnering greater interest than established writers and artists. The Nobel laureate Wisława Szymborska and the Oscar-winning film director Andrzej Wajda still commanded notice as well as respect, but high culture was largely occluded by flashier imports.

It is therefore very difficult to expound with any authority on the state of Polish society and culture in the decades after 1989. In his order disbanding the AK in 1945, General Okulicki made it clear that the war was not over. 'You must not for one moment admit a doubt that this war can only end with the victory of the just cause, the triumph of good over evil, of freedom over slavery,' he wrote. The war did end with the victory of that cause, in 1989. But the wounds inflicted on Polish society during those forty-four years were so deep, so varied and so complex that they would not heal easily.

Some of the most difficult to heal were inflicted in the 1970s and 1980s, when the communist regime forced hundreds of thousands of Poles to spy and report on each other. The Institute of National Remembrance (IPN), established in 1999 and entrusted with all the files of the communist secret services, failed to formulate any coherent policy on how this material was to be treated. Information was released to researchers on a largely *ad-hoc* basis, leading to the exposure of some without in any way clearing the air. While minor informers were denounced and hounded, usually for political reasons, former members of the security services with blood on their hands made successful careers and took their place among the wealthiest people in the country. This created a deep wound within society, one set to fester for some time to come

Pope John Paul II visited his country five times after 1989, and used these occasions to address some of the problems of Polish society. He was Poland's greatest role model, not surprisingly, since the census of 2001 revealed that out of a total population of 38.6 million, 34.6 million were Catholics. But he was also revered and listened to by non-believers. His death on 2 April 2005 not only deprived the country of its greatest role model. It also robbed the Polish Church of its mentor.

After the fall of communism, the Church, which had been at the centre of the struggle for its overthrow and played a vital political role in it, struggled to redefine its mission and find a new place in Polish society. This would not have been easy even if many of its members had not developed a taste for political power and they had all been intellectually up to facing the challenges of a rapidly changing world. It got caught up in major political debates over everything from abortion to EU membership, which revealed internal divisions and damaged its authority.

The destruction of Poland's intellectual, spiritual and social elites by the Nazis and the Soviets between 1939 and 1956, and their continuing emasculation until 1989, had placed the Church in the position of being the only repository and trustee of the values they held dear. With the mission of upholding them and passing them on came great moral authority. Much of that was dissipated after 1989.

Throughout this period there was an evident longing on the part of younger generations for fresh role models and leadership, but no new elite recognised by wider sections of the population emerged. Given an educational system geared to little more than the achievement of grades, it is difficult to see how it could. Similarly, no sense of respect for public institutions was allowed to develop by the squabbles and scandals in the Sejm, the smell of corruption surrounding the media and the police, and, perhaps most important, the corporatism, inefficiency and ineffectuality of the legal system.

As a state, Poland faces geopolitical challenges very similar to those it faced over the past four or five centuries. As a society, it faces the same globalising influences and threats to identity and cohesion as any other, from the most developed and sophisticated to the most recently contacted peoples of Amazonia. Given its social and systemic problems, it would be rash to predict how Polish society will confront these, and whether it will be able to overcome them as successfully as it has survived the onslaughts of the past. Yet that past undoubtedly holds most of the answers.

INDEX

Act of Insurrection (1794) 214
Act of Union, Orthodox-Catholic church,
    Brześć (1596) 139, 140
Acta Henriciana 84, 86, 107–8, 114, 117
Adalbertus, St (Wojciech) 5, 6, 9
Afghanistan 374, 375
Agricultural Society 240–1, 242–3
agriculture 1, 17, 31, 50, 95–6, 120–1, 153–5, 183,
    201–2, 240–1, 242–3, 251–2, 262–3, 265, 269,
    271–2, 307–8, 369
air force 314, 319
AK (Armia Krajowa) 321, 322–3, 325, 326–9, 331,
    332, 333, 336, 342, 344, 363, 367, 390, 407
Alabiano, Garcias 127
Aldobrandini, Cardinal 125
Aleksander, King of Poland 46, 56
Alexander I, Tsar of Russia 221, 224, 225–6, 227, 228
Alexander II, Tsar of Russia 240, 241, 245, 283
Alexander III, Pope 20–1
Alexey, Tsar of Muscovy 147, 154, 155
Algeria 249
Algirdas (Olgierd), Grand Duke of Lithuania 34
Alliance of the Democratic Left (SLD) 389, 391,
    392, 394, 398
American Civil War 248–9
American Food Mission 308
Anabaptists 64
Anders, General Władysław 324, 325, 326
Andrew II, King of Hungary 22
Andropov, Yurii 372, 379
Andruszowo, Treaty of (1667) 151
Andrzejewski, Jerzy 360
Anna Jagiellon, Queen of Poland 106, 108, 109, 125
Annibale di Capua, Papal Legate 113
Antall, Jozsef 401
anti-Semitism *see* Jewish people and culture
Anti-Trinitarians 64; *see also* Arians
architecture: Baroque 170, 171, 175; Bohemian
    52; Burgundian 52; Flemish 52; Franconian 52;

German 52; Kraków 52; nineteenth-century
    230; Renaissance 94, 96–7, 98, 170;
    Romanesque 14; Royal Castle 96, 202, 203;
    seventeenth-century grand country residences
    185–6; Stanislavian period 202; Warsaw 52,
    202, 230; Zamos 96–8
Arciszewski, Krzysztof 135
Arians 64, 65, 73, 75, 76, 99, 125, 126, 127, 128
Armenians 32, 58, 78, 93, 97, 98
army: AK (Armia Krajowa) 321, 322–3, 325, 326–9,
    331, 332, 333, 336, 342, 344, 363, 367, 390,
    407; Commonwealth 90, 111–12, 117, 120;
    'Current Defence Force' 90; foreign legions of
    220–2, 224–6, 236, 248–9; funding 90, 117,
    163; Husaria 134–5; in exile, World War II
    319; *levee en masse* 90, 145; military fashion
    170–1; military science 132; partition and 196;
    Piechota Wybraniecka 133; public attitudes
    towards 90; 'Quarter Troops' 90, 132–3; Sejm
    and 205, 206; size of 90, 121, 233; szlachta and
    133, 134; volunteers 133–4; World War II 314,
    315–16, 326; *see also under individual battle
    and commander*
arts: arcadia, idea of and search for within 98,
    101–2, 253–4; Bible translations 54, 99;
    Catholic Church promotes 53; Commonwealth
    98–105; early Polish 98–9; Enlightenment 197–8;
    fifteenth-century 52–3; influence of Polish arts
    throughout Europe 102; Italian influence upon
    53–4, 85; Jesuit influence upon 128; novel and
    short story 278–9, 281; painting 202, 280;
    People's Republic 346, 352–3, 359–60, 377–8;
    poets 100–2, 103–4, 131–2, 198, 230, 252–3;
    political writing 99–100; Positivist Movement
    277–80, 281; preoccupation with public affairs
    and government 99–100; printing presses first
    used 54, 98, 104; Renaissance 85; Romanticism
    252–7, 279; Stanisław Augustus patronises
    202–3; theatre 198, 278

411

Index

Index

Luxembourg dynasty 42
Lwów 51, 53, 71, 92, 93, 142, 148, 155, 158, 185, 237, 239, 266, 273, 278, 289, 292, 294, 305, 309, 315, 342

Maciejewski, Stanisław 70
Mączyński, Jan 99
Madaliński, General Józef 213
magnates 12, 128; Confederation of Bar, role in 193, 194; constitution and 109, 146, 129, 186; insurrection (1794) and 215; Jesuits and 129; Krakow Lords 33; land ownership 51, 182–4; monarchy, relationship with 109, 119–20, 146, 148, 157, 162, 181, 193; parliamentary system and 159–60, 162, 186, 196; Patriots 205; peasants and 50; private towns 155, 157; starosties and 72–3; supplement income with lucrative or influential public office 51
Magyars 42
Małachowski, Stanisław 205, 207, 222
Malinowski, Joseph ben Mardoch 65
Małopolska (Lesser Poland) 11, 16, 19, 32, 34, 35, 45, 61, 62, 100, 154, 213
March of Brandenburg 26
Marchlewski, Julian 284
Marchocki, Ścibor 202
Marcinkiewicz, Kazimierz 395, 404
Marcinkowski, Karol 277
Maritime Commission 135
Marshall Aid 350
Marx, Karl 217, 248
Marxism xx, 351, 352, 354, 358
Mary I, Queen of England 70
Matejko, Jan 280
Mątwy, Battle of (1666) 161
Maximilian I of Habsburg, Archduke 110, 113, 114
Maximilian II, Holy Roman Emperor 109
Mazarin, Cardinal Jules 146
Mazepa, Ivan 178
Mazovia 16, 20, 21, 26, 30, 43, 45, 61, 62, 67, 71, 92, 154, 158, 307
Mazowiecki, Tadeusz 384, 385, 386, 388, 389
Mazurians 265
Mazzini, Giuseppe 236, 247, 254
Mecklenburg 9, 20
Mehmet IV, Sultan of Turkey 162–3
Melanchthon, Philipp 99
Meller, Stefan 395
Mendelson, Stanisław 284
Mennonites 64
Messner, Zbigniew 380
Metternich, Prince Klemens von 256, 266
Michelet, Jules 254
Michnik, Adam 360, 363, 371, 378, 380, 387, 390
Mickiewicz, Adam 230, 239, 252–5, 257, 278, 352, 361
Mielęcin concentration camp 336
Mielecki, Hetman Mikołaj 111
Mielżyński family 229

Mierosławski, Ludwik 238, 239, 242, 244
Mieszko I, Duke of Poland 3, 4–5, 6, 8, 61
Mieszko II, King of Poland 8–9
Mikołajczyk, Stanisław 319, 325, 326, 327, 330, 332, 334
Miłosz, Czesław 360, 373
Military Council of National Defence (WRON) 379
Mill, John Stuart 277
Miller, Leszek 394
mining 51, 156, 268, 269, 376
Ministry of Public Safety 351, 354
Mniszech, Barbara 75
Mniszech, Jerzy 121
Mniszech, Maryna 121, 122, 123
Moczar, General Mieczysław 358, 360, 361, 362
Moczulski, Leszek 387
Modzelewski, Karol 360, 372
Mohacs, Battle of (1526) 56, 110
Moldavia 56, 78, 95, 132, 141, 142, 143, 144, 145, 146, 204, 219, 404
Molotov, Viacheslav 312, 324, 328
monarchy 45–6, 82–5; Commonwealth 84–6; contract between subjects and 90–1; 1791 constitution and 209; effect of election upon mindset of monarch 156, 157; election of first Commonwealth monarch 84–5; election of monarch (1573) 106–9; election of monarch (1587) 112–13; election of monarch (1632) 136; election of monarch (1669) 162; election of monarch (1673) 163; election of monarch (1696) 175–6; election of monarch (1733) 180; election of monarch (1764) 191; election of monarch, first 84–5; election procedure, attempt to tighten up 113–14; mutinies against (1606 and 1665) 90; oath of loyalty to subjects 90; precedent and 85–6; release clause 90–1, 117–18, 193; source of power in appointments of senior officers 118–19, 157
monasteries 14, 61, 126, 148
Monluc, Jean de, Bishop of Valence 107
Moravia 2, 8, 19
Morges Front 302
Morsztyn, Jan Andrzej 169
Moryson, Fynes 103
Mościcki, Ignacy 300, 301, 302, 319
Moscow 129, 138, 139, 143, 153, 330
Movement for the Defence of Human and Civil Rights (ROPCiO) 368, 371, 397
Mrożek, Sławomir 360
Mścisław 149
Murad II, Sultan of Turkey 56
Murat, Marshal Joachim 221
Muravyov, General 245–6
Muscovy 23, 56–7, 80, 104, 107, 108, 109, 111, 112, 121, 122, 124, 141, 143, 144, 147, 148, 149, 151, 154, 158, 165, 177, 178, 187
museums 203, 229, 309, 338

Index